SEVENTH EDITION

DESIGN BASICS

David A. Lauer

Stephen Pentak

The Ohio State University

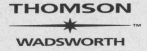

THOMSON
™
WADSWORTH

Australia | Canada | Mexico | Singapore | Spain
United Kingdom | United States

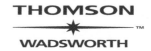

Design Basics, **Seventh Edition**
Lauer/Pentak

Publisher: Clark Baxter
Senior Development Editor: Sharon Adams Poore
Editorial Assistant: Nell Pepper
Development Project Manager: Julie Iannacchino
Executive Marketing Manager: Diane Wenckebach
Marketing Assistant: Aimee Lewis
Marketing Communications Manager: Heather Baxley
Content Project Manager: Jennifer Kostka
Executive Art Director: Maria Epes

Senior Print/Media Buyer: Karen Hunt
Production Service/Compositor: Lachina Publishing Services
Cover/Text Designer: Marsha Cohen/Parallelogram Graphics
Illustrators: Jamie Pentak, Craig Pentak
Rights Acquisition Account Manager, Images: John Hill
Photo Researcher: Seidel Associates
Cover Art: Photograph by Ellen Page Wilson, courtesy of
PaceWildenstein, New York; © Elizabeth Murray, courtesy
PaceWildenstein, New York

Printed in Canada
1 2 3 4 5 6 7 11 10 09 08 07

Library of Congress Control Number: 2007935041

ISBN-13: 978-0-495-50086-5
ISBN-10: 0-495-50086-0

Thomson Higher Education
25 Thomson Place
Boston, MA 02210-1202
USA

For more information about our products, contact us at:
Thomson Learning Academic Resource Center
1-800-423-0563
For permission to use material from this text or product,
submit a request online at **http://www.thomsonrights.com**
Any additional questions about permissions can be submitted
by e-mail to **thomsonrights@thomson.com**

Credits appear on pages 293–294, which constitute a continuation
of the copyright page.

ABOUT THE COVER ART

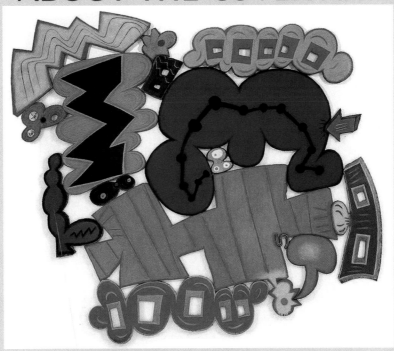

ELIZABETH MURRAY

Bop. 2002–2003. Oil on canvas, 9′ 10″ × 10′ 10$^1/_2$″
(299.7 × 331.5 cm).

Elizabeth Murray was an influential American painter
(1940–2007) who lived and worked in New York. Her abstract
paintings are characterized by playful cartoon-like shapes
deployed in exuberant arrangements. Her work shows that
simplicity and complexity are not contradictory forces in
design. In 2005 Elizabeth Murray's paintings were the subject
of a retrospective exhibition at The Museum of Modern Art
in New York.

To Debbie

CONTENTS

Part 1
DESIGN PRINCIPLES

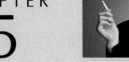

CHAPTER

6

RHYTHM 112

Part 2
DESIGN ELEMENTS

CHAPTER

7

LINE 126

CHAPTER

8

SHAPE/VOLUME 150

CHAPTER

12

VALUE   238

CHAPTER

13

COLOR   250

The seventh edition of *Design Basics* has numerous new images, and some changes that represent a new direction for the text. For the first time, student work is incorporated. Significantly, these student images are incorporated in a way that does not readily identify them as "student work." The goal is to suggest that the best student work can stand side-by-side with the works of masters and professionals.

A second major change is the use of a pair of artworks that repeat in every chapter. The idea here is to emphasize that any example in the book can be a learning tool for many elements and principles. The two artworks selected for this special treatment are: Susan Moore's figure painting titled *Vanity*, and El Lissitzky's *Suprematist Composition from a series of six*. On the face of it, the two could hardly be more different, but over the course of thirteen chapters we find similarities, and equal sophistication of design.

Other new features for this seventh edition include: sections on *pattern* and new thoughts on *movement*. Throughout the text you will find new images that expand the range of cultural sources, and reflect new works of art and design since the last edition.

The revision of this text was assisted by the insights of reviewers who are engaged in teaching and research: Ann Coddington, Eastern Illinois University; K. Genevieve Freeman, Pepperdine University; Herb Goodman, Eastern Kentucky University; Travis Graves, East Tennessee State University; Susan K. Leshnoff, Seton Hall University; David W. Porter, Keystone College; Kimberly Winkle, Tennessee Technological University and David Zdrazil, McLennan Community College. We are grateful for their insights.

RESOURCES

ArtExperience Online

Access to this website is available with all new copies of the text, helping students explore the elements and foundations of art and design through interactive exercises and quizzing. Included are flashcards of the fine art images in the text and *In the Studio* video demonstrations of art techniques, filmed in college art classrooms to allow students to see art and design concepts applied in a familiar setting. **Icons appear throughout the text** to make it easier for students to know when to refer to specific modules for additional practice.

PowerLecture

This presentation tool makes it easy to assemble, edit, and present customized lectures for your course by providing high-resolution images from the text. The zoom feature allows you to magnify selected portions of an image for more detailed display in class. And, you can easily customize your classroom presentation by adding your own images to those from the text.

JoinIn™ Student Response System

JoinIn turns your lecture into a personal, fully interactive experience for your students by allowing you to take attendance, poll students, check student comprehension of difficult concepts, and even administer quizzes without collecting papers or grading.

DESIGN PRINCIPLES

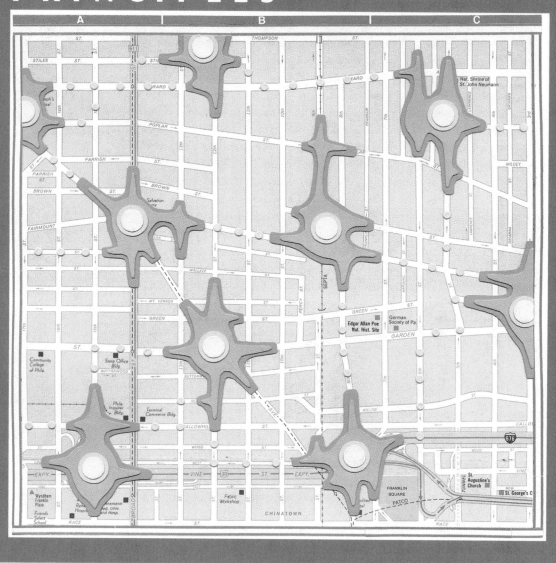

1

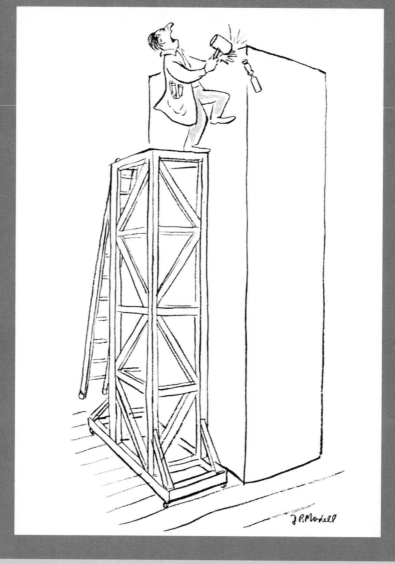

Frank Modell. 1956.
© *The New Yorker Collection* from cartoonbank.com.
All Rights Reserved.

DESIGN PROCESS

DESIGN DEFINED

What do you think of when you hear the word *design*? Do you associate design with fashion, graphics, furniture, or automotive style? Design has a more universal meaning than the commercial applications that might first come to mind. A dictionary definition uses the synonym *plan*: To **design** indeed means to plan, to organize. Design is inherent in the full range of art disciplines from painting and drawing to sculpture, photography, and time-based media such as film, video, computer graphics, and animation. It is integral to crafts such as ceramics, textiles, and glass. Architecture, landscape architecture, and urban planning all apply visual design principles. The list could go on. Virtually the entire realm of two- and three-dimensional human production involves design, whether consciously applied, well executed, or ill considered.

Visual Organization

Design is essentially the opposite of chance. In ordinary conversation, when we say "it happened by design" we mean something was planned—it did not occur just by accident. People in all occupations plan, but the artist or designer plans the arrangement of elements to form a visual pattern. Depending on the field, these elements will vary—from painted symbols to written words to scenic flats to bowls to furniture to windows and doors. But the result is always a visual organization. Art, like other careers and occupations, is concerned with seeking answers to problems. Art, however, seeks visual solutions in what is often called the design process.

The poster shown in **A** is an excellent example of a visual solution. How the letters are arranged is an essential part of communicating the idea. *Math Rules!* **(B)** demonstrates the artist's ability to see a new possibility for numbers as shapes that can form a face. By contrast the message written on

▼ **A**

John Kuchera. *It's Time to Get Organized.* 1986.
Poster. Art Director and Designer: Hutchins/Y&R.

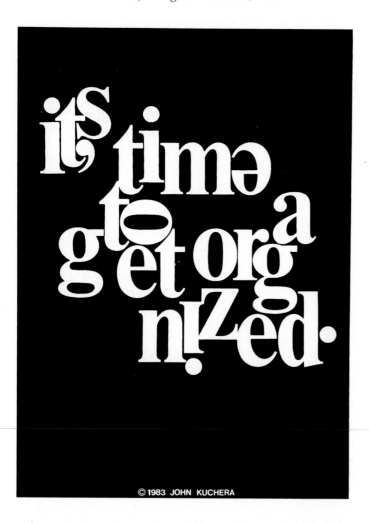

© 1983 JOHN KUCHERA

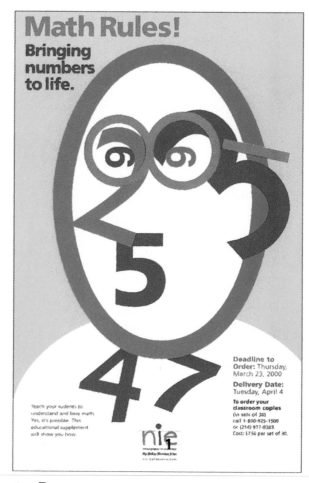

▲ **B**

Steve Chambers. *Math Rules!* 2000. Poster promoting math-oriented educational supplements. Print. *Regional Design Annual*, September/October 2000, p. 140.

the twenty-dollar bill in **C** is a clever verbal confrontation, but the communication is *not* as dependent on the visual composition. All three of these examples are creative; however, the first two are visual, whereas the manipulated currency relies on a simple contrast of "handwritten" text to the engraved words and numbers.

Creative Problem Solving

As we have said, the design process involves seeking visual solutions to problems. The arts are called *creative* fields because there are no predetermined correct answers to the problems. Infinite variations in individual interpretations and applications are possible. Problems in art vary in specifics and complexity. Independent painters or sculptors usually create their own "problems" or avenues they wish to explore. The artist can choose as wide or narrow a scope as he or she wishes. The architect or graphic and industrial designer is usually given a problem, often with very specific options and clearly defined limitations. Students in art classes are often in this "problem-solving" category—they execute a series of assignments devised by the instructor that require rather specific solutions. However, all art or visual problems are similar in that a creative solution is desired.

The creative aspect of art also includes the often-heard phrase "there are no rules in art." This is true. In solving problems visually, there is no list of strict or absolute dos and don'ts to follow. Given the varied objectives of visual art throughout the ages, definite laws are impossible. However, "no rules" may seem to imply that all designs are equally valid and visually successful. This is not true. Artistic practices and criteria have been developed from successful works, of which an artist or designer should be aware. Thus, guidelines (not rules) exist that usually will assist in the creation of successful designs. These guidelines certainly do not mean the artist is limited to any specific solution.

Content and Form

Discussions of art often distinguish between two aspects, **content** and **form**. Content implies the subject matter, story, or information that the artwork seeks to communicate to the viewer. Form is the purely visual aspect, the manipulation of the various elements and principles of design. Content is what artists want to say; form is how they say it. Problems in art can usually concern both categories.

Sometimes the aim of a work of art is purely **aesthetic**. Take, for example, adornment—subject matter can be absent and the only "problem" one of creating visual pleasure. Purely abstract decoration has a very legitimate role in art. Frequently, however, problems in art have a purpose beyond mere visual satisfaction. Art is, and always has been, a means of visual communication.

▶ **C**

"Consume Like Me" on $20 bill. *zingmagazine,* issue #18. Contributed by Andrew Coulter Enright/Tynt Press. Published by Zing LLC.

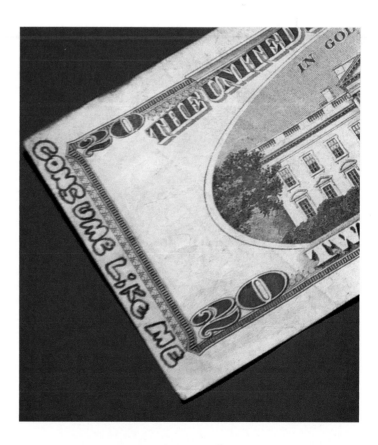

STEPS IN THE PROCESS

We have all heard the cliché "a picture is worth a thousand words." This is true. There is no way to calculate how much each of us has learned through pictures. Communication has always been an essential role for art. Indeed, before letters were invented, written communication consisted of simple pictorial symbols. Today, pictures can function as a sort of international language. A picture can be understood when written words may be unintelligible to the foreigner or the illiterate. We do not need to understand German to grasp immediately that the message of the poster in **A** is pain, suffering, and torture.

Art as Communication

In art, as in communication, the artist or designer is saying something to the viewer. Here the successful solution not only is visually effective but also communicates an idea. Any of the elements of art can be used in communication. Purely abstract lines, color, and shapes can very effectively express ideas or feelings. Many times communication is achieved through symbols, pictorial images that suggest to the viewer the theme or message. The ingenuity of creative imagination exercised in selecting these images can be important in the finished work's success.

In art, as in communication, images are frequently combined with written words. The advertisements we see every day usually use both elements, coordinated to reinforce the design's purpose.

Countless pictures demonstrate that words are not necessary for communication: Here two examples suggest the idea of balance. In the photograph *Balanced Rock* (**B**) no words are needed to communicate the idea. In **C** the visual and intellectual are combined. We read the word, but the uppercase *E* also provides a visual balance to the capital *B*, and the dropped *A* is used as a visual fulcrum.

The Creative Process

These successful design solutions are due, of course, to good ideas. Students often wonder, "How do I get an idea?" Almost everyone shares this dilemma from time to time. Even the professional artist can stare at an empty canvas, the successful writer at a blank page. An idea in art can take many forms, varying from a specific visual effect to an intellectual communication of a definite message. Ideas encompass both content and form.

It is doubtful that anyone can truly explain why or how an answer to something we've been puzzling over appears out of the blue. Our ideas can occur when we are in the shower, mowing the lawn, or in countless other seemingly

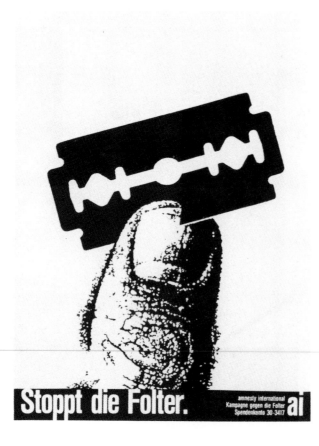

◄ **A**

Stop Torture. 1985. Poster for Amnesty International. Art Director and Designer: Stephan Bundi. Atelier Bundi, Bern, Switzerland.

unlikely situations. But we need not be concerned here with sudden solutions. They will continue to occur, but what happens when we have a deadline? What can we consciously do to stimulate the creative process? What sort of activities can promote the likelihood that a solution to a problem will present itself?

Many people today are concerned with such questions. A number of worthwhile books and articles have been devoted to the study of the creative process, featuring numerous technical terms to describe aspects of this admittedly complex subject. But we suggest three very simple activities with very simple names:

Thinking
Looking
Doing

These activities are not sequential steps and certainly are not independent procedures. They overlap and may be performed almost simultaneously or by jumping back and forth from one to another. Individuals vary; people are not programmed machines in which rigid step-by-step procedures lead inevitably to answers. People's feelings and intuitions may assist in making decisions. Problems vary so that a specific assignment may immediately suggest an initial emphasis on one of these activities. But all three procedures can stimulate the artistic problem-solving process.

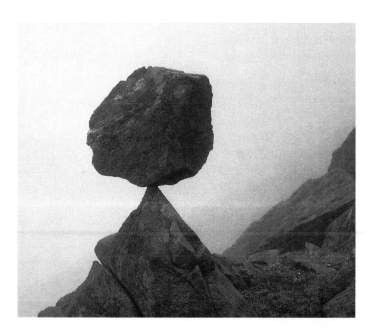

◄ **B**

Andy Goldsworthy. *Balanced Rock* (Misty, Langdale, Cumbria, May 1977). *Andy Goldsworthy: A Collaboration with Nature* (New York: Harry N. Abrams, Inc., Publishers, 1990).

► **C**

The layout of the letters conveys the idea by suggesting the word's meaning.

BALANCE

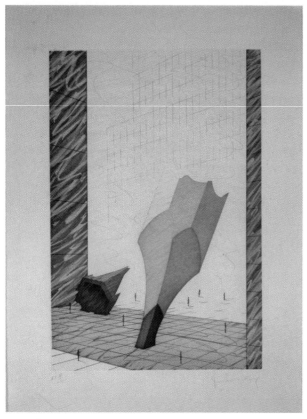

▲ **A**

Claes Oldenburg. *Proposal for a Colossal Monument in Downtown New York City: Sharpened Pencil Stub with Broken-off Tip of the Woolworth Building.* 1993. Etching with aquatint, 2′ 8¹/₂″ × 1′ 10″. Collection of Claes Oldenburg and Coosje van Bruggen.

Having a talent isn't worth much
unless you know what to do with it.

▲ **B**

"Having a talent isn't worth much unless you know what to do with it." 1978. Poster for the School of Visual Arts. Art director: Silas H. Rhodes. Designer/illustrator: Tony Palladino. Copywriter: Dee Ito. Courtesy of School of Visual Arts.

GETTING STARTED

The well-known French artist Georges Braque wrote in his *Cahiers* (notebooks) that "one must not think up a picture." His point is valid; a painting is often a long process that should not be forced or created by formulas to order. However, each day countless designers must indeed "think up" solutions to design problems. Thinking is an essential part of this solution. When confronted by a problem in any aspect of life, the usual first step is to think about it. Thinking is applicable also to art and visual problems. It is involved in all aspects of the creative process. Every step in creating a design involves choices, and the selections are determined by thinking. Chance or accident is also an element in art. But art cannot be created mindlessly, although some art movements have attempted to eliminate rational thought as a factor in creating art and to stress intuitive or subconscious thought.

Even then it is thinking that decides whether the spontaneously created result is worthwhile or acceptable. To say that thinking is somehow outside the artistic process is truly illogical.

Thinking about the Problem

Knowing what you are doing must precede your doing it. So thinking starts with understanding the problem at hand:

Precisely what is to be achieved? (What specific visual or intellectual effect is desired?)

Are there visual stylistic requirements (illustrative, abstract, nonobjective, and so on)?

What physical limitations (size, color, media, and so on) are imposed?

When is the solution needed?

These questions may all seem self-evident, but effort spent on solutions outside the range of these specifications will not be productive. So-called failures can occur simply because the problem was not fully understood at the very beginning.

Thinking about the Solution

Thinking can be especially important in art that has a specific theme or message. How can the concept be communicated in visual terms? A first step is to think logically of which images or pictures could represent this theme and to list them or, better yet, sketch them quickly, because a visual answer is what you're seeking. Let's take a specific example: What could visually represent the idea of art or design? Some obvious **symbols** appear in the designs on these pages, and you will easily think of more. You might expand the idea by discussing it with others. They may offer suggestions you have not considered. Professional designers often consult reports from market surveys that reveal the ideas of vast numbers of people.

Sketch your ideas to see immediately the visual potential. At this point you do not necessarily decide on one idea. But it's better to narrow a broad list to a few ideas worthy of development. Choosing a visual image is only the first step. How will you use your choice? The examples shown use the same source, but in original and unexpected ways:

A fragment of a pencil becomes the subject of a monumental sculpture. **(A)**

Wasted talent is symbolized by a distorted and useless pencil. **(B)**

A carefully sharpened pencil becomes a spiraling ribbon demonstrating art's ability to transform our understanding of form. **(C)**

These designs are imaginative and eye-catching. The image was just the first step. *How* that image or form was used provided the unique and successful solution.

Thinking about the Audience

Selecting a particular symbol may depend on limitations of size, medium, color, and so on. Even thinking of future viewers may provide an influence. To whom is this visual message addressed? An enormous pencil fragment as a piece of sculpture might serve as a monument to the legions of "pencil pushers" in an office complex. The same sculpture located at an art school could pay tribute to the humblest of art-making tools. The ribbon of pencil shaving **(C)** may not engage an audience as a symbol so much as a simple but extraordinary fact.

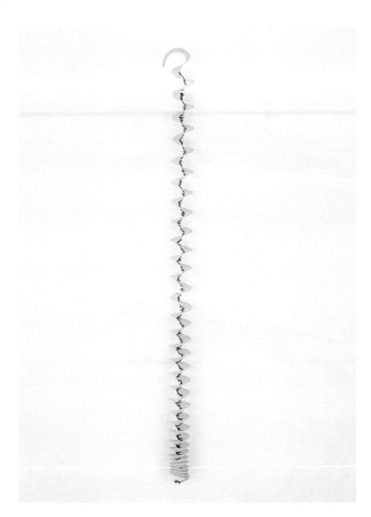

▶ **C**

Tom Friedman. *Untitled (Pencil Shavings)*. 1992. (From an edition of two.) 1′ 11^1/$_2$″ × 1^1/$_2$″ × 1^1/$_2$″.

FORM AND CONTENT

What will be presented, and how will it be presented? The thinking stage of the design process is often a contest to define this relationship of *form* and *content.* The contest may play itself out in additions and subtractions as a painting is revised or in the drafts and sketches of an evolving design concept. The solution may be found intuitively or may be influenced by cultural values, previous art, or the expectations of clients.

Selecting Content

Raymond Loewy's revised logo for the Greyhound Bus Company is an example of content being clearly communicated by the appropriate image or form. The existing logo in 1933 **(A)** looked fat to Loewy, and the chief executive at Greyhound agreed. Loewy's revised version **(B)** (based on a thoroughbred greyhound) conveys the concept of speed, and the company adopted the new logo.

Selecting Form

The form an artist selects can also work in unexpected ways to express content. Edgar Heap of Birds presents just such a contradiction of our expectations for printed words. The word *Sooners* (the name given to the early white settlers of Oklahoma) is presented backward in the billboard shown in **C**. This is an immediate signal that something is wrong, whether or not we know the specific history.

What happens when the same form is used to convey opposing content? A billboard showing a model wearing a De Beers diamond **(D)** is replaced by activists with one depicting a woman from the Bushman group **(E)**. The protest image plays off the familiar advertisement to send an unexpected message: "The Bushmen aren't forever."

Form and content issues would certainly be easier to summarize in a monocultural society. Specific symbols may lose meaning when they cross national, ethnic, or religious borders. Given these obstacles to understanding, it is a powerful testimony to the meaning inherent in form when artworks communicate successfully across time and distance.

Style: Form and Content

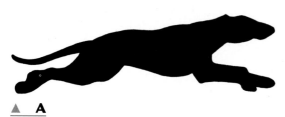

▲ **A**

Raymond Loewy. Original logo for Greyhound Bus Co.

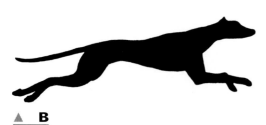

▲ **B**

Raymond Loewy. Redesigned logo, 1933.

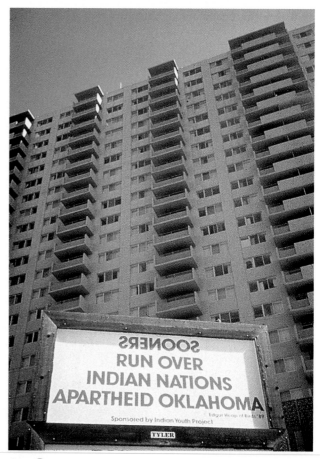

▲ **C**

Hock E Aye Vi (Edgar Heap of Birds). Native American. *Apartheid Oklahoma.* 1989. Billboard.

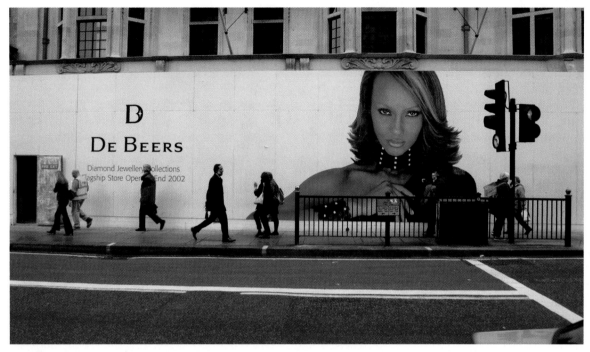

▲ **D**

"A diamond is forever." De Beers diamond advertisement. Photo by Jonathan Player.
The New York Times, Thursday, November 21, 2002, p. W1.

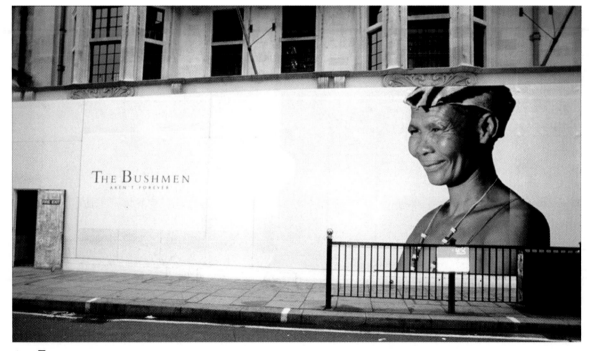

▲ **E**

"The Bushmen aren't forever." De Beers billboard covered by activists. Photo by
Tim Mitchell/Survival International.

FORM AND FUNCTION

Meaning and utility are least ambiguous when the relationship between form and content is clear and uncluttered. This is true of both images and objects. When such clarity is achieved, we say that form follows function. In this case form is determined by content and function is a priority. This relationship is often easiest to see and acknowledge in utilitarian design, such as the furniture design of the American Shaker movement. The interior presented in **A** reveals a simple, straightforward attitude toward furniture and space design. All the furnishings are functional and free from extraneous decoration. The ladder back of the chair exhibits a second utility when the chair is hung on the rail. Everything in this space communicates the Shaker value of simplicity.

The *Spiral Bookworm Shelf* shown in **B** is also functional but in a playful and surprising way. This object's form is not dictated by a strict form-follows-function design approach. This design solution is simple, like Shaker design, but the form expresses a sense of visual delight and humor as well.

Venturi, Scott Brown's addition to the Allen Memorial Art Museum **(C)** is a site-specific architectural design solution that takes into account the context of the original design by Cass Gilbert. The addition stands in striking contrast to the original structure, yet one can readily see a continuity of scale, color, and pattern. In fact, the Cass Gilbert design adapts Italian influences to American Prairie style and in doing so acknowledges the site as an influence on the design. Both parts of the complex illustrate design solutions where the function is not only to house art but also to reflect the historic and geographic context of the museum.

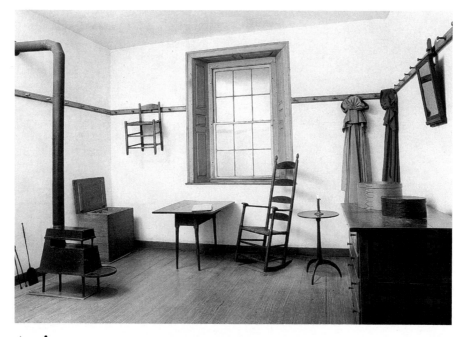

▲ **A**

Shaker interior. Reproduced by permission of the American Museum in Britain, Bath.

▶ **B**

Ron Arad. *Spiral Bookworm Shelf.*
$7^1/_2'' \times 10' 6'' \times 8''$.

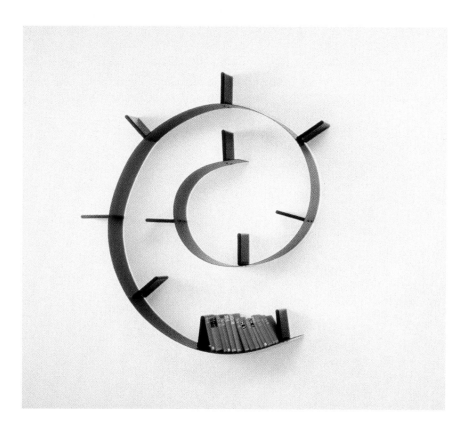

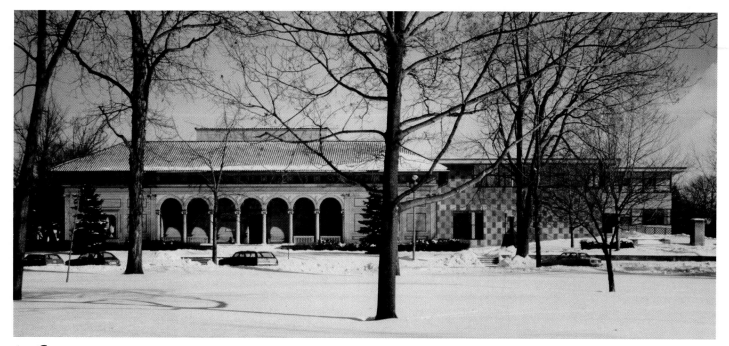

▲ **C**

Allen Memorial Art Museum. Cass Gilbert. Addition by Venturi, Scott Brown and Associates.
The buildings that house the Allen Memorial Art Museum at Oberlin College.

SOURCES: NATURE

Looking is probably the primary education of any artist. This process includes observing both nature and human artifacts, including art, design, and commonplace objects. Most artists are stimulated by the visual world around them and learn of possibilities for expression by examining other art. Studying art from all periods, regions, and cultures introduces you to a wealth of visual creations, better equipping you to discover your own solutions.

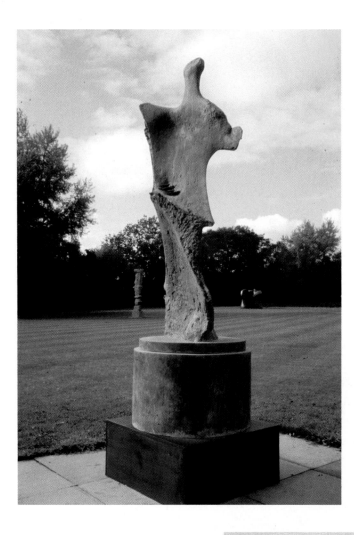

◀ **A**

Henry Moore. *Standing Figure.* 1962. Bronze, height 9′ 4″ (2.84 m). Reproduced by permission of The Henry Moore Foundation.

▼ **B**

Henry Moore's collection of bones. Reproduced by permission of The Henry Moore Foundation.

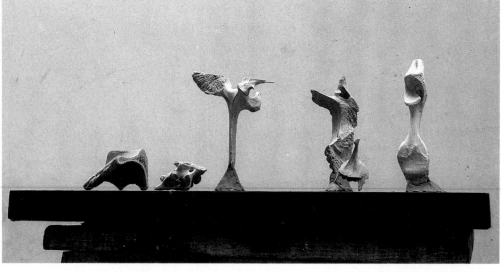

For better or worse we do not create our design solutions in an information vacuum. We have the benefit of an abundance of visual information coming at us through a variety of media, from books to television, websites, and films. On the plus side, we are treated to images one would previously have had to travel to see. On the minus side, it is easy to overlook that we are often seeing a limited (or altered) aspect of the original artwork in a reproduction.

Source versus Subject

Sources in nature and culture are clearly identifiable in the works of some artists, while less obvious in the works of others—perhaps only revealed when we see drawings or preparatory work. In any case a distinction should be made between source and subject. The *source* is a stimulus for an image or idea. For example, a bone can be the source for a work of sculpture. The **subject**, as mentioned previously, is tied to the content of the work or to the artist's ideas and way of seeing.

The sculptor Henry Moore noted that he had a tendency to pick up shells at the beach that resembled his current work in progress. In that way he recognized in nature a resemblance to forms he was already exploring in the studio. His sculpture of a mother embracing a child, for example, resembled the protective wrapping form of a broken shell he found. In turn the forms from nature he collected came to suggest possibilities for new figurative pieces. Moore's *Standing Figure* (**A**) bears a resemblance to various bones in his collection (**B**), but it is not a copy of any of them.

Sometimes the relationship between a model seen in nature and a design it inspires may not be as directly revealed as it is in the case of Henry Moore's sculpture. We can probably assume that the designers of the seaplane shown in **C** did not copy the form or light-dark pattern of the whale (**D**). Similar problems led to similar solutions, however: both plane and whale are streamlined for easy movement through the water. It is safe to assume that the engineers and designers did look at models from nature and that this influenced their solution.

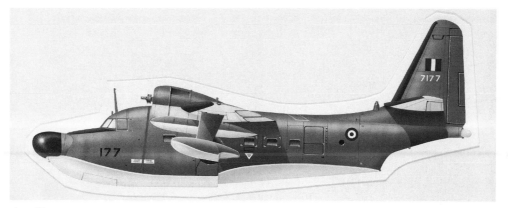

▲ **C**

Grumman HU–16 Albatross, post–World War II utility and rescue amphibian. *Encyclopedia of World Air Power,* Bill Gunston, consultant ed. (London: Aerospace Publishing, 1980), p. 165.

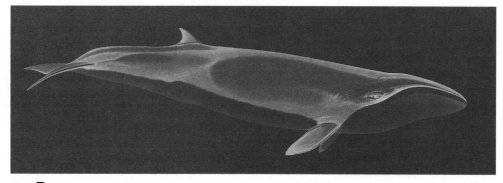

▲ **D**

Pygmy Right Whale (*Caperea marginata*), Southern Hemisphere, 18'–21½' (5.5–6.5 m). From Mark Cawardine and Martin Camm, *Whales, Dolphins, and Porpoises* (London: Dorling Kindersley, 1995), p. 48.

SOURCES: HISTORY AND CULTURE

We expect artists and designers to be visually sensitive people who see things in the world that others might overlook and who look with special interest at the history of art and design.

Jennifer Bartlett's series entitled *In the Garden* consists of dozens of works in a variety of media, including drawings such as **A** and mixed-media studies such as **B**. The source of the imagery is clearly a garden pool. The subject is the many ways of seeing the garden and thinking about painting. A variety of styles is presented in this series, which reflects the processes both of looking at the original source and of looking at art from various periods.

Visual Training and Retraining

The art of looking is not entirely innocent. Long before the training in seeing we get in art and design classes, we are trained by our exposure to mass media. Television,

film, Internet, and print images provide examples that can influence our self-image and our personal relationships. The distinction between "news" and "docudrama" is often a blurry one, and viewers are often absorbed into the "reality" of a movie.

At times it seems that visual training demands a retraining of looking on slower, more conscious terms. "Look again" and "see the relationships" are often heard in a beginning drawing class. Part of this looking process involves examining works of art and considering the images of mass media that shape our culture. Many artists actively address these issues in their art by using familiar images or "quoting" past artworks. Although this may seem like an esoteric exercise to the beginning student, an awareness of the power of familiar images is fundamental to understanding visual communication.

▼ **A**

Jennifer Bartlett. *In the Garden, Drawing #64*. 1980. Pencil on paper, 2′ 2″ × 1′ 7 ¹/₂″ (66 × 49.5 cm). Courtesy Paula Cooper Gallery, New York. Photo: D. James Dee.

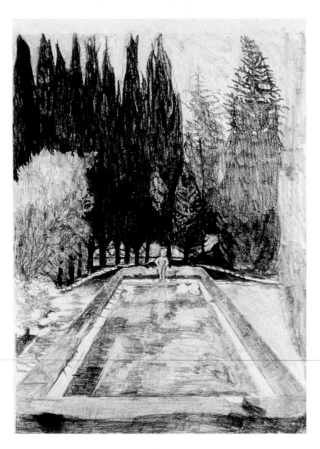

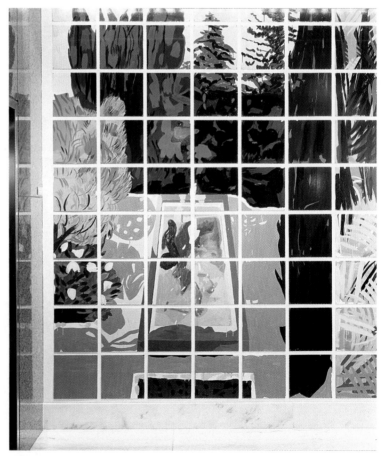

▲ **B**

Jennifer Bartlett. *Study for In the Garden* (detail: 54 of 270 squares). 1980. Pencil, ink, gouache on paper, 2′ × 3′ (61 × 91 cm). Commission, Institute for Scientific Information, Philadelphia. Collection of the artist: Courtesy Paula Cooper Gallery, New York.

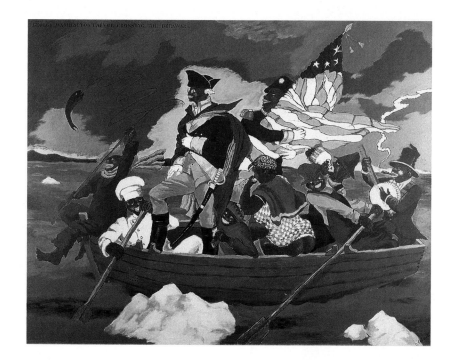

Robert Colescott. *George Washington Carver Crossing the Delaware.* 1975. Acrylic on canvas, 4′ 6″ × 9′. Phyllis Kind Gallery, New York.

▼   **D**

Betty Crocker through the years. Courtesy General Mills.

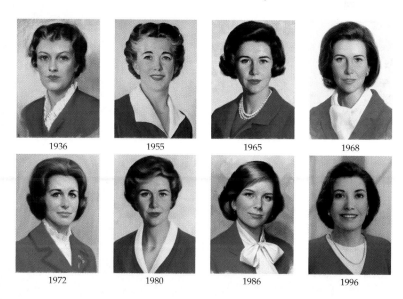

Certain so-called high art images manage to become commonly known, or **vernacular**, through frequent reproduction. In the case of a painting like *Washington Crossing the Delaware*, the image is almost as universally recognized as a religious icon once was. There is a long tradition of artists paying homage to the masters, and we can understand how an artist might study this or other paintings in an attempt to learn techniques. However, *George Washington Carver Crossing the Delaware* (**C**), by the African American artist Robert Colescott, strikes a different relationship to the well-known painting we recognize as a source. Colescott plays with the familiarity of this patriotic image and startles us with a presentation of negative black stereotypes. One American stereotype is laid on top of another, leading the viewer to confront preconceptions about both.

In contrast to the previous fine art examples, the example shown in **D** comes from the world of commercial art. The evolving image of "Betty Crocker" reveals how this icon was visualized at different times. This then reflects where the artist looked for a visual model of "American female." Looking, then, can be influenced by commercial and societal forces, which are as real an aspect of our lives as the elements of nature.

Looking is a complex blend of conscious searching and visual recollections. This searching includes looking at art, nature, and the vernacular images from the world around us, as well as doing formal research into new or unfamiliar subjects. What we hope to find are the elements that shape our own visual language.

THINKING WITH MATERIALS

Doing starts with visual experimentation. For most artists and designers, this means thinking with the materials. Trial and error, intuition, or deliberate application of a system is set into motion. At this point an idea starts to take form, whether in a sketch or in final materials. The artist Eva Hesse got right to the point with her observation on materials:

Two points of view—
1. Materials are lifeless until given shape by a creator.
2. Materials by their own potential created their end.

Eva Hesse is known for embracing apparent contradictions in her work. The studio view **(A)** presents a number of her sculptural works that embody both of the preceding points of view. Hesse gave shape to materials such as papier-mâché, cloth, and wood. Other elements, such as the hanging, looping, and connecting ropes and cords, reflect the inherent potential of the materials.

 In the Studio

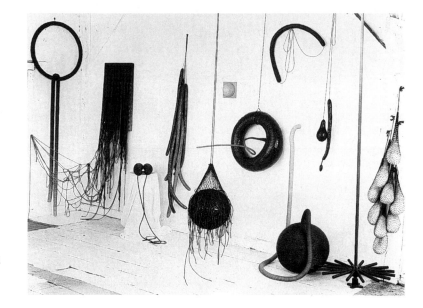

▶ **A**

Eva Hesse. *Studio*. 1966. Installation photograph by Gretchen Lambert. Courtesy Robert Miller Gallery.

◀ **B**

Sarah Weinstock. *Untitled*. 2006. Ink and soap bubbles on paper, $6^{1}/_{2}$″ × $9^{1}/_{2}$″. (Detail.)

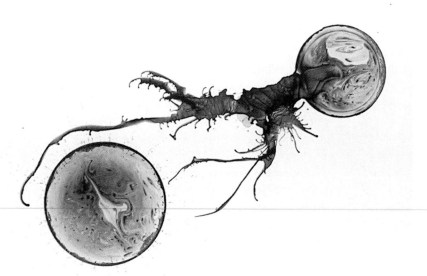

Sarah Weinstock's drawing shown in **B** is the result both of the forces at play with ink spread on soap bubbles and of the artist's coaxing and encouragement of those materials on the paper. The result suggests two organic forms with one reaching out toward the other.

Photographs of the sculptor David Smith at work **(C)** show the playful side of doing. We can see the degree to which he allowed the materials to create their own end.

Just as a child might delight in building blocks becoming a castle, Smith let the forms of cardboard boxes define the proportions of sculpture he would later complete in steel **(D)**. Smith stacked the boxes on a windowsill and taped them to the window as he assembled each study. The influence of the window as a support shows through in the predominantly two-dimensional composition of the final pieces.

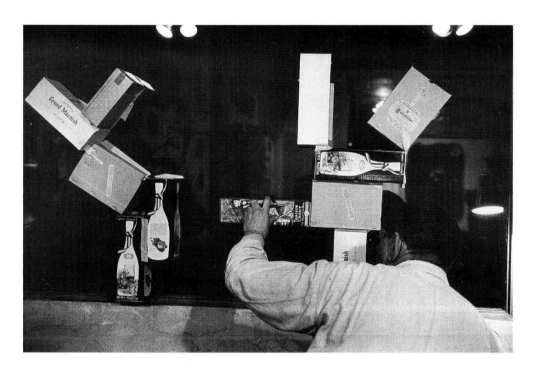

◀ **C**
David Smith assembling liquor boxes as models for his sculptures. Art © Estate of David Smith/ Licensed by VAGA, New York, New York.

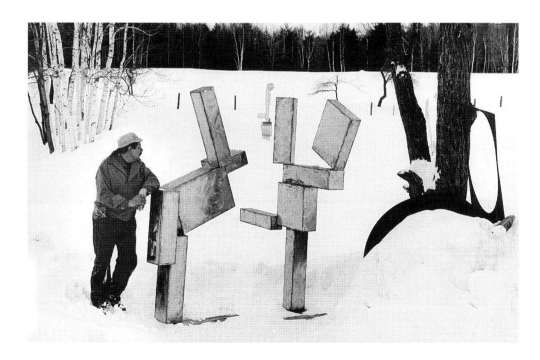

◀ **D**
David Smith with completed sculptures *Cubi IV* and *Cubi V*. Art © Estate of David Smith/ Licensed by VAGA, New York, New York.

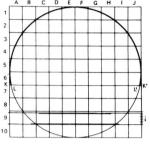
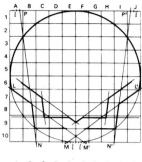
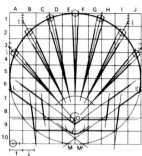
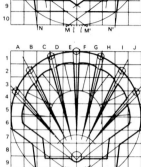
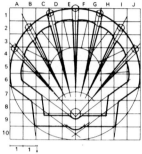

◀ **A**

◀ **A**

Raymond Loewy. Steps in the
development of a new Shell logo, 1971.

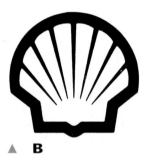

▲ **B**

Raymond Loewy. Revision
of Shell logo, 1971.

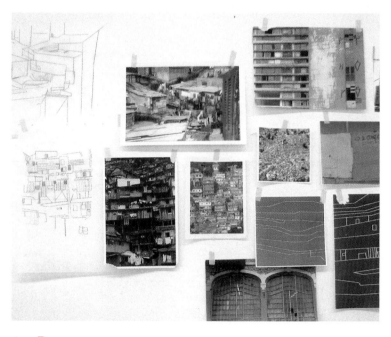

▲ **D**

Sunny Belliston. *Studio Wall.*
2006. Photographs and drawings,
variable dimensions.

DOING AND REDOING

When designers leave a record of their drawings, we are able
in effect to see them doing their work. This is the case with
the construction drawings for Loewy's logo design for Shell
(A). The four steps depicted lay out the defining geometry of the
scallop shell, and the first step shows that a circle provides the
underlying form. These four drawings provide the map to
the final version **(B)**, but undoubtedly other possibilities were
explored before this one was adopted. Today, drawings such
as these would probably be done on a computer, which can
greatly speed up the creation of alternative possibilities.

The process board shown in **C** exhibits all the aspects
of thinking, looking, and doing. Considerations of marketing are recorded, sources and other symbol solutions are
acknowledged, and, finally, the initial idea is shown moving
through stages of doing and redoing leading to finished
refinement.

Sunny Belliston's *Studio Wall* **(D)** can be seen as the
early stages of gathering compositional ideas for one of
her paintings. The collection of photographs and drawings
is also a conversation with earlier work and extends her
investigation of gridlike structures found in architecture
and hillside neighborhoods. This wall is typical of the
studio environment artists create for themselves.

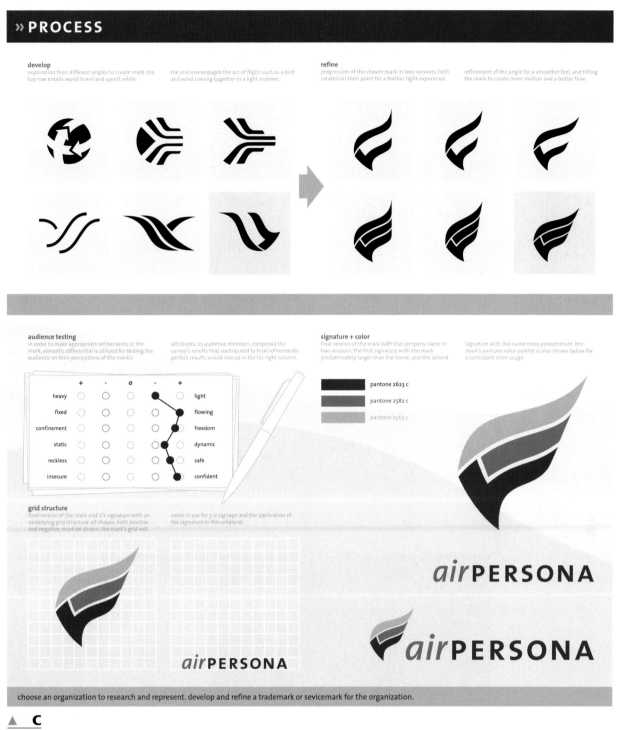

Meredith Rueter. *Process Board: air PERSONA.*

The doing step in the design process obviously involves continuous looking and thinking, yet more than one artist, writer, or composer has observed that doing takes over with a life of its own. An artwork takes shape through you, and as it does you may find yourself wondering where the time went or what you were thinking of when a work session ends. This experience is exhilarating but includes the elements of risk and failure.

A wonderful film of the painter Philip Guston at work ends with him covering his picture with white to begin again. Guston accepted such a setback along the way as normal and even necessary. His experience told him that revision would allow an idea to grow beyond an obvious or familiar starting point.

CRITIQUE

CONSTRUCTIVE CRITICISM

Critique is an integral component of studio education for art students and can take several forms. You could have direct dialogue with a professor in front of a work in progress, or your entire class could review a completed work **(A** and **B)**. Critique can also be a self-critique and take the form of a journal entry. The goal of a critique is increased understanding through examination of the project's successes and shortcomings. A variety of creative people, from artists to composers to authors, generally affirm that criticism is best left for *after* the design or composition is completed. A free and flexible approach to any studio work can be stifled by too much criticism too soon.

The components of a constructive critique can vary, but a critique is most valid when linked to the criteria for the artwork, design, or studio assignment. If a drawing's objective is to present an unusual or unexpected view of an object, then it is appropriate to critique the perspective, size, emphasis, and contrast of the drawing—those elements that contribute to communicating the point of view. Such a critique could also include cultural or historic precedents for how such an object might be depicted. A drawing of an apple that has been sliced in half and is seen from above would offer an unusual point of view. An apple presented alongside a serpent would present a second point of view charged with religious meaning for Jews and Christians. Both approaches would be more than a simple representation and would offer contrasting points of view. Nevertheless, both drawings may be subject to a critique of their composition.

A Model for Critique

A constructive model for critique would include the following:

Description: A verbal account of *what* is there.
Analysis: A discussion of *how* things are presented with an emphasis on relationships (for example, "bigger than," "brighter than," "to the left of").
Interpretation: A sense of the meaning, implication, or effect of the piece.

A simple description of a drawing that includes a snake and an apple might lead us to conclude that the drawing is an **illustration** for a biology text. Further description, analysis, and interpretation could lead us to understand other meanings and the emphasis of the drawing. And, in the case of a critique, thoughtful description, analysis, and interpretation might help the artist (or the viewer) see other, more dynamic possibilities for the drawing.

The many sections devoted to principles and elements of art and design in this text are each a potential component for critique. In fact the authors' observations about an image could be complemented by further critical analysis. For example, the text may point out how color brings emphasis to a composition, and further discussion could reveal the impact of other aspects such as size, placement, and cultural context.

► **A**

A professor critiques a work in progress.

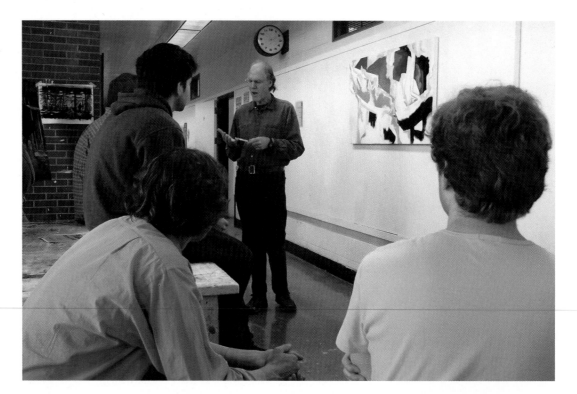

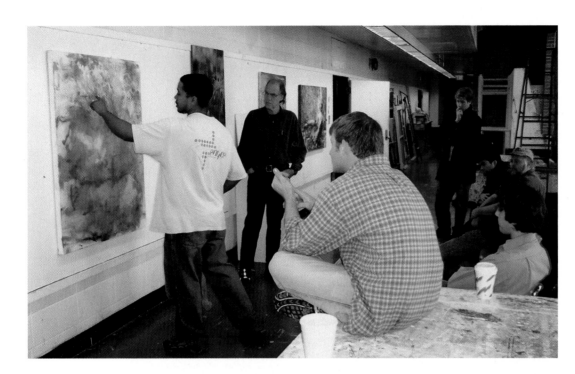

◄ **B**

Students review and critique each other's work.

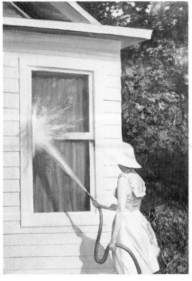
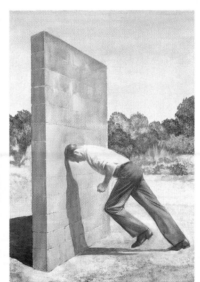
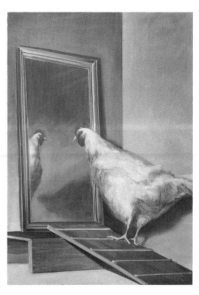

▲ **C**

Mark Tansey. *A Short History of Modernism*. 1982. Oil on canvas, three panels, 4' 10" × 10' overall. Collection of Steve and Maura Shapiro. Courtesy Gagosian Gallery, New York, with permission from the estate of Mark Tansey.

The critique process is an introduction to the critical context in which artists and designers work. Mature artworks are subject to critical review, and professional designers submit to the review of clients and members of their design teams. Future theory and criticism are pushed along by new designs and artworks.

On a lighter note, the critique process can include the range of responses suggested by Mark Tansey's painting shown in **C**:

You may feel your work has been subjected to an aggressive cleansing process.
You may feel you are butting your head against a wall.
And don't forget that what someone takes from an image or design is a product of what she or he brings to it!

COMPARISON AND CONTRAST

The processes of thinking, looking, and doing may seem to be different for graphic design and drawing or painting. The contrasting examples of **A** and **B** appear to be born of differing thought processes. An analysis of these two works will recur throughout the chapters of this text, and the inherent contrasts will be explored, but comparisons will be found as well.

The Susan Moore portrait **(A)** emphasizes the "looking" process. Careful observation is required to register the details and proportions that create a convincing portrait. The looking process is also integral to the challenge of creating this image at the larger-than-life scale. It could be easy to overlook the "thinking" component of such work. What does the artist evoke in confronting the viewer with this large image? What do you make of the title *Vanity*? What is the effect of the physical evidence of the "doing"— that is, the layered texture of the oil-stick medium and marks?

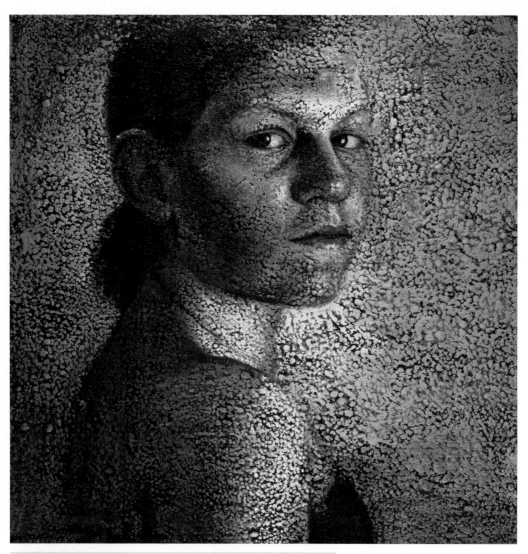

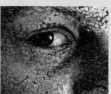 ▲ **A**

Susan Moore. *Vanity (Portrait 1)*. 2000. Oil stick on canvas, 4′ × 3′ 11″.

El Lissitzky's *Of Two Squares: A Suprematist Tale in Six Constructions* **(B)** was a radical approach to art and design in 1922. The text accompanying this group of six studies included the following statement:

Do Not Read, Take [pieces of] Paper, [little] Bars, [building] Blocks, Fold [them], Paint [them], Build

The six-part series tells a story in graphic shapes of an interaction between the red and the black elements that evolves through conflicting forms to conclude in a new construction. The design steps illustrate a revolutionary change leading to the construction of a new visual language consistent with the idealism of the time. The "thinking" process seems to motivate this design, but don't overlook the directions included for "doing." Further, the design creates a dynamic relationship between the few, geometric elements that is evidence of sensitive looking.

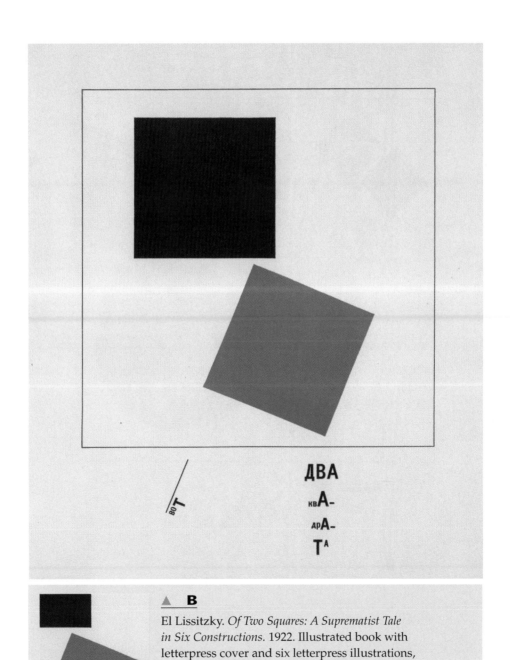

▲ **B**

El Lissitzky. *Of Two Squares: A Suprematist Tale in Six Constructions.* 1922. Illustrated book with letterpress cover and six letterpress illustrations, $10^{15}/_{16}'' \times 8^{7}/_{8}''$ (27.8 × 22.5 cm). Publisher: Skify, Berlin. Gift of the Judith Rothschild Foundation (89.2001.5).

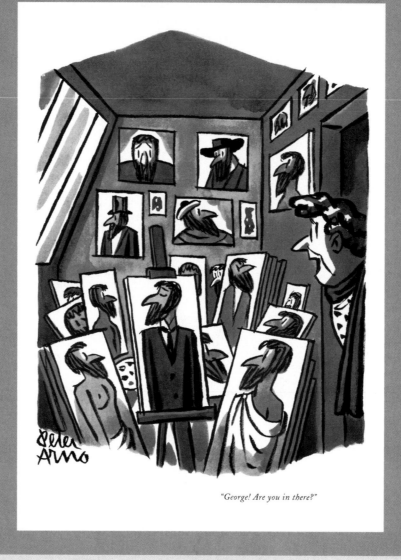

"George! Are you in there?"

Peter Arno. 1959.

CHAPTER 2

UNITY

HARMONY

Unity, the presentation of an integrated image, is perhaps as close to a rule as art can approach. Unity means that a congruity or agreement exists among the elements in a design; they look as though they belong together, as though some visual connection beyond mere chance has caused them to come together. Another term for the same idea is **harmony**. If the various elements are not harmonious, if they appear separate or unrelated, your composition falls apart and lacks unity.

The image in **A** illustrates a high degree of unity. When we look at the elements in this design, we immediately see that they are all somewhat similar. This harmony, or unity, arises not merely from our recognition that all the objects are paint cans. Unity is achieved through the repetition of the oval shapes of the cans. Linear elements such as the diagonal shadows and paint sticks are also repeated. The subtle grays of the metal cans unify a composition accented by a few bright colors. Such a unity can exist with either **representational** imagery or abstract forms.

The landscape photograph in **B** consists of varied shapes with no exact repetitions, yet all the shapes have a similar irregular jigsaw puzzle quality. The harmonious unity of the shapes is reinforced by a similarity of color throughout this **monochromatic** picture.

Seen simply as cutout shapes, the variety of silhouettes in **C** would be apparent. Alex Katz balances this variation with the unity of the repeated portrait of his wife, Ada. This approach of theme and variation is the essence of the concept of unity.

Where Does Unity Come From?

Unity of design is planned and controlled by an artist. Sometimes it stems naturally from the elements chosen, as in these examples. But more often it reflects the skill of the designer in creating a unified pattern from varied elements. Another term for *design* is **composition**, which implies the same feeling of organization. Just as a composition in a writing class is not merely a haphazard collection of words and punctuation marks, so too a visual composition is not a careless scattering of random items around a format.

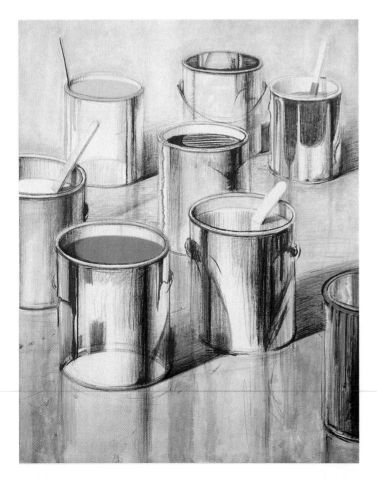

◄ **A**

Wayne Thiebaud. *Paint Cans.* 1990. Lithograph, hand-worked proof, 75.7 × 58.8 cm. DeYoung Museum (gift of the Thiebaud Family, 1995.99.12). Art © Wayne Thiebaud/Licensed by VAGA, New York, New York.

▶ **B**

Damon Winter, personal photograph from Iceland, *Communication Arts*, May/June 2005.

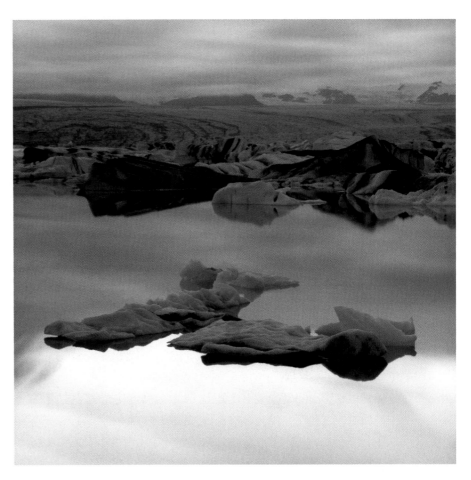

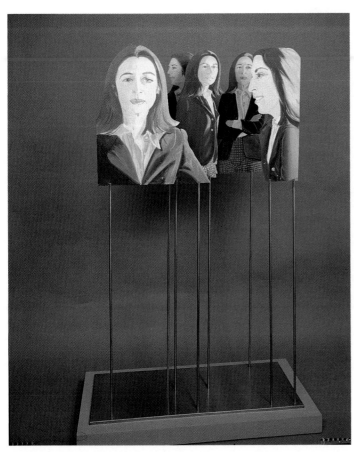

◀ **C**

Alex Katz. *Black Jacket*. 1972. Oil on aluminum (cutout), 5' 2⁵/₈" × 3' ¹/₄" (159 × 92 cm). Des Moines Art Center (gift in honor of Mrs. E. T. Meredith, Permanent Collection, 1978.7). Art © Alex Katz/Licensed by VAGA, New York, New York.

VISUAL UNITY

An important aspect of visual unity is that the whole must predominate over the parts: you must first see the whole pattern before you notice the individual elements. Each item may have a meaning and certainly add to the total effect, but if the viewer sees merely a collection of bits and pieces, then visual unity doesn't exist.

This concept differentiates a design from the typical scrapbook page. In a scrapbook each item is meant to be observed and studied individually, to be enjoyed and then forgotten as your eye moves on to the next souvenir. The result may be interesting, but it is not a unified design.

Exploring Visual Unity

The **collage** in **A** is a design. It is similar to a scrapbook in that it contains many diverse images, but we are aware first of the pattern the elements make together, and then we begin to enjoy the items separately.

Do not confuse intellectual unity with visual unity. Visual unity denotes some harmony or agreement between the items that is apparent to the eye. To say that a scrapbook page is unified because all the items have a common theme (your family, your wedding, your vacation at the beach) is unity of idea—that is, a conceptual unity not observable by the eye. A unifying idea will not necessarily produce a unified visual composition. The fact that all the elements in **A** deal with African American history is interesting but irrelevant to the visual organization.

The unity in **B** does not derive from recognizing all the items in the design as plant specimens. The visual unity stems from the repetition of spiral forms and curvilinear features. Then the variety of thick and thin, dark and light, and arrangement adds interest.

The need for visual unity does not deny that very often there is also an intellectual pleasure in design. Many times the task of a designer is to convey an idea or theme. Now the visual unity function is important along with an intellectual reading of the design. One example can show this dual appreciation. The *Communication Arts* cover in **C** is for an issue of the journal that has the theme "green design." The varied shades of green provide unity and reinforce the title. The repeated, stylized leaf shapes also unify the design with an element that suggests design in harmony with nature.

D B
Module   Visual Unity

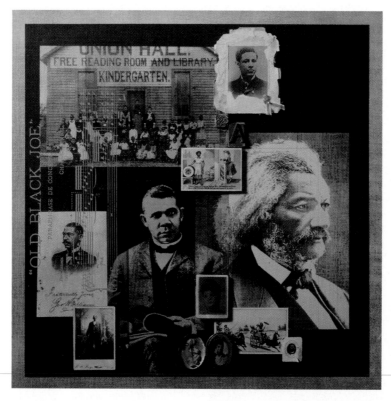

▲ **A**

Fred Otnes, designer. Collage for *National Geographic* magazine.
January 1988.

▶ **B**

Karl Blossfeldt. *Pumpkin Tendrils.*
Works of Karl Blossfeldt by Karl
Blossfeldt Archive. Ann and Jürgen
Wilde, eds., *Karl Blossfeldt: Working
Collages* (Cambridge: MIT Press,
2001), p. 54.

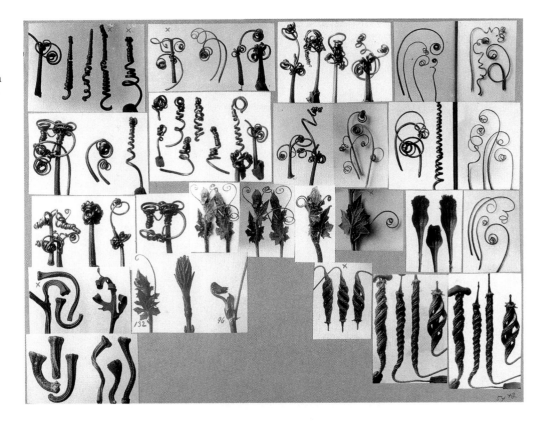

◀ **C**

Cover for *Communication
Arts*, May/June 2005.

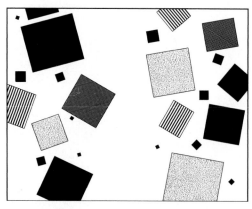

▲ **A**

We instantly see two groups of shapes.

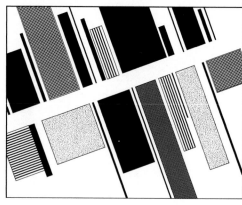

▲ **B**

The white diagonal is as obvious as the two groups of rectangles.

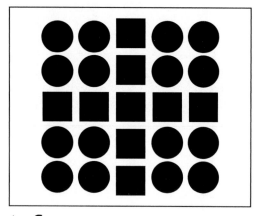

▲ **C**

Grouping similar shapes makes us see a plus sign in the center.

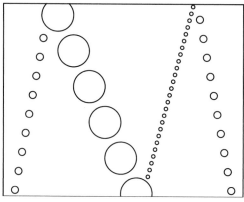

▲ **D**

The circles seem to form "lines," and we see an M shape.

VISUAL PERCEPTION

The designer's job in creating a visual unity is made easier by the fact that the viewer is actually looking for some sort of organization, something to relate the various elements. The viewer does not want to see confusion or unrelated chaos. The designer must provide some clues, but the viewer is already attempting to find some coherent pattern and unity. Indeed, when such a pattern cannot be found, chances are the viewer will simply ignore the image.

Studies in the area of perception have shown this phenomenon. Since early in the twentieth century, psychologists have done a great deal of research on visual perception, attempting to discover just how the eye and brain function together. Much of this research is, of course, very technical and scientific, but some of the basic findings are useful for the artist or designer. The most widely known of these perception studies is called the **gestalt** theory of visual psychology.

How We Look for Unity

Consider a few elementary concepts, which only begin to suggest the range of studies in perception. Researchers have concluded that viewers tend to group objects that are close to each other into a larger unit. Our first impression of **A** is not merely some random squares but two groups of smaller elements.

Negative (or empty) **spaces** will likewise appear organized. In **B** viewers immediately see the many elements as two groups. However, with all the shapes ending on two common boundaries, the impression of the slanted white diagonal shape is as strong as the various rectangles.

Also, our brain will tend to relate and group objects of a similar shape. Hence, in **C** a cross or plus sign is more obvious than the allover pattern of small shapes. In **D** the pattern is not merely many circles of various sizes. Instead our eye will close the spaces between similar circles to form a design of "lines." These diagonal lines organize themselves to give the impression of an M shape.

We easily identify the elements that make up the Richard Prince painting shown in **E** as three ellipses and a circle in a white field. The proximity of the four black shapes forms a constellation, and the smaller parts give way to the organization of the larger pattern. In this case it is possible to see this configuration as a startled clownlike face. This reading is assisted by the title (*My Funny Valentine*) but also reveals how easily we project a "face" onto a pattern.

The impulse to form unity or a visual whole out of a collection of parts can also work on an architectural scale. The Beaubourg **(F)** is a contemporary art center in Paris. The outer shell of the building is formed from conduits and structural features that are usually hidden. The constant repetition of vertical ducts, square structural framing, and circular openings gives visual unity to a potentially chaotic assortment of pipes and scaffolding. This building's distinct appearance stands in contrast to other buildings in the area, further strengthening its visual identity. Our brain looks for similar elements, and when we recognize them we see a cohesive design rather than unorganized chaos.

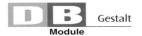
Gestalt

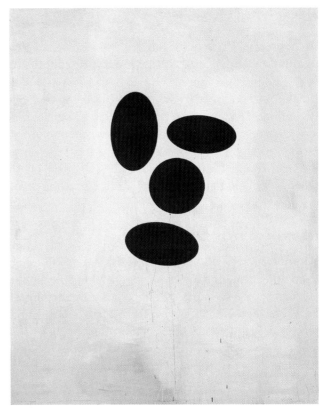

▲ **E**

Richard Prince. *My Funny Valentine.* 2001. Acrylic on silk screen frame, 7′ 2 1/2″ × 5′ 8 1/2″. Courtesy Barbara Gladstone Gallery, New York. © Richard Prince.

▼ **F**

Piano & Rogers; Ova Arup & Partners. Centre National d'Art et de Culture Georges Pompidou (Beaubourg) Paris, 1971–1977. SA4434.

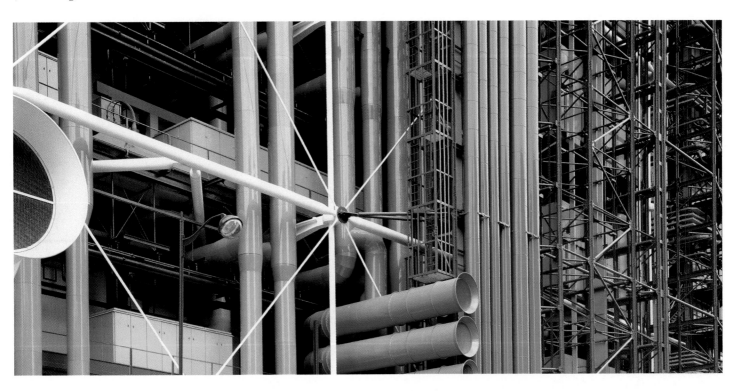

PROXIMITY

An easy way to gain unity—to make separate elements look as if they belong together—is by **proximity**, simply putting the elements close together. The four elements in **A** appear isolated, as floating bits with no relationship to each other. By putting them close together, as in **B**, we begin to see them as a total, related pattern. Proximity is a common unifying factor. Through proximity we recognize constellations in the skies and, in fact, are able to read. Change the proximity scheme that makes letters into words and reading becomes next to impossible.

Proximity in Composition

Thomas Eakins's painting **(C)** of bathers at a swimming hole shows the idea of proximity in composition. The lighter elements of the swimmers' bodies contrast with the generally darker background. However, these light elements are not placed aimlessly around the composition but, by proximity, are arranged carefully to unite visually. Four of the figures form the apex of an equilateral triangle at the center of the painting. This triangle provides a stable unifying effect.

Shirley Kaneda's painting **(D)** is an interesting array of shapes that are grouped in clusters, such as an arc of compressed oval shapes at the bottom of the painting. Elsewhere, shapes that appear to be stretched follow a reversed S curve. Notice how these clusters connect, forming the larger constellation of the whole composition. The elements are visually tied by proximity. Our eyes move smoothly from one item to the next.

Proximity is the simplest way to achieve unity, and many artworks employ this technique. Without proximity (with largely isolated elements), the artist must put greater stress on other methods to unify an image.

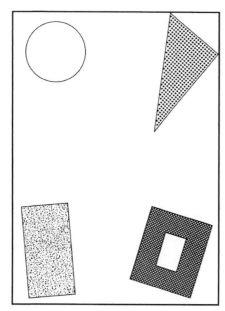

▲ **A**

If they are isolated from one another, elements appear unrelated.

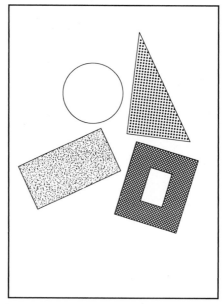

▲ **B**

Placing items close together makes us see them first as a group.

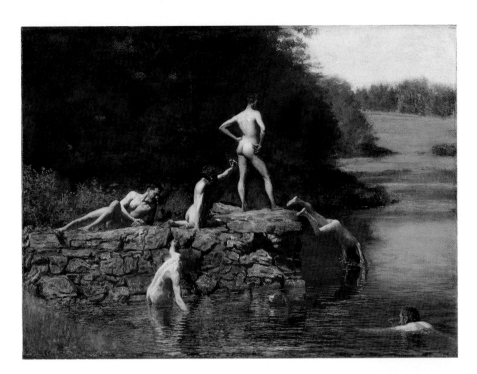

◀ **C**
Thomas Eakins. *Swimming*. 1885. Oil on
canvas, 2′ 3 $^3/_8$″ × 3′ $^3/_8$″. Collection of Amon
Carter Museum, Fort Worth, Texas. (1990.19.1)

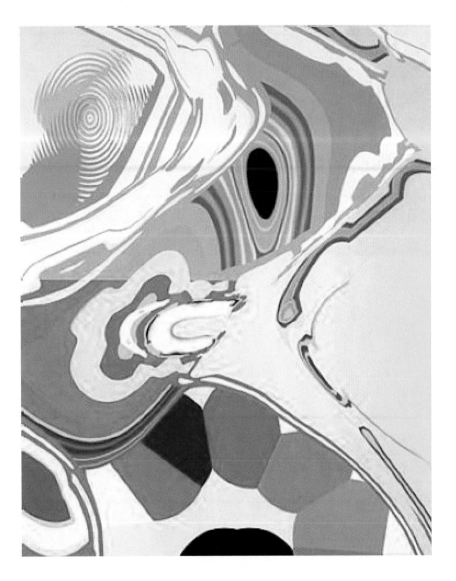

▶ **D**
Shirley Kaneda. *Stable Uncertainty*.
2003. Oil on canvas, 7′ 6″ × 6′ 3″.

REPETITION

A valuable and widely used device for achieving visual unity is **repetition**. As the term implies, something simply repeats in various parts of the design to relate the parts to each other. The element that repeats may be almost anything: a color, a shape, a texture, a direction, or an angle. In the painting by Sophie Taeuber-Arp **(A)**, the composition is based on one shape: a circle with two circular "bites" removed. This shape is repeated in different sizes and positions. The result is a composition that is unified but not predictable.

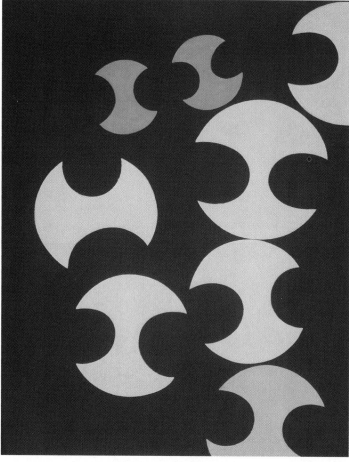

◀ **A**

Sophie Taeuber-Arp. *Composition with Circles Shaped by Curves.* 1935. Gouache on paper, 1' 1 $^7/_8$" × 10 $^5/_8$" (35 × 27 cm). Kunstmuseum Bern (gift of Mrs. Marguerite Arp-Hagenbach).

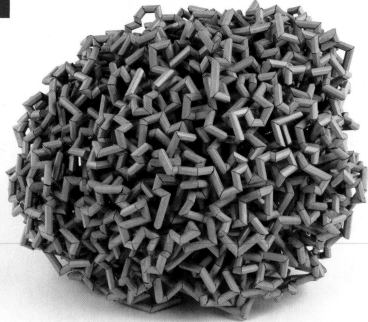

▶ **B**

Tom Friedman. *Untitled.* 1995. Pencils cut at 45-degree angles and glued in a continuous loop, 11" × 1' 2" × 11". *Affinities: Chuck Close and Tom Friedman* (Exhibition Catalog). The Art Institute of Chicago, 1996. Collection of Zoe and Joel Dictrow.

Tom Friedman's sculpture **(B)** also shows unity by repetition. The obvious aspect is the repetition of the cut pencil fragments. The unity created by these many repeated parts is strengthened by the continuous line and cohesive mass of the assembled form.

Repetition is an obvious unifying factor in the patterns found in textiles and the decorative arts. The giddy childlike quality of Murakami's print **(C)** suggests an almost manic wallpaper design for a child's room. In this case the unity created by repeated shapes provides a counterpoint to the raucous variety of colors. Contrast this with the subtle color of **A** and it seems that Murakami barely holds his composition together through repetition.

See also the discussion of *Rhythm* in Chapter 6.

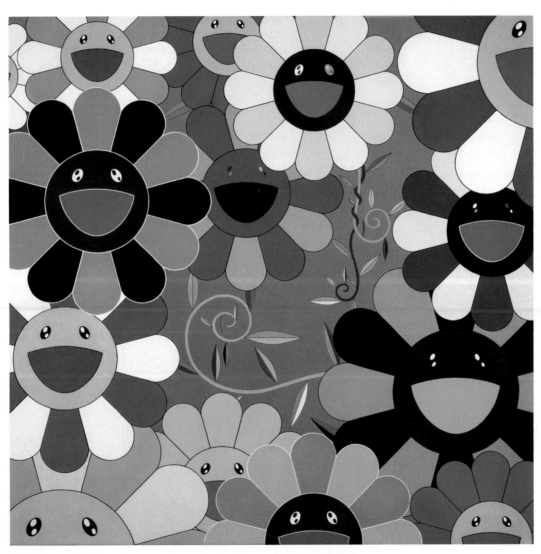

▲ **C**

Takashi Murakami. *Killer Pink.* 2002. Acrylic on canvas, mounted on board, 600 × 600 mm. Courtesy Galerie Emmanuel Perrotin, Paris & Miami. © 2002 Takashi Murakami/Kaikai Kiki Co., Ltd. All rights reserved.

CONTINUATION

A third way to achieve unity is by **continuation**, a more subtle device than proximity or repetition, which are fairly obvious. Continuation, naturally, means that something "continues"— usually a line, an edge, or a direction from one form to another. The viewer's eye is carried smoothly from one element to the next.

The design in **A** is unified by the closeness and the character of the elements. In **B**, though, the shapes seem even more of a unit because they are arranged in such a way that one's vision flows easily from one element to the next. The shapes no longer float casually. They are now organized into a definite, set pattern.

Continuation Can Be Subtle or Deliberate

The edge of the sleeping girl's head and her outstretched arm connect to the curving line of the sofa, forming one line of continuity in *The Living Room* (**C**). Other subtle lines of continuation visually unite the many shapes and colors of what might otherwise be a chaotic composition.

A deliberate or more obvious form of continuation is a striking aspect in many of Jan Groover's photographs. In one series of photographs, she caught passing trucks as an edge of each truck aligned visually with a distant roofline or a foreground pole. This alignment connected these disparate elements for an instant, resulting in a unified image. In **D** Groover employs a more subtle form of continuation, which results in a fluid eye movement around the picture. One shape leads to the next, and alignments are part of this flow.

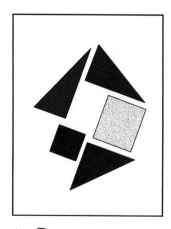

▲ **A**

Proximity and similarity unify a design.

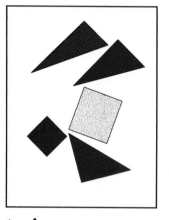

▲ **B**

The unity of the same elements is intensified.

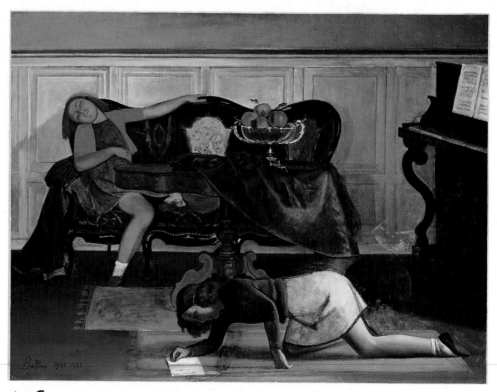

▲ **C**

Balthus (Balthasar Klossowski de Rola). *The Living Room*. 1941–1943. Oil on canvas, 3′ 8 1/2″ × 4′ 9 3/4″. The Minneapolis Institute of Arts.

Three-Dimensional Design

Continuation is an aspect not only of two-dimensional composition. Three-dimensional forms such as the automobile shown in **E** can utilize this design principle.

In this case the line of the windshield continues in a downward angle as a line across the fender. A sweeping curve along the top of the fender also connects the headlight and a crease leading to the door handle.

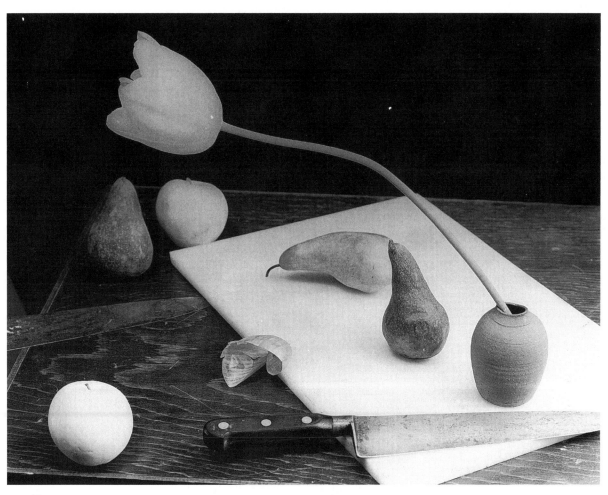

▲ **D**

Jan Groover. *Untitled.* 1987. Silver gelatin print, 11$^{15}/_{16}$" × 1' 2$^{15}/_{16}$" (30 × 38 cm). Janet Borden, Inc.

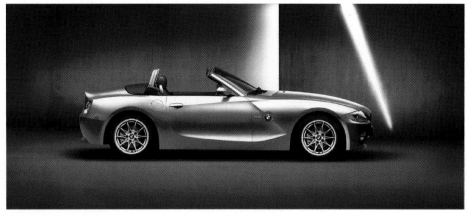

▲ **E**

2003 BMW Z4 Roadster. Courtesy BMW of North America, LLC.

CONTINUITY AND THE GRID

As we have learned, continuation is the planned arrangement of various forms so that their edges are lined up—hence, forms are "continuous" from one element to another within a design.

Serial Design

The artist has almost unlimited choice in how to apply the concept of continuation in a single design. The task changes, however, when there are multiple units. The artist's job now is not only to unify one design but to create several designs that somehow seem to relate to each other. In other words, all the designs must seem part of a "series." In a series the same unifying theme continues in successive designs. This is not an unusual job for a designer. Countless books, catalogs, magazines, pamphlets, and the like all require this designing skill.

▶ **A**

A grid determines page margins and divides the format into areas used on successive layouts.

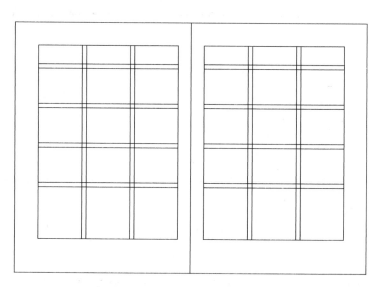

◀ **B**

A grid need not lead to boring regularity in page design.

ARCHITECTURE

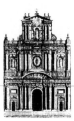
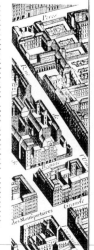

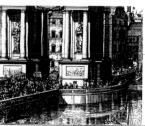

Using a Grid

Continuity is the term often used to denote the visual relationship between two or more individual designs. An aid often used in such serial designs is the grid. The artist begins by designing a **grid,** a network of horizontal and vertical intersecting lines that divide the page and create a framework of areas, such as in **A**. Then this same "skeleton" is used on all succeeding pages for a consistency of spacing and design results throughout all the units. To divide any format into areas or **modules** permits, of course, innumerable possibilities, so there is no predetermined pattern or solution. In creating the original grid, there are often numerous technical considerations that would determine the solution. But the basic idea is easily understood.

Using the same grid (or space division) on each successive page might suggest that sameness, and, hence, boring regularity, would result from repetition. This, however, is not necessarily true. A great deal of variety is possible within any framework, as the varied page layouts in **B** show.

Grid Design on the Internet

As the computer has gained importance in graphic design, formats based on the grid have become even more common and can be seen in website designs on the Internet. The grid alone is no guarantee of a successful composition, however, as can be seen in the range of quality in web page designs. In many cases the grid offers a bland display. **C**, on the other hand, is a lively, active home page for the School of Visual Arts. The grid is obvious as can be seen in distinct vertical columns and horizontal images and text. Visual interest is created in this structure through banners and photographs that change with time, varied color, and a playful patchwork quilt–like border that is also a loose grid. Here the grid provides unity for a changing and varied array of text and images.

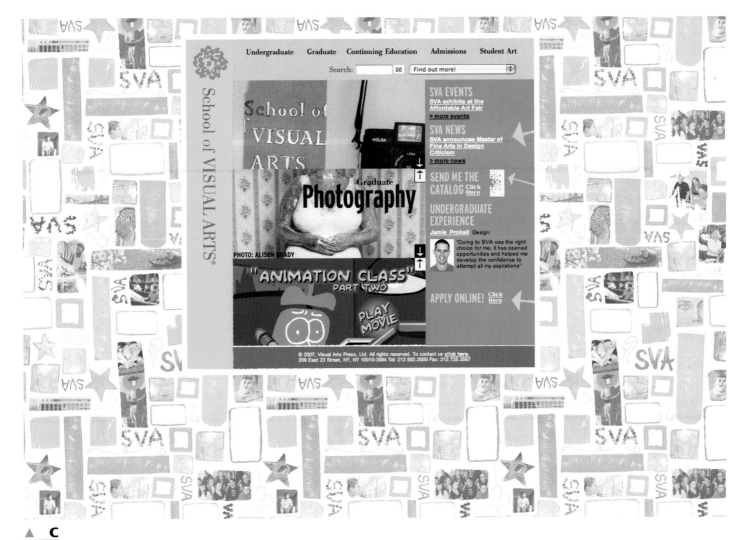

▲ **C**

Screen capture of School of Visual Arts website. http://www.schoolofvisualarts.edu. Courtesy of School of Visual Arts.

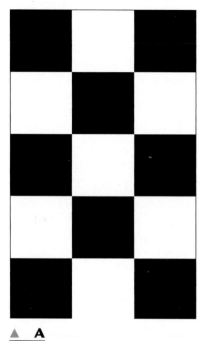

▲ **A**

A checkerboard shows
perfect unity.

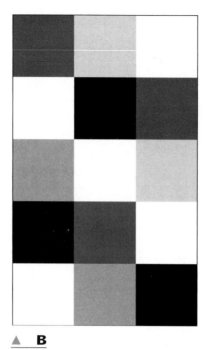

▲ **B**

Some variations in the basic
pattern increase interest.

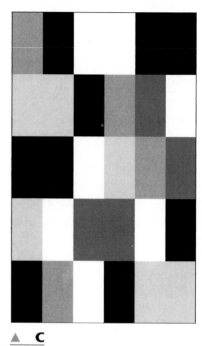

▲ **C**

Variation possibilities
are endless.

THE GRID

The word *design* implies that the various components of a
visual image are organized into a cohesive composition. A
design must have visual unity.

Using the Grid Effectively

The checkerboard pattern in **A** has complete unity. We can
easily see the constant repetition of shape and the obvious
continuation of lined-up edges. Unhappily, the result is also
quite boring. The design in **B** has the same repetitive division
of space, but it doesn't seem quite as dull. Some changes (or
variations) now make this design a bit more interesting to
the eye. In **C** the variations have been enlarged so we can
almost forget the dull checkerboard in **A**, but the same
underlying elements of unity are still present. This is the
basis of the principle of unity with variety. An obvious,
underlying feeling of unity exists, yet variations enliven the
pattern. Shapes may repeat, but perhaps in different sizes;
colors may repeat, but perhaps in different values.

In the painting by Ellsworth Kelly **(D)**, an underlying
feeling of a checkerboard is again the basic space division. The
feeling now is more casual and fluid as the chance arrangement of colors sets up an unpredictable **rhythm** of light
and dark patches not unlike **C**. The chance arrangement
will assure (over a grid with this many squares) a relatively
even distribution of light and dark areas.

Robert Rauschenberg's lithograph **(E)** also conveys an
underlying checkerboard, but the arrangement is playful,
with disruptions to the pattern. The format provides a unity
to a collage of varied historical art images.

The watercolor depiction of animal designs shown in **F**
is organized in a grid but does not resemble a checkerboard.
Each design is unique but is unified by similar style and the
compositional structure of the grid.

A point to remember is that, with a great variety of
elements, a simple layout idea can give needed unity and
be very effective.

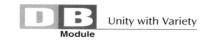

▲ **D**

Ellsworth Kelly. *Spectrum Colors Arranged by Chance.* Oil on wood, 5′ × 5′ (152.4 × 152.4 cm). San Francisco Museum of Modern Art. San Francisco Museum of Modern Art and anonymous private collectors. © Ellsworth Kelly.

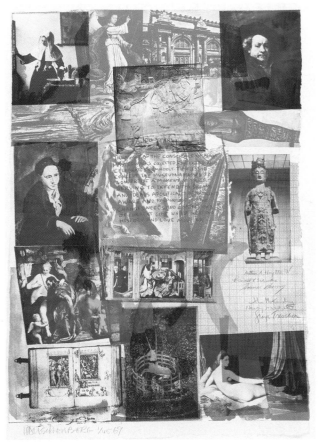

▲ **E**

Robert Rauschenberg. *Centennial Certificate.* 1969. Color lithograph, 2′ 11 7/8″ × 2′ 1″ (91 × 64 cm). The Metropolitan Museum of Art, New York (Florence and Joseph Singer Collection, 1969.630). Art © Robert Rauschenberg/Licensed by VAGA, New York, New York.

▶ **F**

Awa Tsireh. *Animal Designs.* c. 1917–1920. Watercolor on paper sheet, 1′ 8 1/16″ × 2′ 2 1/8″ (50.9 × 66.2 cm). Smithsonian American Art Museum Washington, D.C., Corbin-Henderson Collection (gift of Alice H. Rossin).

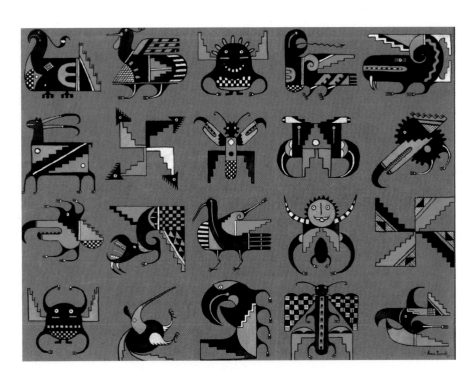

VARIED REPETITION

Is the principle of unity with variety a conscious, planned ingredient supplied by the artist or designer, or is it simply produced automatically by a confident designer? There is no real answer. The only certainty is that we can see the principle in art from every period, culture, and geographic area.

Variety Adds Visual Interest

The sculpture in **A** is composed of three separate forms. Unity is evident in the similar twisting and curved shapes. Variety is achieved by position (standing or reclining), size, and difference in proportion of the curved features.

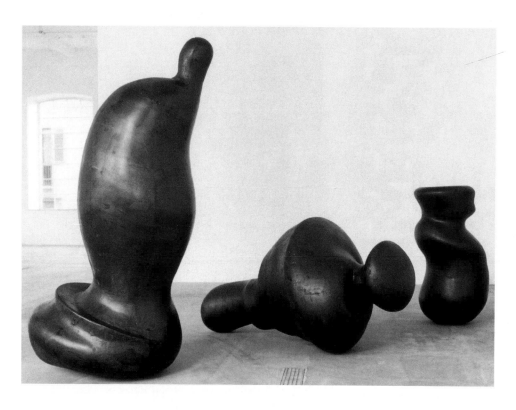

◄ **A**

Tony Cragg. *Rational Beings*. 1995. Styrofoam sheets, carbon fiber mesh, mixed media, 9′ 9″ × 4′ 6″ × 5′. Marian Goodman Gallery, New York.

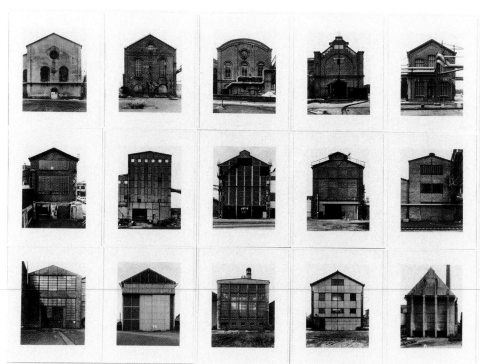

◄ **B**

Bernd and Hilla Becher. *Industrial Facades*. 1970–1992. Fifteen black-and-white photographs, overall: 5′ 8³/₄″ × 7′ 11″ (installed as a group). Albright-Knox Art Gallery, Buffalo, New York (Sarah Norton Goodyear Fund, 1995).

The use of unity with variety displayed in the collection of photographs (**B**) suggests a more rigid approach. The individual subject of industrial buildings might not catch our attention, but the variety displayed in the grid format immediately invites comparison and contrast. The idea of related variations seems to satisfy a basic human need for visual interest that can be achieved without theoretical discussions of aesthetics.

A conscious (or obvious) use of unity with variety does not necessarily lessen our pleasure as viewers. An obvious use of the principle is not a drawback. Unity is immediately apparent in the set of functional ceramic ware in **C**. Eva Zeisel's vessels seem to have evolved their forms as naturally as unfurling leaves or swelling seed pods. A similar small element at the top of each piece works to close a handle in one case and provide a spout in another.

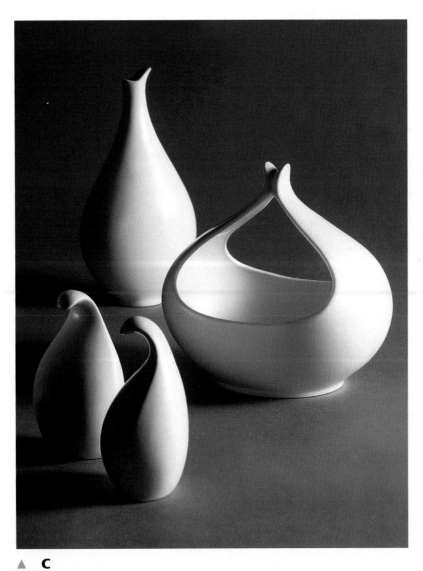

▲ **C**

Eva Zeisel. Classic Century: oil pourer, sauce boat, salt and pepper. Ceramic. Produced by Royal Stafford, England.

EMPHASIS ON UNITY

In the application of any art principle, wide flexibility is possible within the general framework of the guideline. So it is in unity with variety. To say a design must contain both the ordered quality of unity and the lively quality of variety does not limit or inhibit the artist. The principle can encompass a wide variety of extremely different visual images and can even be contradicted for expressive purposes.

Unity through Repetition

These pages show successful examples of emphasis on the unifying element of repetition. Variety is present, but admittedly in a subtle, understated way. Photograph **A** shows thousands of pilgrims in Mecca during the Hajj. The multitude of humanity from all races, nations, and walks of life is united by simple white garments.

We know at a glance that all the plants depicted in **B** are irises. As with other Japanese screens from this period, the composition is strongly unified by repetition of natural forms. But this is not wallpaper. No two leaves or flowers are identical, and the eye is rewarded with subtle variation on a constant theme.

The visual unity gained by repetition is immediately apparent, in fact almost overwhelmingly so, in **C**. Here is an example of a rigid unity quite unlike the graceful unity of the Japanese screen. The thirty-two identical life-size figures seated at the table with palms down on the flat surface and eyes cast downward are unsettling in their unity through repetition. The effect is similar to an irrational bad dream. Unity without variety can evoke our worst feelings about assembly lines and institutions.

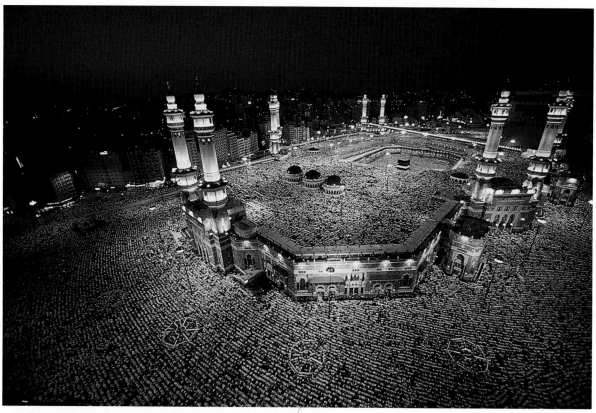

▲ **A**

Grand Mosque, Mecca, Saudi Arabia. More than two million Moslems prostrate themselves at the Grand Mosque in Mecca each year during the Hajj. National Geographic Society.

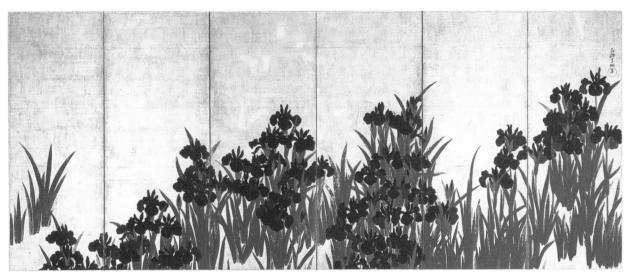

▲ **B**

Ogata Korin. *Irises.* Edo period, c. 1705. Six-fold screen (one of pair), color on gold foil over paper, 150.9 × 338.8 cm. Nezu Art Museum, Tokyo, Japan/The Bridgeman Art Library.

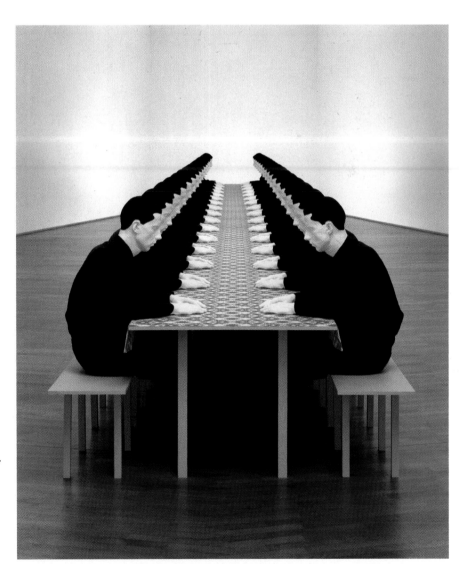

► **C**

Katharina Fritsch. *Tischgesellschaft (Company at Table).* 1988. Thirty-two life-size polyester figures, wooden table and benches, partially painted; printed and bleached cotton, 4′ 7 1/8″ × 52′ 6″ × 5′ 8 7/8″ (1.4 × 16 × 1.75 m). On permanent loan from the Collection of Dresdner Bank Frankfurt am Main to the Museum für Moderne Kunst, Frankfurt am Main.

EMPHASIS ON VARIETY

Two artists argue over a painting:

> "This painting is great because of the unity of similar shapes," says the first.
>
> "You're crazy! It is the variety and contrasts that make it great!" says the second.

And both might be right.

Life is not always orderly or rational. To express this aspect of life, many artists have chosen to underplay the unifying components of their work and let the elements appear at least superficially uncontrolled and free of any formal design restraints. The examples here show works in which the element of variety is strong.

Variety in Form, Size, Color, and Gesture

The sculpture shown in **A** demonstrates unity by an emphasis on serpentine curves flowing through the clustered figures. Continuation is a strong feature as the viewer's eye is led through the complex arrangement by the arms linked hand-in-hand and by the arc of one figure leading to the central figure's upraised arm. Unity is also emphasized by the white of the stone. Variety is emphasized through the almost infinite subtle differences possible in the human form.

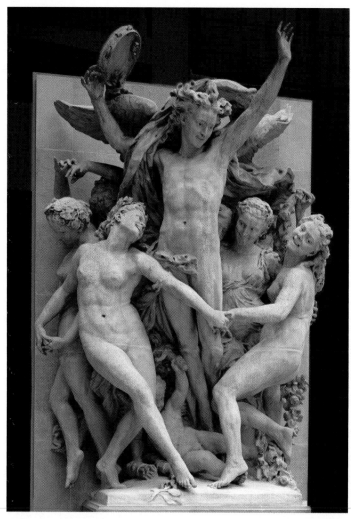

▲ **A**

Jean-Baptiste Carpeaux. *The Dance*. 1863–1869. Limestone, 4.2 × 2.98 × 1.45 m. Musée d'Orsay, Paris.

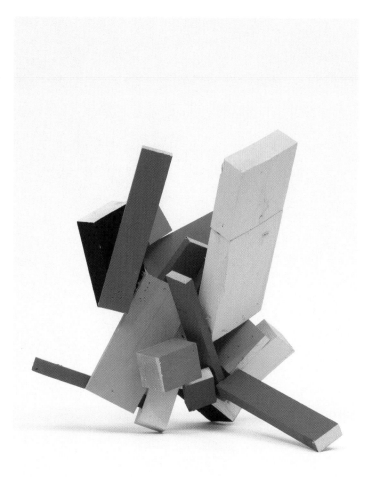

▲ **B**

Joel Shapiro. *Study, 20 Elements*. 2004. Wood and casein, 1′ 4¹/₂″ × 1′ 2³/₄″ × 1′ 3″ (41.9 × 37.5 × 38.1 cm). © Joel Shapiro. Finished sculpture, painted wood: H 3.1 m; B 3.35 m; D 2.16 m. Courtesy Pace Wildenstein, New York. Photograph by Kerry Ryan McFate.

Joel Shapiro's study for *20 Elements* shown in **B** is an unlikely mate to Carpeaux's *Dance* shown in **A**. Shapiro created this piece in response to Carpeaux, and, in fact, many of Shapiro's geometric sculptures suggest the **gesture** of a figure. His *20 Elements* has an obvious unity built upon only rectangular forms. In this case the dynamism of Carpeaux's piece is answered by *Study, 20 Elements* with a variety of size, position, and color: no two rectangular forms are alike. Both Carpeaux and Shapiro express dynamism through variety and rely on unifying elements to hold it all together.

An aggressive near ugliness pervades the chaotic jumble of battered texts in George Herms's **assemblage** sculpture **(C)**. A first impression might be of materials out of control and barely hanging together. One can find, however, an intellectual unity of purpose in the imagery and visible text. A visual unity is also at work in the strong crosslike structure and a limited range of colors dominated by brown, black, and white.

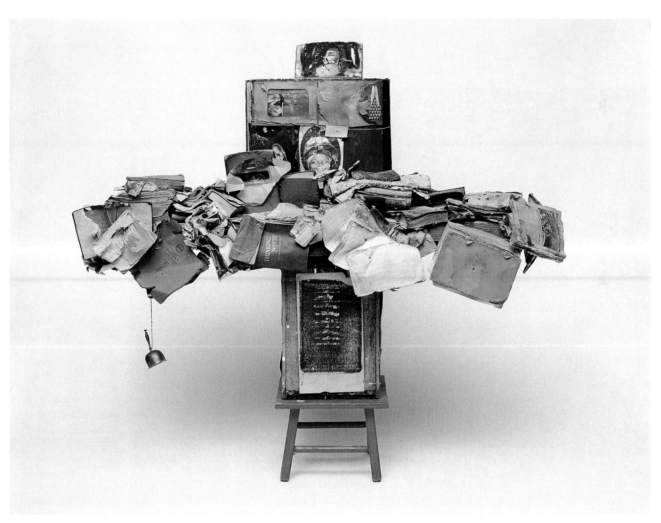

▲ **C**

George Herms. *The Librarian.* 1960. Assemblage: wood box, papers, brass bell, books, painted stool, 4′ 9″ × 5′ 3″ × 1′ 9″ (1.4 m × 1.6 m × 53 cm). Norton Simon Museum, Pasadena (gift of Molly Barnes, 1969).

CHAOS AND CONTROL

Without some aspect of unity, an image or design becomes chaotic and quickly "unreadable." Without some elements of variety, an image is lifeless and dull and becomes uninteresting. Neither utter confusion nor utter regularity is satisfying.

The photograph of a commercial strip shown in **A** reveals a conflicting jumble of **graphic** images, each vying for our attention. In this case information overload cancels out the novelty or variety of any single sign and leaves us confused with the chaotic results.

The photo in **B** reveals the bland unity of a housing subdivision. There is an attempt at variety in the facades, but the backs of the homes are identical. After a number of years, personal variations may show in paint color, landscaping, and sometimes eccentric renovations. Such expressions can bring about conflict between conformity and individuality.

The model for the Frank Gehry–designed Guggenheim Museum at Bilbao **(C)** offers a dramatic but coherent emphasis on variety. The various sweeping curves provide a contrast to the straight and angular architectural features and to the surrounding built environment. Within the curves is a variety of directions, sizes, and shapes. In this case a variety of architectural forms was made possible by the use of computer design software developed for airplane design. Here you can see the power of variety to offer contrast within a unified whole.

▼ **A**

Signs create a visual clutter along old Route 66 in Kingman, Arizona.

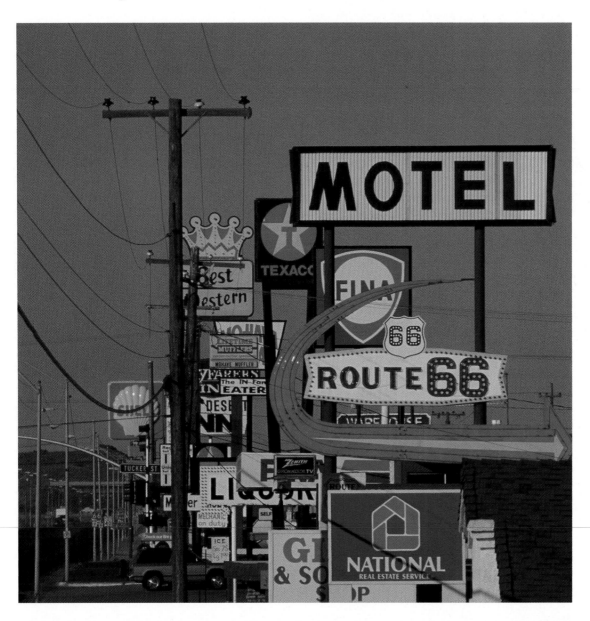

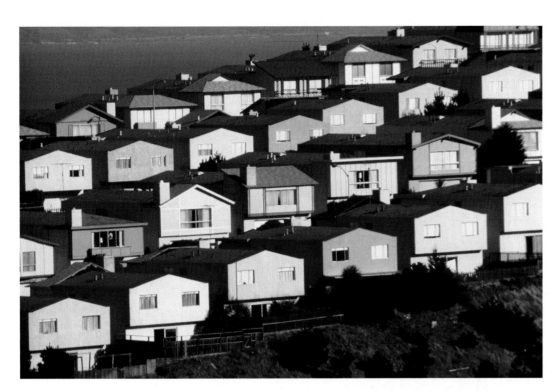

◄ **B**

The bland unity of a housing subdivision.

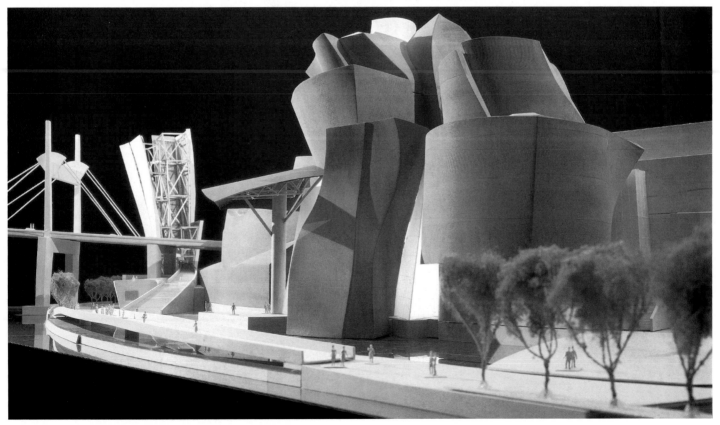

▲ **C**

Frank Gehry. Model of Guggenheim Museum. Bilbao, Spain.

FIGURATIVE AND NONOBJECTIVE

The earlier discussion of the works by Carpeaux and Joel Shapiro (see **A** and **B** on page 48) examined unity and variety within both figurative and nonobjective artworks. Unity is not simply a property of related organic shapes or of related geometric elements. An apprehension of unity is a simple and immediate sense of connections resonating throughout a composition. The elements that build that unity may be simple as well, or they may be subtle and more complex.

El Lissitzky's composition **(A)** has a simple and obvious unity based on the repetition of the square. The contrast of red and black and the position of each square create variety. The limited palette serves to unify this single composition and creates a connecting unity with the five other variations that complete the series (not shown.) Unity in this single composition is also a result of continuation as a path is suggested from the black square through the diagonal of the red square to the trail of text at the bottom.

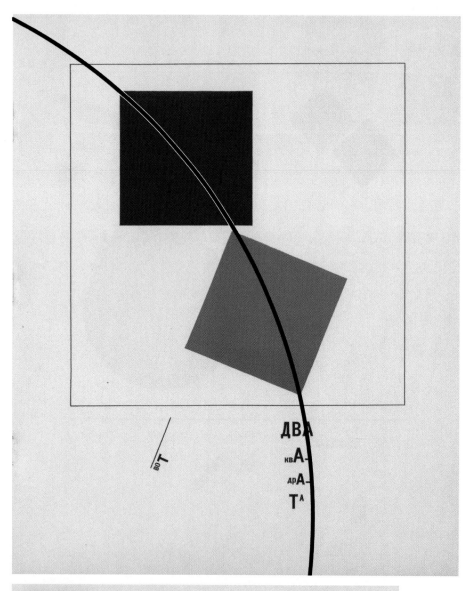

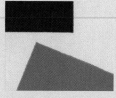 ▲ **A**

Shapes and text follow a line of continuation. El Lissitzky. *Of Two Squares: A Suprematist Tale in Six Constructions.* 1922. Diagram.

Susan Moore's portrait **(B)** reminds us of the powerful gestalt presented by the human face. Even in a childish or "bad" portrait we will grasp the unity of the component shapes and see a face first and foremost. In Moore's more sophisticated and accomplished artwork we not only grasp the unity of the face but also appreciate the unity built of repeated textural marks and a subdued palette of related or **analogous colors**.

The unity in Lissitzky's work helps build a coherent series of compositions from otherwise meaningless components. The unity at work in Moore's portrait creates the whole artwork, not just the face.

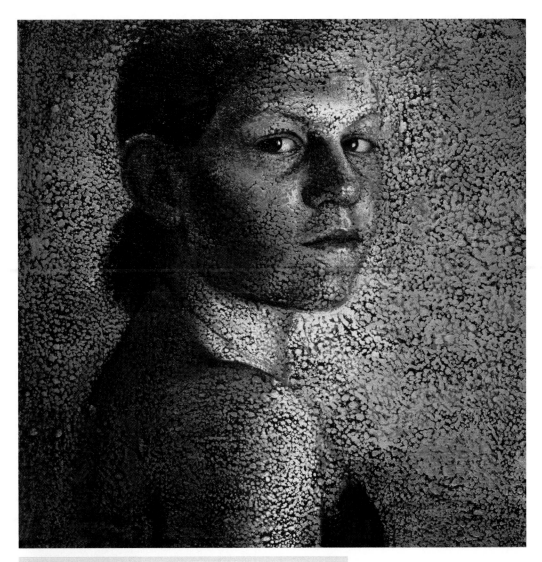

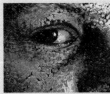

▲ **B**

Susan Moore. *Vanity (Portrait 1).* 2000. Oil stick on canvas, 4′ × 3′ 11″.

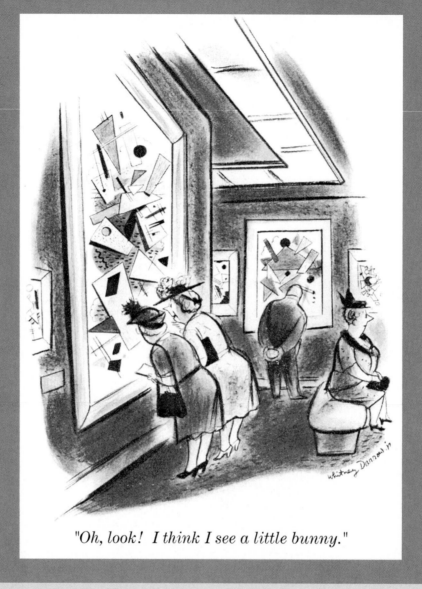

"Oh, look! I think I see a little bunny."

Whitney Darrow, Jr. 1946.
© *The New Yorker Collection* from cartoonbank.com.
All Rights Reserved.

EMPHASIS AND FOCAL POINT

ATTRACTING ATTENTION

Very few artists or designers do not want people to look at their work. In past centuries, when pictures were rare, almost any image was guaranteed attention. Today, with photography and an abundance of books, magazines, newspapers, signs, and so on, all of us are confronted daily with hundreds of pictures. We take this abundance for granted, but it makes the artist's job more difficult. Without an audience's attention, any messages, any artistic or aesthetic values, are lost.

How does a designer catch a viewer's attention? How does the artist provide a pattern that attracts the eye? Nothing will guarantee success, but one device that can help is a point of emphasis or **focal point**. This emphasized element initially can attract attention and encourage the viewer to look closer.

Using Focal Point for Emphasis

Every aspect of the composition in **A** emphasizes the grapefruit at center stage. The grapefruit shape is large, centered, light, and yellow (compared with darker gray surroundings), and even the lines of the sections point to the center. All these elements bring our focus to the main character or subject. This is the concept of a focal point.

The painting by Henri Matisse **(B)** does not have the central, obvious target that is evident in **A**, but the focal point is unambiguous and even humorous. The small red turtle is emphasized by contrast of size, unique color, and isolation. The figures direct our attention as well as we follow their gaze to the focal point. In this case even a very small area of emphasis is powerful enough to need balancing counterpoints such as the bright hair of the left-hand figure and the abstracted blue stripe of water at the top of the painting.

The photograph in **C** is a view of an ordinary street scene. The large pine tree might go unnoticed in a stroll through the neighborhood. Several things contribute to the emphasis on this tree in the photograph: placement near the center, large size, irregular shape, and dark value against the light sky.

There can be more than one focal point. Sometimes an artwork contains secondary points of emphasis that have less attention value than the focal point. These serve as accents or counterpoints as in the Matisse picture. However, the designer must be careful. Several focal points of equal emphasis can turn the design into a three-ring circus in which the viewer does not know where to look first. Interest is replaced by confusion: When everything is emphasized, nothing is emphasized.

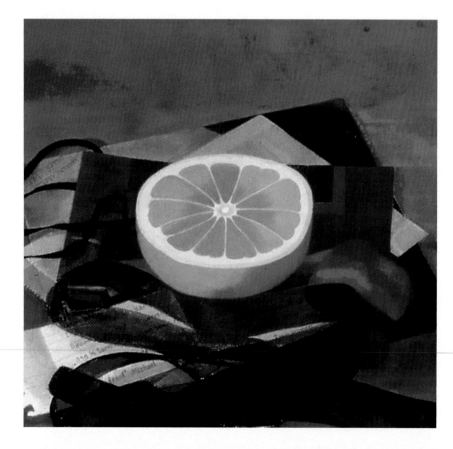

◄ **A**

Susan Jane Walp. *Grapefruit with Black Ribbons.* 2000. Oil on linen, 8" × 8¼". Tibor de Nagy Gallery, New York.

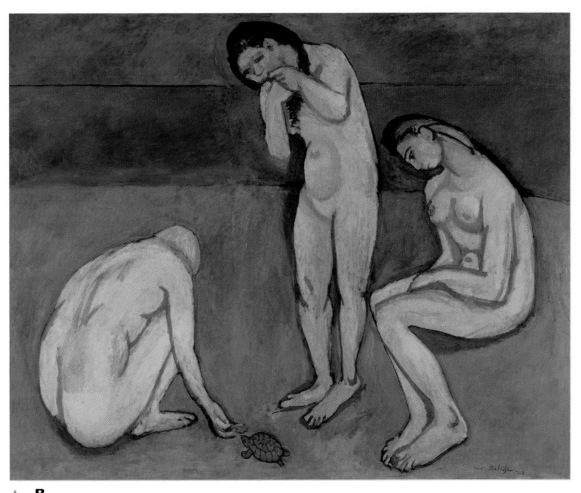

▲ **B**

Henri Matisse. *Bathers with a Turtle.* 1908. Oil on canvas. The St. Louis Museum of Art, Missouri.

▶ **C**

Jeff Wall. *The Pine on the Corner.* 1990.
3′ 10³/₄″ × 3′ 10¹/₄″ (1.19 × 1.48 m). Edition
of 3. Marian Goodman Gallery, New York.

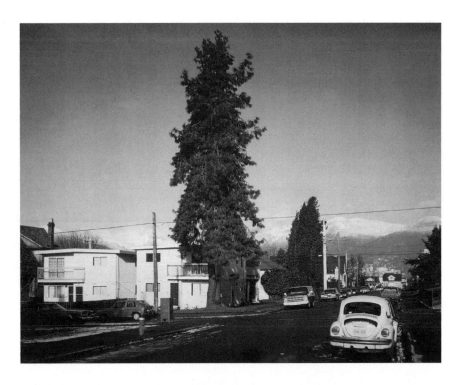

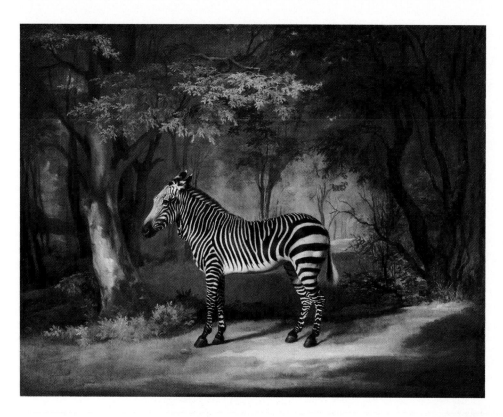

◄ **A**

George Stubbs. *A Zebra.* 1763. Oil on canvas. © Yale Center for British Art, Paul Mellon Collection, USA/The Bridgeman Art Library.

EMPHASIS BY CONTRAST

Very often in art the pictorial emphasis is clear, and in simple compositions (such as a portrait) the focal point is obvious. But the more complicated the pattern, the more necessary or helpful a focal point may become in organizing the design.

Creating a Focal Point through Contrast

As a rule, a focal point results when one element differs from the others. Whatever interrupts an overall feeling or pattern automatically attracts the eye by this difference. The possibilities are almost endless:

> When most of the elements are dark, a light form breaks the pattern and becomes a focal point.
> When most of the elements are muted or soft-edged, a bold contrasting pattern will become a focal point **(A)**.
> In an overall design of distorted expressionistic forms, the sudden introduction of a naturalistic image **(B)** will draw the eye for its very different style.
> Text or graphic symbols will be a focal point (in this case, the eye is drawn to the number *16*) **(C)**.
> When the majority of elements are shapes, an irregular line will stand out, such as the black line with a loop at the center of **D**.

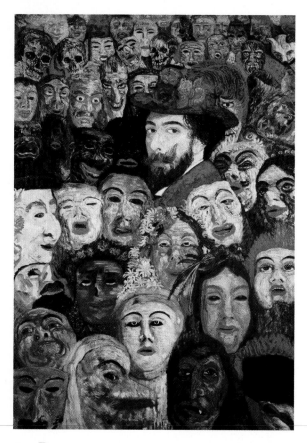

▲ **B**

James Ensor. *Self-Portrait Surrounded by Masks.* 1899. Oil, 3′ 11¹/₂″ × 2′ 7¹/₂″ (121 × 80 cm). Sammlung Cleomir Jussiant, Antwerp.

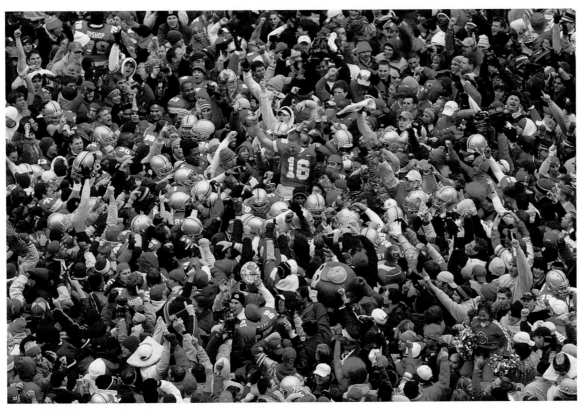

▲   **C**

Karl Kuntz (photographer). *Columbus Dispatch,* Sunday, November 24, 2002.

▶   **D**

Stuart Davis. *Ready-to-Wear.* 1955. Oil on canvas, 4′ 8″ × 3′ 6″ (142.9 × 106.7 cm). The Art Institute of Chicago (restricted gift of Mr. and Mrs. Sigmund Kunstadter and Goodman Fund, 1956.137). Art © Estate of Stuart Davis/licensed by VAGA, New York, NY.

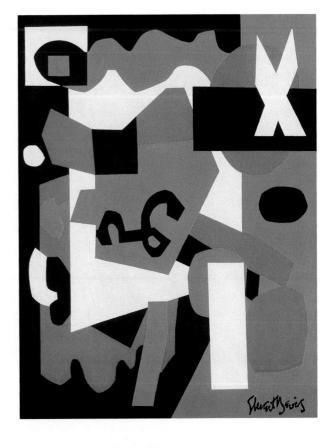

This list could go on and on; many other possibilities will occur to you. Sometimes this idea is called *emphasis by contrast.* The element that contrasts with, rather than continues, the prevailing design scheme becomes the focal point.

Color is often used to achieve emphasis by contrast. A change in color or a change in brightness can immediately attract our attention.

See also *Devices to Show Depth: Size,* page 196; *Value as Emphasis,* page 244; and *Color as Emphasis,* page 268.

 Ways to Achieve Emphasis

EMPHASIS BY ISOLATION

A variation on the device of emphasis by contrast is the useful technique of emphasis by isolation. There is no way we can look at the design in **A** and not focus our attention on that element at the bottom. It is identical to all the elements above. But simply by being set off by itself, it grabs our attention. This is contrast, of course, but it is contrast of placement, not form. In such a case, the element, as here, need not be any different from the other elements in the work.

Creating a Focal Point through Isolation

In the painting by Eakins **(B)** the doctor at left repeats the light **value** of the other figures in the operating arena. All the figures in this oval stand out in contrast to the darker figures in the background. Isolation gives extra emphasis to this doctor at the left.

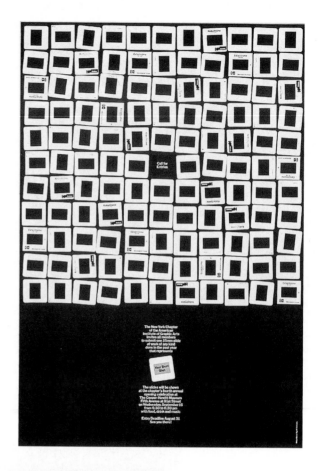

▶ **A**

Call for entries for AIGA/New York show, "Take Your Best Shot." Designer: Michael Beirut, Vignelli Associates, New York.

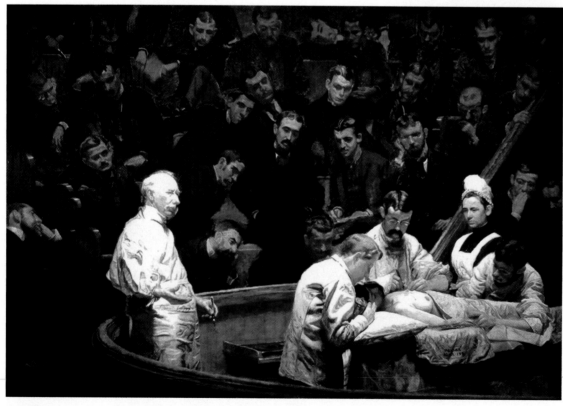

▲ **B**

Thomas Eakins. *The Agnew Clinic.* 1889. Oil on canvas, 6′ 2¹/₂″ × 10′ 10¹/₂″ (1.9 × 3.3 m). University of Pennsylvania Art Collection, Philadelphia.

Murillo's painting *Little Boy Begging* (**C**) uses isolation to evoke an emotional or psychological impact. The young boy is situated in the right half of the painting and further isolated by a stark black background with even greater contrast than the Eakins painting. The depiction of the window as a light source on the left side of the painting provides balance and even the potential for hope as the figure is illuminated. Tension is created between two isolated focal points.

In neither of these examples is the focal point directly in the center of the composition. This placement could appear too obvious and contrived. However, it is wise to remember that a focal point placed too close to an edge will tend to pull the viewer's eye right out of the picture. Notice in Eakins's painting (**B**) how the curve of the oval on the left side and the doctor looking toward the action at right keep the isolated figure from directing our gaze out of the picture. In **C** a water jug in the lower left corner and the boy's head right of center keep our attention in the picture.

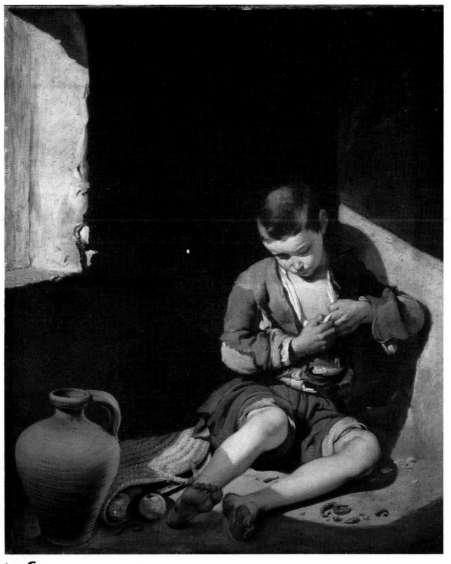

▲ **C**

Bartolomé Esteban Murillo. *Little Boy Begging*. 1650. Oil on canvas, 134 × 100 cm. The Louvre, Paris.

EMPHASIS BY PLACEMENT

The placement of elements in a design may function in another way to create emphasis. If many elements point to one item, our attention is directed there, and a focal point results. A radial design is a perfect example of this device. Just as all forms radiate from the convergent focus, so they also repeatedly lead our eyes back to this central element. As **A** illustrates, this central element may be like other forms in the design; the emphasis results from the placement, not from any difference in character of the form itself.

Creating a Focal Point through Placement

Radial designs are more common in architecture or the craft areas than in two-dimensional art. In pictures, perspective lines can lead to a point of emphasis and the result can be a radial design. In Vermeer's painting **(B)** the girl is the focal point, and the perspective lines of the interior all direct our eyes back to the figure. It is a mark of the subtlety and complexity of Vermeer's work that the painting is not simply constructed to point to the main figure but also unfolds other areas of interest and keeps our attention and involvement.

The placement of the most famous apple of all time is also near the center of **C**. The painting is busy and crowded, and the passing of the apple takes place at the intersection of the tree trunk and the lines formed by the arms of Adam and Eve. The composition has an equal balance to the left and right of this focal point, and the key element is emphasized. Both **B** and **C** succeed because the focal point for each does not have to compete with other elements for prominence.

See also *Symmetrical Balance,* pages 94 and 96, and *Radial Balance,* page 108.

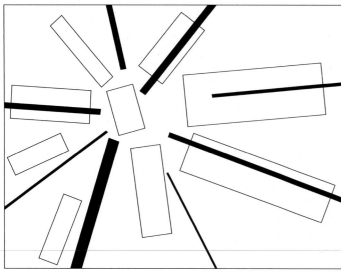

▲ **A**

Our eyes are drawn to the central element of this design by all the elements radiating from it.

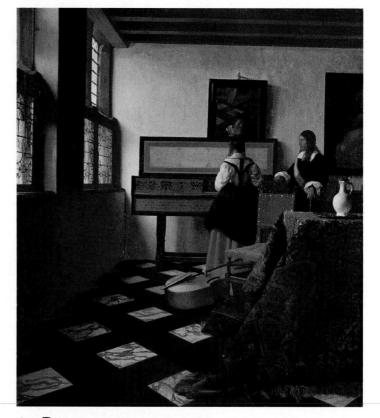

▲ **B**

Jan Vermeer. *A Lady at the Virginals with a Gentleman (The Music Lesson).* 1662–1664. Oil on canvas, 2' 5" × 2' 1". The Royal Collection, London.

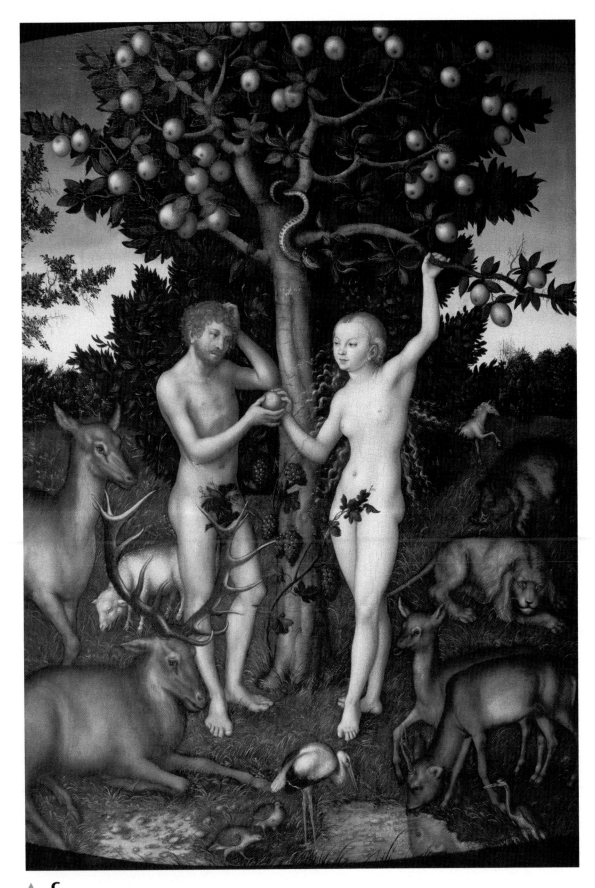

▲ **C**

Lucas Cranach the Elder. *Adam and Eve.* 1526. Oil on panel, 3′ 10$\frac{1}{8}$″ × 2′ 7$\frac{3}{4}$″ (117 × 80 cm).
Courtauld Institute of Art Gallery, London, P.1947.LF.77.

ONE ELEMENT

A specific theme may, at times, call for a dominant, even visually overwhelming focal point. The use of a strong visual emphasis on one element is not unusual.

In the graphic design of newspaper advertisements, billboards, magazine covers, and the like, we often see an obvious emphasis on one element. This emphasis can be necessary to attract the viewer's eye and present the theme (or product) in the few seconds most people look casually at such material. Such increased focus is also needed when an idea is being promoted, as in the illustration for an editorial shown in **A**. Here the intent is to grab our attention in the hope that we will read the commentary. The striking red circle creates a mouth and gives voice to the marginalized subject in a plea for peace.

Maintaining Unity with a Focal Point

A focal point, however strong, should remain related to and a part of the overall design. The red circle in **A** is visually strong yet is related to other elements of strong contrast: the black head and white doves. Contrast the effect in **A** with that in **B**. In Bonnard's painting **(B)** the isolated black oval tray in the center foreground is clearly a focal point. In this case it seems too dominant; this sudden dark spot seems out of keeping with the subtle value and color changes in the rest of the painting. In fact it is a witty way to have us *not* notice a dog at the table as the first thing to catch our eye!

In general, the principle of unity and the creation of a harmonious pattern with related elements are more important than the injection of a focal point if this point would jeopardize the design's unity. In the playful illustration by Maurice Vellekoop **(C)**, the unusual shape of the orange dress is accentuated by the blue figure and background. The figure dissolves into the blue, and the dress literally pops! The strength of this focal point is integrated into the unity of the total composition. The established focal point is not a completely unrelated element. The curving shapes are balanced by other similar shapes, and the orange is echoed by the brown of the man's suit.

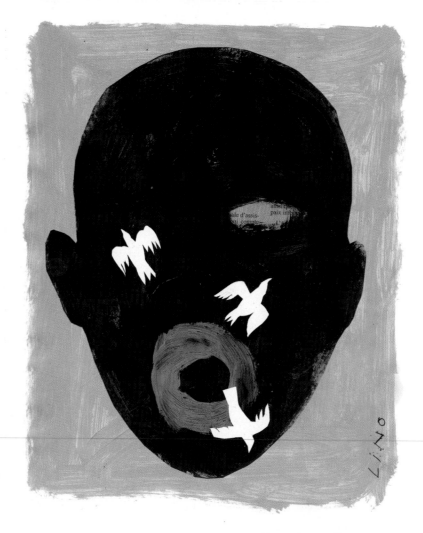

▶ **A**

Lino. *Communication Arts*, May/June 2005, p. 115. Editorial for *Courier International* (France). Art Director: Pascal Phillipe.

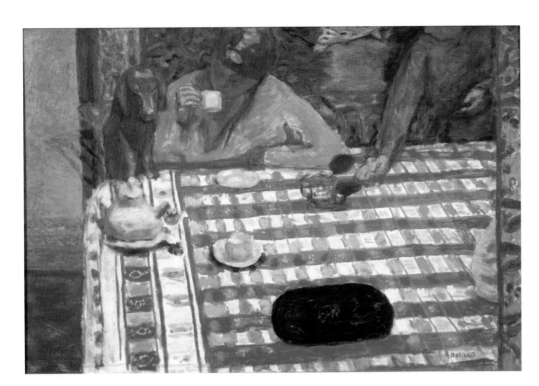

◄ **B**

Pierre Bonnard. *Coffee.* c. 1915.
Oil on canvas, 2′ 4³/₄″ × 3′ 5⁷/₈″
(73 × 106.4 cm). Tate Gallery,
London. Reproduced by courtesy
of Trustees.

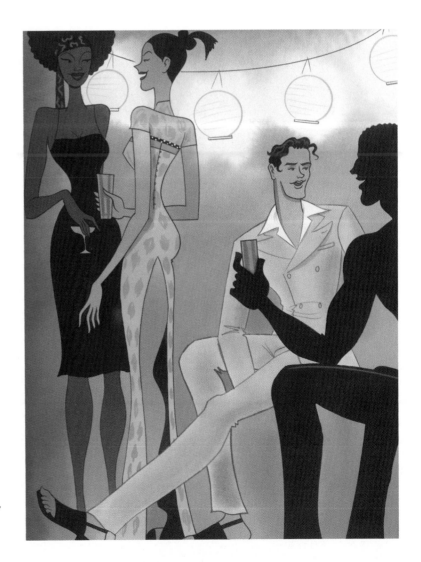

► **C**

Maurice Vellekoop. *Christian Dior Boutique,
Valentino.* Watercolor on paper. Wallpaper,
November/December 1997.

EMPHASIZING THE
WHOLE OVER THE PARTS

A definite focal point is not a necessity in creating a successful design. It is a tool that artists may or may not use, depending on their aims. An artist may wish to emphasize the entire surface of a composition over any individual elements. Lee Krasner's painting (**A**) is an example. Similar shapes and textures are repeated throughout the painting. These shapes and textures form loose rows and columns and a kind of grid. The artist creates an ambiguous visual environment that is puzzling. Dark and light areas repeat over the surface in an even distribution, and no one area stands out. The painting has no real starting point or visual climax.

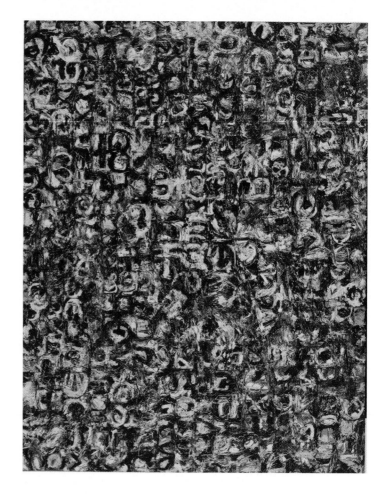

▶ **A**

Lee Krasner. *Untitled.* 1949. Oil on composition board, 4′ × 3′ 1″ (122 × 94 cm). The Museum of Modern Art, New York (gift of Alfonso A. Ossorio).

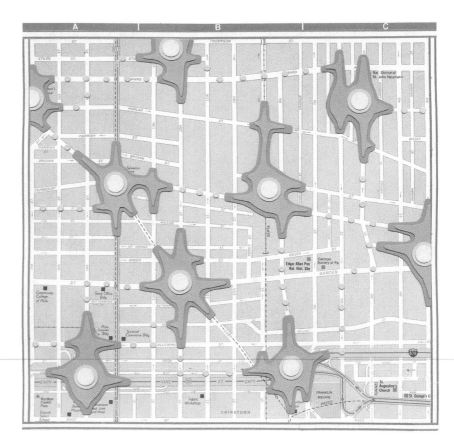

▶ **B**

Mark Keffer. *Altered Map. Esopus,* Number 3 (Fall 2004), p. 1.

The **collage** painting by Mark Keffer shown in **B** is less dense than **A**, and by comparison it seems open and airy. Here the grid is that of a street map. The added elements of pink shapes and circles punctuate different intersections. If only one shape or circle had been added, it would create a focal point, but the repetition and suggested continuation beyond the edge of the composition emphasize the whole over the parts.

The still photograph of Bill Viola's video **installation** *The World of Appearances* **(C)** exhibits no emphasis or focal point. This artwork develops slowly as a video in extreme slow motion. At one time a figure becomes a strong focal point. Later, after a dramatic splash, the image of water settles into a surface of ripples and waves with no distinct focus. Tension is followed by activity, and that is followed by a quieter, contemplative play of light and color. In an installation such as this, the viewer can replace a depicted figure as the focal point.

See also *Crystallographic Balance,* page 110.

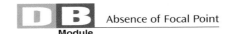

Absence of Focal Point

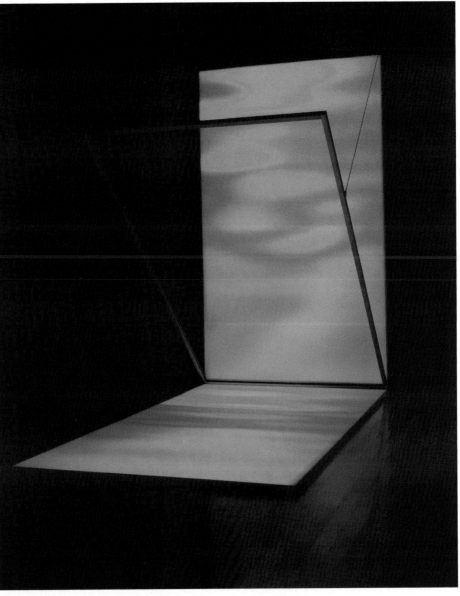

▲   **C**

Bill Viola. *The World of Appearances.* 2003. Video installation at James Cohan Gallery, New York.

OPTICAL AND PSYCHOLOGICAL

The mechanics of visual perception and the psychology of visual perception are both at work in the experience of emphasis in art and design. This may seem obvious but can be overlooked. Returning to our two recurring examples, we can see the weight of both the optical nature of perception and the psychology of looking.

El Lissitzky's composition of a few geometric elements **(A)** takes advantage of our color perception to emphasize the red square. We humans are blessed with color perception (most mammals have a lower level of color vision). This allows us to see the attention-getting bright red flower or the warning coloration of red stripes on a venomous snake. Red is also associated with passion and has a psychological impact. The result is not just *that* we see it, but *how* we see it. Little wonder that the red square of Lissitzky's design is the focal point.

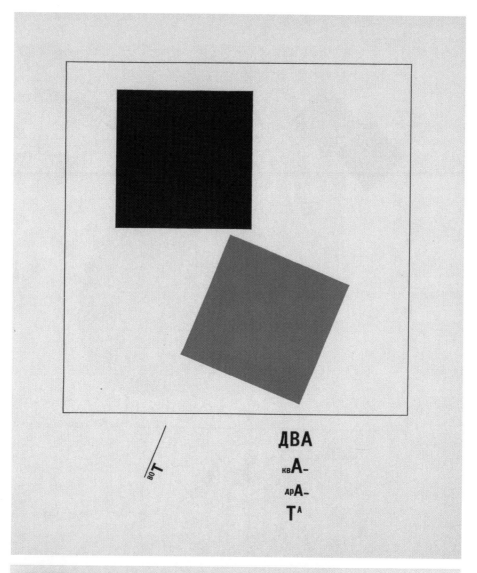

▲ **A**

El Lissitzky. *Of Two Squares: A Suprematist Tale in Six Constructions*. 1922. Illustrated book with letterpress cover and six letterpress illustrations, $10^{15}/_{16}'' \times 8^{7}/_{8}''$ (27.8 × 22.5 cm). Publisher: Skify, Berlin. Gift of the Judith Rothschild Foundation (89.2001.5).

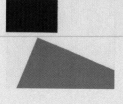

From infancy the face is a target of our strongest attention. Parents get face-to-face with their newborn children, and a bond is formed. So, it is no wonder that the face will be the emphasis of Susan Moore's painting **(B)**, even if it occupies only a fraction of the total painted surface. Furthermore, the figure's right eye falls along the vertical center of the painting, reinforcing the strength of the returned gaze of the model. This structure offers a less passive version of the model as a focus of our attention.

See also *Color as Emphasis,* page 268.

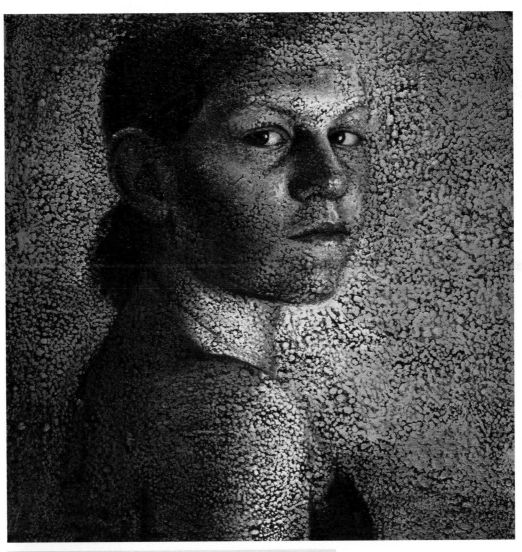

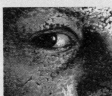

▲   **B**

Susan Moore. *Vanity (Portrait 1).* 2000. Oil stick on canvas, 4′ × 3′ 11″.

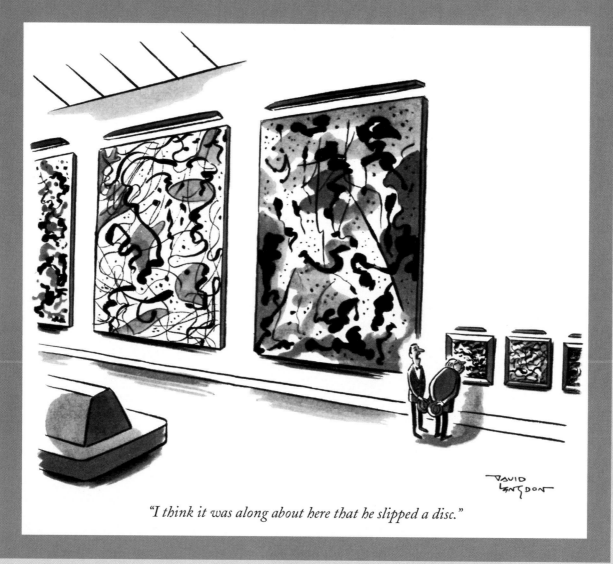

"I think it was along about here that he slipped a disc."

David Langdon. 1959.

SCALE AND PROPORTION

SCALE AND PROPORTION

Scale and *proportion* are related terms: Both basically refer to size. Scale is essentially another word for size. "Large scale" is a way of saying big, and "small scale" means small. Big and small, however, are relative. What is big? "Big" is meaningless unless we have some standard of reference. A "big" dog means nothing if we do not know the size of an average dog. This is what distinguishes the two terms. **Proportion** refers to relative size—size measured against other elements or against some mental norm or standard.

The small stool and the clues given by the architecture of the space provide a scale reference for judging the size of the sphere in **A**. Because a sphere has no inherent scale reference, we depend on the context to judge its size. In **A** the sphere is almost oppressively large in proportion to the setting. Imagine the same sphere outdoors seen from an airplane. It might have the same visual impact as a period on this page.

We often think of the word *proportion* in connection with mathematical systems of numerical ratios. It is true that many such systems have been developed over the centuries. Artists have attempted to define the most pleasing size relationships in items as diverse as the width and length of sides of a rectangle to parts of the human body.

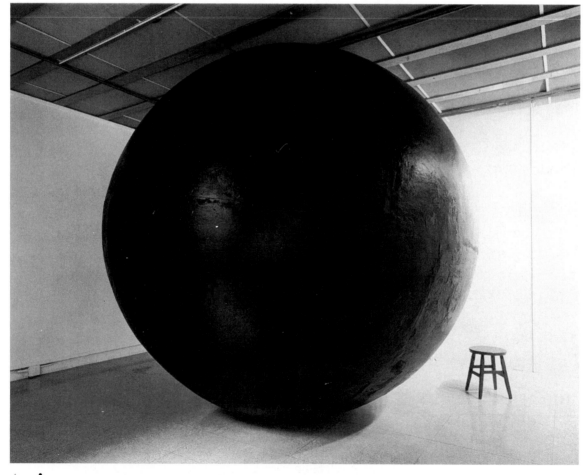

▲ **A**

Richard Roth. *Untitled*. 1983. Installation: 11' diameter (3.4 m) sphere with red stool.
© 1993 Richard Roth. Photo: Fredrik Marsh.

Using Scale and Proportion for Emphasis

Scale and proportion are closely tied to emphasis and focal point. The lemon and strawberry depicted in Glen Holland's painting **(B)** are at a one-to-one (1:1) scale, so the painting is obviously small. However, the proportion of these subjects to the rest of the painting and the unusual point of view lend a monumental feeling to these humble subjects.

In past centuries visual scale was often related to thematic importance. The size of figures was based on their symbolic importance in the subject being presented. This use of scale is called **hieratic scaling**. Saint Lawrence is unnaturally large compared with the other figures in the fifteenth-century painting in **C**. The artist thus immediately not only establishes an obvious focal point but also indicates the relative importance of Saint Lawrence to the other figures.

See also *Devices to Show Depth: Size,* page 196.

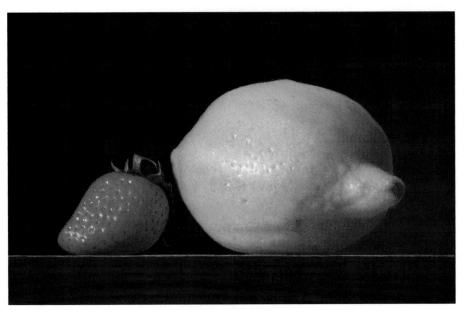

 B

Glen Holland. *Sweet & Sour.* 1998. Oil on wood, actual size 4′ 6″ × 7′. Fischbach Gallery, New York.

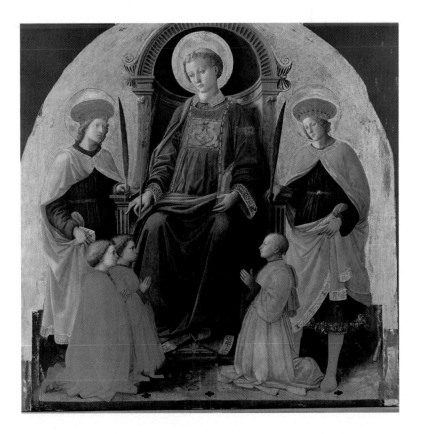

▶ **C**

Fra Filippo Lippi. *Saint Lawrence Enthroned with Saints and Donors.* c. late 1440s. Altarpiece from the church of the Villa Alessandri, Vincigliata Fiesole, central panel only. Tempera on wood, gold ground; overall, with arched top and added strips: 3′ 11³/₄″ × 3′ 9¹/₂″ (121.3 × 115.6 cm). The Metropolitan Museum of Art, Rogers Fund, 1935 (35.31.1a).

HUMAN SCALE REFERENCE

One way to think of artistic scale is to consider the scale of the work itself—its size in relation to other art, in relation to its surroundings, or in relation to human size. Unhappily, book illustrations cannot show art in its original size or scale. Unusual or unexpected scale is arresting and attention-getting. Sheer size does impress us.

When we are confronted by **frescoes** such as the Sistine Chapel ceiling, our first reaction is simply awe at the enormous scope of the work. Later we study and admire details, but first we are overwhelmed by the magnitude. The reverse effect is illustrated in the Chinese medallion in **A**. A world of details—figures, landscape, and architecture—is compressed into a 3½-inch-diameter circle. An immensity of information is rendered with delicate precision on an intimate scale.

The Power of Unusual Scale

If large or small size springs naturally from the function, theme, or purpose of a work, an unusual scale is justified. We are acquainted with many such cases. The gigantic pyramids made a political statement of the pharaohs' eternal power. The elegant miniatures of the religious Book of Hours **(B)** served as inspirational illustrations for the private devotionals of medieval nobility. The small scale is appropriate to private reflection.

The scale of **C** illustrates the opposite approach. Kent Twitchell's enormous wall painting rivals today's large billboards. As trees have grown to eclipse these portraits of musicians, a humorous juxtaposition occurs. Naturalistic images blown up to such monumental scale cannot be ignored, and they alter the urban environment.

In **D** we see a different application of human scale with a satiric effect. This parody of Leonardo's *Mona Lisa* is startling and even grotesque. Intuitively we know the right proportion for head to body, and the large head in Botero's painting is unsettling and out of scale.

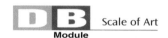

Scale of Art

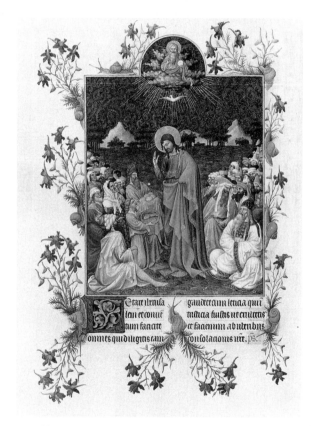

▲ **B**

Limbourg Brothers. *Multiplication of the Loaves and Fishes,* from the Book of Hours *Les Très Riches Heures du Duc de Berry.* 1416. Manuscript illumination, 6¼″ × 4⅜″ (16 × 11 cm). Musée Condé, Chantilly.

◀ **A**

Chinese medallion. Ming Dynasty, late 16th–early 17th century. Front view: carved in high relief with scene of the return by moonlight of a party from a "spring outing." Ivory, diameter: 3⅜″ (8.6 cm). The Metropolitan Museum of Art, purchase, Friends of Asian Art Gifts, 1993 (1993.176).

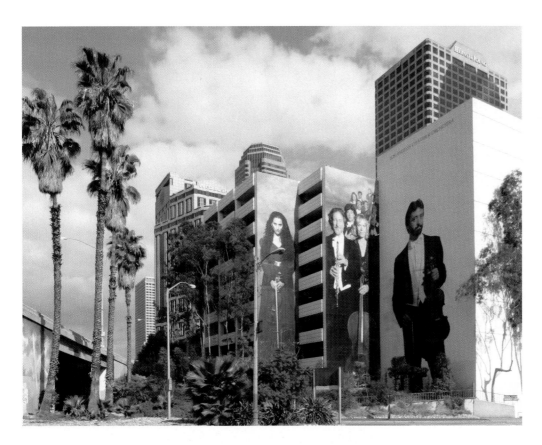

◀ **C**

Kent Twitchell. *Harbor Freeway Overture*. 1993. Acrylic mural. Los Angeles. Photo: 2007 by you-are-here.com.

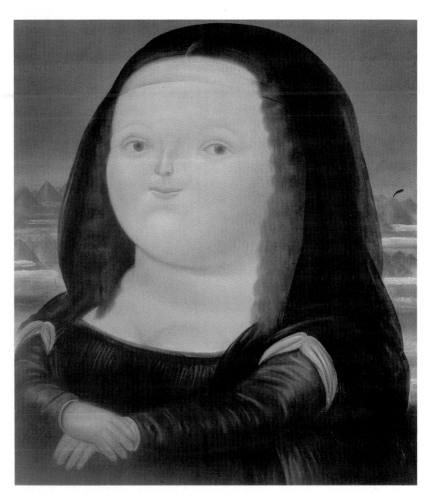

▶ **D**

Fernando Botero. *Mona Lisa*. 1977. Oil on canvas, 6′ × 5′ 5²/₅″ (183 × 166 cm). © Fernando Botero, courtesy Marlborough Gallery, New York.

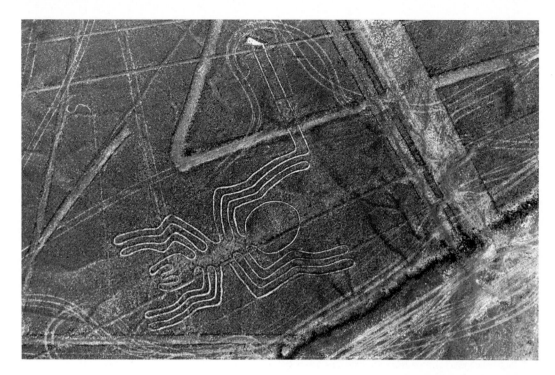

Nazca earth drawing. *Spider.*
Approximately 150′ long.

CONTEXT

Earthworks are unique in the grandeur of their scale. The Nazca earth drawing **(A)** is pre-Columbian in origin. Its original function or meaning has been lost and is the subject of much speculation. With a length of 150 feet it can really only be seen properly from the air! A sense of scale can be determined by the tire tracks around the perimeter of the spider.

Claes Oldenburg has made use of a leap of scale in his *Typewriter Eraser* **(B)**. As with the work of other **pop artists**, this piece calls attention to an everyday object not previously considered worthy of aesthetic consideration. Oldenburg transforms the object by elevating it to a monumental scale. A magnification such as this allows us to see the form with fresh eyes, and, as a result, we might discover new associations, such as the graceful strands of the brush, which project upward like a fountain. It can also be argued that Oldenburg makes monuments appropriate to a consumer culture.

► **B**

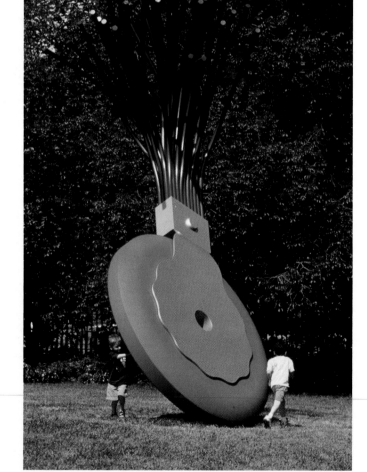

Claes Oldenburg and Coosje van Bruggen. *Typewriter Eraser, Scale X.* 1999. Stainless steel and cement, approximately 20′ tall. National Gallery of Art, Sculpture Garden, Washington, D.C. (gift of The Morris and Gwendolyn Cafritz Foundation, 1998.150.1).

The ad for Emirates Airline shown in **C** is stunning even if we have grown accustomed to supersize billboards such as those that crowd Times Square in New York and many other cities. In this case the poster spans most of a fifty-five-story building. The sheer size may lead us to overlook other considerations of context: The extended arm of the Statue of Liberty is echoed by the shape of the building itself, and the location of this image in the Arab city of Dubai is an affirmation of American and Arab connection, not discord.

The Anti Ad Agency fosters other considerations of large-scale images in public space and critiques the insistent message to consume implicit in such ubiquitous advertising. The child's scribble drawing "proposed" for a billboard **(D)** creates a surprisingly delicate and witty counterpoint to the usual sales pitch. In fact, a blow-up of scribbles would be difficult to convey at a large scale.

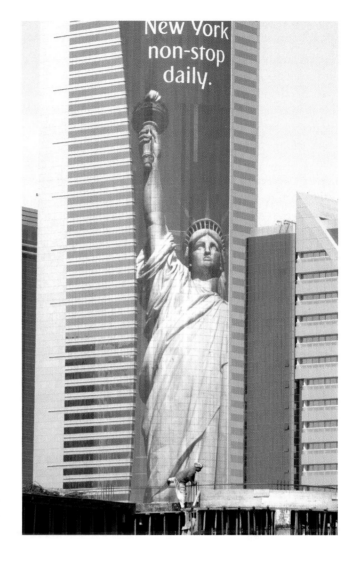

▶ **C**

Emirates Airlines. Ad for air service between Dubai and New York, 180 m tall. Displayed on a fifty-five-story building in Emirates' home base of Dubai.

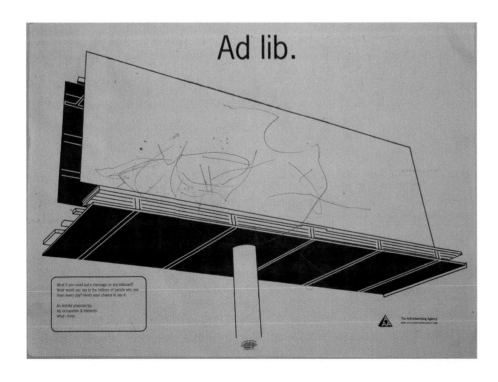

◀ **D**

The Anti-Advertising Agency. *Some Kid.* PDF submission of proposed billboard by "some kid."

INTERNAL PROPORTIONS

The second way to discuss artistic scale is to consider the size and scale of elements within the design or pattern. The scale here, of course, is relative to the overall area of the format—a big element in one painting might be small in a larger work. Again, we often use the term *proportion* to describe the size relationships between various parts of a unit. To say an element in a composition is "out of proportion" carries a negative feeling, and it is true that such a visual effect is often startling or unsettling. However, it is possible that this reaction is precisely what some artists desire.

The three examples in **A** contain the same elements. But in each design the scale of the items is different, thus altering the proportional relationships between the parts. This variation results in very different visual effects in the same way that altering the proportion of ingredients in a recipe changes the final dish. Which design is best or which we prefer can be argued. The answer would depend on what effect we wish to create.

Using Scale to Effect

Look at the difference scale can make in a painting. The images in **B** and **C** both deal with the same topic: the well-known story of Christ's last supper with His disciples before the crucifixion. In Ghirlandaio's painting **(B)** all the figures are quite small relative to a large, airy, and open space. The figures are life-size in a 25-foot-long architectural painting. The regular placement of the figures at the table and the geometric, repeating elements of the architecture give a feeling of calm and quiet order. *The Last Supper* by Nolde **(C)** is, indeed, in a different style of painting, but a major difference between the two works is the use of scale within the picture. In fact the figures in both paintings are similar in size! However, Nolde's figures are crammed together and overlap in the constricting space of a modest canvas. The result is crowded and claustrophobic. Nolde focuses our attention on the intense emotions of the event. The harsh drawing, agitated brushwork, and distortion of the figures enforce the feeling. Both artists relate the same story, but they have very different goals. The choice of scale is a major factor in achieving each artist's intention.

D B Scale Within Art
Module

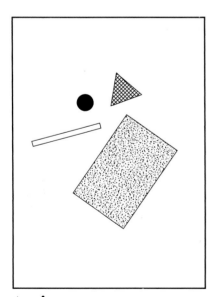
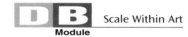
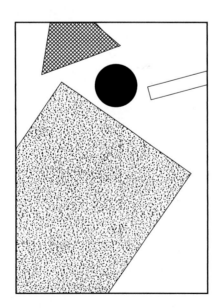
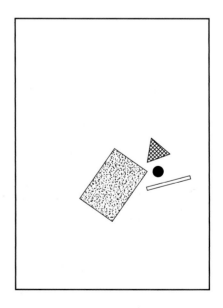

▲ **A**

Changes in scale within a design also change the total effect.

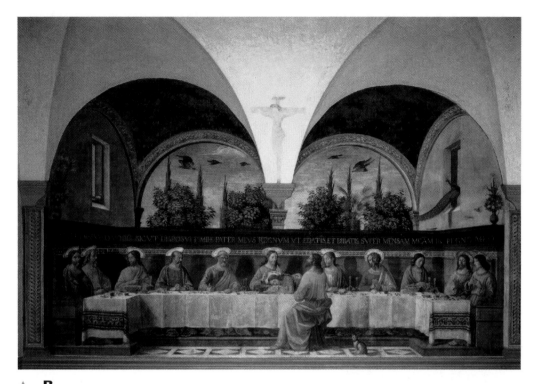

▲ **B**

Domenico Ghirlandaio. *Last Supper.* c. 1480. Fresco, 25′ 7″ (8 m) wide. San Marco, Florence.

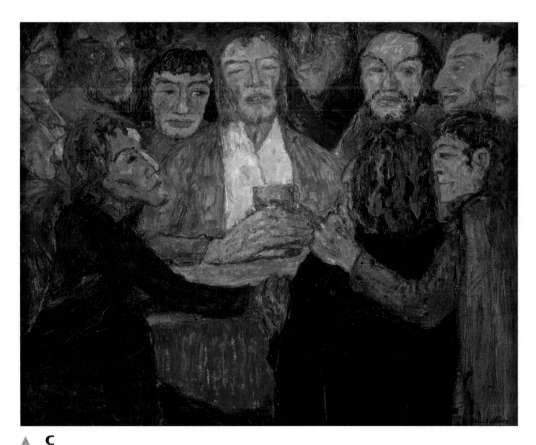

▲ **C**

Emil Nolde. *The Last Supper.* 1909. Oil on canvas, 2′ 10⅝″ × 3′ 6½″ (88 × 108 cm).
Statens Museum for Kunst, Copenhagen.

CONTRAST OF SCALE

Unexpected or Exaggerated Scale

An artist may purposely use scale to attract our attention in different ways. For example, we notice the unexpected or exaggerated, as when small objects are magnified or large ones are reduced. The wash drawing in **A** is startling, here seen enlarged to page-filling size. Just the extreme change in scale attracts our attention. The opposite approach is shown in **B**. Here the purposeful use of the very tiny figures contrasts with a vast space, evoking anxiety. We can see upon revisiting Lissitzky's composition **(C)** that the small text gives a sense of large presence to the red square in an effect not unlike that of **B**.

Unexpected scale is often used in advertising. As visual attention must be directed to a product, we regularly see layouts with a large package, cookie, automobile grille, or cereal flake, for example. A sudden scale change surprises us and gets our attention.

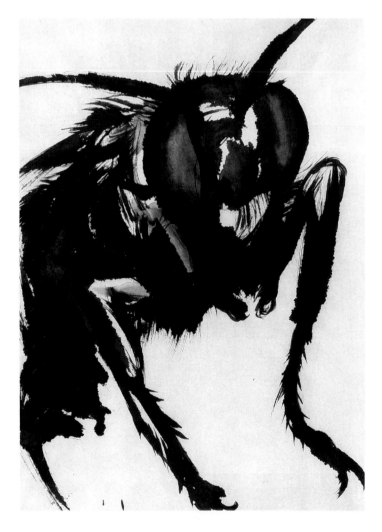

◄ **A**

Mark Fennessey. *Insects IV.* 1965–1966. Wash, 2′ 5″ × 1′ 8″ (73.6 × 50.7 cm). Yale University Art Gallery (transfer from the Yale Art School).

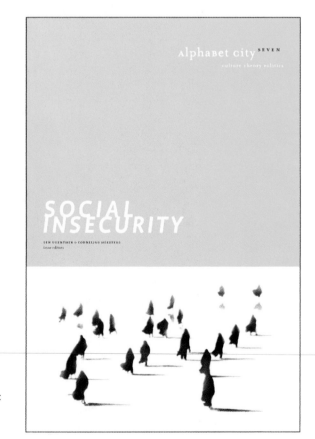

► **B**

Gilbert Li. *Social Insecurity.* 2001. Design Firm: Up Inc. (Toronto, Canada). Client: Alphabet City, Inc. 7³/₈″ × 10⁷/₈″, 342 pages.

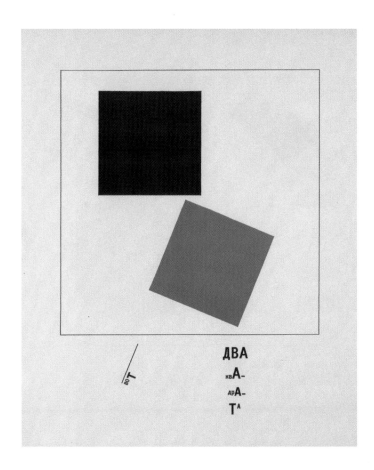

ДВА
кв A–
ар A–
T ᴬ

Large and Small Scale Together

Either large or small scale is often employed in painting or design. However, a more common practice is to combine the two for a dramatic contrast. In John Moore's *Blue Stairway* **(D)**, a foreground plant is presented in front of a distant building. This juxtaposition results in their similarity of size within the painting and encourages a visual dialogue between these otherwise contrasting forms.

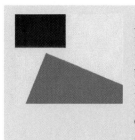

◀ **C**

El Lissitzky. *Of Two Squares: A Suprematist Tale in Six Constructions.* 1922. Illustrated book with letterpress cover and six letterpress illustrations, $10^{15}/_{16}''\times8^{7}/_{8}''$ (27.8 × 22.5 cm). Publisher: Skify, Berlin. Gift of the Judith Rothschild Foundation (89.2001.5).

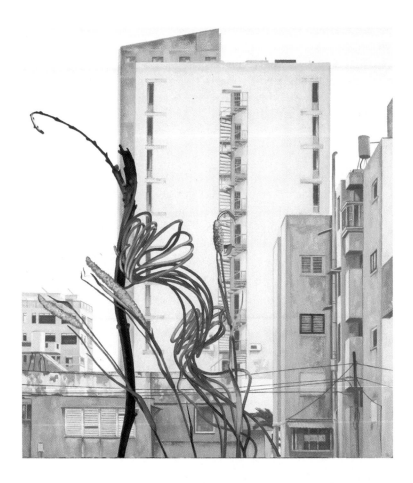

◀ **D**

John Moore. *Blue Stairway.* 1998. Oil on canvas, 2′ 4″ × 2′. Photo courtesy of Hirschl & Adler Modern, New York, NY.

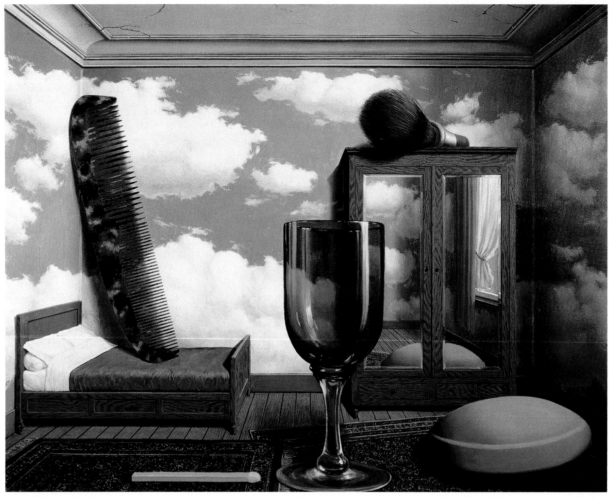

▲ **A**

René Magritte. *Personal Values (Les Valeurs Personnelles).* 1952. Oil on canvas, 2′ 7¹/₂″ × 3′ 3³/₈″ (80.01 × 100.01 cm).

SURREALISM AND FANTASY

The deliberate changing of natural scale is not unusual in painting. In religious paintings many artists have arbitrarily increased the size of the Christ or Virgin Mary figure to emphasize philosophic and religious importance.

Some artists, however, use scale changes intentionally to intrigue or mystify us rather than to clarify the focal point. **Surrealism** is an art form based on paradox, on images that cannot be explained in rational terms. Artists who work in this manner present the irrational world of the dream or nightmare—recognizable elements in impossible situations. The **enigmatic** painting by Magritte **(A)** challenges the viewer with a confusion of scale. We identify the various elements easily enough, but they are all the wrong size and strange in proportion to each other. Does the painting show an impossibly large comb, shaving brush, bar of soap,

and other items, or are these normal-size items placed in a dollhouse? Neither explanation makes rational sense.

A scale change can be an element of fantasy like the small door that Alice can't fit through until she shrinks in *Alice in Wonderland.* The city skyline shown in **B** is almost convincing but also more than just a bit "off." In fact, it is the New York–New York Hotel in Las Vegas. The cars in the photograph betray the actual size of this Vegas fantasy.

Charles Ray's *Family Romance* **(C)** radically demonstrates the impact of a side-by-side scale change. In this case the adult figures are reduced in scale, and the children are presented at closer to actual scale. This comparison reveals the difference in bodily proportions for adults and children.

Magritte would say that such artworks provoke a "crisis of the object." They cause us to pause and reconsider how we know things.

▶ **B**

New York–New York Hotel
& Casino. Las Vegas, Nevada.

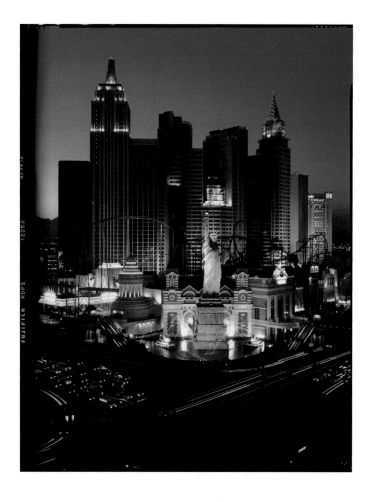

▼ **C**

Charles Ray. *Family Romance*. 1993. Mixed media,
4′ 6″ × 8′ × 2′ (137 × 244 × 61 cm). Edition of 3.
Regen Projects, Los Angeles.

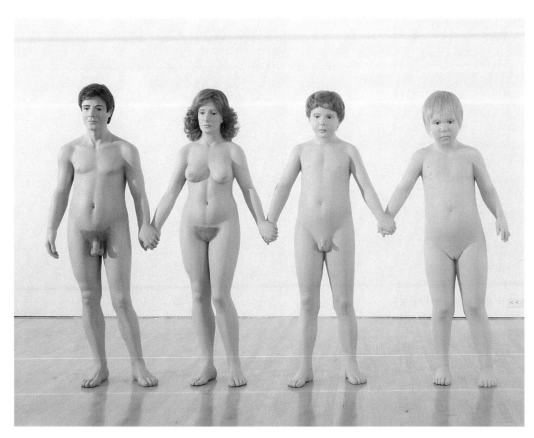

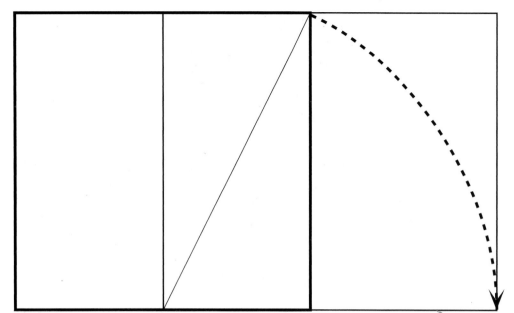

A golden rectangle can be created by rotating the diagonal of the half-square.

NOTIONS OF THE IDEAL

Proportion is linked to ratio. That is to say, we judge the proportions of something to be correct if the ratio of one element to another is correct. For example, the ratio of a baby's head to its body is in proportion for an infant but would strike us as out of proportion for an adult. In a life drawing class, you might learn that an adult is about seven and one-half heads tall. Formulas for the ideal figure have at times had the authority of a rule or canon. Contemporary art or design seldom seems based on such canons, but you may have noticed the apparent standard of "ten heads tall" in the exaggerated proportions of fashion illustration.

The ancient Greeks desired to discover ideal proportions, and these took the form of mathematical ratios. The Greeks found the perfect body to be seven heads tall and even idealized the proportions of the parts of the body. In a similar fashion they sought perfect proportions in rectangles employed in architectural design. Among these rectangles the one most often cited as perfect is the **golden rectangle**. Although this is certainly a **subjective** judgment, the golden rectangle has influenced art and design throughout the centuries. The fact that this proportion is found in growth patterns in nature (such as the chambered nautilus shell, plants, and even human anatomy) and lends itself to a modular repetition has given it some authority in the history of design.

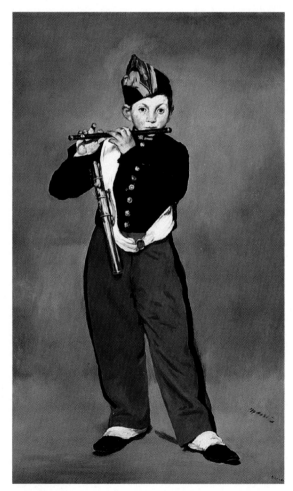

▲ **B**

Édouard Manet. *The Fifer.* 1866. Oil on canvas, 5′ 3″ × 3′ 2⅝″ (160 × 98 cm). Signed lower right: Manet. Musée d'Orsay, Paris (bequest of Count Isaac de Camondo, 1911, RF 1992).

Finding the Golden Rectangle

The proportions of the golden rectangle can be expressed in the ratio of the parts to the whole. This ratio (called the ratio of the **golden mean**) is width is to length as length is to length plus width (w:l as l:l + w). This rectangle can be created by rotating the diagonal of a half-square, as shown in **A**. Both the entire rectangle created and the smaller rectangle attached to the original square are golden rectangles in their proportions.

The ratio of the golden mean can be found in the Fibonacci sequence, a counting series where each new number is the sum of the previous two: 1, 1, 2, 3, 5, 8, 13, 21, 34, and so on. The irrational number $^{21}/_{34}$ is approximately 0.618 and is represented by the Greek letter Φ.

We see this 3:5 ratio expressed in music (harmonies of thirds, fifths, and octaves), and we find it in growth patterns in nature. With research you can find numerous examples of these proportions in nature, the human body, and design. In art the 3:5 proportion is well suited to figure (vertical) **(B)** and landscape (horizontal) **(C)** paintings. Returning to Susan Moore's portrait, we can find the golden proportion in the area occupied by the figure **(D)** within the larger square composition.

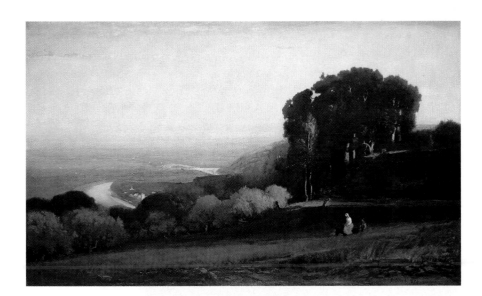

◄ **C**

George Inness. *View of the Tiber near Perugia.* 1872–1874. Oil on canvas, 3′ 2 $^9/_{16}$″ × 5′ 3 $^9/_{16}$″ (98 × 161.5 cm). National Gallery of Art, Washington, D.C. (Ailsa Mellon Bruce Fund, 1973.16.1).

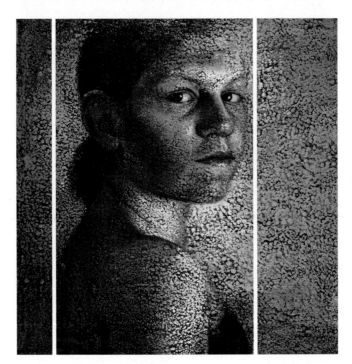

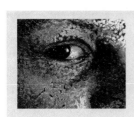

◄ **D**

Susan Moore. *Vanity (Portrait 1).* 2000. Oil stick on canvas, 4′ × 3′ 11″. Diagram.

ROOT RECTANGLES

Like the golden rectangle, other rectangles are derived from the square. These are called *root rectangles* and have proportions such as 1:√2, 1:√3, and 1:√5. It is interesting to explore the dynamics of these shapes and find their expression in art and design.

Rotation of the diagonal of the half-square describes a half-circle and creates a new rectangle with a square at the center flanked by two golden rectangles. This rectangle can be seen in the **facade** of the Parthenon, shown in **A**. The center square contains the four center columns.

Root Five Rectangles

This rectangle, a derivative of the golden rectangle, is called a root five (√5) rectangle because its proportions are 1:√5. Masaccio's *The Tribute Money* (**B**) exploits the properties of this rectangle in depicting a three-part narrative with grace and subtlety. In the center area (the square), the tax collector demands the tribute money from Christ, who instructs Peter to get the money from the fish's mouth. On the left Peter kneels to get the money, and on the right he pays the tax collector.

Exploring Roots in Art and Design

The inherent geometry of rectangles such as the golden rectangle and root five rectangle not only provides an agreeable proportion; the diagonals and other interior structural lines often conform to significant features in a composition as is evident in **B**. These proportions do not provide a formula for design success, however. As with other visual principles, the attributes of the golden mean offer an option for design exploration, and this option continues to interest many contemporary designers, architects, and artists.

The altered appearance of the "street rod" shown in **C** may seem odd after looking at a Greek temple and Masaccio's fresco, and the car was probably not designed with the golden mean in mind. What it does reveal is the power of altered proportions to get our attention and cause us to notice a form. In this case any notion of normal proportion is abandoned and replaced with a personal vision of what looks right. The roofline of this street rod is immediately recognizable as altered in proportion from our expected image of a car. In fact it bears a striking resemblance to the diagrams in **A** and **B**.

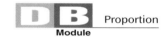
D B Proportion
Module

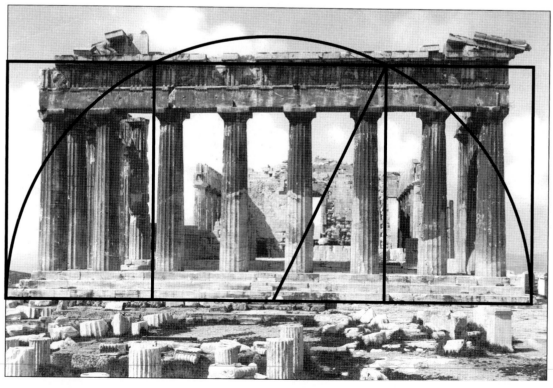

▲ **A**

Parthenon, East Facade, Athens. The root five rectangle and golden rectangle are part of the geometry of the facade. Diagram.

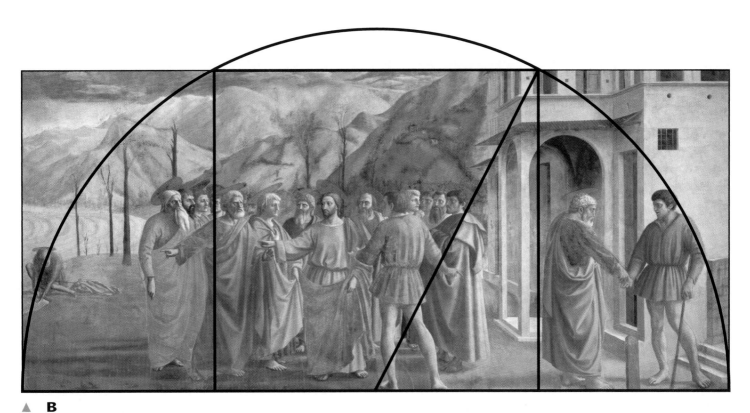

▲   **B**

The geometry of root five and golden rectangles divides this three-part painting at significant locations. Masaccio. *The Tribute Money.* c. 1427. Fresco, 8′ 4″ × 19′ 8″ (2.54 × 5.99 m). Santa Maria del Carmine, Florence, Italy.

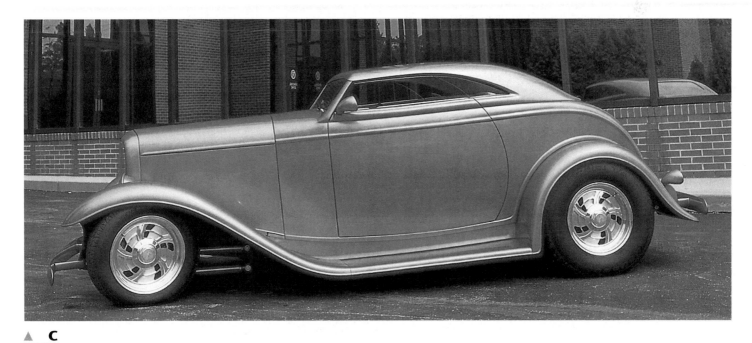

▲   **C**

Modified 1932 Ford ("Deuce") Street Rod. Designer: Thom Taylor. Source: Timothy Remus, *Ford '32 Deuce Hot Rods and Hiboys: The Classic American Street Rod 1950s–1990s* (Motorbooks International Publishers and Wholesalers).

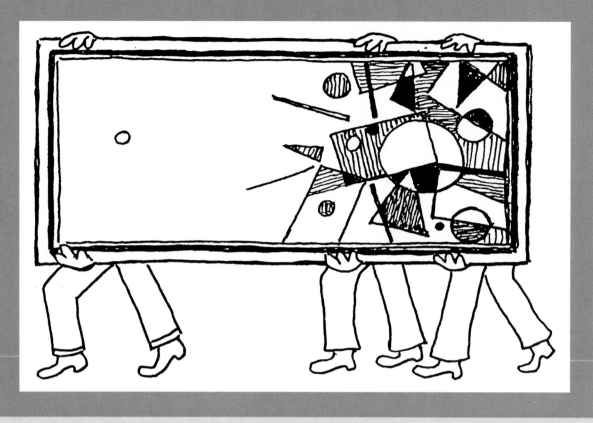

David Lauer

BALANCE

Funeral under Umbrellas (**A**) is a striking picture. What makes it unusual concerns the principle of **balance** or distribution of visual weight within a composition. Here all the figures and visual attention seem concentrated on the right-hand side. The left-hand side is basically empty. The diagonal sweep of the funeral procession is subtly balanced by the driving rain that follows the other diagonal. The effect seems natural and unposed. The result looks like many of the photographs we might see in newspapers or magazines.

A sense of balance is innate; as children we develop a sense of balance in our bodies and observe balance in the world around us. Lack of balance, or imbalance, disturbs us. We observe momentary imbalance such as bodies engaged in active sports that quickly right themselves or fall. We carefully avoid dangerously leaning trees, rocks, furniture, and ladders. But even where no physical danger is present, as in a design or painting, we still feel more comfortable with

a balanced composition. The bookshelf designed by Josef Albers (**B**) is lively in design as the shelves alternate in their extension left and right. The overall pattern is balanced and lends a sense of stability to the design.

Pictorial Balance

In assessing pictorial balance, we always assume a center vertical **axis** and usually expect to see some kind of equal weight (visual weight) distribution on either side. This axis functions as the fulcrum on a scale or seesaw, and the two sides should achieve a sense of **equilibrium**. When this equilibrium is not present, as in **C**, a certain vague uneasiness or dissatisfaction results. We feel a need to rearrange the elements in the same way that we automatically straighten a tilted picture on the wall.

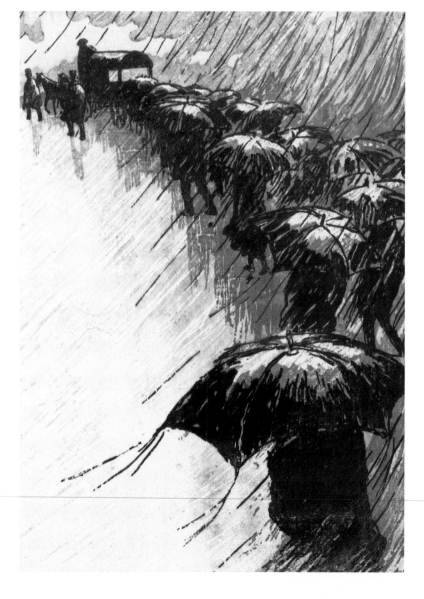

 A

Henri Rivière. *Funeral under Umbrellas.* c. 1895. Etching, 8 1/2″ × 7″ (21.5 × 17.7 cm). Paris, Bibliothèque Nationale de France, Cabinet des Estampes.

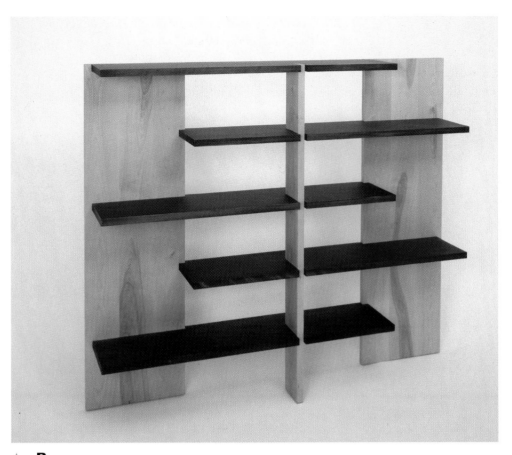

▲ **B**

Josef Albers. *Bookshelf.* 1923. Reproduction by Rupert Deese (1999). Baltic birch, 4′ 9 1/8″ × 5′ 8 3/8″ × 11 3/8″. The Josef and Anni Albers Foundation.

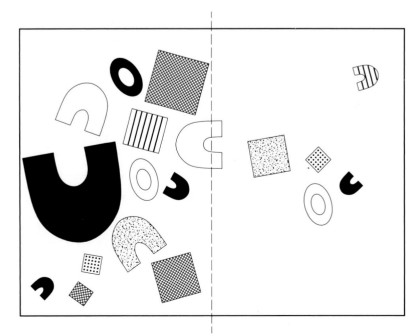

▶ **C**

An unbalanced design leaves the viewer with a vague uneasiness.

HORIZONTAL AND VERTICAL PLACEMENT

Balance—some equal distribution of visual weight—is a universal aim of composition. The vast majority of pictures we see have been consciously balanced by the artist. However, this does not mean there is no place in art for purposeful **imbalance**. An artist may, because of a particular theme or topic, expressly desire that a picture raise uneasy, disquieting responses in the viewer. In this instance imbalance can be a useful tool.

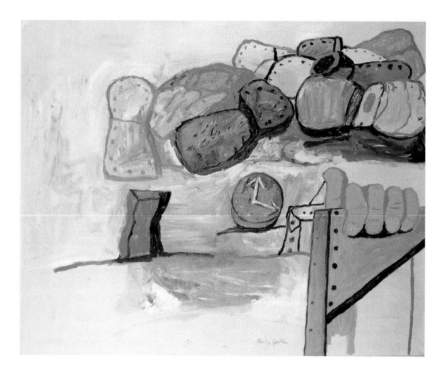

▶ **A**

Philip Guston. *Transition.* 1975. Oil on canvas, 5′ 6″ × 6′ 8¹/₂″ (167.6 × 204.5 cm). Smithsonian American Art Museum, Washington, D.C. Bequest of Musa Guston.

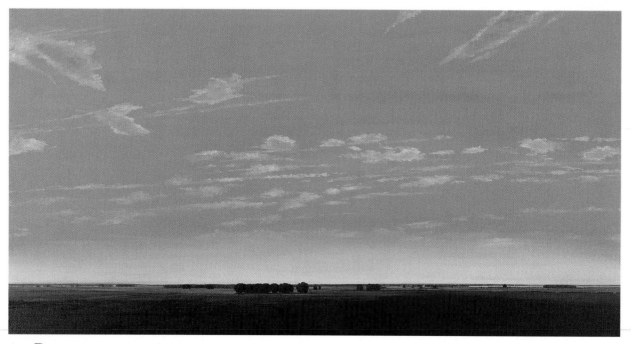

▲ **B**

Keith Jacobshagen. *In the Platte River Valley.* 1983. Oil on canvas, 2′ 6″ × 4′ 8¹/₄″. Sheldon Memorial Art Gallery and Sculpture Garden, University of Nebraska–Lincoln (gift of Wallis, Jaime, Sheri, and Kay in memory of their parents, Joan Farrar Swanson and James Hovland Swanson, 1984.U-3729). Photo: © Sheldon Memorial Art Gallery.

Using Imbalance to Create Tension

Philip Guston's *Transition* **(A)** is weighted to the right-hand side of the painting. Even the hands of the clock seem to point to the mass of enigmatic forms. The off-balance shift in weight seems in keeping with the title: A body off balance tends to be in transition until balance is reached.

In speaking of pictorial balance, we are almost always referring to horizontal balance, the right and left sides of the image. But artists consider vertical balance as well. An imagined horizontal axis divides a work top and bottom. Again, a certain general equilibrium is usually desirable. However, because of our sense of gravity, we are accustomed to seeing more weight toward the bottom, with a resulting stability and calmness **(B)**. The farther up in the format the main distribution of weight or visual interest occurs, the more unstable and dynamic the image becomes.

The effect of a high center of visual interest can be seen in Paul Klee's whimsical *Tightrope Walker* **(C)**; the instability of the image expresses the theme perfectly. The linear patterns build up vertically until we reach the teetering figure near the top. The artist can manipulate the vertical balance freely to fit a particular theme or purpose.

At first glance, **D** appears imbalanced with an awkward void in the center and right side of the composition. Our attention is drawn to the graceful white handle depicted on the left and the white lettering in the text at top and bottom. The "empty" area reveals a subtle shadow of the pitcher suggesting that what we see first and most emphatically is not the whole story.

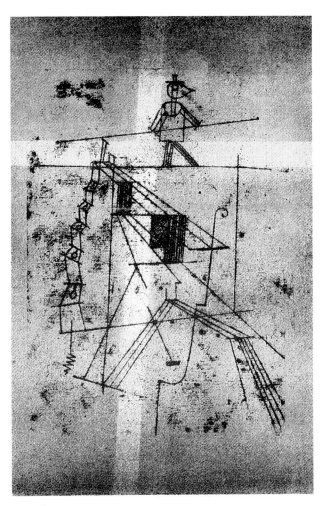

▲ **C**

Paul Klee. *Tightrope Walker,* plate 4 from the portfolio *Mappe der Gegenwart (Map of the Future).* 1923. Color lithograph, 1' 5³/₁₆" × 10⁵/₈" (43.6 × 27 cm). The Museum of Modern Art, New York (given anonymously).

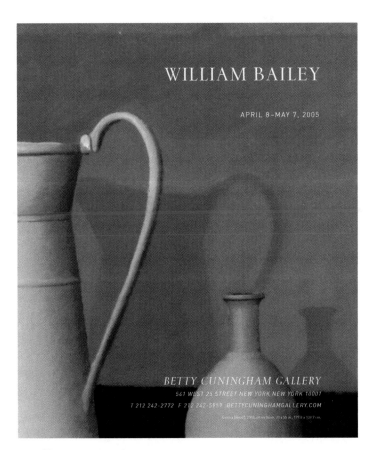

▲ **D**

William Bailey. Detail from *TURNING.* 2003. Oil on linen, 5' 10" × 4' 7" (177.8 × 139.7 cm). WB10092. Advertisement for Betty Cunningham Gallery. *Art in America,* April 2005.

BILATERAL SYMMETRY

The simplest type of balance, both to create and to recognize, is called *symmetrical balance.* In symmetrical balance, like shapes are repeated in the same positions on either side of a vertical axis. This type of **symmetry** is also called **bilateral symmetry**. One side, in effect, becomes the mirror image of the other side. Symmetrical balance seems to have a basic appeal for us that can be ascribed to the awareness of our bodies' essential symmetry. In the case of the shirt shown in **A,** the symmetry is clearly in response to this symmetry of the body.

Formal Balance

Conscious symmetrical repetition, while clearly creating perfect balance, can be undeniably **static**, so the term *formal balance* is used to describe the same idea. There is nothing wrong with quiet formality. In fact, this characteristic is often desired in some art, notably in architecture. Countless examples of architecture with symmetrical balance can be found throughout the world, dating from most periods of art history. The continuous popularity of symmetrical design is not hard to understand. The **formal** quality in symmetry imparts an immediate feeling of permanence, strength, and stability. Such qualities are important in public buildings to suggest the dignity and power of a government. So statehouses, city halls, palaces, courthouses, and other government monuments often exploit the properties of symmetrical balance.

    The state Capitol in Albany, New York **(B)**, has a repetitive pattern, and the result is a sedate, calm, and dignified facade. Such an effect is often termed **classical**, alluding to the many ancient Greek and Roman buildings in which symmetrical design imparted the same feeling of clarity and rational order. This symmetry is continued in the newer buildings that frame this entrance to the capitol. This ordered balance provides an anchor to the rest of the plaza, which is not symmetrical in design.

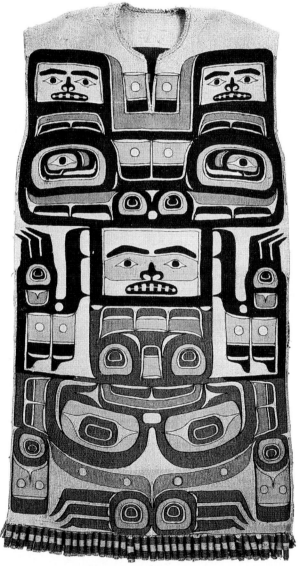

▲ **A**

Man's (Chilkat Tlingit) shirt (front view), Alaska. c. 1890. Woven from goat's hair on a cedarbark base, 3′ 8³/₄″ (114 cm) long. Courtesy National Museum of the American Indian, Smithsonian Institution. Photo by Carmelo Guadagno (neg. no. 20961).

Symmetry Unifies

Symmetrical balance does not, by itself, preordain any specific visual result. Both **B** and **C** are examples of symmetrical architecture, but here the similarity ends. The simplicity of the Capitol complex, with its orderly progression of repeated shapes and a calm, regular rhythm of dark and light, is certainly not present in the church interior **(C)**. The latter is a busy, exciting, ornate space with only the symmetrical organization molding the masses of niches, columns, and statuary into a unified and coherent visual pattern. Symmetry is often associated with altars and religious artworks where stability and order reinforce enduring values.

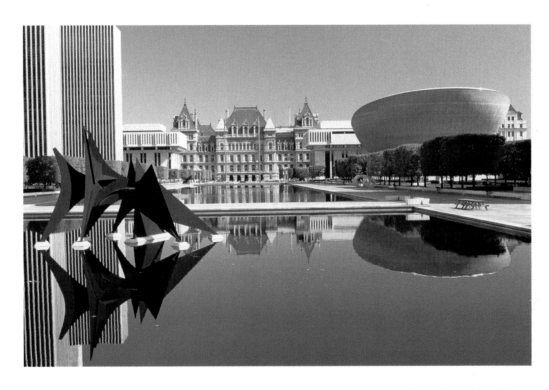

◄ **B**

New York State Capitol Building, Albany, NY (South Facade). Architect: H. H. Richardson (with Leopold Eidlitz), 1876–1883.

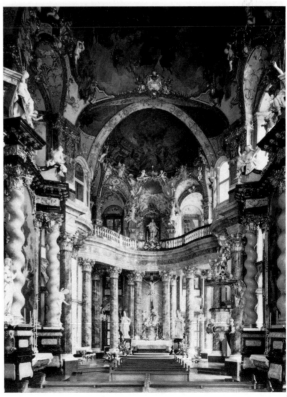

▶ **C**

Balthasar Neumann. Würzburg, Residenz Court Church Interior. 1732–1744. Stuccoes by Bossi. Frescoes by Byss.

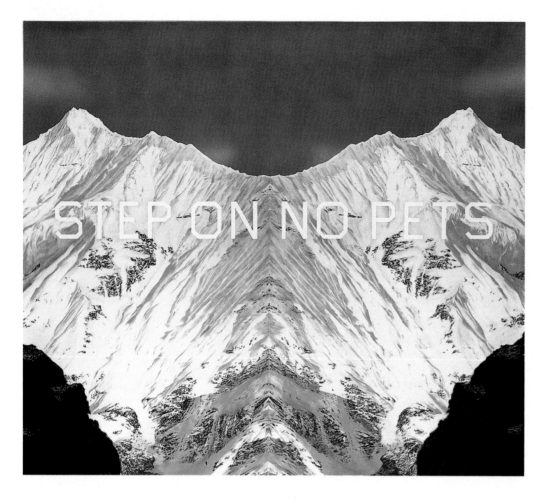

◄ **A**

Ed Ruscha. *Step on No Pets*. 2002.
Acrylic on canvas, 5′ 4 1/8″ × 6′ 1/8″.
Gagosian Gallery, New York.

EXAMPLES FROM VARIOUS ART FORMS

Symmetrical balance is rarer in painting or photography than in architecture. In fact, relatively few two-dimensional artworks would fit a strict definition of symmetry.

Using Symmetry of Nature

Sometimes the subject matter of a painting makes symmetrical balance an appropriate compositional device. Ed Ruscha turns a mountain landscape **(A)** into a symmetrical shape like a Rorschach test. Superimposed over this image is a palindrome, the verbal equivalent of bilateral symmetry.

The photo **(B)** shows a symmetry found easily in the natural world. A reflection in still water creates symmetry along a horizontal axis. In this case the two halves of the symmetrical arrangement nearly complete a dark circle at the center of the photograph. The remainder of the photograph includes less-emphatic asymmetrical elements typical of the "messiness" of the real world. In **B** we see one distinct advantage to symmetrical compositions: the immediate

creation and emphasis of a focal point. With the two sides being so much alike, whatever element is placed on the center axis has an obvious visual importance.

A Vertical Axis and the Body

Susan Moore's portrait **(C)** presents the model in a pose that is *not* symmetrical. The young woman glances back over her shoulder, and we see her head in three-quarter view. Nevertheless, her right eye falls along the vertical centerline of the painting, giving emphasis to her gaze. We sense that she could complete her turn and her pose would be symmetrical.

Margaret Wharton transforms a wooden chair into a *Mocking Bird* **(D)** through a process of slicing and reassembling. In this case we can, once again, trace the origins of the sculpture's symmetry back to the human figure. The symmetry of the chair derives from the human body for which it is designed. Wharton's cut and reassembled version takes on the winged symmetry of a birdlike form. In this case symmetry results in a whimsical, lighthearted artwork, rather than a solemn image.

◄ **B**
Anna Shteynshleyger. *Bush.* 2001.
Digital C-print, 2′ 6″ × 3′ 4″. Courtesy
of the artist.

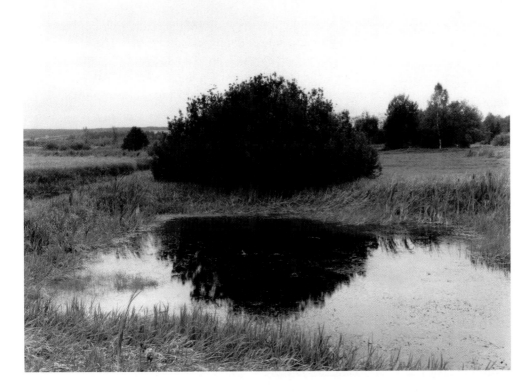

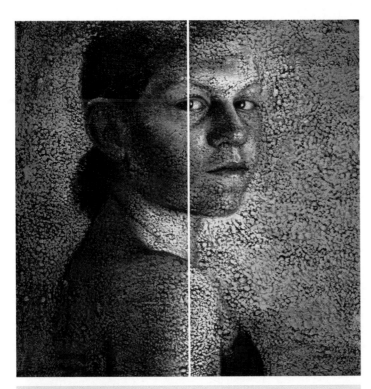

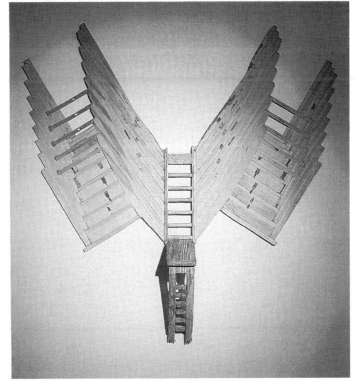

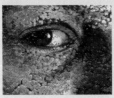

▲ **C**
Susan Moore. *Vanity
(Portrait 1).* 2000. Oil stick
on canvas, 4′ × 3′ 11″.
Diagram.

▲ **D**
Margaret Wharton. *Mocking Bird.* 1981. Partially stained
wooden chair, epoxy glue, paint, wooden dowels, 5′ ×
5′ × 1′ 1″ (152 × 152 × 33 cm). Courtesy of the artist and
Jean Albano Gallery, Chicago.

ASYMMETRICAL BALANCE

INTRODUCTION

The second type of balance is called **asymmetrical balance**. In this case balance is achieved with dissimilar objects that have equal visual weight or equal eye attraction. Remember the children's riddle, "Which weighs more, a pound of feathers or a pound of lead"? Of course, they both weigh a pound, but the amount and mass of each vary radically. This, then, is the essence of asymmetrical balance.

Informal Balance

In Nan Goldin's photograph **(A)** the figure gazes out at us from the right side of the picture. But the composition is not off balance. Left of center are the hand and cigarette, which balance the face as a natural point of interest. Balance is maintained as the two sides of the picture each provide a visual emphasis.

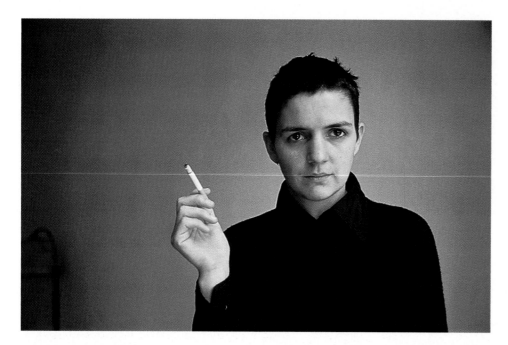

◄ **A**

Nan Goldin. *Siobhan with a cigarette, Berlin.* 1994. Photograph.

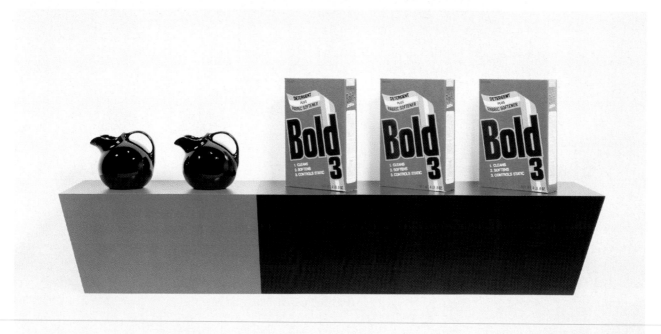

▲ **B**

Ham Steinbach. *supremely black.* 1985. Plastic laminated wood shelf, ceramic pitchers, cardboard detergent boxes, 2′ 5″ × 5′ 6″ × 1′ 1″ (74 × 168 × 33 cm). Sonnabend Gallery and Jay Gorney Modern Art, New York.

Goldin's photograph shows one advantage of asymmetrical balance: The feeling is more casual than that of a formal symmetrical portrait. Another term for asymmetrical balance is, appropriately, **informal balance**. The human face is a strong target for our attention. Presented in absolute symmetry the result can be a static or boring portrait. Goldin's use of a more informal balance is in keeping with the delicate sense of balance in the lives of real people.

Symmetry can appear artificial, as our visual experiences in life are rarely symmetrically arranged. Some buildings and interiors are so designed, but even here, unless we stand quietly at dead center, our views are always asymmetrical.

Carefully Planning Asymmetry

Asymmetry appears casual and less planned, although obviously this characteristic is misleading. Asymmetrical balance is actually more intricate and complicated to use than symmetrical balance. Merely repeating similar elements in a mirror image on either side of the center is not a difficult design task. But attempting to balance dissimilar items involves more complex considerations and more subtle factors.

The sculpture by Ham Steinbach **(B)** shows how two can balance three in an asymmetric arrangement. Two black pitchers sit on a red shelf adjacent to three red Bold 3 detergent boxes on a black shelf. This asymmetric pairing invites us to find the visual rhymes and contrasts that exist across the dividing line. The visual interest in comparing the unequal sides results in a balanced composition, and the number of elements feels correct.

Careful planning takes on a different level of significance in the engineering and design of a bridge where function and safety are paramount. The expressive asymmetry of Calatrava's bridge **(C)** confounds our usual expectation of stability, and the result is a dynamic, unforgettable design.

▼ **C**

Alamillo Bridge/Cartuja Viaduct, Seville, Spain. Architect: Santiago Calatrava.

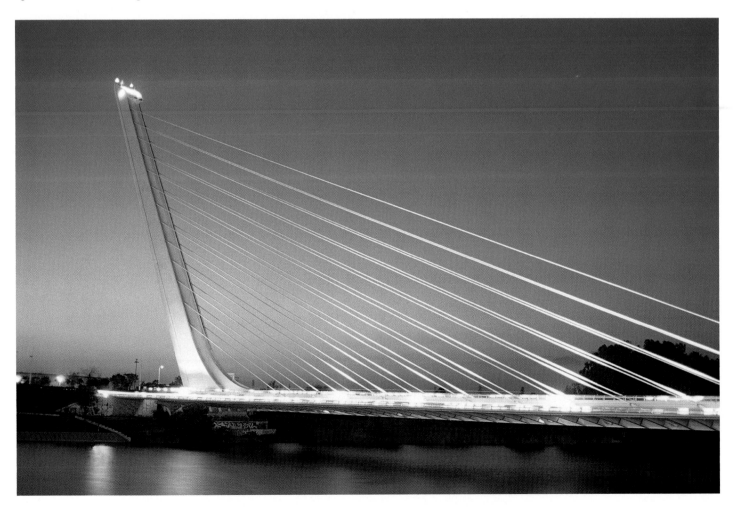

BALANCE BY VALUE AND COLOR

Value

Asymmetrical balance is based on equal eye attraction—dissimilar objects are equally interesting to the eye. One element that attracts our attention is **value** difference, a contrast of light and dark. As **A** illustrates, black against white gives a stronger contrast than gray against white; therefore, a smaller amount of black is needed to visually balance a larger amount of gray.

The photograph of the cathedral at York (**B**) reverses the values but shows the same balance technique. The left side of the composition shows many details of the angled wall of the church nave. However, the receding arches, piers, columns, and so on are shown in subtle gradations of gray, all very close and related in value. In contrast, on the right side is the large black **silhouette** of a foreground column and the small window area of bright white. These two sharp visual accents of white and black balance the many essentially gray elements on the left.

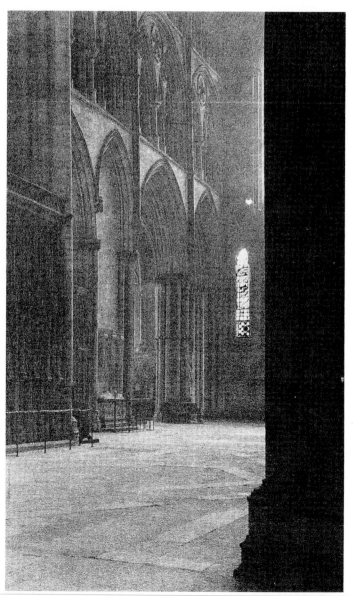

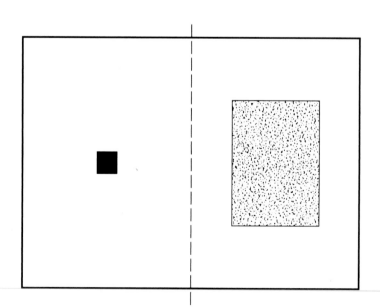

▲ **A**

A darker, smaller element is visually equal to a lighter, larger one.

▲ **B**

Frederic H. Evans. *York Minister, Into the South Transept.* 1900. Platinum print, 8 1/4″ × 4 3/4″ (20.9 × 12.1 cm). The Metropolitan Museum of Art, Alfred Stieglitz Collection, 1933 (33.43.368).

Color

The illustration in **C** suggests motion as the figure exits the left side of the composition. The design is quite abstract and breaks into jigsaw puzzle–like shapes. This dynamic arrangement is countered by the bold expanse of yellow that dominates the right half of the image.

Balance by value or color is a great tool, allowing a large difference of shapes on either side of the center axis and still achieving equal eye attraction.

See also *Color and Balance*, page 270, and *Ways to Suggest Motion*, pages 232, 234, and 236.

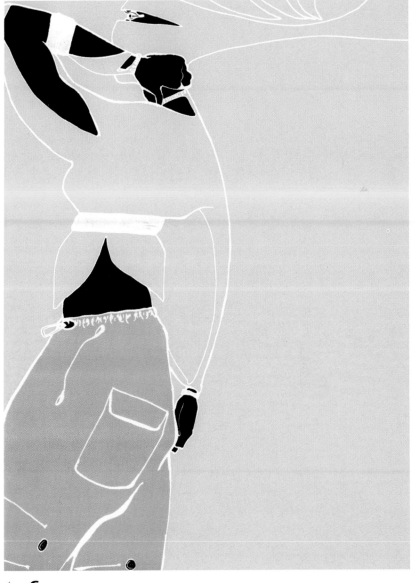

▲ **C**

Kristian Russell, Art Department. 1998.

BALANCE BY TEXTURE AND PATTERN

The diagram in **A** illustrates balance by shape. Here the two elements are exactly the same value and texture. The only difference is their shape. The smaller form attracts the eye because of its more complicated contours. Though small, it is more interesting than the much larger, but duller, rectangle.

Texture Adds Interest

Any visual **texture** with a variegated dark and light pattern holds more interest for the eye than does a smooth, unrelieved surface. The drawing in **B** presents this idea: The smaller, rough-textured area balances the larger, basically untextured area (smoothness is, in a sense, a texture).

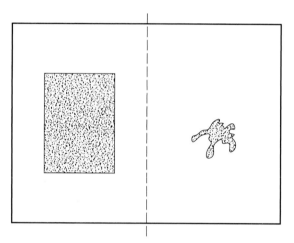

▲ **A**

A small, complicated shape is balanced by a larger, more stable shape.

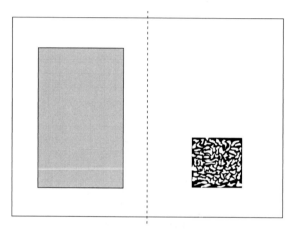

▲ **B**

A small, textured shape can balance a larger, untextured one.

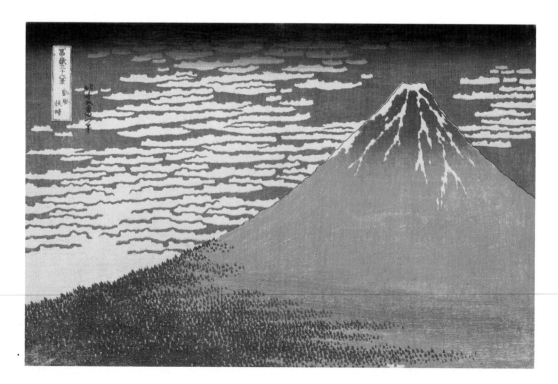

◄ **C**

Katsushika Hokusai. *South Wind, Clear Dawn* from *Thirty-Six Views of Mount Fuji*. Woodblock print, 10″ × 1′ 2⁷/₈″ . The Metropolitan Museum of Art, bequest of Henry L. Phillips, 1939 (JP 2960).

Using Texture and Pattern for Balance

The balance of the elements in the Japanese woodcut **(C)** shows how a large, simple form can be balanced by an intricate pattern or texture. The large, simple triangular mass of the mountain is positioned to the right. The left side is balanced by the pattern of clouds and sky and by a texture that suggests a forest of trees. Pattern and texture balance the strength of the large red mountain shape.

The still-life painting by Henri Fantin-Latour **(D)** offers a surprising composition. A pitcher sits on top of a broad expanse of white linen, and this focal point is balanced by the intricate pattern of foliage on the right.

Texture in Commercial Design

Printed text consisting of letters and words in effect creates a visual texture. The information is in symbols that we can read, but the visual effect is nothing more than a gray-patterned shape. Depending on the typeface and the layout, this gray area varies in darkness, density, and character, but it is visually textured. Very often in advertisements or editorial page layouts, an area of "textured" printed matter will balance photographs or graphics. The pages of this text are similarly composed.

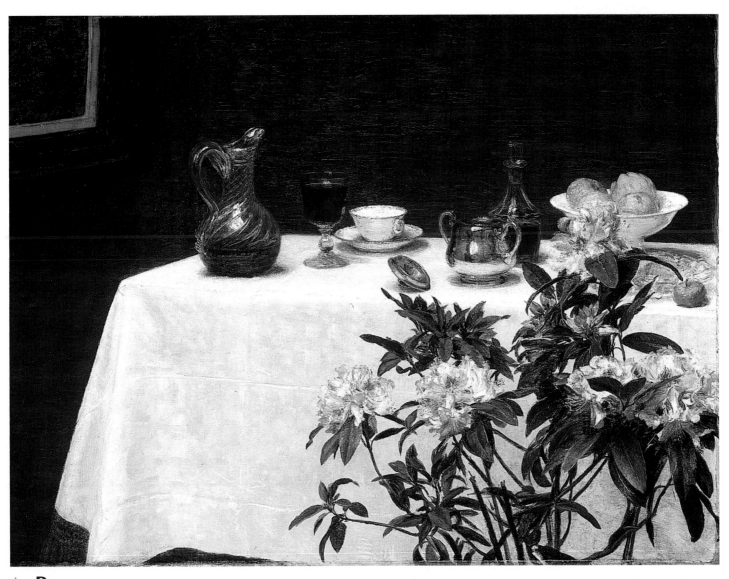

▲ **D**

Henri Fantin-Latour. *Still Life: Corner of a Table.* 1873. Oil on canvas, 3′ 1⁵/₁₆″ × 4′ 1³/₁₆″ (96.4 × 125 cm). The Art Institute of Chicago (Ada Turnbull Hertle Endowment, 1951.226).

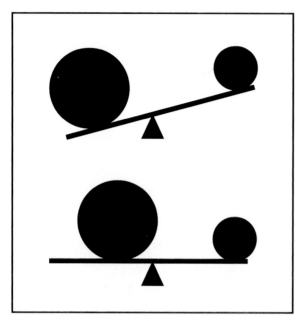

▲ **A**

A large shape placed near the middle of a design can be balanced by a smaller shape placed toward the outer edge.

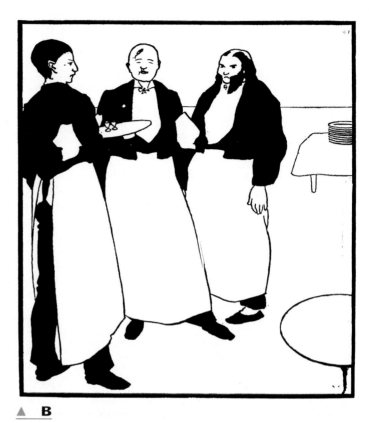

▲ **B**

Aubrey Beardsley. *Garçons de Café*. 1894. Line block drawing originally published in *The Yellow Book*, vol. II, July.

BALANCE BY POSITION AND EYE DIRECTION

A well-known principle in physics says that two items of unequal weight can be brought to equilibrium by moving the heavier inward toward the fulcrum. In design this means that a large item placed closer to the center can be balanced by a smaller item placed out toward the edge. The two seesaw diagrams in **A** illustrate this idea of balance by position.

Achieving Casual Balance

Balance by position often lends an unusual, unexpected quality to the composition. The effect not only appears casual and unplanned but also can make the composition seem, at first glance, to be in imbalance. This casual impression is evident in the illustration by Aubrey Beardsley (**B**). The three "garçons" are grouped in the left-hand portion of the composition. Notice how much of these figures is actually

the white aprons, which lighten the weight of the figure grouping. Two tables, one stacked with plates, on the right-hand edge of the picture provide sufficient balancing lines and shapes to this informal group.

Connecting the Eyes

At first glance, the *Annunciation* fresco by Fra Angelico (**C**) seems heavily weighted to the left side of the composition. The angel has prominent wings with bright color and darker values. The figure of Mary, on the other hand, is pale, almost dissolving into the background. This imbalance is offset by subtle eye direction. We connect the figures through the line of their gaze and the arches sweeping across the top of the painting.

Although not usually the only technique of balance employed by artists, eye direction is a commonly used device. Eye direction is carefully plotted, not only for balance but also for general compositional unity.

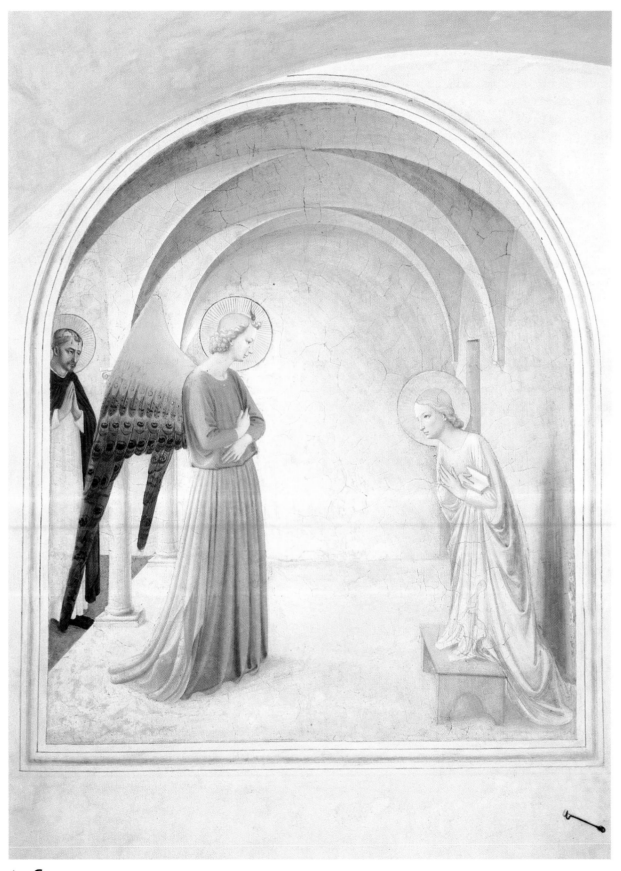

▲ **C**

Fra Angelico. *The Annunciation*. 1442. Fresco, 6′ 1 $^1/_2$″ × 5′ 1 $^3/_4$″ (187 × 157 cm).
Museo di San Marco dell'Angelico, Florence, Italy / The Bridgeman Art Library.

ANALYSIS SUMMARY

In looking at works of art, you will realize that isolating one technique of asymmetrical balance as we have done is a bit misleading because the vast majority of works employ several of the methods simultaneously. For the sake of clarity, we discuss these methods separately, but the principles often overlap and are frequently used together. Let us look at just a few examples that use several of the factors involved in asymmetrical balance.

Combining Asymmetrical Techniques

The title of Martin Puryear's sculpture shown in **A** is appropriate for the asymmetric balance that is achieved. *Lever No. 3* presents a quirky and unexpected form with a small circular loop cast off from a more massive body. This loop sits like a head atop a long neck and visually balances the weight of the grounded body. The effect is like that of the smaller weight at the end of a long lever arm, but our visual interest is drawn to the space inside the loop more powerfully than if it were simply a solid circle. This added complexity helps offset the much larger bulk of the left side.

We have seen how most of the elements in **B** form a cluster along an arc. This creates a minor imbalance in the composition weighted to the right side. The small bit of text and the line at lower left are just enough to provide balance without neutralizing the dynamism of the large sweeping constellation.

Garry Winogrand's photograph **(C)** appears to be essentially symmetrical with elements balanced to the left and right of the center. In fact it is the *asymmetrical* aspects of the composition that keep us engaged:

> The white car on the left blends into the light sand, while the blue picnic stand on the right echoes the sky.
> The open door and figure on the left balance two figures on the right.
> The clouds are distributed equally left and right but the shapes vary.

The Winogrand photograph seems remarkably symmetrical for an unposed, spontaneous moment. The picture is, in fact, a play between the asymmetrical balance of lively casual elements and a symmetry that evokes a staged or artificial quality.

 Symmetrical and Asymmetrical Balance

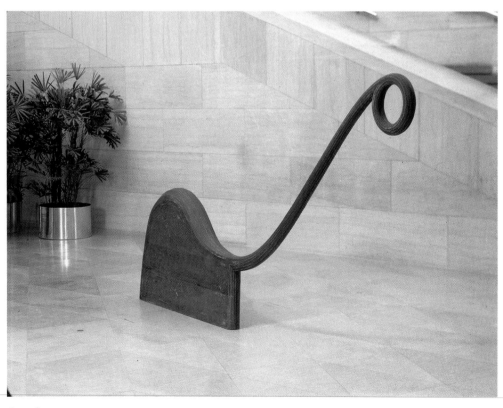

▲ **A**

Martin Puryear. *Lever No. 3.* 1989. Wood, carved and painted, 7' 1/2" × 13' 6" × 1' 1" (214.6 × 411.5 × 33 cm). National Gallery of Art, Washington, D.C. (gift of the Collectors Committee, 1989.71.1). Image © Board of Trustees, National Gallery of Art, Washington.

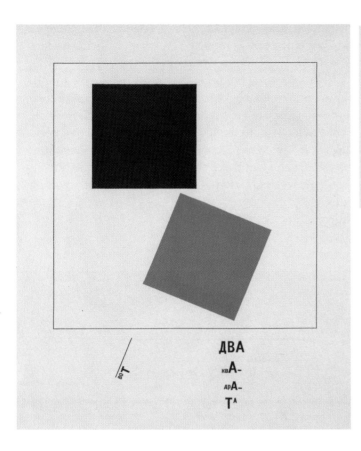

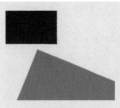

◄   **B**

El Lissitzky. *Of Two Squares: A Suprematist Tale in Six Constructions.* 1922. Illustrated book with letterpress cover and six letterpress illustrations, $10^{15}/_{16}'' \times 8^{7}/_{8}''$ (27.8 × 22.5 cm). Publisher: Skify, Berlin. Gift of the Judith Rothschild Foundation (89.2001.5).

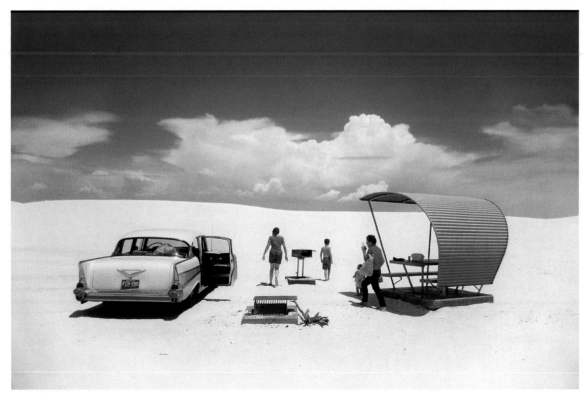

▲   **C**

Garry Winogrand. *White Sands National Monument.* 1964. Courtesy of Estate of Garry Winogrand, Center for Creative Photography, University of Arizona.

EXAMPLES IN NATURE AND ART

A third variety of balance is called **radial balance**. Here all the elements radiate or circle out from a common central point. The sun with its emanating rays is a familiar symbol that expresses the basic idea. Radial balance is not entirely distinct from symmetrical or asymmetrical balance. It is merely a refinement of one or the other, depending on whether the focus occurs in the middle or off center.

Radial patterns are abundant in the natural world. The form of the flower shown in **A** is a visual expression of its growth outward from the stem. Each small floret echoes this pattern. This same pattern is seen in Josiah McElheny's sculpture **(B)**, which is modeled on what physicists understand about a certain stage of the big bang.

Circular forms abound in craft areas, where the round shapes of ceramics, basketry, and jewelry often make radial balance a natural choice in decorating such objects. Radial balance can be found in the playful design based on a bicycle wheel in **C**. This whirligig, fashioned from a wheel and funnels to catch the wind, exemplifies a rotational structure also seen in the weather patterns of a hurricane or the vortex of water in a whirlpool.

▶ **A**

Queen Anne's Lace.

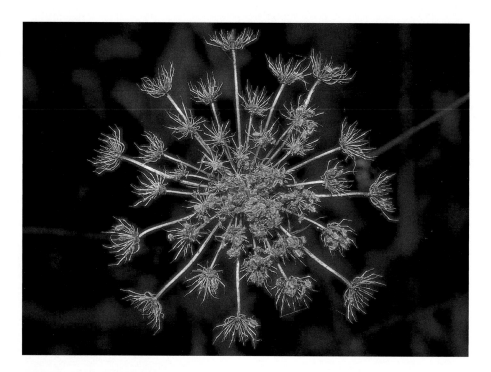

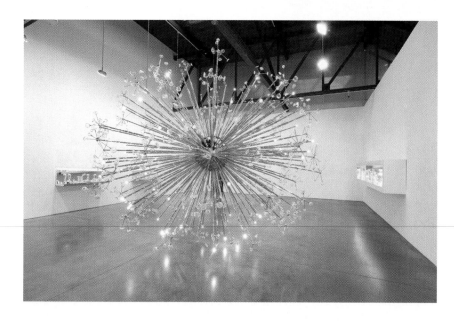

◀ **B**

Josiah McElheny. *An End to Modernity.* 2005. Chrome-plated aluminum, electric lighting, handblown glass, 12′ × 15′ × 15′ . Courtesy Donald Yound Gallery, Chicago and Andrea Rosen Gallery, New York.

Cultural Symbols

Radial balance has been used frequently in architecture. The round form of domed buildings such as the Roman Pantheon or our nation's Capitol will almost automatically give a radial feeling to the interior. Such a design has a symbolic function of giving emphasis to the center as a place of cultural significance. Many cultures employ radial balance as part of their spiritual imagery and designs. These range from Tibetan **mandalas** to the rose windows of Gothic cathedrals.

The advantage of such a design is the clear emphasis on the center and the unity that this form of design suggests.

The Rose, a painting by Jay DeFeo (**D**), is literally radiant with a light center. This is a surprising contrast to the texture and apparent weight of the rest of the painting's surface.

Radial Balance

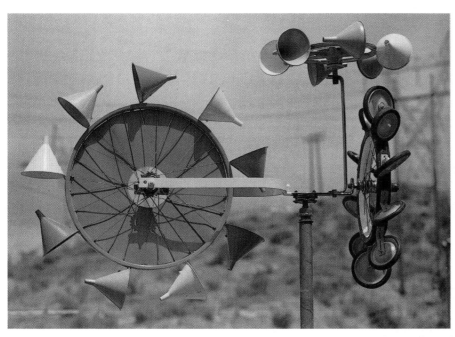

▲ **C**

Anonymous. "Whirligig."

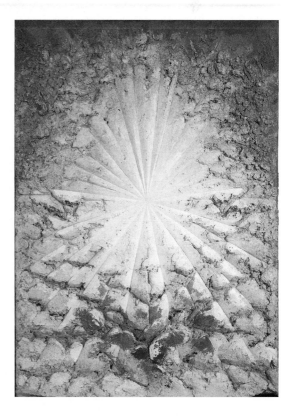

▶ **D**

Jay DeFeo. *The Rose.* 1958–1966. Oil with wood and mica on canvas, 10′ 8⁷/₈″ × 7′ 8¹/₄″ × 11″ (327.3 × 234.3 × 27.9 cm). Frame: 10′ 11¹/₁₆″ × 7′ 10³/₈″ × 5″ (332.9 × 239.7 × 12.7 cm). Collection of Whitney Museum of American Art (gift of the Estate of Jay DeFeo and purchased with funds from the Contemporary Painting and Sculpture Committee and the Judith Rothschild Foundation, 95.170).

ALLOVER PATTERN

One more specific type of visual effect is often designated as a fourth variety of balance. The examples here illustrate the idea. These works all exhibit an equal emphasis over the whole format—the same weight or eye attraction literally everywhere.

This technique is officially called **crystallographic balance**. Because few people can remember this term—and even fewer can spell it—the more common name is **allover pattern**. This technique is, of course, a rather special refinement of symmetrical balance. The constant repetition of the same quality everywhere on the surface, however, creates an impression truly different from our usual concept of symmetrical balance.

Allover Pattern in Art and Design

In the *Signature Quilt* **(A)**, emphasis is uniform throughout. The many blocks are the same size, with each defined in the same degree of contrast to the black background. Each signature on each block is accorded the same value, whether that of a president (Lincoln, for example) or a lesser-known individual. There is no beginning, no end, and no focal point—unless, indeed, the whole quilt is the focal point.

An allover pattern may suggest the geometry of a quilt, but the same effect can be achieved with a more irregular structure such as a map. A map may lead us to look for a point of emphasis such as a major city; however, Jasper Johns's map **(B)** has no such emphasis. Shattered patches of color are distributed in similar amounts and defy most boundaries of the map. The result is more raucous than **A** but similarly suggests that the whole composition is the focus.

The wall of photographs shown in **C** is intended for quiet reflection or contemplation. Here are photos of many of the predominantly Jewish residents of an eastern European town. The Jewish community was eliminated by the Nazis, and this wall gives testimony to the loss with each individual having an equal place of commemoration. A balance is present between the unique nature of each photograph and frame, emphasizing the loss of distinct individuals, and the whole collection, which gives some sense of the larger community.

▲ **A**

Adeline Harris Sears. *Signature Quilt.* 1856–63. Silk with inked signatures, 6′ 5″ × 6′ 8″ (195.6 × 203.2 cm). The Metropolitan Museum of Art, Purchase, William Cullen Bryant Fellow Gifts, 1996 (1996.4).

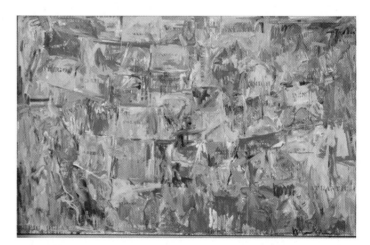

▲ **B**

Jasper Johns. *Map.* 1961. Oil on canvas, 6′ 6″ × 10′ 3 1/8″. Gift of Mr. and Mrs. Robert C. Scull (277.1963). Art © Jasper Johns/licensed by VAGA, New York, NY.

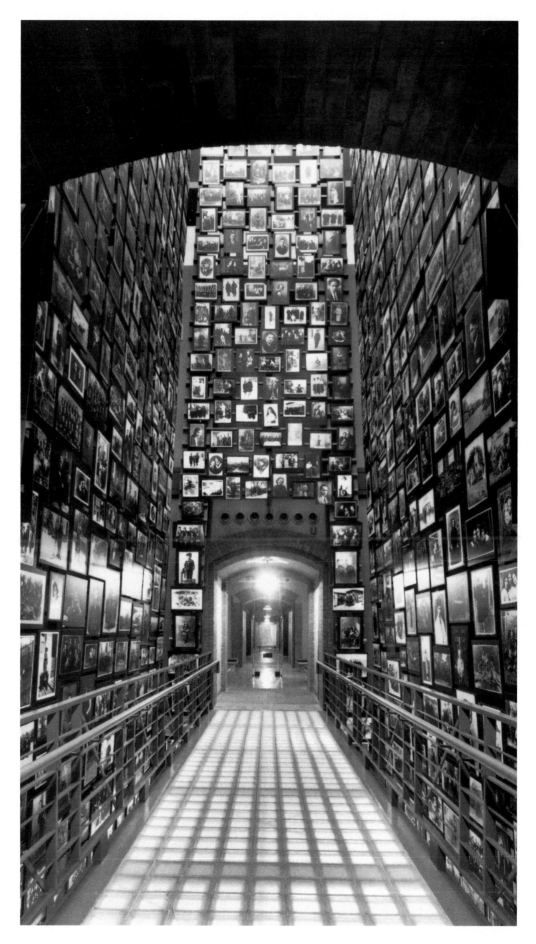

◄ **C**
Ralph Appelbaum. Hallway in the
United States Holocaust/Memorial
Museum, Washington, D.C.

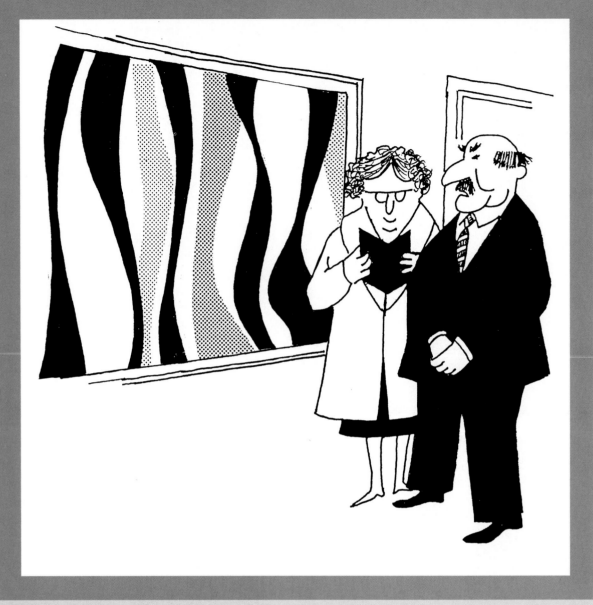

Frankly, Martha, NO!! It does NOT make me feel like dancing!
David Lauer.

RHYTHM

VISUAL RHYTHM

Rhythm as a design principle is based on repetition. Repetition, as an element of visual unity, is exhibited in some manner by almost every work of art. However, rhythm involves a clear repetition of elements that are the same or only slightly modified.

In conversation we might refer to Bridget Riley's painting **(A)** as having a rhythmic feeling. This might seem a strange adjective to use because **rhythm** is a term we most often associate with the sense of hearing. Without words, music can intrigue us by its pulsating beat, inducing us to tap a foot or perhaps dance. Poetry often has *meter*, which is a term for measurable rhythm. The pace of words can establish a cadence, a repetitive flow of syllables that makes reading poems aloud a pleasure. But rhythm can also be a visual sensation. We commonly speak of rhythm when watching the movement displayed by athletes, dancers, or some workers performing manual tasks. In a similar way the quality of rhythm can be applied to the visual arts, in which it is again basically related to movement. Here the concept refers to the movement of the viewer's eye, a movement across recurrent motifs providing the repetition inherent in the idea of rhythm.

The painting in **A** has this feeling of repetition in the curved vertical stripes that vary from thick to thin. The contrasts of color enhance the sense of undulation. The senses of sight and hearing are indeed so closely allied that we often relate them by interchanging adjectives (such as "loud" and "soft" colors). Certainly this relationship is shown in Riley's visual rhythm.

Not only **nonobjective** shapes are capable of producing an undulating rhythm. A similar effect is present in the photograph shown in **B**. Here tree trunks produce a sinuous and graceful rhythm. In **A** and **B** the linear elements that create the rhythm are obvious. If we look past the figure in **C**, we will find convex and concave contours and edges that, taken together, support the composition with a fluid rhythm.

The chair shown in **D** has a crisp rhythm in the repetition of vertical slats. The squares formed by crossing horizontals create a rhythmic pattern as well. This second rhythm gains emphasis toward the top of the chair. The curve of the chair's back subtly alters these patterns. In this case a few simple design elements work together to make a dramatic, more complex rhythm.

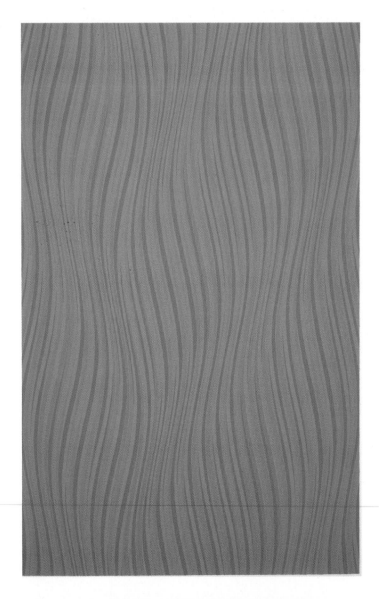

▶ **A**

Bridget Riley. Series 35. *Olive Added to Red and Blue, Violet and Green, Single Reversed Diagonal.* 1979. Gouache on paper, 3' 2 1/8" × 2' 3/8".

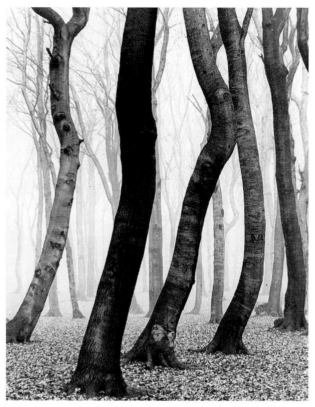

▲ **B**

Albert Renger-Patzsch. *Buchenwald in Herbst (Beech Forest in Autumn).* 1936. Silver gelatin print, 8³/₄″ × 6³/₈″ (22.2 × 16.2 cm). The Metropolitan Museum of Art, Warner Communications, Inc., purchase fund, 1980; 1980.1063.1.

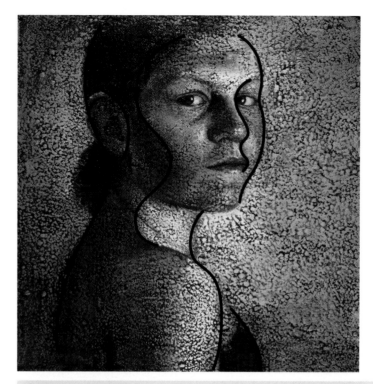

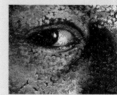

▲ **C**

Susan Moore. *Vanity (Portrait 1).* 2000. Oil stick on canvas, 4′ × 3′ 11″. Diagram.

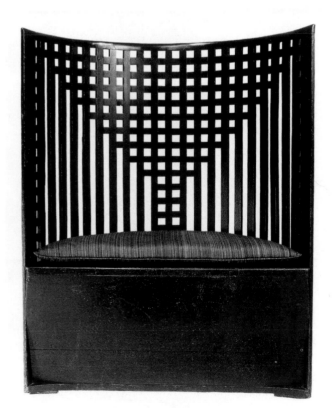

◀ **D**

Charles Rennie Mackintosh. *Chair.* 1904. Ebonized oak, reupholstered with horsehair, 3′ 10⁹/₁₆″ × 3′ 1″ × 1′ 4¹/₂″ (118 × 94 × 42 cm). Collection of Glasgow School of Art, Glasgow.

SHAPES AND REPETITION

We may speak of the rhythmic repetition of colors or textures, but most often we think of rhythm in the context of shapes and their arrangement. In music, some rhythms are called **legato**, or connecting and flowing. The same word could easily be applied to the visual effect in **A**. The photograph of Death Valley shows the sand dune ridges in undulating, flowing, horizontal curves. The dark and light contrast is quite dramatic, but in several places the changes are soft with smooth transitions. The feeling is relaxed and calm.

A similar rhythm occurs in the sixteenth-century illuminated manuscript by Hoefnagel **(B)**. Here the rhythm is faster with more repetitions and more regularity or consistency in the repeated curves. The fluid strokes carry our eye across the text and mark both the beginning and end of the passage with a flourish.

Manipulating Rhythm

It is true that the rhythmic pattern an artist chooses can quickly establish an emotional response in the viewer. For contrast, look at the painting in **C**. The effect here is also rhythmic, but now of an entirely different sort. Small, bold, blue and red squares move horizontally and vertically around the light canvas. The shapes are rigidly defined with the value changes sudden and startling. Again, music has a term for this type of rhythm: **staccato**, meaning abrupt changes with a dynamic contrast. The recurrence of these dark squares establishes a visual rhythm. The irregular spacing of the small squares causes the pattern (and rhythm) to be lively rather than monotonous. The artist, Piet Mondrian, titled this painting *Broadway Boogie Woogie.* He has expressed in the most abstract visual terms not only the on/off patterns of Broadway's neon landscape but also the rhythmic sounds of 1940s instrumental blues music. The effect for us today is almost like the jumpy, always changing patterns we see in video games.

The rhythms of **B** and **C** are indeed different, but the two examples are also alike in that the rhythm initially established is then consistent and regular throughout the composition. This regularity is not present in Alan Crockett's painting *Doodle de do* **(D)**; however, even the title suggests a playful rhythm. Elements repeat, but in less-predictable ways and always with some variation. The analogy here might be to the dynamic but often unsettling rhythms of improvised jazz.

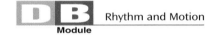

Rhythm and Motion

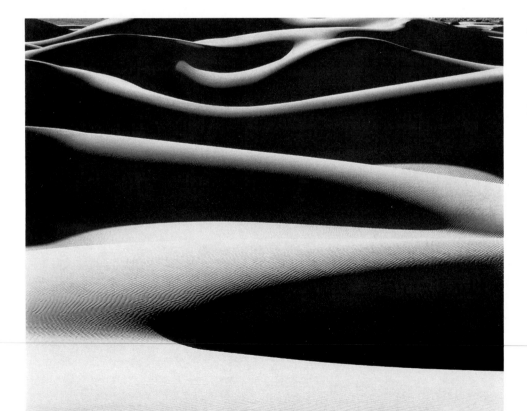

◀ **A**

Bruce Barnbaum. *Dune Ridges at Sunrise, Death Valley.* 1976. Silver gelatin print, $10^3/4'' \times 1' 1^1/4''$ (27.3 × 33.6 cm). Courtesy of the photographer.

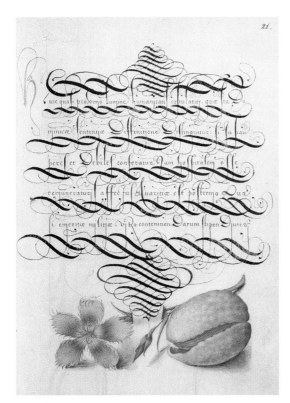

▲ B

Joris Hoefnagel (illuminator) and Georg Bocskay (scribe). *Dianthis and Almond* from *Mira Calligraphiae Monumenta (Model Book of Calligraphy)*, folio 21r. 1561–1562. Pen and ink, watercolors on vellum and paper, 6 ⁹/₁₆″ × 4 ¹³/₁₆″ (16.6 × 12.3 cm). The J. Paul Getty Museum, Los Angeles (86.MV.527).

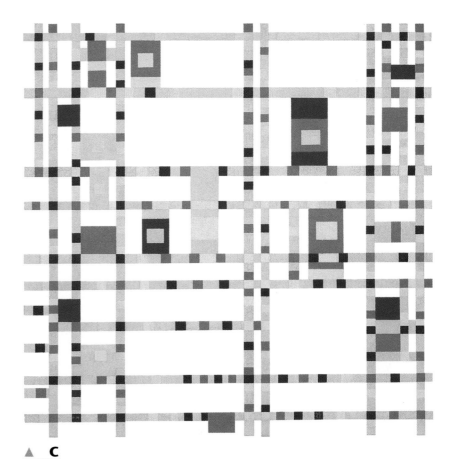

▲ C

Piet Mondrian. *Broadway Boogie Woogie*. 1942–1943. Oil on canvas, 4′ 2″ × 4′ 2″ (127 × 127 cm). © 2007 Mondrian/Holtzman Trust c/o HCR International, Warrenton, Virginia.

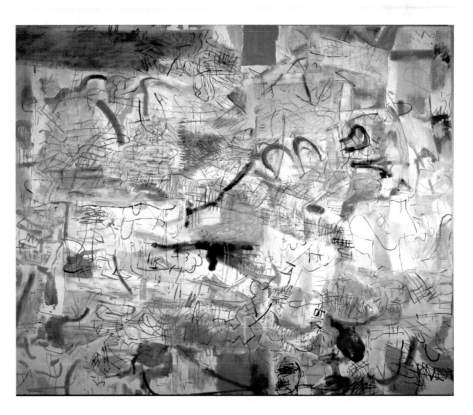

▶ D

Alan Crockett. *Doodle de Do*. 2006. Oil on canvas, 5′ × 6′.

PATTERNS AND SEQUENCE

Rhythm is a basic characteristic of nature. The pattern of the seasons, of day and night, of the tides, and even of the movements of the planets, all exhibit a regular rhythm. This rhythm consists of successive patterns in which the same elements reappear in a regular order. In a design or painting, this would be termed an **alternating rhythm**, as motifs alternate consistently with one another to produce a regular (and anticipated) sequence. This predictable quality of the pattern is necessary, for unless the repetition is fairly obvious, the whole idea of visual rhythm becomes obscure.

The pattern in Edna Andrade's *Interchange* (**A**) produces a bouncy alternating rhythm. Our eye flips back and forth due to the **vibrating colors** and alternating direction of diagonal lines and circles. A musical term for the "bouncing bow" applied to the violin is *spiccato*. If Mondrian's painting (**C** on page 117) is staccato, then Andrade's is spiccato.

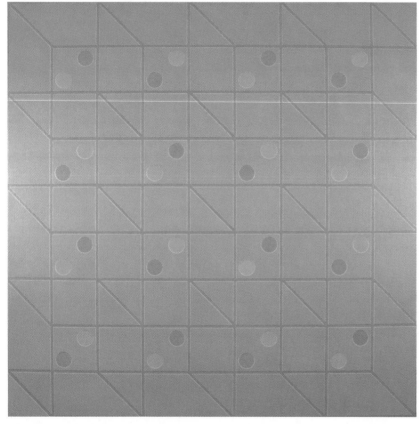

▲ **A**

Edna Andrade. *Interchange.* 1976.
Acrylic on canvas, 3′ 4³/₄″ × 3′ 4³/₄″.

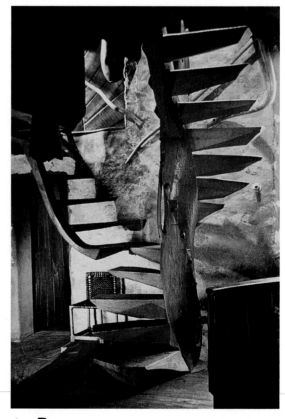

▲ **B**

Wharton Esherick. *Spiral Staircase.* 1930. The Wharton Esherick Museum, Paoli, Pennsylvania.

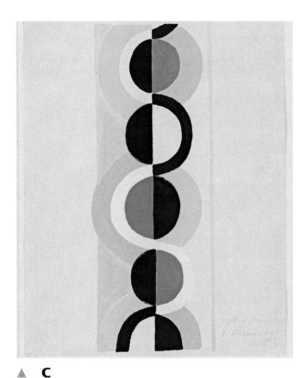

▲ **C**

Robert Delaunay. *"Rhythme sans fin" (Rhythm Without End)*. 1934. Gouache, brush and ink, on paper, $10^5/_8$″ × $8^5/_8$″ (27 × 21 cm). The Museum of Modern Art, New York (given anonymously 34.1936).

Details in Architecture and Art

We can see a familiar example of alternating rhythm in a building with columns, such as a Greek temple. The repeating pattern of light columns against darker negative spaces is clearly an alternating rhythm. Architectural critics often speak of the rhythmic placement of windows on a facade. Again, it is an alternating pattern—dark glass against a solid wall. The spiral stairway of Wharton Esherick's home (**B**) shows this type of rhythm. The design involves a sequence of forms that not only alternate in dark and light areas but shift regularly back and forth as figure and ground alternate for our attention. Notice that exactly the same description of alternating themes could be used for the painting in **C**. The artist, Robert Delaunay, titled this work, appropriately, *Rhythm Without End.*

The light and dark areas alternate consistently along the top band of the brick cornice shown in **D**. The lowest decorative band presents an alternating rhythm of *X* and *O* blocks. Alternating rhythms and rhythmic variety can relieve the large surface of predictable patterns such as a brick wall.

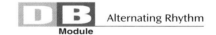 Alternating Rhythm

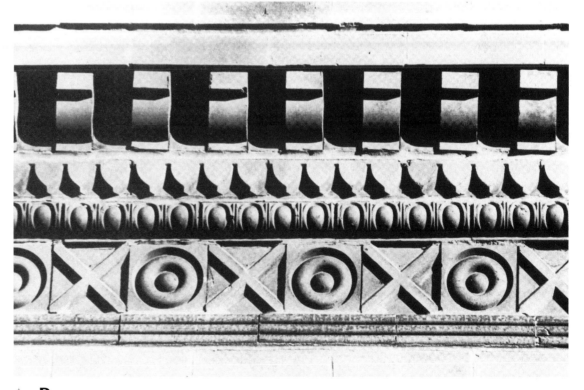

▲ **D**

Brick cornice. Published in James Stokoe, *Decorative and Ornamental Brickwork* (New York: Dover Publications, 1982), p. 6.

CONVERGING PATTERNS

Another type of rhythm is called *progression,* or **progressive rhythm**. Again, the rhythm involves repetition, but repetition of a shape that changes in a regular manner. There is a feeling of a sequential pattern. This type of rhythm is most often achieved with a progressive variation of the size of a shape, though its color, value, or texture could be the varying element. Progressive rhythm is extremely familiar to us; we experience it daily when we look at buildings from an angle. The perspective changes the horizontals and verticals into a converging pattern that creates a regular sequence of shapes gradually diminishing in size.

Inherent Rhythm

In **A** the rhythmic sequence of lines moving vertically across the format is immediately obvious. A more subtle progressive rhythm appears when we notice the dark shapes of the oil stains in the parking spaces. These change in size, becoming progressively smaller farther away from the building. In this photograph from an aerial vantage point, a rhythm is revealed in the ordinary pattern of human habits.

Progressive rhythms are rather commonplace in nature, although they may not always be readily apparent. Edward Weston's extreme close-up of an artichoke cut in half **(B)** shows a growth pattern. The gradual increase in size and weight creates a visual movement upward and outward. Other natural forms (such as chambered nautilus shells) cut in cross section would also reveal progressive rhythms.

The photographs in **A** and **B** are quite different, yet they both make visible progressive rhythms from the world around us, whether in the pattern of human activity or in natural forms. It is not surprising, then, that we should sense a growthlike pattern in the abstract sculpture by Louise Bourgeois **(C)**. This piece is more architectural than organic in its individual parts, yet the progression upward and outward from smaller to larger forms is similar to **B**.

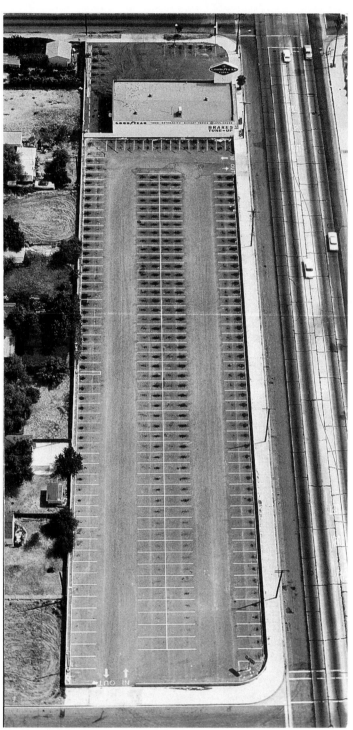

▲ **A**

Edward Ruscha. *Goodyear Tires, 6610 Laurel Canyon, North Hollywood.* 1967. Photograph, 8$^{1}/_{4}$″ × 3$^{7}/_{8}$″ (21 × 10 cm). From the book *Thirty-Four Parking Lots in Los Angeles* (1974), published by the author.

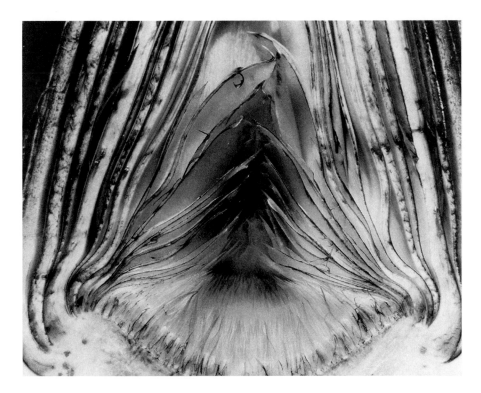

◄ **B**

Edward Weston. *Artichoke, Halved*. 1930. Silver gelatin print, 7 1/2″ × 9 1/2″ (19 × 24.1 cm). © 1981. Center for Creative Photography, Arizona Board of Regents.

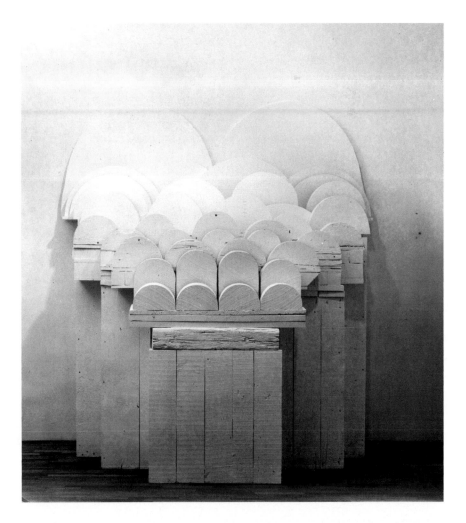

► **C**

Louise Bourgeois. *Partial Recall*. 1979. Wood, 9′ × 7′ 6″ × 5′ 6″ (274.3 × 228.5 × 167.6 cm). Private collection. Art © Louise Bourgeois/ Licensed by VAGA, New York, New York.

ENGAGING THE SENSES

Rhythmic structures in visual art and design are often described (as they have been here) in terms borrowed from music vocabulary. The connection between visual rhythms and musical rhythms can be more than a simile or metaphor. In some cases the visual rhythms composed by an artist seem to resonate with memories or associations in our other senses. When a visual experience actually stimulates one of our other senses, the effect is called **kinesthetic empathy**.

Evoking Sight, Sound, and Touch

Charles Burchfield's painting **(A)** is, on one level, a depiction of the roofline of a building set among trees and plants. This description does not tell us the subject of *The Insect Chorus*, however. A description of the painting's many rhythmic patterns would come closer to explaining the title. Repeated curves, zigzags, and straight linear elements throughout the picture literally buzz and create the sensation of a hot summer afternoon alive with the sound of cicadas. Even the sensation of heat is evoked by the rhythm of wavering lines above the rooftop.

▶ **A**

Charles Burchfield. *The Insect Chorus.* 1917. Opaque and transparent watercolor with ink and crayon on paper, 1′ 7⁷/₈″ × 1′ 3⁷/₈″ (50 × 40 cm). Munson-Williams-Proctor Institute. Museum of Art, Utica, New York (Edward W. Root Bequest), 58.104.

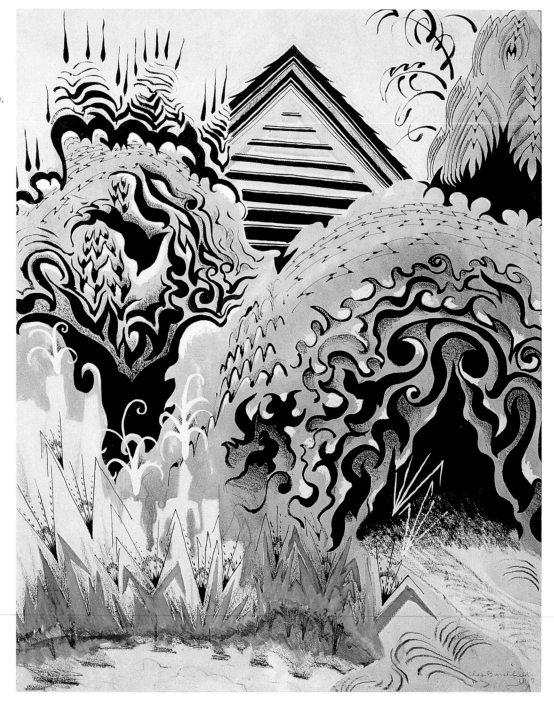

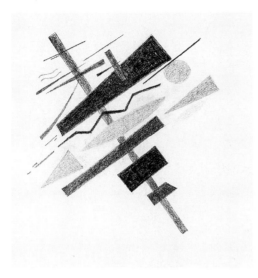

▲ **B**

Kasimir Malevich. *Suprematist Composition: Sensation of Metallic Sounds.* 1915. Pencil, 8" × 6¹⁄₂" (20.9 × 16.4 cm). Kunstmuseum Basel, Kupferstichkabinett (1969.51.11).

The drawing shown in **B** attempts to convey the sensation of "metallic" sounds. This early experiment in Russian **Suprematism** from 1915 reflects the interest in industrial subjects of that era. The jumpy arrangement of shapes, almost lacking in any rhythmic pattern, seems to echo the harsh, dynamic sounds of a factory.

A second drawing by Malevich **(C)** is titled *Sensation of Movement and Resistance.* In this case our physical experiences of moving through the world are simulated. The drawing appeals to our sense of touch and "muscle memory" by repeating horizontal lines of varying weight along a curved path. The rhythmic interruption of the heavier, darker rectangles offers the "resistance" referred to in the title.

The resemblance between Malevich's and Lissitzky's work **(D)** is not a coincidence. They were contemporaries and shared similar ideas. Lissitzky's image is an abstract proclamation for a new "movement" that had to overcome "resistance." Lissitzky's composition evokes a sensation similar to **C** through comparable rhythmic structures.

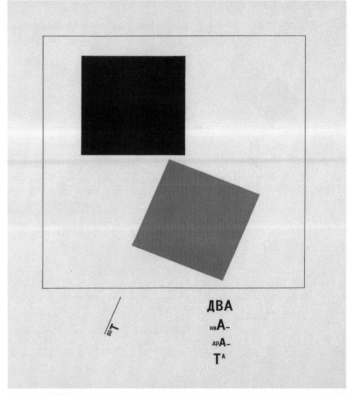

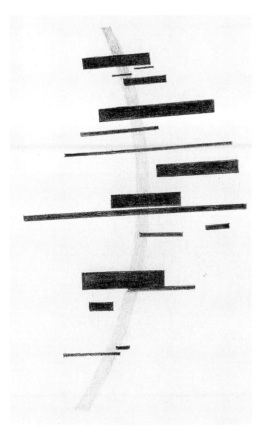

▲ **C**

Kasimir Malevich. *Suprematist Composition: Sensation of Movement and Resistance.* 1915. Pencil, 10¹⁄₂" × 8" (26.5 × 20.5 cm). Kunstmuseum Basel, Kupferstichkabinett (1969.51.17).

▲ **D**

El Lissitzky. *Of Two Squares: A Suprematist Tale in Six Constructions.* 1922. Illustrated book with letterpress cover and six letterpress illustrations, 10¹⁵⁄₁₆" × 8⁷⁄₈" (27.8 × 22.5 cm). Publisher: Skify, Berlin. Gift of the Judith Rothschild Foundation (89.2001.5).

DESIGN ELEMENTS

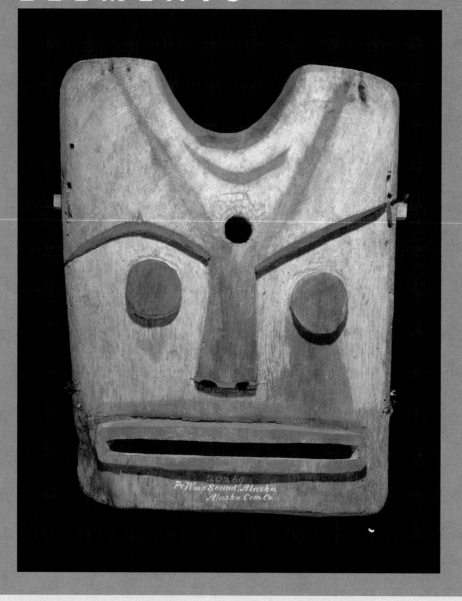

LINE

A POINT SET IN MOTION

What is a **line**? If we think of a point as having no dimensions (neither height nor width), and then we set that point in motion, we create the first dimension: line. In theory, line consists only of the dimension of its length, but, in terms of art and design, we know line can have varying width as well. The pathways in **A** are fashioned from irregular rocks, yet we instantly perceive the serpentine paths as lines.

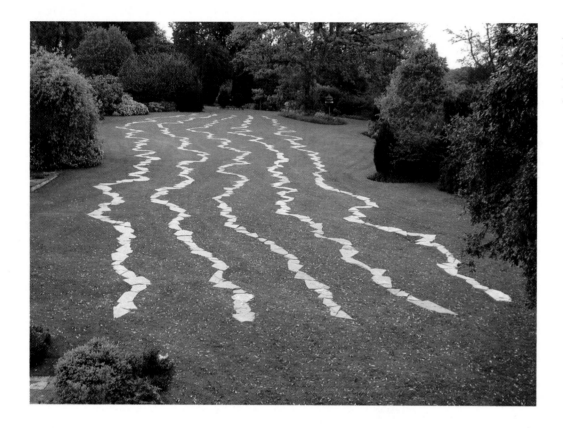

◄ **A**

Richard Long. *Five Paths*. 2002. Delabole slate, 61.1 × 17.4 m. New Art Centre Sculpture Park & Gallery, Wiltshire, UK.

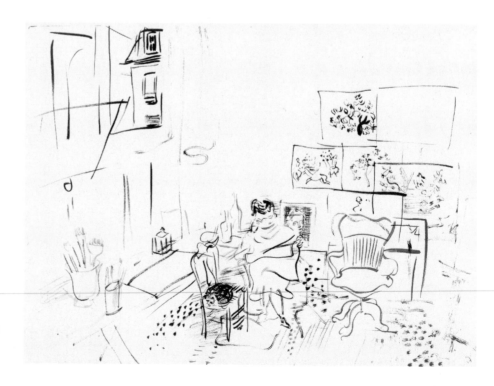

► **B**

Raoul Dufy. *The Artist's Studio*. c. 1942. Brush and ink on paper, 1′ 7⁵/₈″ × 2′ 2″ (49.7 × 66 cm). The Museum of Modern Art, New York (gift of Mr. and Mrs. Peter A. Rubel).

Of all the elements in art, line is perhaps the most familiar. Most of our writing and drawing tools are pointed, and we have been making lines constantly since we were young children. Our simplest notion of line comes from our first experiences with outlines such as those in coloring books. But line is more than mere border or boundary. Figure **B** is a line drawing describing the many items in the artist's studio and even the view out the window. The use of line is sufficiently descriptive so that we understand the whole scene. We see the brushstrokes as vivid paths in search of the edges of the forms. These lines are loose and free in the spirit of Paul Klee's idea that a line "is a point set in motion."

Lines Convey Mood and Feeling

Line is created by movement and is capable of infinite variety. The image in **C** shows just a few of the almost unlimited variations possible in the category of line. A curious feature of line is its power of suggestion. What an expressive tool it can be for the artist! A line is a minimum statement, made quickly with a minimum of effort, but able to convey all sorts of moods and feelings. The lines pictured in **C** are truly abstract elements: they depict no objects. Yet we can read into them emotional and expressive qualities. Think of all the adjectives we can apply to lines. We often describe lines as being nervous, angry, happy, free, quiet, excited, calm, graceful, or dancing and as having many other qualities. The power of suggestion of this basic element is great, as **D** makes obvious with a delightful wit.

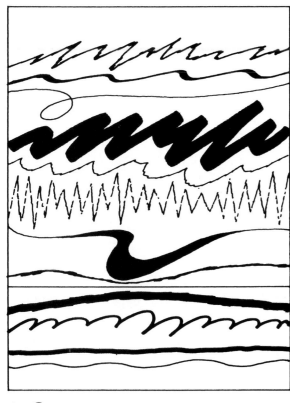

▲ **C**

Line has almost unlimited variations.

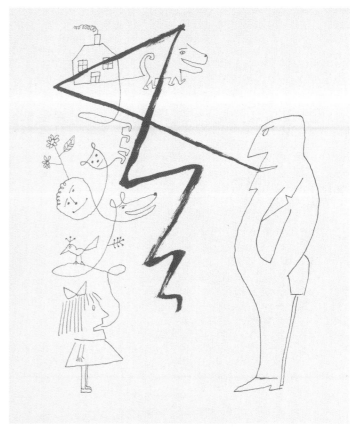

▲ **D**

Saul Steinberg. *Untitled.* c. 1959. Ink on paper. Originally published in *The New Yorker*, March 14, 1959. © The Saul Steinberg Foundation/Artists Rights Society (ARS), New York.

DEFINING SHAPE AND FORM

Line is important to the artist because it can describe shape, and by shape we recognize objects. For example, **A** is immediately understood as a picture of a flower. It does not have the dimension or mass of a flower; it does not have the color or texture of a flower; it is not the actual size of a flower. Nevertheless, we recognize a flower. Ellsworth Kelly has shown us, through his economical use of line, those shapes he felt to be most characteristic of the calla lily.

Artistic Shorthand

Example **B** is a line drawing—a drawing of lines that are not present in the photograph (**C**) or in the original collection of objects. In the photograph, of course, no black line runs around each object. The lines in the drawing actually show edges, whereas in **C** areas of different value (or color) meet, showing the end of one object and the beginning of another. Line is, therefore, artistic shorthand, useful because with comparatively few strokes, an artist can describe and identify shapes through outline and contour.

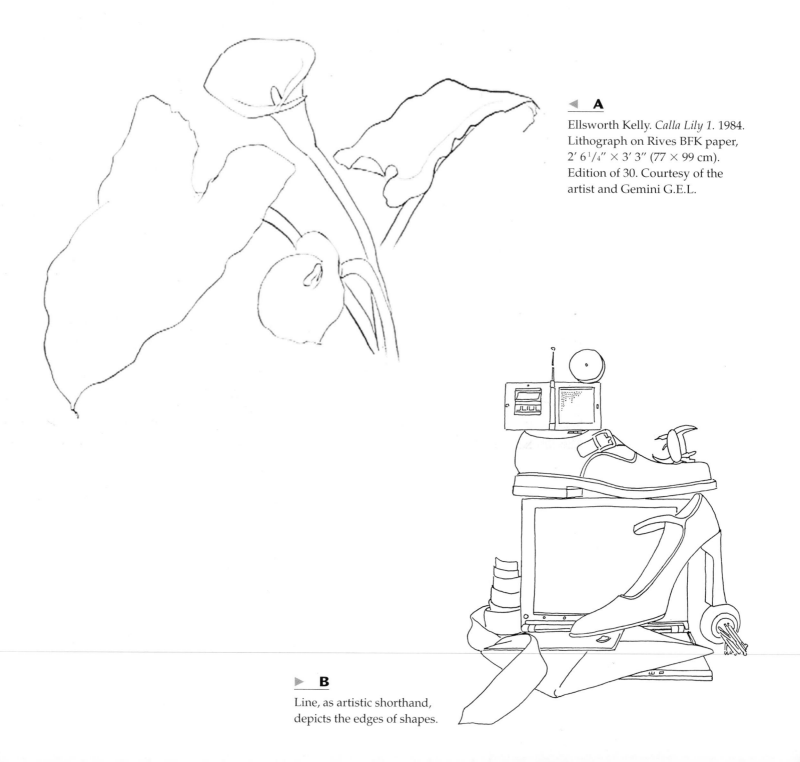

◀ **A**

Ellsworth Kelly. *Calla Lily 1*. 1984. Lithograph on Rives BFK paper, 2′ 6¹⁄₄″ × 3′ 3″ (77 × 99 cm). Edition of 30. Courtesy of the artist and Gemini G.E.L.

▶ **B**

Line, as artistic shorthand, depicts the edges of shapes.

Cross Contour Describes Form

The white lines of the fabric billowing in the wind **(D)** are not outlines; rather, they reveal the flowing topography of the material. The textural stretch marks on the bark of a gray birch **(E)** suggest lines that go around the limb of this tree. This photograph reveals the cross-contour lines inherent in round forms. In these two examples, line defines form by means other than mere outline.

▼ **C**

Advertisement from *New York Times* Advertising Supplement, Sunday, November 11, 1998, p. 14A. Photo: Thomas Card. Fashion direction: Donna Berg and Heidi Godoff for Twist Productions. Prop styling: Caroline Morrison. Advertorial produced by Comer & Company.

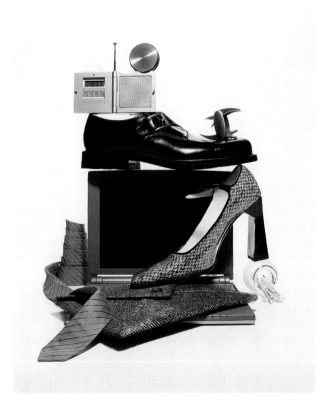

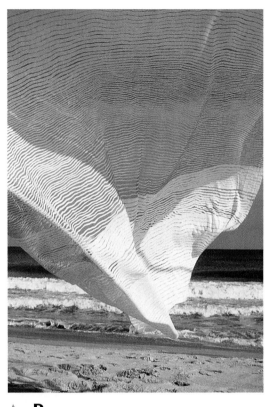

▲ **D**

Jack Lenor Larsen. *Seascape.* 1977.

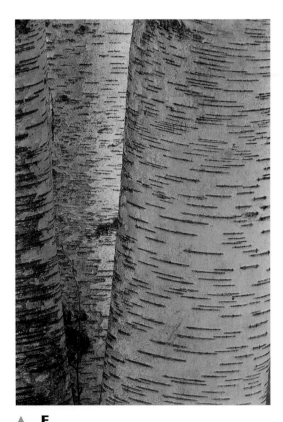

▲ **E**

Lines in the bark reveal the cross contours of the tree. Mark Newman/www.bciusa.com.

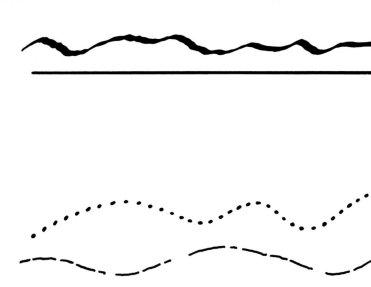

A

There are many types of actual lines, each varying in weight and character.

B

The points in an implied line are automatically connected by the eye.

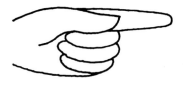

C

When one object points to another, the eye connects the two in a psychic line.

ACTUAL, IMPLIED, AND PSYCHIC LINES

Line has served artists as a basic tool ever since cave dwellers drew with charred sticks on the cave walls. Actual lines **(A)** may vary greatly in weight, character, and other qualities. Two other types of line also figure importantly in pictorial composition.

An **implied line** is created by positioning a series of points so that the eye tends automatically to connect them. The dotted line is an example familiar to us all **(B)**. Think also of the line waiting for a bus; several figures standing in a row form an implied line.

A **psychic line** is illustrated in **C**. There is no real line, not even intermittent points, yet we feel a line, a mental connection between two elements. This connection usually occurs when someone or something looks or points in a certain direction. Our eyes invariably follow, and a psychic line results.

Interpreting Lines

All three types of line are present in Georges de La Tour's *Fortune Teller* **(D)**. Actual lines clearly delineate the edges of figures and garments. An implied line is created between the victim's hand on his hip and the fortune-teller's left hand. Along this line we spy (in the shadows) hands at work relieving the victim of his valuables **(E)**. A second such line is created by the continuation of the pickpocket's arm on the left through the bottom of the victim's jacket and along to the fortune-teller on the right. Psychic lines occur as our eyes follow the direction in which each figure is looking.

Artists have the potential to lead a viewer's eye movement, and the various types of lines can be a valuable tool to that end.

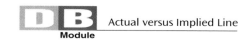
DB Module — Actual versus Implied Line

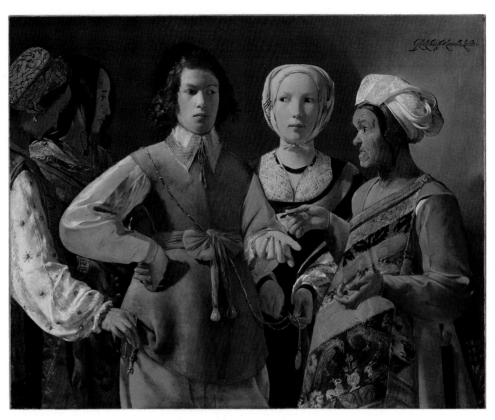

▲ **D**

Georges de La Tour. *The Fortune Teller.* Probably 1630s. Oil on canvas, 3′ 4 1/8″ × 4′ 5/8″
(102 × 123.5 cm). The Metropolitan Museum of Art, Rogers Fund, 1960 (60.30).

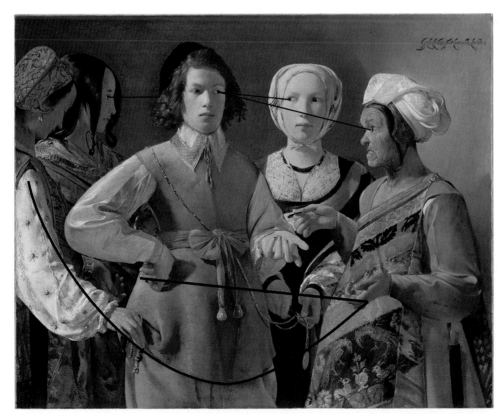

◀ **E**

Actual, implied, and psychic
lines organize the composition.

HORIZONTAL, VERTICAL, AND DIAGONAL LINES

One important characteristic of line that should be remembered is its direction. A horizontal line implies quiet and repose, probably because we associate a horizontal body posture with rest or sleep. A vertical line, such as a standing body, has more potential of activity. But the diagonal line most strongly suggests motion. In so many of the active movements of life (skiing, running, swimming, skating) the body is leaning, so we automatically see diagonals as indicating movement. Whereas **A** is a static, calm pattern, **B** is changing and exciting.

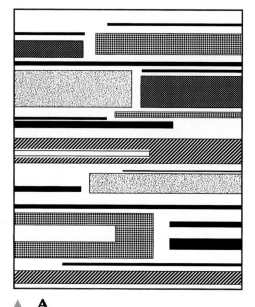

▲ **A**

Horizontal lines usually imply rest or lack of motion.

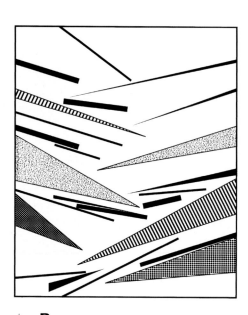

▲ **B**

Diagonal lines usually imply movement and action.

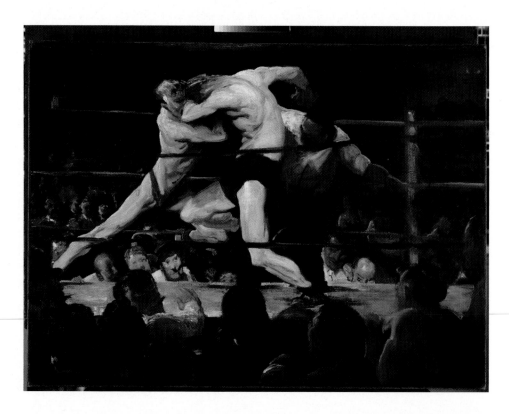

▶ **C**

George Bellows. *Stag at Sharkey's.* 1909. Oil on canvas, 110 × 140.5 × 8.5 cm. © The Cleveland Museum of Art (Hinman B. Hurlbut Collection 1133.1922).

Reinforcing the Format

One other factor is involved in the quality of line direction. The outside format of the vast majority of drawings, designs, paintings, and so forth is rectangular. Therefore, any horizontal or vertical line within the work is parallel to, and repetitive of, an edge of the format. The horizontal and vertical lines within a design are stabilizing elements that reduce any feeling of movement. The lines in **A** are parallel to the top and bottom, but none of the lines in **B** is parallel to any of the edges.

Analyzing Lines in Paintings

George Bellows's painting **(C)** is dominated by a diagonal line that begins with the one fighter's leg on the left and continues through the second fighter's shoulder and arm. Other diagonals within the figures create the dynamism of the fight scene. The diagonal gesture of the referee balances the group of three figures and completes a triangle. The verticals and horizontals of the fight ring stabilize the composition and provide a counterpoint to the action depicted.

John Moore's *Evangeliste* **(D)** has a subtle but strong underlying structure of verticals and horizontals that lend a calm serenity to the scene. The window frame provides the anchor to this pattern, but the table and building seen outside the window repeat vertical and horizontal lines. The more chaotic line directions on the tabletop and other curved and diagonal lines provide a lyric variety within the dominant order of vertical and horizontal.

The painting shown in **D** does not suggest the kind of dynamic movement of the Bellows work **(C)**, but it does show that a composition based on verticals and horizontals does not have to be boring!

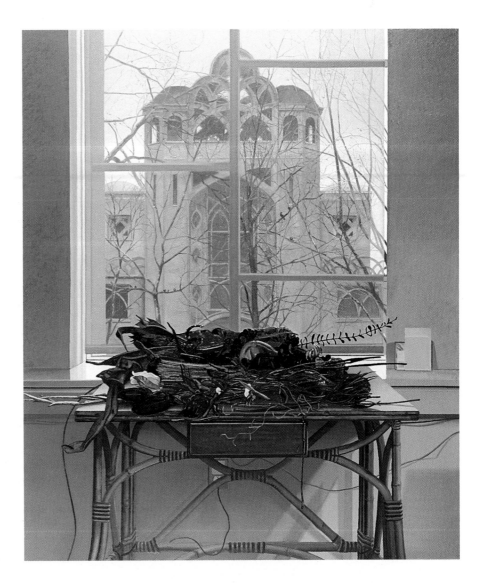

▶ **D**

John Moore. *Evangeliste*. 2001. Oil on canvas, 5′ × 4′ 2″. Hirschl & Adler Modern, New York.

PRECISION OR SPONTANEITY

Regardless of the chosen medium, when line is the main element of an image, the result is called a drawing. There are two general types of drawings: **contour** and **gesture**.

Contour Drawings

When line is used to follow the edges of forms, to describe their outlines, the result is called a contour drawing. This is probably the most common use of line in art; **A** is an example. This portrait by Ingres is a precise drawing with extremely delicate lines carefully describing the features and the folds of the clothing. The slightly darker emphasis of the head establishes the focal point. We cannot help but admire the sureness of the drawing, the absolute accuracy of observation.

The self-portrait by Giacometti **(B)** is not composed of the precise contours we find in **A**. Instead, we see many lines which, taken together, suggest the mass and volume of the head. The result is more active, and we can more readily observe the artist's process of looking and recording. Many of Giacometti's lines follow the topography of the head and find surface contours within the form of the head, not merely at the outer edge.

Gesture Drawings

The other common type of drawing is called a gesture drawing. In this instance, describing shapes is less important than showing the action or the dynamics of a pose. Line does not stay at the edges but moves freely within forms. Gesture drawings are not drawings of objects so much as drawings of movement, weight, and posture. Because of its very nature, this type of drawing is almost always created quickly and spontaneously. It captures the momentary changing aspect of the subject rather than recording nuances of form. Rembrandt's *Christ Carrying the Cross* **(C)** is a gesture drawing. Some quickly drawn lines suggest the contours, but most of the lines are concerned with the action of the falling, moving figures.

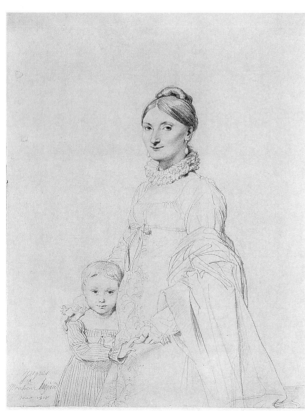

▲ **A**

Jean-Auguste-Dominique Ingres. *Portrait of Mme. Hayard and Her Daughter Caroline.* 1815. Graphite on white wove paper, 11 1/2″ × 8 11/16″ (29.2 × 22 cm). University of Harvard Art Museums, Fogg Art Museum (bequest of Grenville L. Winthrop) (1943.843).

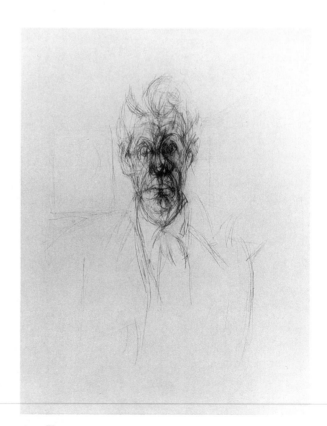

▲ **B**

Alberto Giacometti. *Self-Portrait.* 1954. Pencil, 1′ 4″ × 1′ (40.5 × 31 cm).

Deborah Butterfield's *Tango* (**D**) is a sculpture that conveys a sense of drawing in three dimensions. The found objects and steel scraps suggest the presence of a horse with almost scribble-like lines. These lines largely define the horse from the inside of the form and the gesture of the pose. Butterfield's work has a spontaneous appearance we would more likely associate with brush and ink than welded steel.

Combining Styles

Although quite different approaches to drawing, the two categories of contour and gesture are not mutually exclusive. Many drawings combine elements of both, as can be seen in Giacometti's *Self-Portrait* (**B**). And, as is the case with **D**, the elements of contour or gestural line can be found in artworks other than traditional drawings.

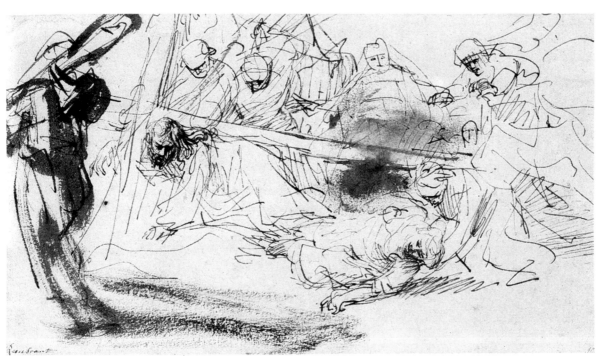

▲ **C**

Rembrandt. *Christ Carrying the Cross.* c. 1635. Pen and ink with wash, 5⁵/₈″ × 10¹/₈″ (14 × 26 cm). Kupferstichkabinett, Staatliche Museen, Berlin.

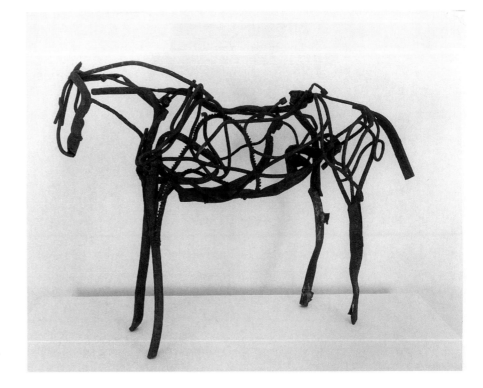

▶ **D**

Deborah Butterfield. *Tango.* 1987. Steel, 2′ 4¹/₂″ × 3′ 6¹/₂″ × 1′ 3″ (72 × 107 × 38 cm). Edward Thorp Gallery, New York.

CREATING VARIETY AND EMPHASIS

To state that an artist uses line is not very descriptive of the artist's work because line is capable of infinite variety. To imagine the qualities that a line may have, just think of an adjective you can place before the word *line,* such as *thin, thick, rough,* or *smooth.* The illustrations on these two pages give only a sampling of the linear possibilities available to the artist or designer.

Volume

Example **A** shows a drawing by Henry Ossawa Tanner. This figure study shows how varied **line quality** can define three-dimensional form, create emphasis, and transform a flat piece of paper into a spatial experience. Darker, heavier lines create emphasis on the light paper and draw our attention to the figure's hand and face. The darker contour along the back blends into shaded areas, giving **volume** to the figure.

Lighter contours along the left arm do not merely suggest an unfinished drawing. These lines allow the figure to subtly emerge from the page.

Expressing Mood and Motion

The untitled drawing by Susan Rothenberg shown in **B** is characterized by heavy, blunt contours echoed by thinner, coarse lines. The brutal line quality that describes dismembered horse shapes is as appropriate to this imagery as the varied and graceful lines are for the nude.

The print by Judy Pfaff **(C)** takes advantage of a variety in line quality from bold to light, from elegant to awkward. Some thin lines perform figures like an ice skater, while the heavier lines sag like the drips of spilled paint. This print does not use line as **calligraphy**, nor is it representational. In this case, line exists for its own expressive qualities.

The lines in **D** quiver and reverberate, suggesting movement. Notice how difference in line weight suggests motion.

The linear technique you choose can produce emotional or expressive qualities in the final pattern. Solid and bold, quiet and flowing, delicate and dainty, jagged and nervous, or countless other possibilities influence the effect on the viewer of your drawing or design.

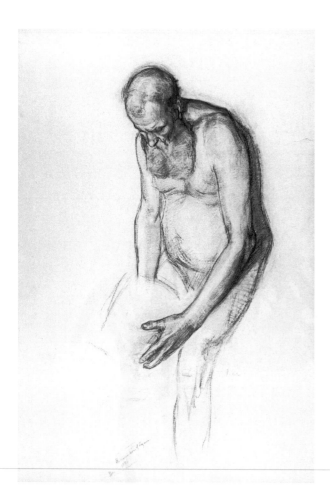

▲ **A**

Henry Ossawa Tanner. *Study of a Man for the Resurrection of Lazarus.*

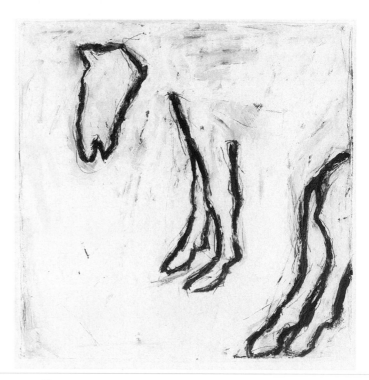

▲ **B**

Susan Rothenberg. *Untitled.* 1978. Acrylic, flashe, pencil on paper, 1′ 8″ × 1′ 8″ (51 × 51 cm). Collection of Walker Art Center, Minneapolis (Art Center Acquisition Fund, 1979).

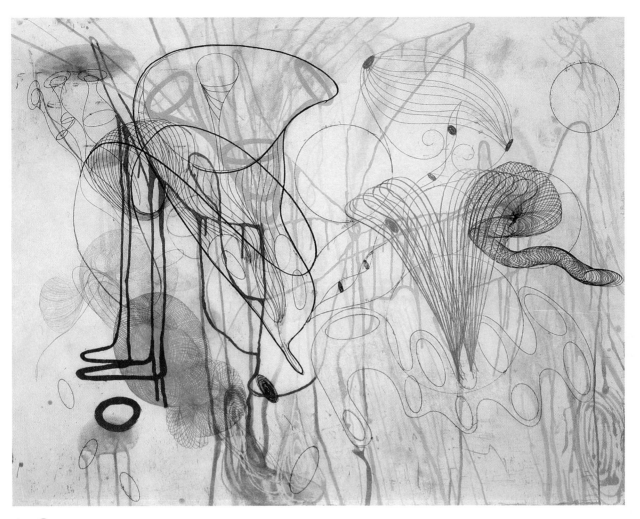

▲ **C**

Judy Pfaff. *Che Cosa è Acqua* from *Half a Dozen of the Other*. 1992. Color drypoint with spit bite and sugar lift aquatints, and soft ground etching, 3′ × 3′ 9″ on 3′ 6⁷/₈″ × 4′ 2³/₄″ sheet. Edition of 20. Printed by Lawrence Hamlin.

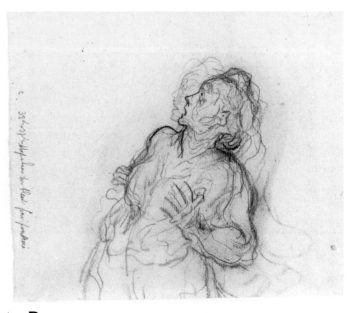

▲ **D**

Honoré Daumier. *Frightened Woman*. 1828–1879. Charcoal with black crayon, on ivory laid paper, 21 × 23.9 cm. The Art Institute of Chicago, gift of the Print and Drawing Club, 1923.944.

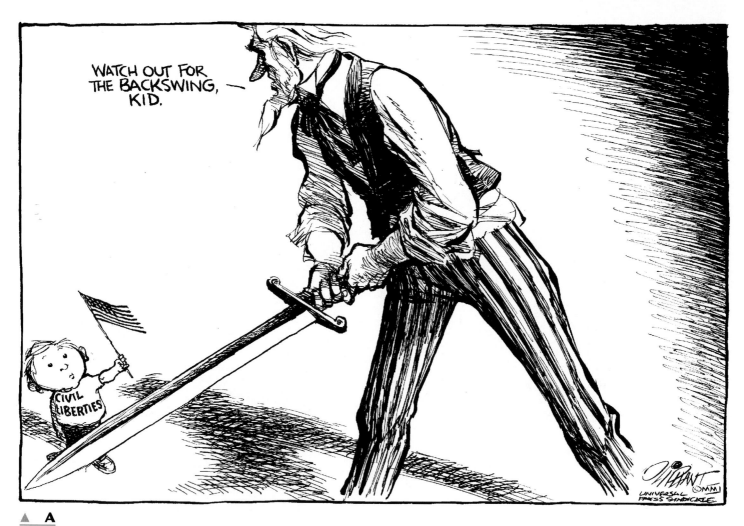

WATCH OUT FOR THE BACKSWING, — KID.

CIVIL LIBERTIES

▲ **A**

Oliphant. © 2001 Universal Press Syndicate. Reprinted with permission. All rights reserved.

USING LINES TO CREATE DARK AND LIGHT

A single line can show the shape of objects. But an outlined shape is essentially flat; it does not suggest the volume of the original subject. The artist can, by placing a series of lines close together, create visual areas of gray. By varying the number of lines and their proximity, the artist can produce an almost limitless number of grays. These resulting areas of dark and light (called areas of value) can begin to give the three-dimensional quality lacking in a pure contour line. Again, the specific linear technique and the quality of line can vary a great deal among different artists.

Cross-Hatching

Traditionally, editorial cartoonists have had to make the most of the limitations imposed by black ink on newsprint. This constraint challenged the artists to be inventive in all aspects of their design. Hatching and cross-hatching are techniques often employed by these artists to suggest a broad gamut of **values**. Pat Oliphant's cartoon in **A** shows a light-to-dark gradation on the right side of the composition created by a series of parallel ("hatching") lines that increase in density. To the left, Uncle Sam casts a shadow that is made up of intersecting patterns of pen strokes—or cross-hatching.

The same cross-hatching technique is clear in **B**. But in this etching, the artist, Rembrandt, has used the lines in a looser manner. The various densities of line suggest the values and textures of sky and landscape.

Applying Line as Value to Textiles

These techniques are by no means limited to drawings and prints. The woven fabric in **C** uses fibers as lines to create different values out of differing densities of the dark threads. Our eye reads the weave of darks and lights to create optical mixtures of various values.

See also *Value: Techniques*, page 248.

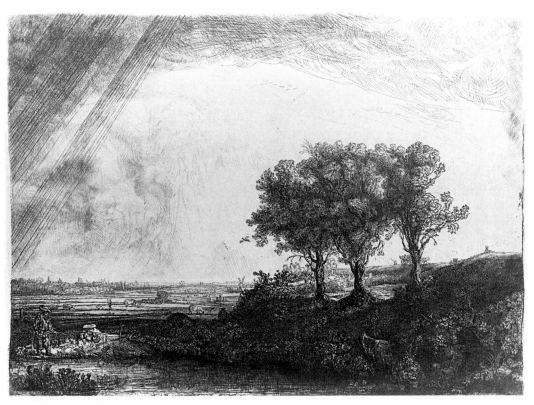

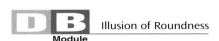 **B**

Rembrandt. *The Three Trees.* 1643. Etching with drypoint and burin, only state. Courtesy of Wetmore Print Collection of Connecticut College.

D B Illusion of Roundness
Module

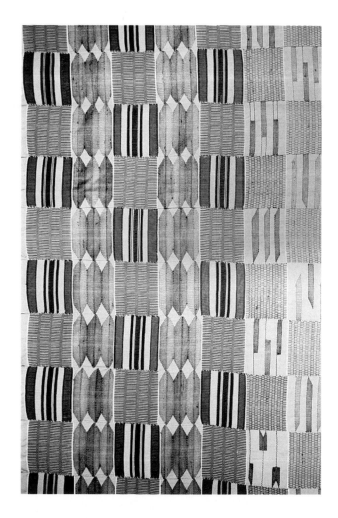

▶ **C**

West African Kente cloth. No date. Cotton, 6′ 10 1/4″ × 11′ 1/2″ (23 × 3.5 m). Anacostia Community Museum, Smithsonian Institution, Washington, D.C.

LINE IN PAINTING

OUTLINE OF FORMS

Line can be an important element in painting. Because painting basically deals with areas of color, its effect is different from that of drawing, which limits the elements involved. Line becomes important to painting when the artist purposely chooses to outline forms, as Alice Neel does in her portrait **(A)**. Dark lines define the edges of the figure and the sofa. The lines are bold and quite obvious.

Line can be seen in the detail of Venus from Botticelli's famous painting **(B)**. The goddess's hair is a beautiful pattern of flowing, graceful, swirling lines. The hand is delineated from the breast by only the slightest value difference; a dark, now quite delicate line clearly outlines the hand.

Adapting Technique to Theme

Compare the use of line in Botticelli's painting with that in **A**. Both works stress the use of line, but the similarity ends there. *Crying Girl,* by Roy Lichtenstein **(C)**, employs the extremely heavy, bold line—almost a crude line typical of the drawing in comic books. Each artist has adapted his technique to his theme. Compare the treatment of the hair. Venus **(B)** is portrayed as the embodiment of all grace and beauty, her hair a mass of elegant lines in a delicate arabesque pattern. The *Crying Girl*'s hair **(C)**, by contrast, is a flat, colored area boldly outlined, with a few slashing heavy strokes to define its texture.

Dark Line Technique

The use of a black or dark line in a design is often belittled as a crutch. There is no doubt that a dark linear structure can often lend desirable emphasis when the initial color or **value pattern** seems to provide little excitement. Many artists, both past and present, have purposely chosen to exploit the impact of dark lines to enhance their work. The heavy lines support the theme of construction in *The Constructors* **(D)**. Both **C** and **D** balance the dark lines with an equally bold red, yellow, and blue color structure.

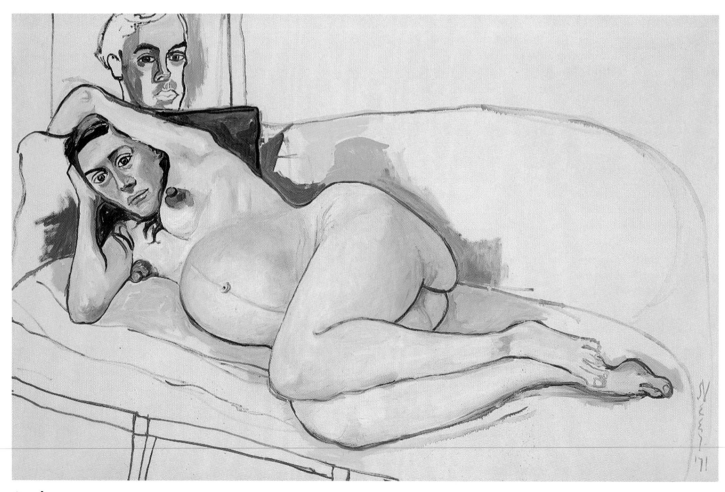

▲ **A**

Alice Neel. *The Pregnant Woman.* 1971. Oil on canvas, 3' 4" × 5'. © The Estate of Alice Neel.

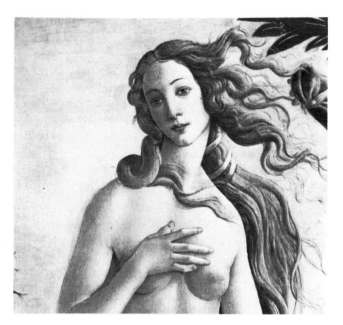

▲ **B**

Sandro Botticelli. *The Birth of Venus* (detail). c. 1480. Oil on canvas; entire work: 5′ 8⁷/₈″ × 9′ 1⁷/₈″ (1.75 × 2.79 m). Galleria degli Uffizi, Florence, Italy.

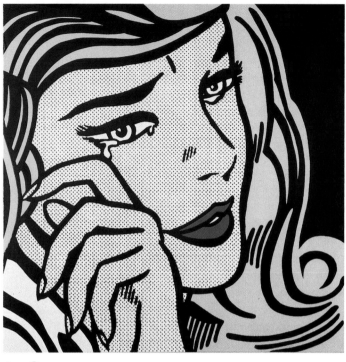

▲ **C**

Roy Lichtenstein. *Crying Girl.* 1964. Enamel on steel, 3′ 10″ square. © Roy Lichtenstein.

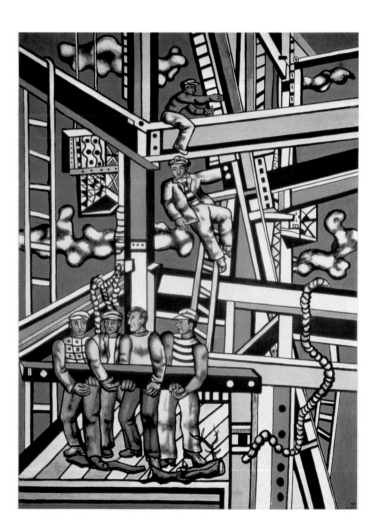

◀ **D**

Fernand Léger. *The Constructors.* 1950. © Musée Leger, Biot, France/The Bridgeman Art Library.

EXPLICIT LINE

Explicit line is obvious in an image such as the computer-generated trees in **A**. In this case every element from thick trunk to delicate branch is recognizable as line. Such explicit lines can be evident in a variety of media from computer animation to painting.

Defining Shape and Form

Line becomes important in a painting when the contours of the forms are sharply defined and the viewer's eye is drawn to the edges of the various shapes. The still life painting by Louisa Mathiasdottir (**B**) contains no actual outlines as we have seen in other examples. However, the contour edges of the objects and the tablecloth are very clearly defined. A clean edge separates each of the elements in the painting, so that a line tracing of these edges would be complete. The color adds interest, but we are most aware of the essential drawing underneath. Despite the absence of actual lines, the Mathiasdottir painting would be classified as a linear painting.

Applying Color

Explicit lines can play other roles in painting besides the clear definition of shape or form. Some artists use a linear technique in applying color. The color areas are built up by repeated linear strokes that are not smoothed over. *The Artist's Daughter, Julie, with Her Nanny* (**C**) by Berthe Morisot is an example of this technique, which was employed by many artists of the **Impressionist** period.

Karin Davie's painting (**D**) is composed of serpentine lines that create a complex pattern. The varying color of the lines creates different spatial levels and shifting areas of interest or emphasis. Although these "lines" are wide brushstrokes, they still convey Paul Klee's idea of a "point set in motion."

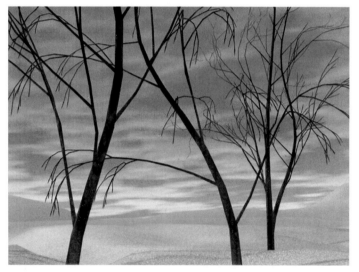

▲ **A**

Janet Lucroy. Computer-generated image.

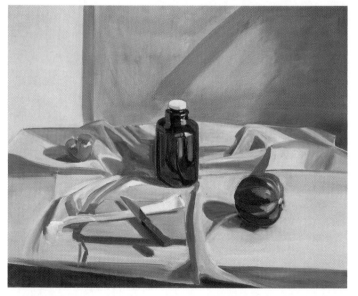

▲ **B**

Louisa Mathiasdottir (Icelandic American, b. 1917).
Still Life with Celery. c. 1983. Oil on canvas. 3' 3" × 4'.
National Museum of Women in the Arts, Washington,
D.C., gift of the American Academy of Arts and Letters:
Hassam, Speicher, Betts and Symons Fund.

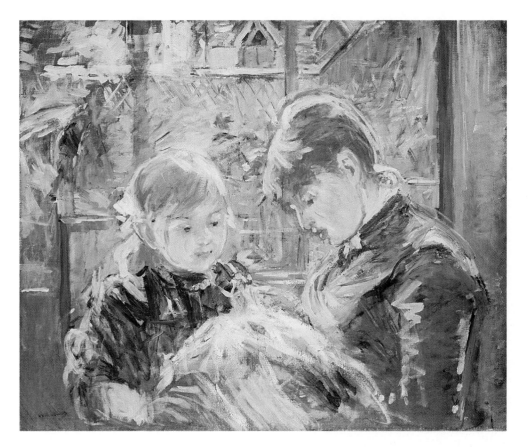

◀ **C**

Berthe Morisot. *The Artist's Daughter, Julie, with her Nanny.* c. 1884. Oil on canvas, 1′ 11″ × 2′ 4″. The Minneapolis Institute of Arts (John R. Van Derlip Fund).

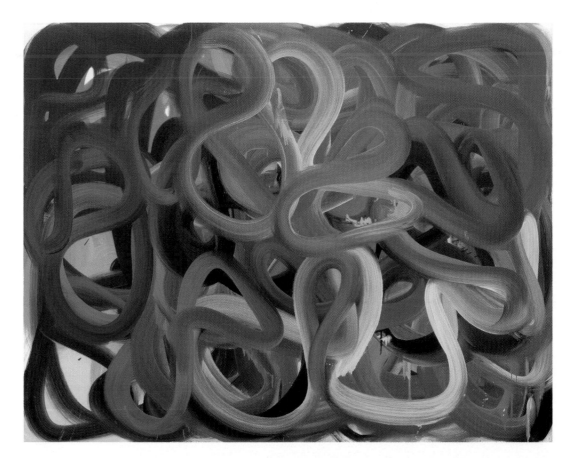

◀ **D**

Karin Davie. *Between My Eye and Heart No. 12.* 2005. Oil on canvas, 5′ 6″ × 7′. Mary Boone Gallery, New York.

SUGGESTIONS OF FORM

Salome with the Head of John the Baptist **(A)** is a painting by Caravaggio that puts more emphasis on color and value than on line. In each of the figures, only part of the body is revealed by a sharp contour, but the edge then disappears into a mysterious darkness. This is termed **lost-and-found contour**:

Now you see it, now you don't. The artist gives us a few clues, and we fill in the rest. For example, when we see a sharply defined profile, we will automatically assume the rest of the head is there, although we do not see it. A line interpretation **(B)** of this painting proves that we do not get a complete scene but merely suggestions of form. Bits and pieces float, and it is more difficult to understand the image presented.

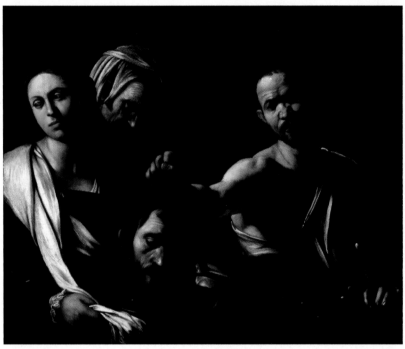

▲ **A**

Caravaggio. *Salome with the Head of John the Baptist*. c. 1609. Oil on canvas, 116 × 140 cm. National Gallery, London, Great Britain.

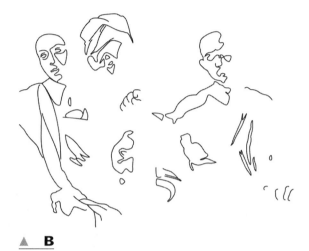

▲ **B**

Only some contours are visible in the painting.

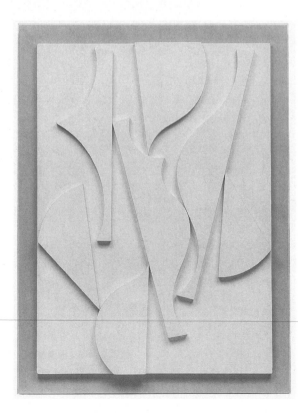

▶ **C**

Sophie Taeuber-Arp. *Parasols*. 1938. Painted wood relief, 2' 10" × 2' (86 × 61 cm). Rijksmuseum Kröller-Múller, Otüterlo, Netherlands.

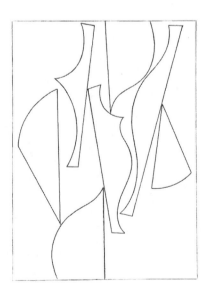

▲ **D**

Sophie Taeuber-Arp. *Untitled (Study for Parasols)*. 1937. Black crayon, 1' 1 1/2" × 10" (34 × 25 cm). Foundation Jean Arp and Sophie Taeuber-Arp, Rolandseck, Germany.

Relative Clarity

A strong linear contour structure in a painting provides clarity. Lost-and-found contour gives only relative clarity but is in fact closer to our natural perception of things. Seldom do we see everything before us in equal and vivid contrast. The relief shown in **C** presents a rhythmic linear composition created by only those edges cast in shadow. In this case of a white-on-white relief, it is the illuminated edges that disappear. We can get a better idea of the "lost" contours from the study drawing shown in **D**. Obviously a different composition of lines in **C** would be revealed with a change in the direction of light.

Selected Lighting

Photographers often choose the lighting for a subject to exploit the emotional and expressive effects of lost-and-found contour. Illustration **E** is just one of the countless photographs that have used the technique. Here a very beautiful and dramatic image has been produced from a simple architectural detail.

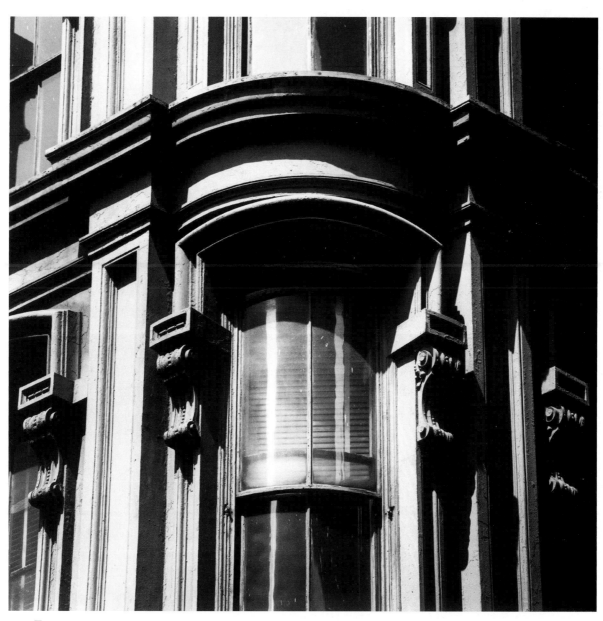

▲ **E**

Mark Feldstein. *Untitled.* Photograph.

STRUCTURE OF THE RECTANGLE

Any rectangular composition has inherent in its format a whole series of lines tied to the geometry of that shape. Take any rectangular piece of paper: Fold it in half, then fold it in half again. Now fold from corner to corner, and again from the opposite corners. A whole web of lines will appear, dividing quadrants and tracing diagonals. The intersections of these lines suggest further possible folds and lines. Whether explicitly drawn or implicitly left unmarked, these lines form an underlying structure that can create a foundation for a visual composition.

Returning to our familiar examples, we can see that such a substructure of inherent compositional lines can exist in both figurative and nonfigurative artworks. The vertical midline intersects the near eye in Susan Moore's painting **(A)**. Follow the other lines and you will see that

the head is essentially within the top half of the space
the features of the face are contained in a rectangle
an isosceles triangle connects the ear, chin, and eye

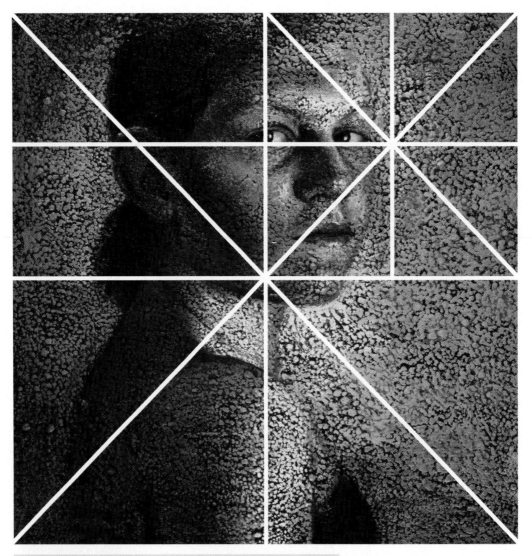

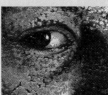

▲ **A**
Susan Moore. *Vanity (Portrait 1)*. 2000. Oil stick on canvas, 4′ × 3′ 11″. Diagram.

Lissitzky's composition is explicitly geometric, yet that may be just part of the story as revealed in **B**. Perhaps most significantly, the "tipping" red square rests on a pivot point near the intersection of many of the underlying diagonals and quadrant lines. These inherent compositional lines reinforce the already dominant role of the red square.

Some artists will consciously employ an awareness of geometry. Others prefer a more intuitive, less conscious approach. In either case we will often find that a riveting composition owes much to the arrangement of elements within the web of inherent lines.

See also *Proportion: Root Rectangles,* page 86.

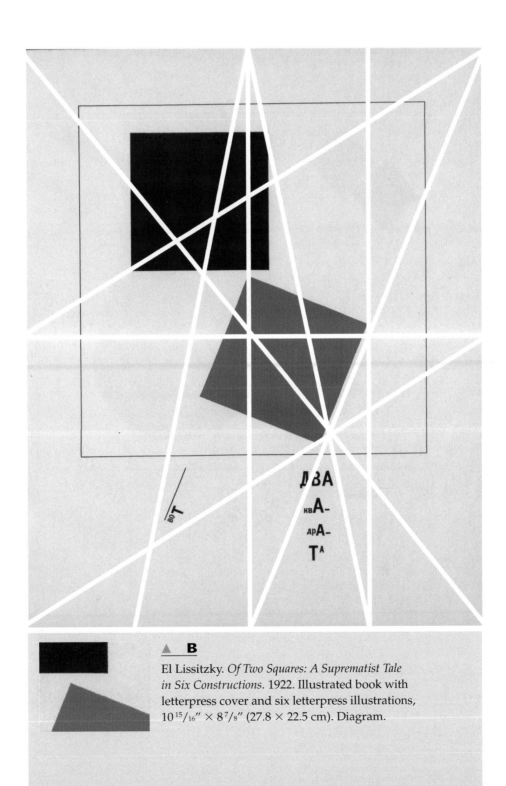

▲ **B**

El Lissitzky. *Of Two Squares: A Suprematist Tale in Six Constructions.* 1922. Illustrated book with letterpress cover and six letterpress illustrations, 10 $^{15}/_{16}$″ × 8 $^{7}/_{8}$″ (27.8 × 22.5 cm). Diagram.

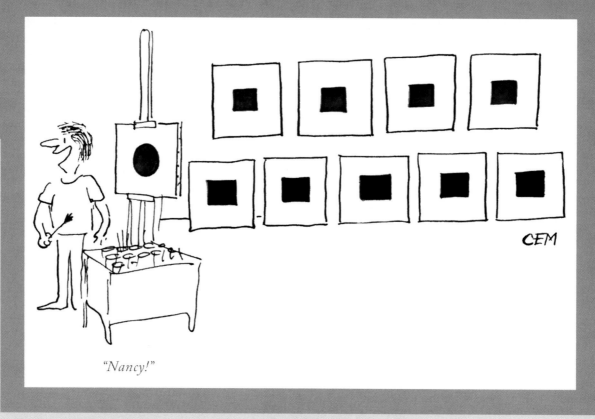

"Nancy!"

Charles E. Martin. 1968.
© *The New Yorker Collection* from cartoonbank.com.
All Rights Reserved.

SHAPE/VOLUME

A **shape** is a visually perceived area created either by an enclosing line or by color or value changes defining the outer edge. A shape can also be called a **form**. The two terms are generally synonymous and are often used interchangeably. *Shape* is a more precise term because *form* has other meanings in art. For example, *form* may be used in a broad sense to describe the total visual organization of a work, including color, texture, and composition. Thus, to avoid confusion, the term *shape* is more specific.

Design, or composition, is basically the arrangement of shapes. The still life painted by the contemporary painter Sydney Licht **(A)** is dominated by oval shapes in various sizes and combinations. Of course, the color, texture, and value of these shapes are important, but the basic element is shape, including the shapes defined by the spaces between objects and the more complex shapes created through groups or clusters of simple shapes. The pattern on the tablecloth serves as a simple and more abstract echo of the shapes and negative shapes found in the asparagus bundles.

Pictures certainly exist without color, without any significant textural interest, and even without line, but rarely do they exist without shape. In representational pictures, only the most diffuse atmospheric images of light can be said almost to dispense with shape. The image in **B** is one of Monet's impressions of the Rouen Cathedral that emphasizes light and atmosphere over shape. Illustration **C** is a further exaggeration of these qualities by Lichtenstein. The shape of the cathedral in **C** barely flickers into focus, and the many dots make the image compete with the shapes of the architectural elements for our attention.

If you look closely, you can see that the dots in **C** are small circles, and so this image has one level of connection with the still life in **A**. Everything else may be different, but at the level of shape they have a common element.

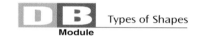

Types of Shapes

Module

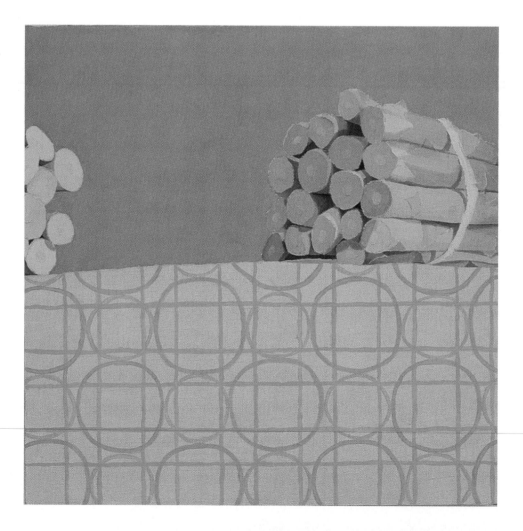

► **A**

Sydney Licht. *Still Life with Two Bunches.* Oil on linen, 1′ × 1′. Kathryn Markel Fine Arts. Courtesy of the artist.

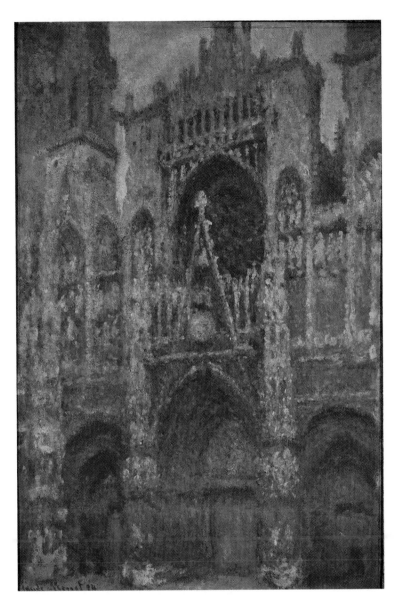

 B

Claude Monet. *Rouen Cathedral: Portal, Grey Weather.*
1892. Oil on canvas. Musée d'Orsay, Paris.

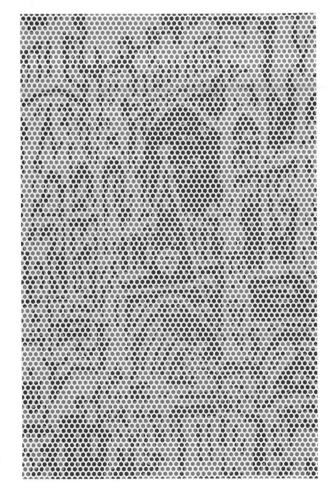

► **C**

Roy Lichtenstein. *Cathedral #2 from the Cathedral Series.*
1969. Color lithograph and screen print in red and blue,
4′ $^5/_{16}$″ × 2′ 8$^3/_8$″ (123 × 82.5 cm). Fine Arts Museums of
San Francisco, Anderson Graphic Arts Collection (gift of
Harry W. and Margaret Anderson Charitable Foundation,
1996.74.239).

WORKING IN TWO AND THREE DIMENSIONS

Shape usually is considered a two-dimensional element, and the words *volume* and *mass* are applied to the three-dimensional equivalent. In simplest terms, paintings have shapes and sculptures have masses. The same terms and distinctions that are applied to shapes apply to three-dimensional volumes or masses. Although the two concepts are closely related, the design considerations of the artist can differ considerably when working in two- or three-dimensional media.

Angle of Perception

A flat work, such as a painting, can be viewed satisfactorily from only a limited number of angles and offers approximately the same image from each angle, but three-dimensional works can be viewed from countless angles as we move around them. The three-dimensional design changes each time we move: the forms are constantly seen in different relationships. Unless we purposely stop and stare at a sculpture, our visual experience is always fluid, not static. The two photographs of the piece of sculpture by David Smith **(A)** show how radically the design pattern can change depending on our angle of perception.

Thus, in composing art of three-dimensional volume or mass, the artist faces more complex considerations. We may simply step back to view the progress of our painting or drawing. With sculpture we must consider the work from a multitude of angles, anticipating all the viewpoints from which it may be seen.

Architecture is the art form most concerned with three-dimensional volumes. Architecture creates three-dimensional shapes and volumes by enclosing areas within walls. Some artists, in both the past and present, have selected to work with the architecture, not independent from it.

Combining Two- and Three-Dimensional Work

A sharp, clear-cut label for art as either two- or three-dimensional is not always possible. Relief sculptures are three-dimensional, but because the carving is relatively shallow with a flat back, they function more as paintings without color. Many contemporary artists now incorporate three-dimensional elements by attaching items to the canvas or presenting them with the canvas. In the work by Jennifer Bartlett **(B)**, a painting of boats is juxtaposed against three-dimensional versions of the same image. These sculptural elements refer more to the shapes in the painting than to real boats. They are cropped at the same points as the images are cropped in the painting. In this case, the three-dimensional form seems to copy the painting, rather than the usual idea of the painting following the appearance of the three-dimensional form.

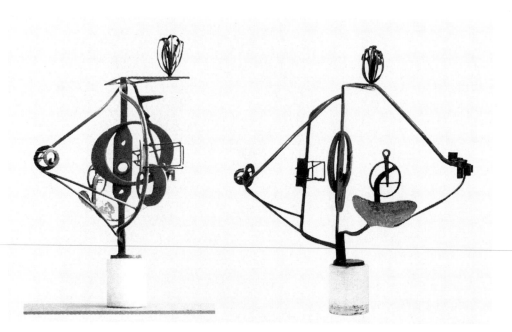

◄ **A**

David Smith. *Blackburn: Song of an Irish Blacksmith* (front and side views). 1949–1950. Steel and bronze, 3′ 10 1/4″ × 3′ 5″ × 2′ (117 × 104 × 61 cm); height of base 8″ (20 cm), diameter 7 1/4″ (18 cm). Wilhelm Lehmbruck Museum, Duisburg, Germany. Art © Estate of David Smith/Licensed by VAGA, New York, New York.

Many artists today attempt to break down the dividing barriers between painting, drawing, sculpture, and architecture. Julian Opie's *Shahnoza* **(C)** accomplishes just this and goes farther in breaking down distinctions between "high brow" and "low brow." The vinyl line drawings of a "pole dancer" were placed to interact in a witty dialogue with an installation of Henry Moore's massive abstracted figures.

The Opie drawings are also quite abstract: note the circles for heads. The position of the drawings aligns the poles with the architectural grid of the ceiling, humorously suggesting that, like ancient **caryatids**, they are holding up the building. Opie accomplishes all this with drawings that emphasize flat shapes, not three-dimensional volumes.

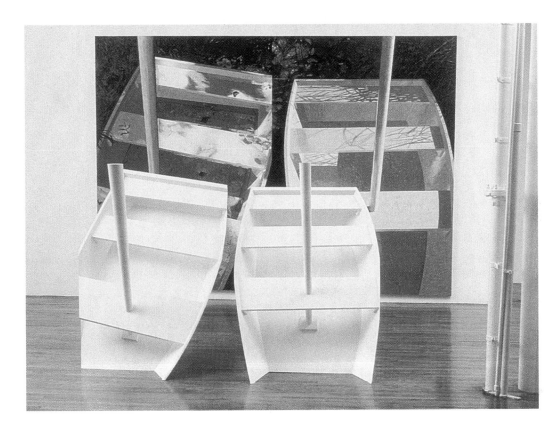

◄ **B**

Jennifer Bartlett. *Boats.* 1987. Sculpture: painted wood, steel support, pine mast, 5′ 6 1/2″ × 3′ 11 1/2″ × 3′ 10″ each (169 × 121 × 117 cm); painting: oil on canvas, 9′ 10″ × 14′ (3 × 4.3 m). Courtesy Paula Cooper Gallery, New York.

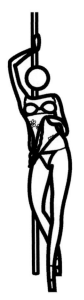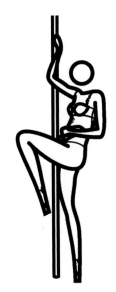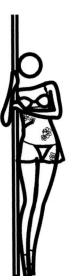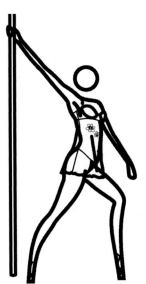

▲ **C**

Julian Opie. *Shahnoza.* 2006. Wallworks installation. Courtesy of Julian Opie's Studio, London, England.

► **A**

Russell Connor. *The New Yorker* cover drawing. November 23, 1992.

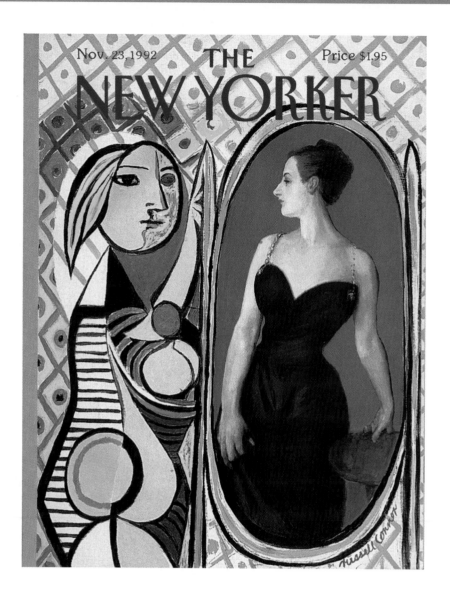

EXAGGERATED SHAPES

The magazine cover in **A** shows the difference between **naturalism** and **distortion**. Through a clever adaptation of two well-known paintings, we can see the contrast. The woman on the right (from a Sargent painting) would be described as "naturalistic." The artist has skillfully reproduced the visual image, the forms and proportions seen in nature, with an illusion of volume and three-dimensional space.

Naturalism is what most people call **realism**, meaning, of course, visual realism. On the left side of **A**, another woman (from a Picasso painting) is shown in what is called "distortion." In using distortion, the artist purposely changes or exaggerates the forms of nature. Sometimes distortion is meant to provoke an emotional response on the part of the viewer; sometimes it serves to emphasize the design elements inherent in the subject matter.

Distortion Old and New

Many people think that distortion is a twentieth-century development. Now that the camera can easily and cheaply reproduce the appearance of the world around us—a role formerly filled by painting—distortion has greatly increased in contemporary art to one degree or another. However, distortion has been a recurrent facet of art. Hans Holbein the Younger included a distorted skull streaking across the front of his painting *The Ambassadors* **(B)**. This is not simply a stylistic flourish but a carefully constructed distortion or **anamorphic** shape. Seen from an extreme side viewpoint, the ambiguous form resolves into a human skull.

The advertisement shown in **C** distorts the human form through elongation. The result is an image that communicates visually the stretching, leaping, and reaching inherent in a basketball game. This distortion puts an emphasis on the action over a naturalistic view of the body.

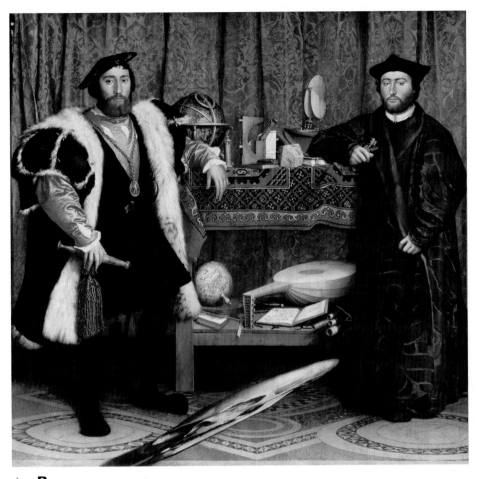

▲ **B**

Hans Holbein the Younger. *The Ambassadors.*
1553. Oil on panel. © National Gallery, London,
UK/The Bridgeman Art Library.

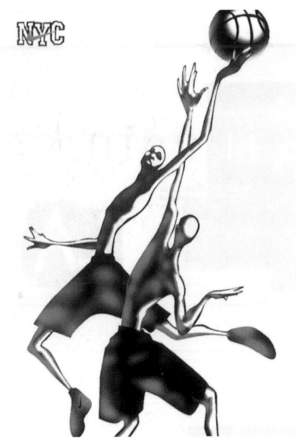

▶ **C**

Advertisement for Nike Sportswear. 1995. NYC
Campaign. Art Director: John C. Jay. Designer: Pao.
Illustrator: Javier Michaelski. Creative Directors:
Dan Wieden, Susan Hoffman. Source: *Print,*
March/April 1996, p. 87.

NATURE IMPROVED

Naturalism is concerned with appearance. It gives the true-to-life, honest visual appearance of shapes in the world around us. In contrast, there is a specific type of artistic distortion called **idealism**. Idealism reproduces the world not as it is but as it should be. Nature is improved on. All the flaws, accidents, and incongruities of the visual world are corrected.

Idealism in Art

The self-portrait by Catherine Murphy **(A)** is naturalistic. Even in painting herself, the artist has indulged in no flattery. The artist's face is in shadow, and the emphasis is less on the portrait than the naturalistic presentation of the artist's studio. The fifth-century B.C. statue **(B)** illustrates the opposite approach—idealism. This statue was a conscious attempt to discover the ideal proportions of the human body. No human figure was copied for this sculpture. The statue represents a visual paragon, a conceptual image of perfection that nature simply does not produce.

Idealism is a recurrent theme in art, as it is in civilized society. We are all idealistic; we all strive for perfection. Despite overwhelming historical evidence, we continue to believe we can create a world without war, poverty, sickness, or social injustice. Obviously, art will periodically reflect this dream of a utopia.

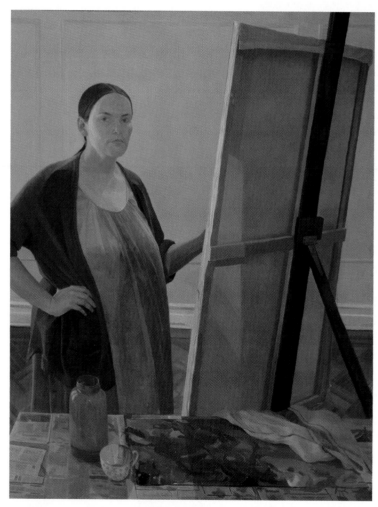

▲ **A**

Catherine Murphy. *Self-Portrait*. 1970. Oil on canvas, 4′ 1 1/2″ × 3′ 1 1/8″ (125.7 × 94.3 cm). Museum of Fine Arts, Boston (gift of Michael and Gail Mazur, 1998.416). Photograph © 2007 Museum of Fine Arts, Boston.

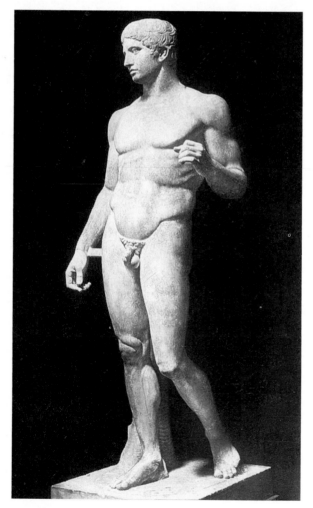

▲ **B**

Polyclitus. *Doryphorus (Spear Bearer)*. Roman copy after Greek original of c. 450–440 B.C. Marble, height 6′ 11″ (1.98 m). Museo Archeologico Nazionale, Naples, Italy.

Idealism in Advertising and Propaganda

Today, we are all familiar with a prevalent, if mundane, form of idealism. Large numbers of the advertisements we see daily are basically idealistic. Beautiful people in romantically lit and luxurious settings evoke an atmosphere that is far different from the daily lives of most of us. Fashion illustration suggests body types that are rare or unreal. Governments also often employ idealistic images to convince the world (or themselves) that their particular political system is superior. The heroic "worker" shown in **C** has the idealized muscles of a comic superhero.

▼ **C**

Artist unknown. *Completely Smash the Liu-Deng Counter-Revolutionary Line.* Collection © The University of Westminster. All rights reserved.

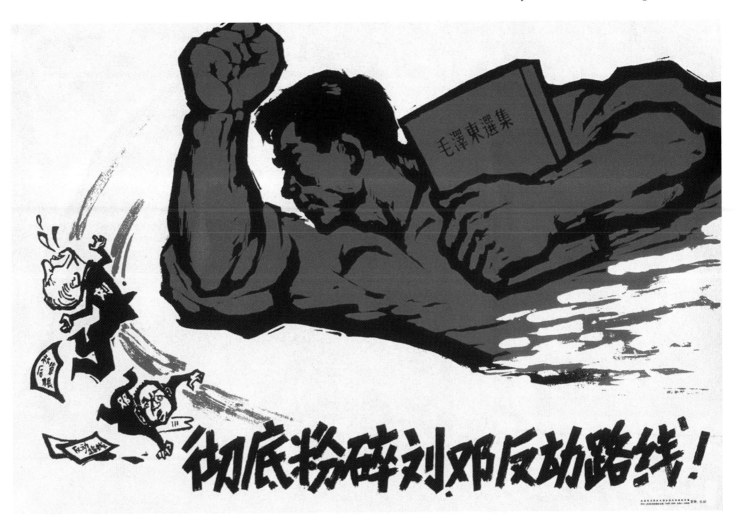

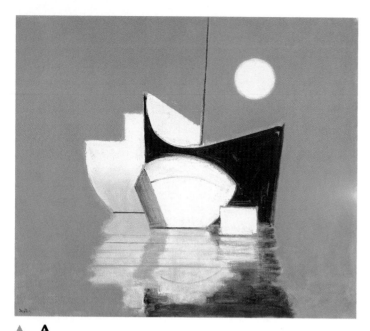

▲ **A**

Paul Resika. *July.* 2001. Oil on canvas, 4′ 4″ × 5′.
Salander-O'Reilly Galleries, LLC, New York, New York.

ESSENCE OF SHAPE

A specific kind of artistic distortion is called **abstraction**. Abstraction implies a simplification of natural shapes to their essential, basic character. Details are ignored as the shapes are reduced to their simplest terms. The painting in **A** is an example of abstraction.

Abstraction for Effect

Because no artist, no matter how skilled or careful, can possibly reproduce every detail of a natural subject, any painting could be called an abstraction. But the term *abstraction* is most often applied to works in which simplification is visually obvious and important to the final pictorial effect. Of course, the degree of abstraction can vary. In **A** all the elements have been abstracted to some extent. Most details have been omitted in reducing the boats to basic geometric shapes (primarily sections of circles and rectangles). Still, the subject matter is immediately recognizable, even though we are several steps removed from a naturalistic image. This form of abstraction, where elements are simplified to building blocks, is sometimes called "reductive."

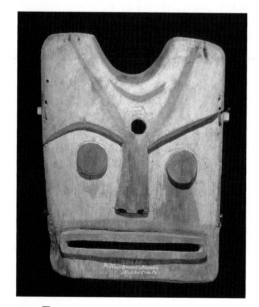

▲ **B**

Chugach (Sugpiaq) mask from Prince William Sound. Painted wood, 38 cm high. © Chugach Alaska Corporation.

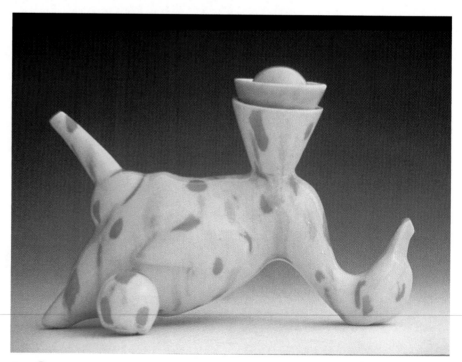

▲ **C**

Rebecca Harvey. *Systema Naturae.* 1998. Department of Art, Ohio State University.

For the Love of Shapes

Abstraction is not a new technique; artists have employed this device for centuries. If anything, the desire for naturalism in art is the more recent development. The Chugach mask in **B** clearly shows abstracted forms. Although the result is quite different from **A**, many of the shapes in this mask also seem to suggest geometric forms. This aspect illustrates a widely accepted principle: All form, however complex, is essentially based on, and can be reduced to, a few geometric shapes.

Abstracted form does not always lead simply to an alternative representation of a naturalistic form. Abstraction often arises from a love of shape and form for its own sake and from a delight in manipulating form. The teapot shown in **C** transforms a given mold form of a duck in an unexpected way.

Biomorphic Shapes

Not all abstraction necessarily results in a geometric conclusion, and abstraction can result in imagery that is not as directly derived from natural references as the previous examples. The simple petal-like shapes in Arshile Gorky's *Garden in Sochi* (**D**) suggest plants, and even human anatomy, without explicitly resembling anything nameable. Abstract shapes such as these, which allude to natural, organic forms, are called **biomorphic**.

▼ **D**

Arshile Gorky. *Garden in Sochi*. c. 1943. Oil on canvas, 2′ 7″ × 3′ 3″ (78.7 × 99 cm). The Museum of Modern Art, New York (acquired through the Lillie P. Bliss Bequest, 492.1969).

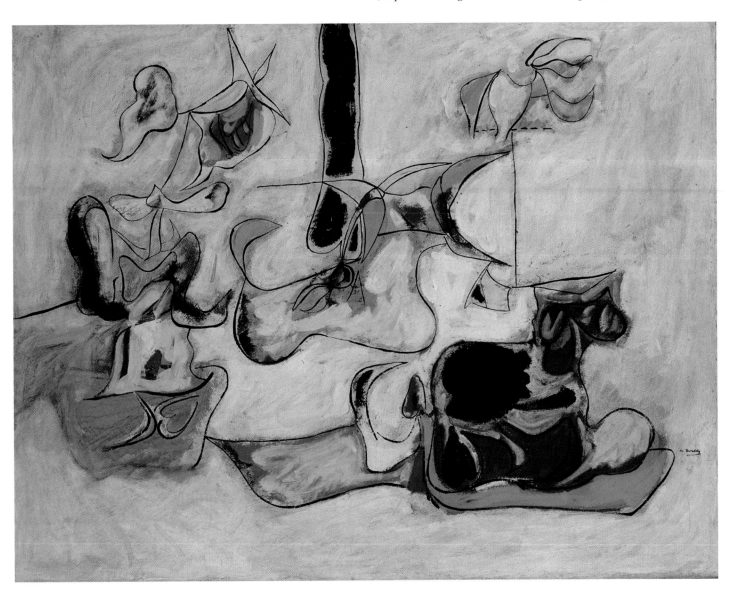

PURE FORMS

According to common usage, the term *abstraction* might be applied to the collage in **A**. This would be misleading, however, because the shapes in this work are not natural forms that have been artistically simplified. They do not represent anything other than the geometric forms we see. Rather, they are pure forms. A better term to describe these shapes is **nonobjective**—that is, shapes with no object reference and no subject matter suggestion.

Visual Design

Most of the original design drawings in this book are non-objective patterns. Often, it is easier to see an artistic principle or element without a distracting veneer of subject matter. In a similar way, many twenty-first-century artists are forcing us to observe their works as visual patterns, not storytelling narratives. Without a story, subject, or even identifiable shapes, a painting must be appreciated solely as a visual design. Lack of subject matter does not necessarily eliminate emotional content in the image. Some nonobjective works are cool, aloof, and unemotional. Paintings or collages such as **A** present purely nonobjective, geometric shapes that are, as Plato said, "free from the sting of desire." Illustration **B** is equally nonobjective, but the shapes are not geometric and seem to have developed from the inherently fluid quality of the paint. The canvas seems to be a record of the paint flowing and pooling under the artist's direction.

Shape Associations

Whether any shape can be truly nonobjective is a good question. Can we really look at a circle just as a circle without beginning to think of some of the countless round objects in our environment? Artists often make use of this instinctive human reflex. A work such as Daniel Wiener's sculpture **(C)** appears to be a totally nonobjective pattern of forms, yet it is reminiscent of structures we know from nature: the roots of a tree or spider legs, to name just two.

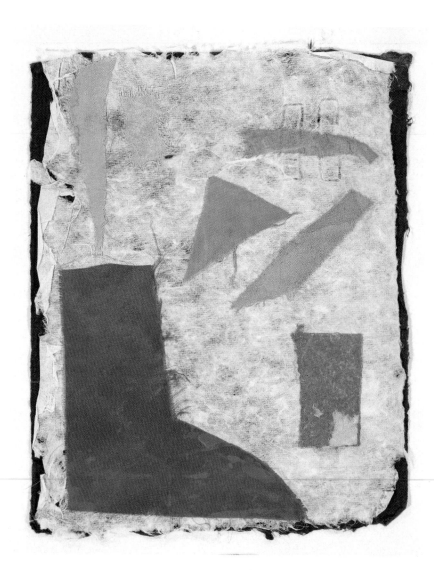

◄ **A**

Anne Ryan. *No. 492.* 1948–1954. Fabric and paper collage, 8" × 7" unframed. Walker Art Center (gift of Elizabeth McFadden, 1979.21).

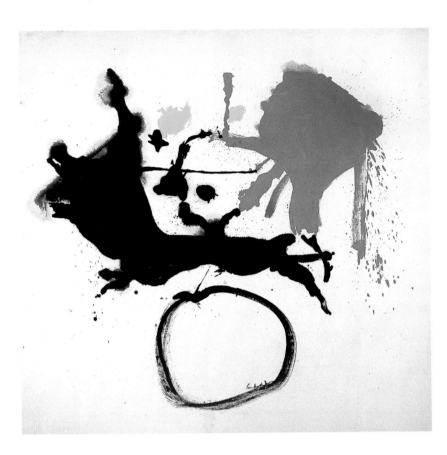

◀ **B**

Helen Frankenthaler. *Over the Circle.* 1961. Oil on canvas, 7′ 1/8″ × 7′ 3 7/16″ (2.13 × 2.21 m). Jack S. Blanton Museum of Art, The University of Texas at Austin (gift of Mari and James A. Michener, 1991.213).

▼ **C**

Daniel Wiener. *Chorus.* 1993. Hydrocal, acrylic, wire, dyed muslin, 15′ 5 1/2″ × 13′ × 7′ 7″ (1.66 × 3.96 × 2.31 m). Gorney Bravin & Lee, New York.

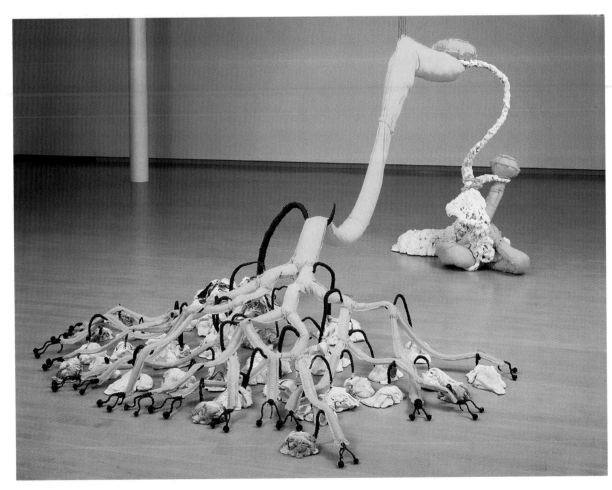

Figures **A** and **B** illustrate the difference between two terms that are commonly applied to shapes: **curvilinear** and **rectilinear**. Two objects with functional priorities are visually quite different in design. The chair in **A** is one continuous curve mounted on a tubular frame—

an example of curvilinear design. The prefabricated house **(B)** emphasizes right angles and rectangular planes—all the forms have straight edges, giving a sharp, angular feeling. *Rectilinear* is the term to describe this visual effect. Interestingly enough, interior photographs of this home show chairs similar to **A**.

The painting by Yeardley Leonard **(C)** is clearly a rectilinear design. The emphasis of this painting is on color intervals and relationships. A rectilinear composition keeps the focus on planes of color, and these planes repeat the overall format of a rectangular painting.

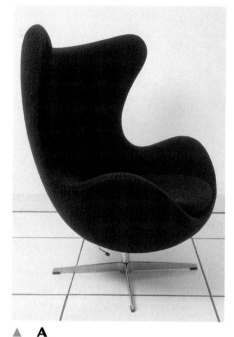

▲ **A**

Arne Jacobsen. *The Egg Chair.* 1957 (in production since 1958). 107 × 86 × 79 cm. Photo: Jean-Claude Planchet. Musée National d'Art Moderne, Centre Georges Pompidou, Paris, France.

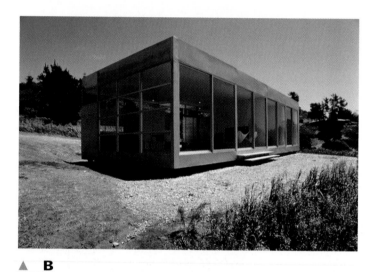

▲ **B**

Rocio Romero. *Prefabricated Home* ("LV Home," designed as a second vacation home—production beginning Summer 2003).

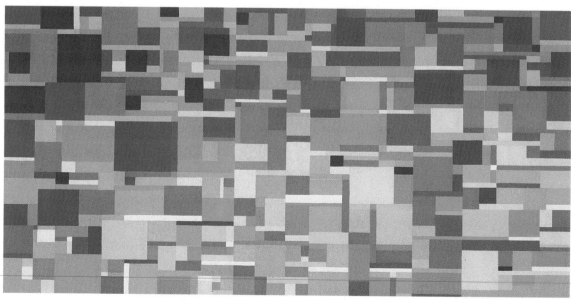

▲ **C**

Yeardley Leonard. *Sita.* 2001. Acrylic on linen on panel, 1′ 4$^{1}/_{2}$″ × 2′ 9″. Elizabeth Dee Gallery, New York, New York.

The poster in **D** shows an equal emphasis on the opposite curvilinear type of shape. There is barely a straight line to be found. This poster is a product of a late nineteenth-century style called **art nouveau**, which put total pictorial emphasis on curvilinear or natural shapes.

We do think of curvilinear shapes as natural, reflecting the soft, flowing shapes found in nature. Rectilinear shapes, being more regular and precise, suggest geometry and, hence, appear more artificial and manufactured. Of course, these are very broad conclusions. In fact, geometric shapes abound in nature, especially in the microscopic structure of elements, and people design many objects with irregular, free-form shapes.

Examples **C** and **D** concentrate exclusively on a single type of shape. Most art and design combine both types. In architecture we may think of rectilinear design dominating, with the verticals and horizontals of doors, windows, and walls. The simple curve of an arch can provide visual relief. Or, as in **E**, a dramatically curved section of the building seems to send a ripple or wave through the design of the rest of the building, even affecting the pattern of rectangular windows.

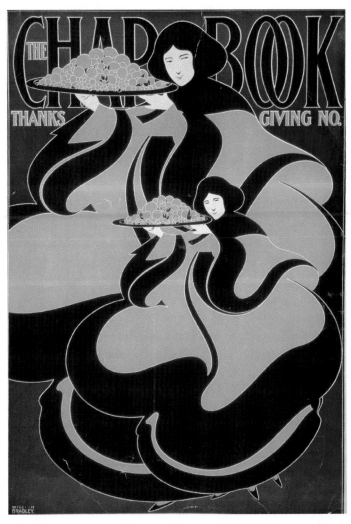

▲ **D**

William H. Bradley. Magazine cover, *The Chap Book*, Thanksgiving Number, USA, 1894. Lithograph. © Victoria and Albert Museum, London, UK/ The Bridgeman Art Library.

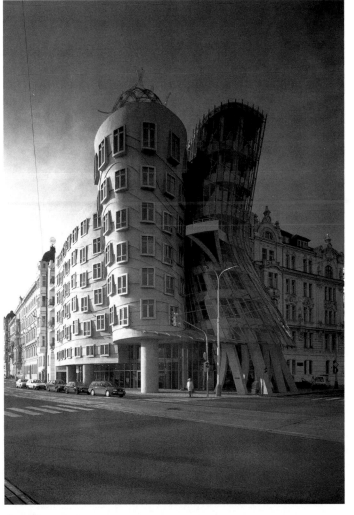

▲ **E**

Nationale-Nederlanden Building. Prague. 1996. Architects: Vladimir Milunic, Frank Gehry. The Metropolitan Museum of Art (1984.1202.7.155E). Photo: © Tim Griffith/Esto. All rights reserved.

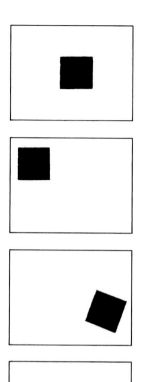

◀ **A**

The location of shapes in space organizes the space into positive and negative areas.

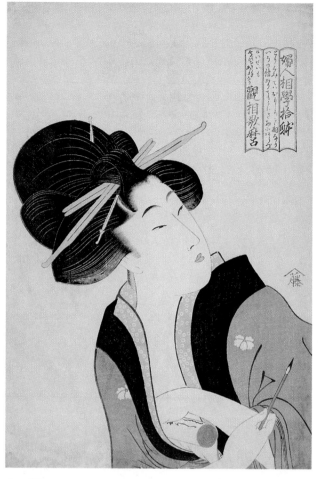

▲ **B**

Utamaro. *Ten looks of women's physiognomy/enjoyable looks.* The Japan Ukiyo-e Museum, Matsumoto, Japan.

INTRODUCTION

The four examples in **A** illustrate an important design consideration that is sometimes overlooked. In each of these patterns, the black shape is identical. The very different visual effects are caused solely by its placement within the format—the location of the black shape immediately organizes the empty space into various shapes. We often refer to these as **positive** and **negative shapes**. The black shape is a positive element; the white empty space, the negative shape or shapes. **Figure** and **ground** are other terms used to describe the same idea, the black shape being the figure.

Negative Spaces Are Carefully Planned

In paintings with subject matter, the distinction between object and background is usually clear. It is important to remember that both elements have been thoughtfully designed and planned by the artist. The subject is the focal point, but the negative areas created are equally important in the final pictorial effect. Japanese art often intrigues the Western viewer because of its unusual design of negative spaces. In the Japanese print **(B)**, the unusual bend of the

central figure and the flow of the robes to touch the edges of the picture create two varied and interesting negative spaces. A more usual vertical pose for this figure would have formed more regular, symmetrical shapes in the negative areas. In this composition the dominant shapes are actually the hair and black borders on the robe. The light ground blends with the face and head; only a delicate line marks the boundary of figure and ground here.

Negative shapes are also an aspect of letter design and typography. In this case a black letter may be the "figure" and the white page, the "ground." Aaron Siskind's photograph *Chicago 30* **(C)** is apparently a sideways letter *R*. By cropping in on his subject, Siskind has given almost equal weight to the white negative areas, thus giving emphasis to the shapes of both. The play of light and dark or figure and ground is similar to the print by Utamaro **(B)**.

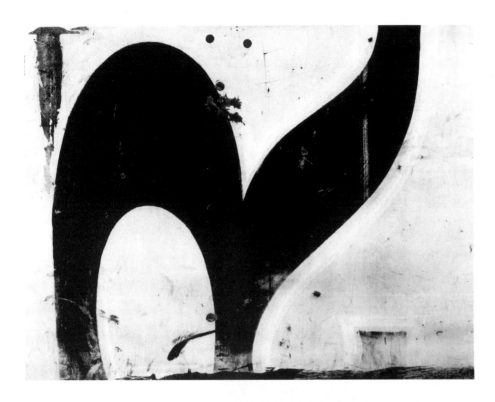

◄   **C**

Aaron Siskind. *Chicago 30.* 1949. Silver
gelatin, 1′ 1⁷/₈″ × 1′ 5⁵/₈″. International
Center of Photography, New York.

▶   **D**

Richard Serra. *Joe.* The Pulitzer
Foundation, St. Louis.

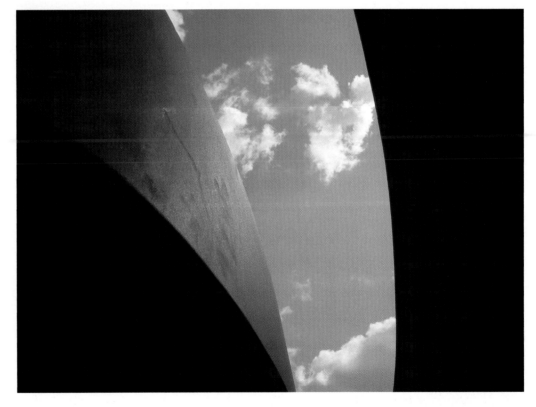

Using Negative Space
in Three Dimensions

The same positive/negative concept is applicable to three-
dimensional art forms. The sculpture shown in **D** is first
perceived as large arcs of steel. As you move about the

labyrinth-like arrangement, the space becomes not a mere
leftover but a positive component of the composition. A view
skyward reveals the power of the negative shapes.

ISOLATION OR INTEGRATION

Design themes and purposes vary, but some integration between positive and negative shapes is generally thought desirable. In **A** the shapes and their placement are interesting enough, but they seem to float aimlessly within the format. They also have what we call a "pasted-on" look, because there is little back-and-forth visual movement between the positive shapes and the negative white background. An unrelieved silhouette of every shape is usually not the most interesting spatial solution. The image in **B** shows similar shapes in the same positions as those in **A**, but the "background" is now broken into areas of value that lend interest as well as greater positive/negative integration. The division into positive and negative is flexible: that is, some squares serve *both* as a ground (negative) that hosts smaller square shapes and as a figure (positive) within the larger ground of the entire composition.

At first glance Lissitzky's composition **(C)** seems more akin to **A** because the two squares float unanchored in the space. Notice the size of these two characters and the tension created by the small space between them. There is no doubt that they are the principal actors or characters in the design. The figure/ground relationship is simple and unambiguous. Their position suggests a dynamic or conflicting relationship. The fact that they are not tethered to other lines or shapes suggests the potential for change or movement. In fact this composition is part of a series, and the shapes do change position in the subsequent compositions.

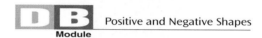
Positive and Negative Shapes

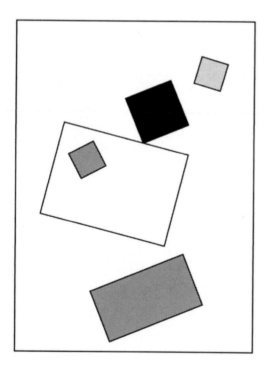

▲ **A**

When positive and negative spaces are too rigidly defined, the result can be rather uninteresting.

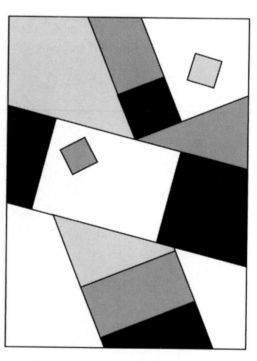

▲ **B**

If the negative areas are made more interesting, the positive/negative integration improves.

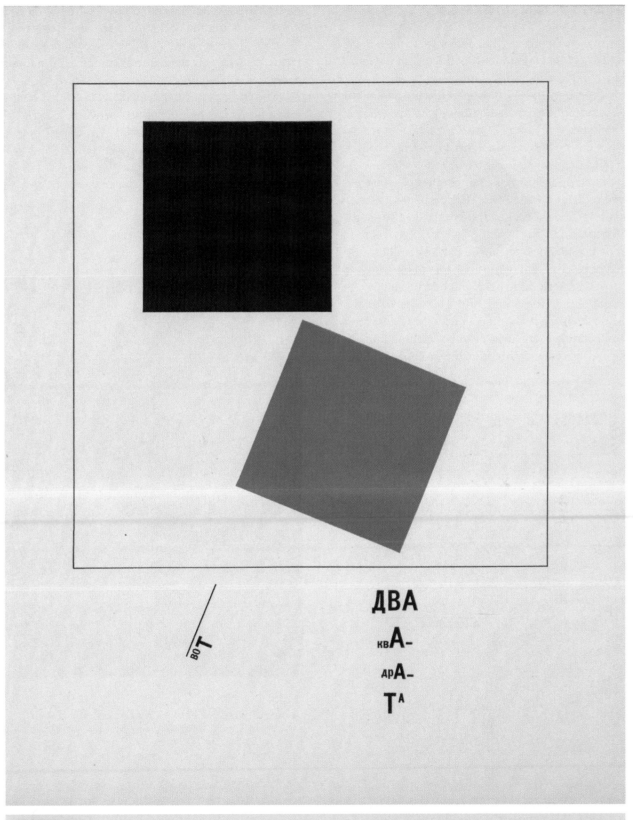

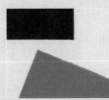

▲   **C**

El Lissitzky. *Of Two Squares: A Suprematist Tale in Six Constructions*. 1922. Illustrated book with letterpress cover and six letterpress illustrations, $10^{15}/_{16}''$ × $8^{7}/_{8}''$ (27.8 × 22.5 cm). Publisher: Skify, Berlin. Gift of the Judith Rothschild Foundation (89.2001.5).

EMPHASIS ON INTEGRATION

Three drawings by Georges Seurat demonstrate three degrees of positive/negative integration. The drawing of the female figure shown in **A** presents the figure as a dark shape against a lighter background. For the most part this is a silhouette; positive and negative (figure and ground) are presented as a simple contrast.

The relationship of positive and negative is more complex in **B**. The left side of the figure is dark against a lighter ground, and the right side of the figure is light against a darker ground. This alternation of dark and light makes us aware of the negative shapes, and they take on a stronger visual interest than in **A**.

The composition of **C** presents the most complex integration of positive and negative shapes of the three Seurat drawings. Here, dark, light, and middle values are present as both figure and ground. There are areas of sharp distinction, such as the edge of the arm against the background, and there are areas of soft or melting transitions where the eye moves smoothly from foreground to middle ground to background. The soft boundaries of the hair melt into the surrounding background shapes. This is true as well in Susan Moore's painting **(D)**, where color is an additional factor. We will view the figure as complete even though there are places where figure and ground dissolve.

The range of positive/negative integration can be found in abstract or nonobjective artworks as well as in representational images. The shapes in **C** work both as representations (head and wall, for example) and as an abstract composition of light and dark shapes.

See also *Lost-and-Found Contour,* page 146.

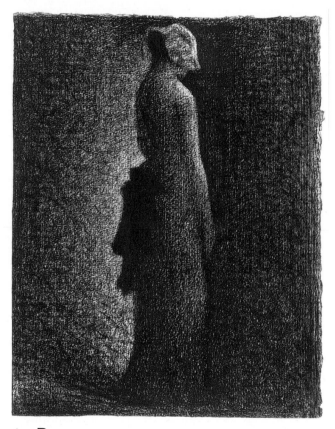

▲ **B**

Georges Seurat. *The Black Bow.* c. 1882. Conté crayon, 1'³/₁₆" × 9¹/₁₆" (31 × 23 cm). Musée d'Orsay, Paris.

▲ **A**

Georges Seurat. *Silhouette of a Woman.* 1882–1884. Conté crayon on paper, 1' × 8⁷/₈" (30.5 × 22.5 cm). Collection of McNay Art Museum, San Antonio, Texas (bequest of Marion Koogler McNay).

▶ **C**

Georges Seurat. *Embroidery: The Artist's Mother (Woman Sewing)*. 1882–1883. Conté crayon, 1′⁵/₈″ × 9⁷/₁₆″ (31.2 × 24 cm). Metropolitan Museum of Art (Purchase, Joseph Pulitzer Bequest, 1951; acquired from The Museum of Modern Art, Lillie P. Bliss Collection, 55.21.1).

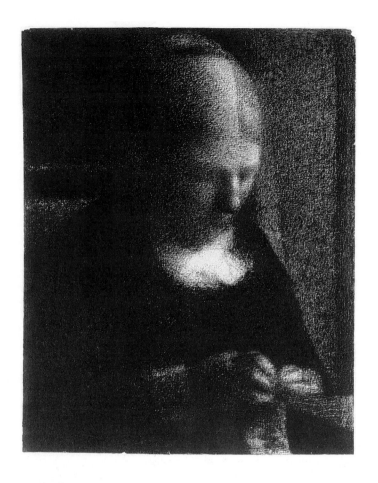

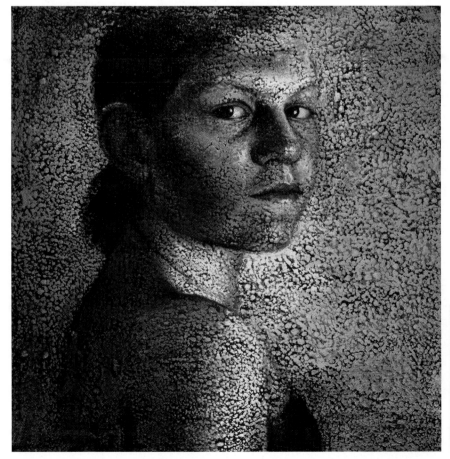

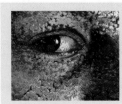

◀ **D**

Susan Moore. *Vanity (Portrait 1)*. 2000. Oil stick on canvas, 4′ × 3′ 11″.

CONFUSION

Sometimes positive and negative shapes are integrated to such an extent that there is truly no visual distinction. When we look at the painting in **A**, we are conflicted in our response to the bulbous central shape. The convex curves suggest a positive form or figure framed by a yellow border. The small wedges of dark color along the edge of the painting can visually connect with the dark center shape, and then it becomes possible to see the dark area as a space, like a dark entryway. The artist has purposely made the positive/negative relationship ambiguous. The big shape can be *both* figure and ground.

The film poster in **B** has this same quality, as our eyes must shift back and forth from dark to light in seeking the positive element. We may at first see two black heads, one in top hat, silhouetted against a light shape. Then we notice the light area is a woman's profile. The image is appropriate for the title, *The Bartered Bride.*

Deliberate Blending of Positive/Negative Shapes

In most paintings of the past, the separation of object and background was easily seen, even if selected areas merged visually. But several twentieth-century styles literally did away with the distinction. We can see that the subject matter of the painting in **C** is a figure. Despite the **cubist** abstractions of natural forms into geometric planes, we can discern the theme. But it is difficult to determine just which areas are part of the figure and which are background. The artist, Picasso, also broke up the space in the same cubist manner. There is no clear delineation of the positive from the negative.

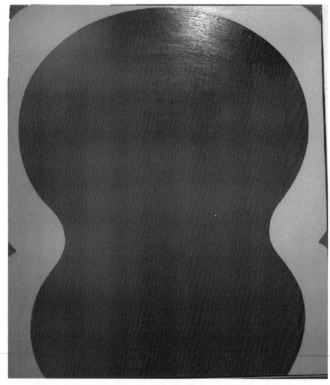

▲ **A**

Al Held. *Helena.* 1963. Acrylic on canvas, 7′ × 6′. Art © Estate of Al Held/Licensed by VAGA, New York, New York.

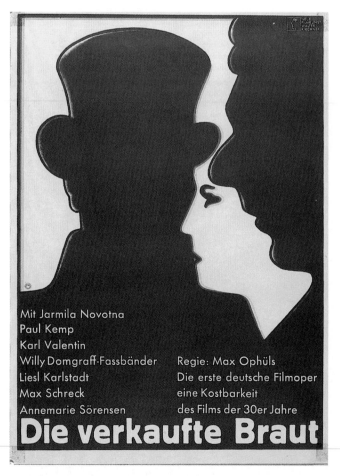

▲ **B**

Hans Hillmann. Poster for the film *The Bartered Bride.* 1972. Source: *Print,* March/April 1988, p. 105.

Deliberate Delineation of Positive/Negative Shapes

Picasso's painting invites the viewer to a slow reading of figure and ground relationships. In graphic design the goal more often is to make a quicker impact. An integration of positive and negative shapes not only is a way to get a viewer's attention with high-contrast simple forms, but often it can present surprising or memorable results. The logo for Multicanal, an Argentine cable company **(D)**, takes advantage of an alternating figure ground reading. Our attention is captured by the back-and-forth reading of stars and *M*.

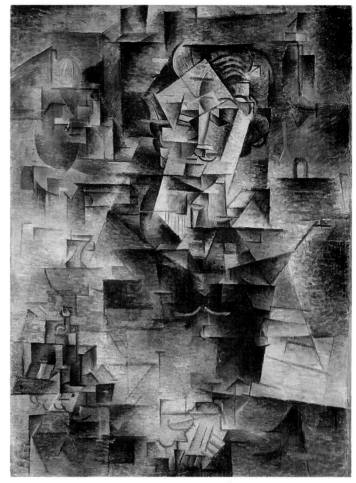

▲ **C**

Pablo Picasso. *Daniel-Henry Kahnweiler.* 1910. Oil on canvas, 3′ 3⁵/₈″ × 2′ 4⁵/₈″ (101.1 × 73.3 cm). The Art Institute of Chicago (gift of Mrs. Gilbert W. Chapman in memory of Charles B. Goodspeed, 1948.561).

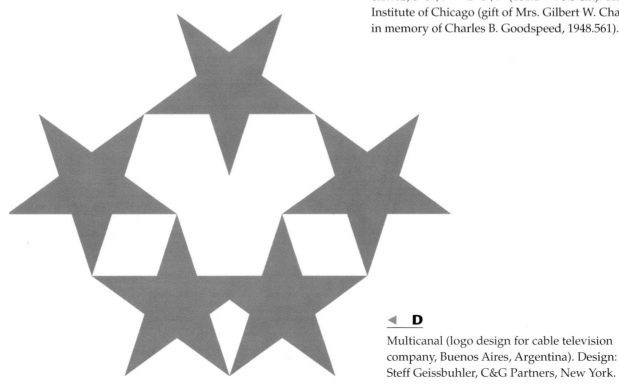

◄ **D**

Multicanal (logo design for cable television company, Buenos Aires, Argentina). Design: Steff Geissbuhler, C&G Partners, New York.

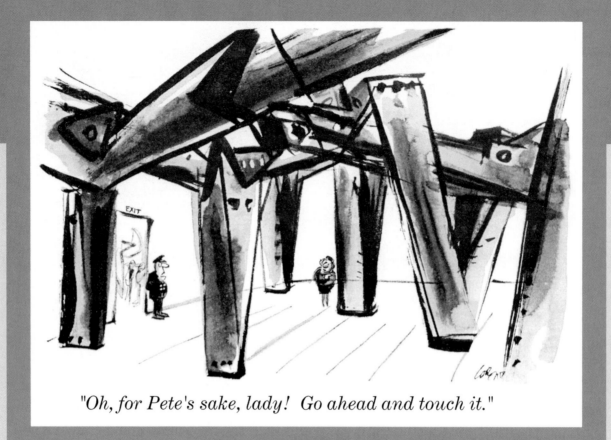

"Oh, for Pete's sake, lady! Go ahead and touch it."

Lee Lorenz. 1968.

PATTERN AND TEXTURE

CREATING VISUAL INTEREST

Pattern is a term ubiquitous to design. It has one meaning when we think of a "dress pattern" or template, and it has another, more general meaning referring to repetition of a design motif. This latter meaning is intrinsic to the human thought process. We say we need to change our patterns of thought or actions when we want to break a habit. We speak of "pattern recognition" when we search for meaning in facts or information. Humankind's earliest discoveries relating to the cosmos came with the recognition of the patterns of seasons and lunar cycles. Though "pattern"—in the visual sense of the word—is often linked to a superficial idea of decoration, our very human interest in pattern clearly has deeper roots.

Psychologists speak of "*horror vacui*" or a need to fill up empty spaces, and that is a basic human impulse. This explains a desire to add visual interest to an empty surface or space. When this surface activation is accomplished through repeated marks or shapes we have the beginnings of pattern. The photograph in **A** shows the walls of a young man's room filled with photos similar enough to create a "wallpaper" effect and form an ad hoc pattern.

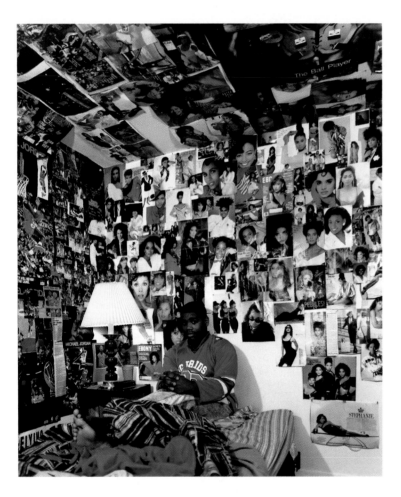

◄ **A**

Adrienne Salinger. *Fred H.* Photograph from *Teenagers in their Bedrooms* (Chronicle Books, 1995).

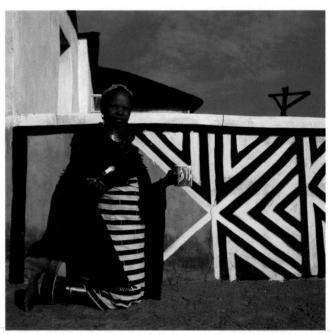

▲ **B**

Margaret Courtney-Clarke. *Anna Mahlangu Painting Her Home for a Ceremonial Occasion.* 1985. Photograph. Mabhokho, Kwandebele, South Africa.

Pattern can be intricate or simple. The pattern being created in **B** is both simple and bold. Further, it echoes the pattern of the woman's dress, suggesting her preference for such motifs! The pattern for wallpaper created by Anni Albers is more subtle in nature **(C)**, and the pattern of blocks created by her husband, Josef **(D)**, actually creates a wall. An empty wall is a strong motive for pattern!

One effect of an expanse of patterned surface is the creation of a visual rhythm. The examples here suggest some of those rhythmic possibilities.

See also *Introduction*: *Visual Rhythm, Rhythm and Motion*, and *Alternating Rhythm*, pages 114, 116, and 118.

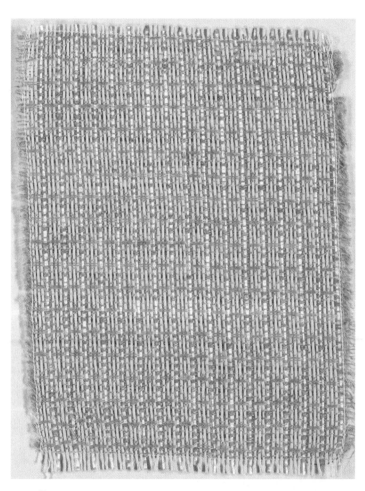

▲ **C**

Anni Albers. *Sample of wall covering*. 1928. Jute, twisted yellow paper, and cellophane, basket weave, 6¼″ × 4½″ (15.9 × 11.5 cm). Harvard University Art Museums, Busch-Reisinger Museum, Gift of Anni Albers, BR48.32. Copyright: © Josef and Anni Albers Foundation.

▼ **D**

Josef Albers. *Fireplace*. 1955. Off-white Firebrick, 7′ 3″ × 5′ 4″ (221 × 162.6 cm). Irving Rouse House, New Haven, Connecticut. Photo © Robert Walker photography.

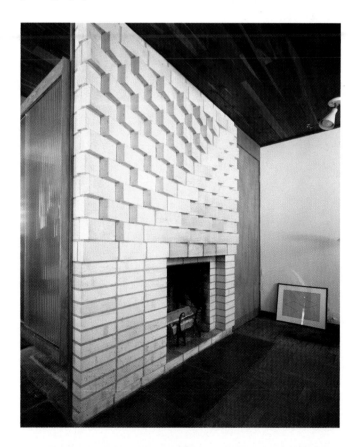

ORDER AND VARIETY

Pattern begins with a unit or shape that is repeated. It is common to find pattern based on floral designs evoking the richness of a garden. Such floral motifs can be representational and flow like a rambling vine, or more abstract and geometric as in example **A**. This shows just a section of the wallpaper pattern, but we can see the elements that will continue and repeat on the larger wall.

Most patterns can be reduced to a grid of some sort, and the result is a crystallographic balance or order. A highly disciplined version of this is seen in the Alhambra tiles shown in **B**. Here we can see both the individual units or tiles and the larger expanse of the patterns. Such elaborate patterns are built on complex symmetries, repetitions, and rotations.

The drawings of M. C. Escher continue the tradition of highly mathematical pattern making we see in the Alhambra. Figure **C** shows the basic triangular unit that is the core of one such pattern. Notice the symmetry along lines formed by each side of the triangle. Each curve or shape has an equal and opposite curve or shape across the line. These shapes are balanced by radial symmetry around the center of the line. Example **D** reveals the hexagon that orders the pattern of fish shapes. Slide the hexagon down and to the right on a 30-degree axis and the pattern is created. Each point of pinwheel-like rotation conforms to a radial symmetry. The magic of such a pattern is a complete unity of figure and ground. Every space is also a fish!

▲ **A**

Wallpaper pattern: Geometric R-580. 1960s. French.

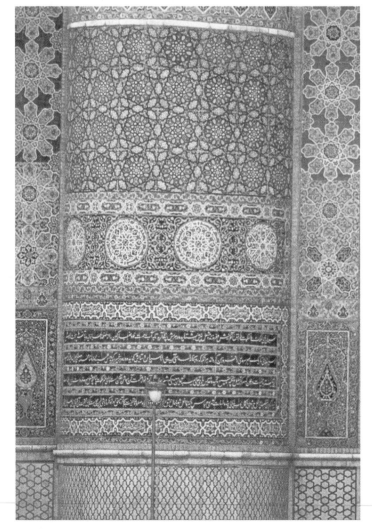

▲ **B**

Tile patterns from the Alhambra, Granada, Spain. Close-up of ornamental mosaic. Photo: © Howard Davis/ArtificeImages.

The examples we have seen thus far are closely related to architecture or graphics. In painting, an artist may include pattern as one element among others such as line or shape or color. Gustav Klimt gains some of the dazzle of the Alhambra in his juxtaposition of two patterns in the painting *Hope, II* **(E)**. The patterns in this case are distinct from each other and do not conform to a strict order (you can find variety in each).

See also *Positive/Negative Shapes*, pages 166, 168, 170, and 172, and *Radial Balance*, page 108.

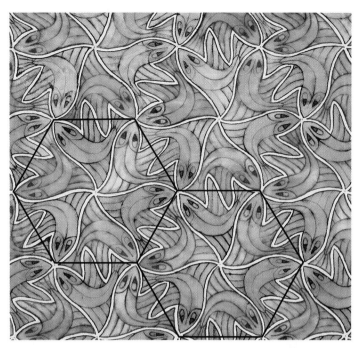

▲ **D**

M. C. Escher. *Pattern Drawing* (detail). Hexagon repeat. M. C. Escher's *Symmetry Drawing E94* © 2007 The M. C. Escher Company, Holland. All rights reserved. www.mcescher.com.

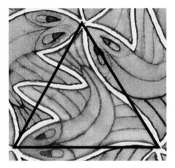

▲ **C**

M. C. Escher. *Pattern Drawing* (detail). Triangular module. M. C. Escher's *Symmetry Drawing E94* © 2007 The M. C. Escher Company, Holland. All rights reserved. www.mcescher.com.

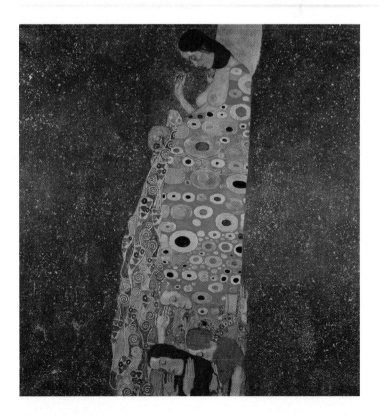

▶ **E**

Gustav Klimt. *Die Hoffnung II* (*Hope, II*). 1907–1908. Oil and gold paint on canvas. © Fischer Fine Art Ltd., London, United Kingdom / The Bridgeman Art Library.

SIMILARITIES AND DIFFERENCES

It would be difficult to draw a strict line between texture and pattern. Pattern is usually defined as a repetitive design, with the same motif appearing again and again. Texture, too, often repeats, but its variations usually do not involve such perfect regularity. The difference in the two terms is admittedly slight. The texture of a material such as burlap would be readily identified by touch, yet the surface design is repetitive enough that a photograph of burlap could be called pattern.

The essential distinction between texture and pattern seems to be whether the surface arouses our sense of touch or merely provides designs appealing to the eye. In other words, although every texture makes a sort of pattern, not every pattern could be considered a texture. Some suggestion of a three-dimensional aspect to the surface, such as shadows or glossiness, no matter how subtle, will visually evoke texture.

Evoking Our Sense of Touch

This distinction between what the eye takes to be simply pattern and the qualities that evoke our sense of touch can be seen in the three examples beginning with **A**. This decorative motif is regular, high in contrast, and representational of a plant. It is clearly a pattern. The image in **B** is also a Victorian-era decorative motif, but its irregular pattern and lack of a representational image allow it to be read as a series of ridges and thus it has some textural associations. The image in **C** is a close-up of pleated silk. The pattern is again rippled, but there is also a variety of grays. It is more complex than **B** and more suggestive of texture. An irony is that the resulting image in **C** is rather like tree bark and might not be recognized as silk due to this close-up view.

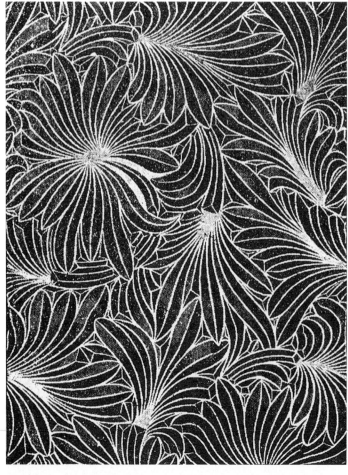

▲ **A**
Figured glass.

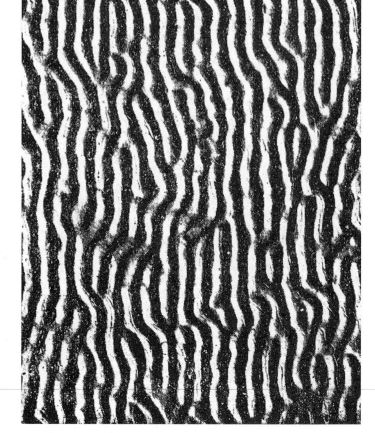

▲ **B**
Figured glass.

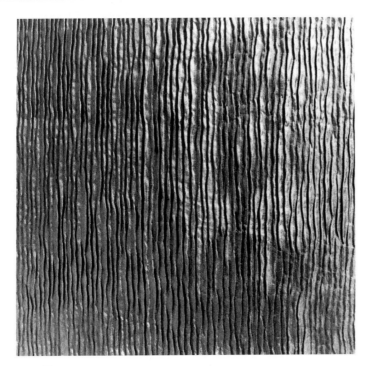

▲ **C**

Gretchen Belinger (fabric designer). *Isadora* (pleated silk fabric). 1981. From *Contemporary Designers* (London: St. James Press, 1990).

The small, intricate designs that dominate the illustration in **D** read predominantly as pattern and create decorative areas that do not appeal to our sense of touch. However, as with **B**, some areas do evoke texture, especially when viewed from a distance. Some areas take on a prickly appearance and others seem pebbly. The simple areas of white for the two faces emerging from the patterned surface provide a startling contrast.

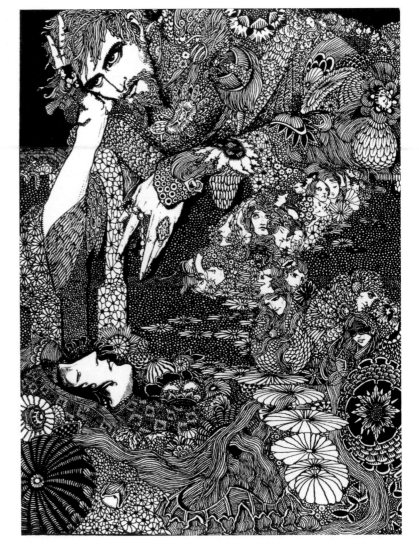

▶ **D**

Harry Clarke. *Illustration to Edgar Allan Poe's "Tales of Mystery and Imagination."* 1919. Half-tone engraving, 10″ × 7¹/₂″ (25.3 × 19 cm). General Research Division, The New York Public Library, New York, New York.

CREATING VISUAL INTEREST

Texture refers to the surface quality of objects. Texture appeals to our sense of touch. Even when we do not actually feel an object, our memory provides a sensory reaction or sensation of touch. In effect, the various light and dark patterns of different textures give visual clues so that we can enjoy the textures vicariously. Of course, all objects have some surface quality, even if it is only an unrelieved smooth flatness. The element of texture is illustrated in art when an artist purposely exploits contrasts in surface to provide visual interest.

Texture in Craft Forms

Many art forms have a basic concern with texture and its visual effects. In most of the craft areas, texture is an important consideration. Ceramics, jewelry, and furniture design often rely heavily on the texture of the materials to enhance the design effect. In weaving and the textile arts, texture is a primary consideration. The interior designer must be sensitive to the visual effects that textural contrasts can achieve.

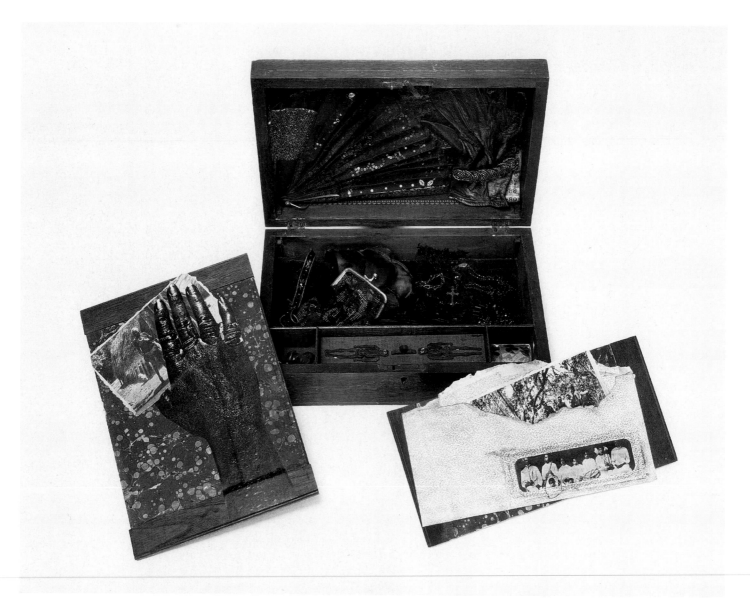

▲ **A**

Betye Saar. *The Time Inbetween.* 1974. Wooden box containing photographs, magazine illustrations, paint, envelope, 3¹/₂″ × 11⁵/₈″ × 8¹/₈″ (8.89 × 29.53 × 20.64 cm). San Francisco Museum of Modern Art (purchase). © Betye Saar.

Texture in Sculpture

In sculpture exhibits, Do Not Touch signs are a practical (if unhappy) necessity, for so many sculptures appeal to our enjoyment of texture that we almost instinctively want to touch. The smooth translucence of marble, the rough grain of wood, the polish or patina of bronze, the irregular drop of molten solder—each adds a distinctive textural quality.

Textural Variety

Betye Saar's *The Time Inbetween* (**A**) contains a variety of textures and seems to invite us to explore this intimate collection by handling it. Beads, feathers, bone, and velvet provide a variety of tactile sensations. A photocopy of the artist's hand underscores the primacy of the sense of touch for this artwork.

The photograph in **B** shows a contrast between the smooth eggs and the rough stones. It also shows the effect of scale on our visual impression of texture. At close range we might observe an individual rock or stone. At a distance, a textural pattern takes over. At an even farther distance, the pattern becomes finer and textural contrasts apparently soften. When seen from an airplane, a hillside cloaked in trees may appear to be soft in texture.

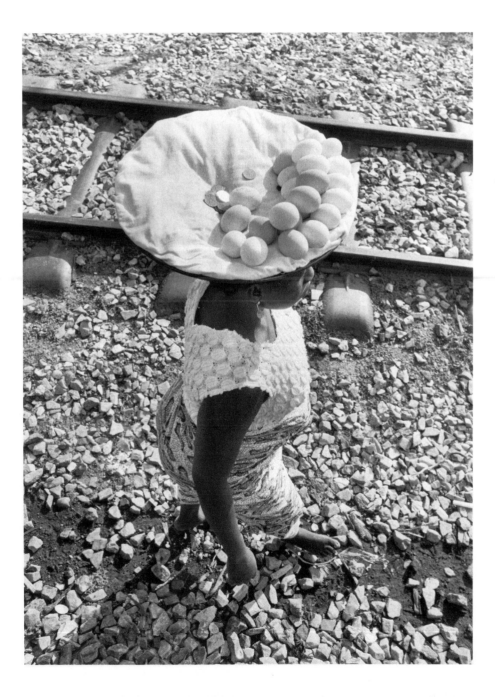

▶ **B**

Chester Higgins. *Egg vendor along commuter rail tracks in Ghana.* 1974. Photograph.

TACTILE TEXTURE

ACTUAL AND IMPLIED

There are two categories of artistic texture—tactile and visual. Architecture and sculpture have what is called **tactile texture**—texture that can actually be felt. In painting, the same term describes an uneven paint surface, produced when an artist uses thick pigment (a technique called **impasto**) to create a rough, three-dimensional paint surface.

Texture as Paint on Canvas

As the need and desire for illusionism in art faded, tactile texture became a more common aspect of painting. Paintings now could look like what they truly were—paint on canvas. Modifying the painting's surface became another option available to the artist. Van Gogh was an early proponent of the application of paint as an expressive element. The detail in **A** shows how short brushstrokes of thick, undiluted paint are used to build up the agitated, swirling patterns of van Gogh's images. The ridges and raised edges of the paint strokes are obvious to the viewer's eye.

The Next Step

The "relief painting" by Thornton Dial (**B**) shows a next step in bringing tactile texture into a painting. This painting is so complex with contrasts of value (light and dark) and added materials that we have to look closely at some parts to determine what is tactile texture and what is implied texture. In this case materials include cans, bottles, and a desiccated cat! The surprising result is one of paint and other materials working together to create a unified composition. The dividing line between painting and sculpture disappears in many such contemporary works when physical items are attached to the painted surface.

Texture in Architecture

Wharton Esherick designed a home (**C**) with gentle curves, muted colors, and the textures of stone, wood, and shingles. All these elements echo the surrounding tactile textures of the environment. In this case the sense of touch can accompany that of sight. Tactile texture can be felt as well as seen in an architectural context.

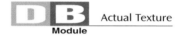

D B Module   Actual Texture

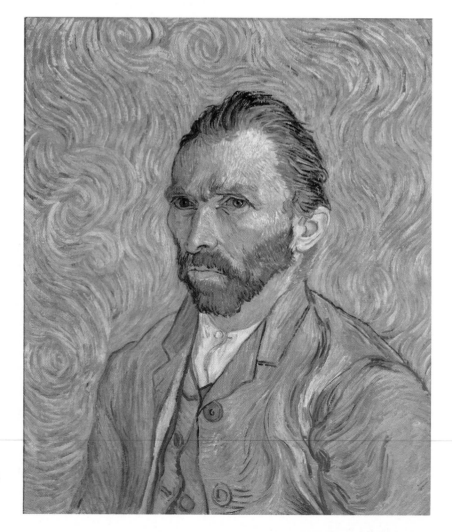

► **A**

Vincent van Gogh. *Portrait of the Artist.* 1889. Oil on canvas, 65 × 54.5 cm. Musée d'Orsay, Paris.

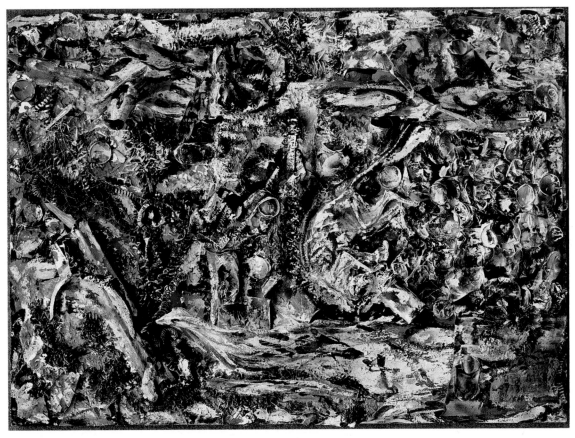

▲ **B**

Thornton Dial. *Contaminated Drifting Blues.* 1994. Desiccated cat, driftwood, aluminum cans, glass
bottle, found metal, canvas, enamel, spray paint, industrial sealing compound on surplus plywood,
5′ 7″ × 4′ 1″ × 1′ 5¹/₂″ (170 × 124 × 44 cm). Collection of William S. Arnett.

▶ **C**

Wharton Esherick. *Esherick
House.* Wharton Esherick
Museum, Paoli, Pennsylvania.

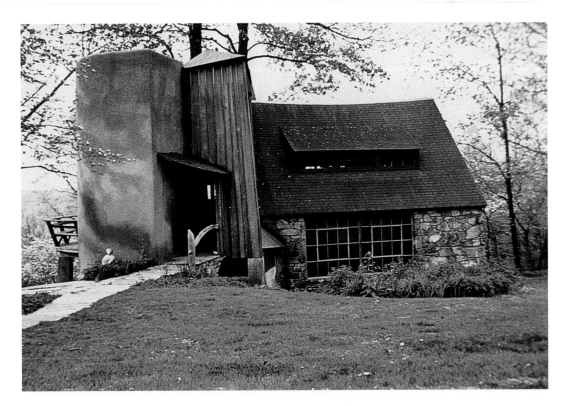

COLLAGE

Creating a design by pasting down bits and pieces of colored and textured papers, cloth, or other materials is called **collage**. This artistic technique has been popular for centuries, mainly in the area of **folk art**. Only since the twentieth century has collage been seriously considered a legitimate medium of the fine arts.

Why Collage?

The collage method is a very serviceable one. It saves the artist the painstaking, often tedious task of carefully reproducing textures in paint. Collage is an excellent **medium** for beginners. Forms can be altered or reshaped quickly and easily with scissors. Also, compositional arrangements can more easily be tested (before pasting) than when the design is indelibly rendered in paint.

Creating a Range of Tactile Sensations

Mary Bauermeister's collage titled *Progressions* **(A)** is composed of stones and sand on board. Even in the reproduction, one can imagine a range of tactile sensations, from bumpy to rough. Bauermeister has emphasized the textural qualities of her materials by reducing the composition to a few squares of progressively larger size. Within two of the squares there is also a progression in the size of the pebbles, creating a gradation in texture from fine to coarse. The physical presence of the materials can be seen in the shadows cast by this collage.

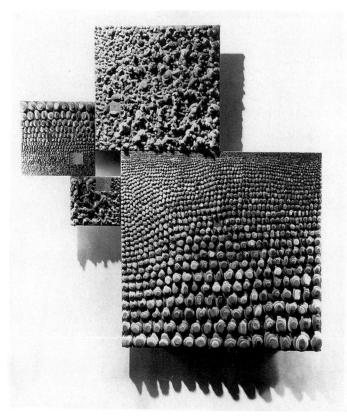

▲ **A**

Mary Bauermeister. *Progressions.* 1963. Pebbles and sand on four plywood panes, 4′ 3¹/₄″ × 3′ 11³/₈″ × 4³/₄″ (130.1 × 120.4 × 12 cm). The Museum of Modern Art, New York (Matthew T. Mellon Foundation Fund).

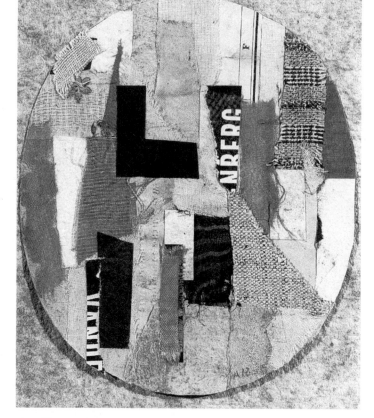

▲ **B**

Anne Ryan. *Untitled, No. 129.* c. 1948–1954. Collage on paper, 4³/₄″ × 4¹/₄″ (12.1 × 10.8 cm). Courtesy Joan T. Washburn Gallery, New York.

Anne Ryan, an American, worked mainly in collages of cloth. Her untitled collage in **B** shows various bits of cloth in contrasting weaves and textures interspersed with some scraps of printed papers. The dark and light pattern is interesting, but our attention is drawn mainly to the contrast of tactile textures.

Using Found Materials

Folk art is often characterized by an inventive use of found materials and may be considered one of the oldest forms of collage. Uninhibited by academic conventions about "appropriate" art materials, artists outside the mainstream have frequently taken joy in transforming trash into treasure. The many bottle caps in **C** take on a new life as the "skin" of a fantasy giraffe.

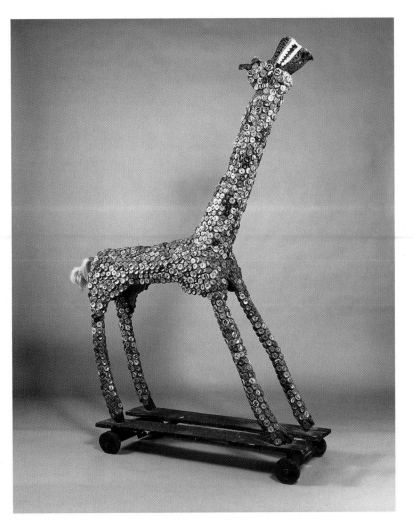

▲ **C**

Unidentified Artist. *Bottlecap Giraffe*. c. 1966. Bottle caps on painted wood with marbles and animal hair and fur, 6′ ¹/₂″ × 4′ 6″ × 1′ 5¹/₂″ (184.2 × 137.2 × 44.5 cm). Smithsonian American Art Museum, Washington, D.C. (gift of Herbert Waide Hemphill, Jr., and Museum Purchase made possible by Ralph Cross Johnson).

VISUAL IMPRESSION

In painting, artists can create the impression of texture on a flat, smooth painted surface. By reproducing the color and value patterns of familiar textures, painters encourage us to see textures where none actually exists. This is called **visual texture**. The impression of texture is purely visual; it cannot be felt or enjoyed by touch. It is only suggested to our eyes.

Choosing Subject Matter Rich in Texture

One of the pleasures of still-life paintings is the contrast of visual textures. These works, lacking story or emotional content, can be purely visual delights as the artist plays one simulated texture against another. Figure paintings can also delight the viewer with an emphasis on visual texture. The painting in **A** shows how the sheen of satin subtly reflects color from the surroundings and reveals one more aspect of that texture. This is an expected role for painting: to create such evocative visual texture. The painting in **B** conforms to this expectation in creating the qualities of smoothness for the eyes, cheeks, and lips, but elsewhere rougher marks suggest grainy "out of focus" areas. The transition from rough to smooth leads our eye to the focus of the painting.

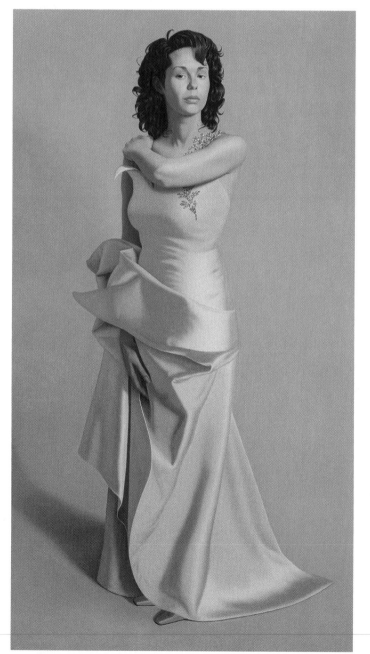

▲ **A**

Kurt Kauper. *Diva Project #12.* 1999.
Deitch Projects, New York.

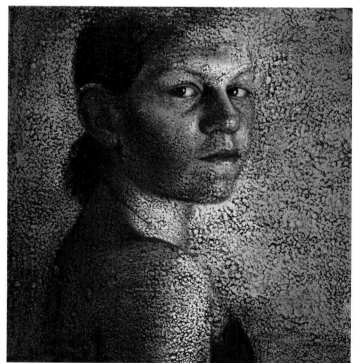

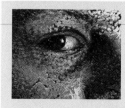

▲ **B**

Susan Moore. *Vanity (Portrait 1).* 2000.
Oil stick on canvas, 4′ × 3′ 11″.

Texture as Design Element

Visual texture can be an interesting design element even without subject matter or any pictorial reference. The work in **C** is titled *Exploration with a Pencil*. The artist used pencil and watercolor to create a composition based solely on areas of contrasting visual textures.

In contrast, Lissitzky's composition (see the detail in **D**) evokes a purity not of the everyday world. Such geometric precision calls for a smooth, manufactured perfection.

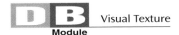 Visual Texture

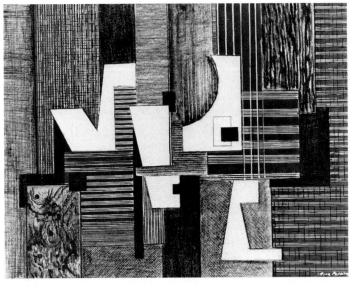

▲ **C**

Irene Rice Pereira. *Exploration with a Pencil.* 1940. Pencil, gouache, and metallic paint, 1′ 1⁷/₈″ × 1′ 5¹/₂″ (35.8 × 44.4 cm). The Museum of Modern Art, New York (gift of Mrs. Marjorie Falk).

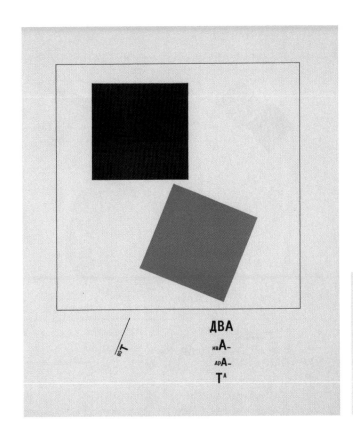

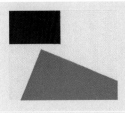

◄ **D**

El Lissitzky. *Of Two Squares: A Suprematist Tale in Six Constructions.* 1922. Illustrated book with letterpress cover and six letterpress illustrations, 10¹⁵/₁₆″ × 8⁷/₈″ (27.8 × 22.5 cm). Publisher: Skify, Berlin. Gift of the Judith Rothschild Foundation (89.2001.5).

TROMPE L'OEIL

The ultimate point in portraying visual texture is called **trompe l'oeil**, a French term meaning "to fool the eye." This style is commonly defined as "deceptive painting." In trompe l'oeil, the objects, in sharp focus, are delineated with meticulous care. The artist copies the exact visual color and value pattern of each surface. A deception occurs because the appearance of objects is so skillfully reproduced that we are momentarily fooled. We look closer, even though our rational brain identifies the image as a painting and not the actual object.

Continuing Popularity

You might think that now, with the camera able to capture easily all the details of appearance, we would have lost our appreciation for this type of painting. But we seem as intrigued as our ancestors in admiring the skill of an artist who can produce these effects. The 13-inch-high contemporary painting by Michael Flanagan **(A)** is incredible in the amount of tiny detail the artist has meticulously rendered.

◀ **A**

Michael Flanagan. *Chalybeate Springs*. 1991. Acrylic, ink, and graphite on composition board, 1' 1" × 1' 5" (33 × 43 cm). Courtesy of the artist.

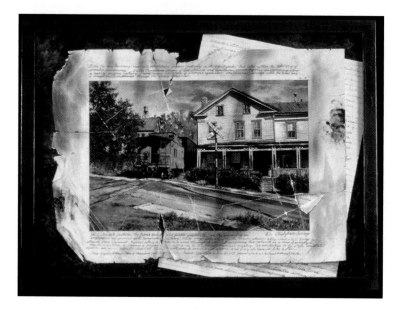

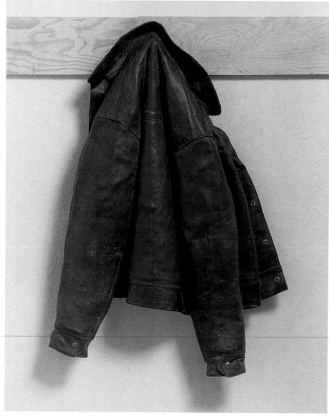

▶ **B**

Marilyn Levine. *Thom's Jacket*. 1989. Ceramic and mixed media, 2' 10³/₄" × 1' 11" × 5" (88 × 58 × 13 cm). OK Harris Works of Art, New York.

Trompe L'oeil in Sculpture, Painting, and Architecture

Certainly, twentieth- and twenty-first-century artistic emphasis has been on abstractions, distortion, and nonobjective patterns. But in much art the trompe l'oeil tradition continues. In sculpture, the hanging jacket **(B)** by Marilyn Levine is incredibly realistic. But it is made of ceramic. The illusion is superb, and we enjoy being visually fooled.

Artists working in this area often purposely arrange contrasting textures as in **C**. Here the reflective glass and cold metal contrast with the powdery sugar inside the container.

It would also be a mistake to think of trompe l'oeil art as confined to painters with fine brushes laboring over easel paintings. More and more today in our cities, we are seeing examples of trompe l'oeil art such as **D**. This "painting" is truly enormous in scale. The entire blank wall of the side of a building has been painted with carefully rendered architectural features and details matching the actual three-dimensional facade.

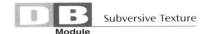

Subversive Texture

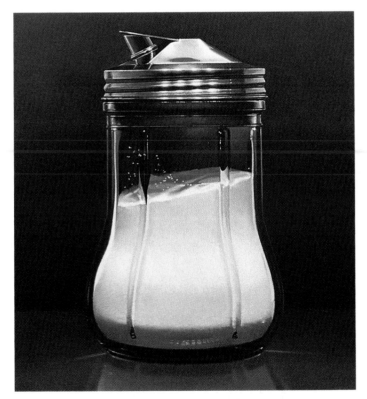

▲ **C**

Ralph Goings. *Sugar Shaker.* 2002. Oil on canvas, 2′ 11″ × 2′ 8″ (40.64 × 50.8 cm). OK Harris Works of Art, New York.

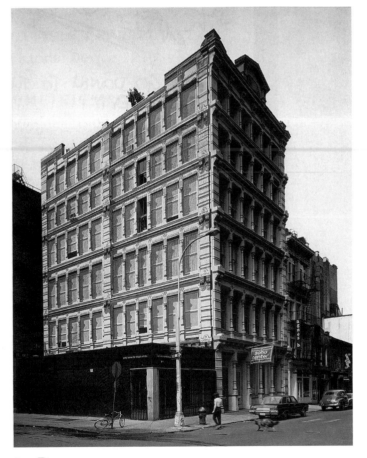

▲ **D**

Richard Haas. *112 Prince Street Facade, Prince and Greene Streets, New York.* 1974–1975. Painted building commissioned by City Walls, Inc. Brooke Alexander, Inc., New York. Art © Richard Haas/Licensed by VAGA, New York, New York.

TRANSLATING SPACE TO TWO DIMENSIONS

Several art forms are three-dimensional and therefore occupy space: ceramics, jewelry and metalwork, weaving, and sculpture, to name a few. In traditional sculpture or in a purely abstract pattern of forms, it is important for us to move about and enjoy the changing spatial patterns from various angles. Architecture, of course, is an art form mainly preoccupied with the enclosure of three-dimensional space. A photograph of architecture such as that of the interior court of BCE Place in Toronto **(A)** can only hint at the spectacular feeling of space and volume we experience when actually in the area. The many arches form a concave shell when seen from the interior, yet our feeling of the *space* is that of a convex volume pushing upward.

In two-dimensional art forms, such as drawings, paintings, and prints, the artist often wants to convey a feeling of space or depth. Here space is an illusion, for the images rendered on paper, canvas, or boards are essentially flat.

Exploring Options

This illusion of space is an option for the artist. The photograph in **B** emphasizes the rhythm of trees on a hillside and is most interesting as a flat pattern. A different photograph by the same photographer taken the same day in the same region emphasizes the space of the Western landscape **(C)**. *Gros Ventre #3* **(C)** creates a sense of this space with many spatial clues: overlap, diminishing size, and effects of atmosphere.

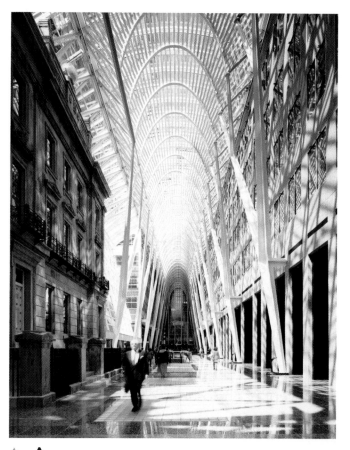

▲ **A**

The Galleria, BCE Place, Toronto.

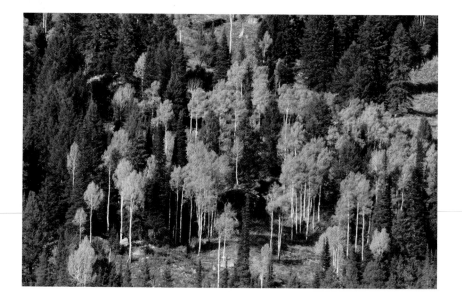

▶ **B**

Michel Taupin. *Rhythm Study.* 2006. Digital photograph.

The photograph in **B** and the painting in **D** have a surprising commonality: a vertical line at the center which taken alone would tend to flatten the space. In **B** this line is suggested by the continuation of a few light tree trunks. In **D** a lamppost divides the painting into two rectangular areas. Nevertheless, Gustave Caillebotte's painting in **D** pierces the **picture plane**. We are encouraged to forget that a painting is merely a flat piece of canvas. Instead, we are almost standing with the figures in the painting, and our eyes are led to the distant buildings across the plaza and down the streets that radiate from the intersection.

Caillebotte's images suggest three-dimensional forms in a real space. The picture plane no longer exists as a **plane**, but becomes a window into a simulated three-dimensional world created by the artist. A very convincing illusion is created. Artists throughout the centuries have studied this problem of presenting a visual illusion of space and depth. By the nineteenth century a variety of devices were known and used. With the advent of photography these devices became less important to many painters.

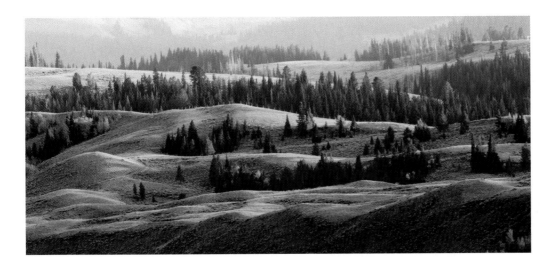

◀   **C**

Michel Taupin. *Gros Ventre #3.*
2006. Digital photograph.

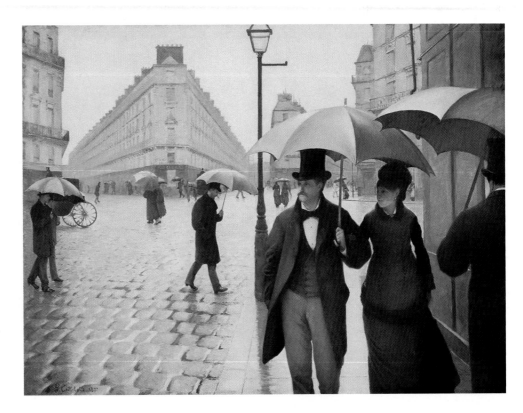

▶   **D**

Gustave Caillebotte. *Rue de Paris;
Temps de Pluie (Paris Street, Rainy Day).*
1877. Oil on canvas, 6′ 11¹/₂″ × 9′³/₄″
(212.2 × 276.2 cm). The Art Institute
of Chicago (Charles H. and Mary F. S.
Worcester Fund Collection, 1964.336).

SIZE

The easiest way to create an illusion of space or distance is through size. Very early in life we observe the visual phenomenon that as objects get farther away they appear to become smaller. Complex naturalistic artworks will employ many spatial clues, but it is possible to find artworks that choose a more limited vocabulary effectively. Abraham Walkowitz's painting **(A)** relies primarily on contrast of size. In this case the elements of the landscape are painted as flatter shapes; however, the foreground figures are larger than those in the middle and far distance. Size difference conforms with our understanding of how we perceive space, yet the artist is able to emphasize the shapes of rocks and figures and even glimpses of the ocean by playing down other effects of space.

Spatial Effect with Abstract Shapes

Notice that the size factor can be effective even with abstract shapes, when the forms have no literal meaning or representational quality **(B)**. The smaller squares automatically begin to recede, and we see a spatial pattern. With abstract figures, the spatial effect is more pronounced if (as in **B**) the same shape is repeated in various sizes. The device is less effective when different shapes are used **(C)**. The repetition of figures and rocks in **A** is consistent with the example shown in **B**.

In **D** we see an example that purposefully rejects change in size. The two squares are different colors and in different positions but offer no real spatial contrast. Later in the series **(E)** these two "actors" take on contrasting roles and the red square (now larger than the black) advances in the space.

 Relative Size and Linear Perspective
Module

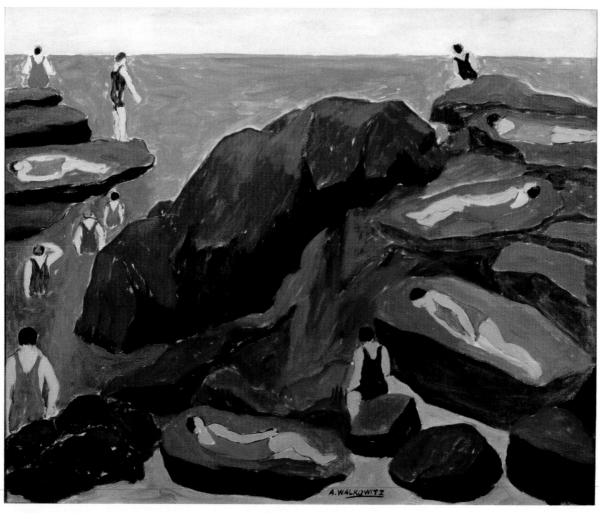

▲ **A**

Abraham Walkowitz. *Bathers on the Rocks.* 1935. Oil on canvas, 2′ 1″ × 2′ 6⅛″.
Tampa Museum of Art Collection, Museum Purchase (1984.15).

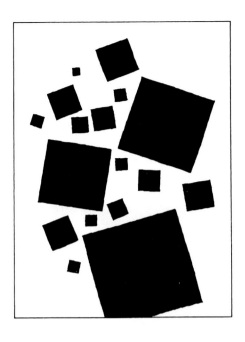

◀ **B**

If the same shape is repeated in different sizes, a spatial effect can be achieved.

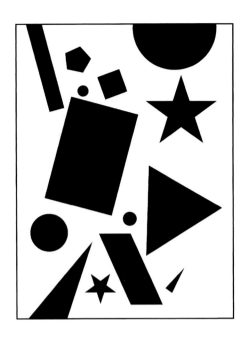

▶ **C**

With differing shapes, the spatial illusion is not as clear.

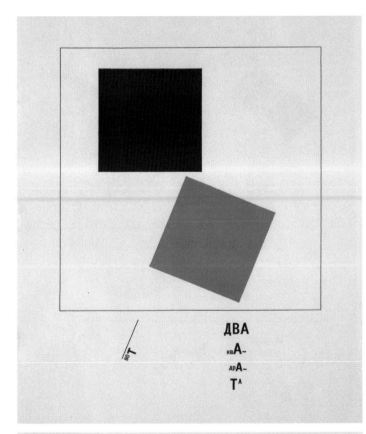

▲ **D**

El Lissitzky. *Of Two Squares: A Suprematist Tale in Six Constructions.* 1922. Illustrated book with letterpress cover and six letterpress illustrations, 10 15/16″ × 8 7/8″ (27.8 × 22.5 cm). Publisher: Skify, Berlin. Gift of the Judith Rothschild Foundation (89.2001.5).

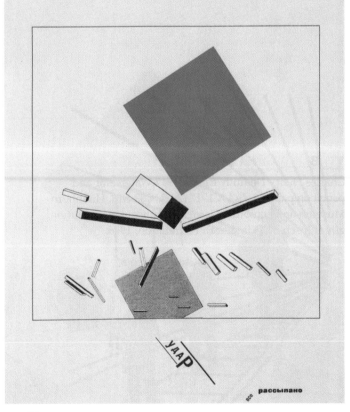

▲ **E**

El Lissitzky. *Of Two Squares: A Suprematist Tale in Six Constructions.* 1922. Illustrated book with letterpress cover and six letterpress illustrations, 10 15/16″ × 8 7/8″ (27.8 × 22.5 cm). Publisher: Skify, Berlin. Gift of the Judith Rothschild Foundation (89.2001.5).

OVERLAPPING

Overlapping is a simple device for creating an illusion of depth. When we look at the design in **A**, we see four elements and have no way to judge their spatial relationships. In **B** the relationships are immediately clear due to overlapping. Each shape hides part of another because it is on top of or in front of the other. A sense of depth is established.

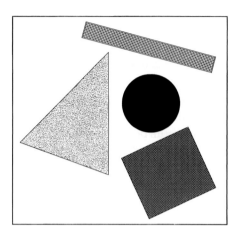

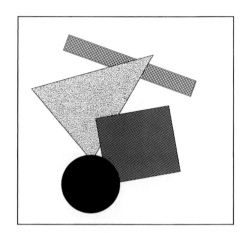

◄ **A**

No real feeling of space or depth can be discerned.

► **B**

Simple overlapping of the shapes establishes the spatial relationships.

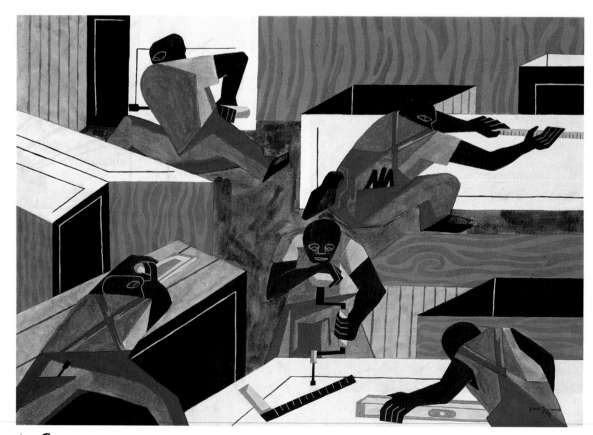

▲ **C**

Jacob Lawrence. *Cabinet Makers.* 1946. Gouache with pencil underdrawing on paper; sheet: 1′ 10″ × 2′ 6³/₁₆″ (55.9 × 76.6 cm), image: 1′ 9³/₄″ × 2′ 6″ (55.2 × 76.1 cm). Hirshhorn Museum and Sculpture Garden, Smithsonian Institution, gift of Joseph H. Hirshhorn, 1966 (66.2915).

Emphasizing Figure

As the image in **B** shows, the
a composition can emphasiz
architectural features. These
a blanket, the card table, and
more importance than an ac
relationships.

The painting and collag
shows that this device can b
of the work are "photorealis
see an arrangement based on
cloth pattern and other verti
arranged within this grid, an
based mainly on vertical loca

Overlapping with and without Size Differences

In Jacob Lawrence's painting **(C)**, there is no size difference
between the cabinetmakers in the front and those in back.
But we do understand their respective positions because
of the overlapping that hides portions of the figures.
Because overlapping is the primary spatial device used,
the space created is admittedly very shallow. The pattern
of two-dimensional shapes is stronger than an illusion of
depth. Notice that when overlapping is combined with size
differences, as in Hayllar's painting **(D)**, the spatial sensation
is greatly increased.

Spatial Depth with Abstract Shapes

The same principle can be illustrated with abstract shapes,
as the designs in **E** show. The design on top, which combines
overlapping and size differences, gives a much more effective
feeling of spatial recession.

See also *Transparency,* page 222.

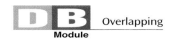 Overlapping

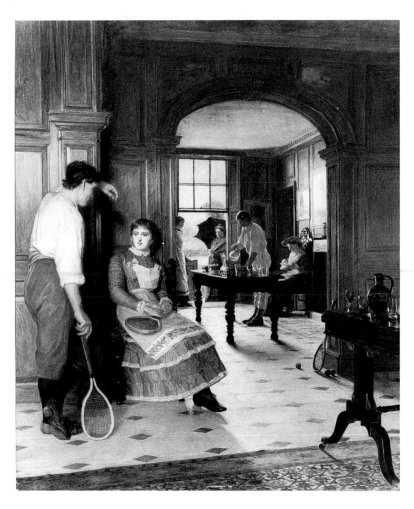

▲ **C**

Tom Wesselmann. *Still Life #12*
of fabric, photogravure, metal
(1.22 × 1.22 m). Smithsonian *A*
Washington, D.C. Art © Tom W
VAGA, New York, New York.

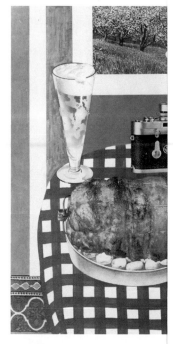

◄ **D**

Edith Hayllar. *A Summer Shower.* 1883. Oil
on panel, 1' 9" × 1' 5²/₅"(53.4 × 44.2 cm).
The Bridgeman Art Library.

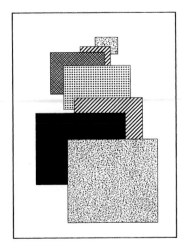

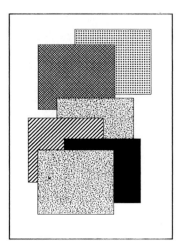

► **E**

The design on the bottom does not give as
much feeling of spatial depth as the one on top.

VERTICAL LOCA

Vertical location is a spatial
the page or format indicates a
higher an object, the farther b
painting shown in **A**, the artis
location to give us a sense of
eyes, the effect, though charm
to have little suggestion of de
almost on top of each other al
device was used widely in Ne
Oriental art and was immedia
cultures.

AERIAL PERSPECTIVE

Aerial, or *atmospheric*, **perspective** describes the use of color
or value (dark and light) to show depth. The photograph
in **A** illustrates the idea: The value contrast between distant
objects gradually lessens, and contours become less distinct.
Greater contrast advances, diminished contrast retreats.
The color would change also, with objects that are far away
appearing more neutral in color and taking on a bluish
character.

Using Size with Value
to Create Perspective

In **B** the feeling of spatial recession is based entirely on
differences in size. Illustration **C** shows the same design,
but the spatial feeling is greatly increased because the
smaller shapes become progressively darker and show
less value contrast with the background.

▶ **A**

Miskina. *The*
1593–1595. F
on paper, 30
rights reserv

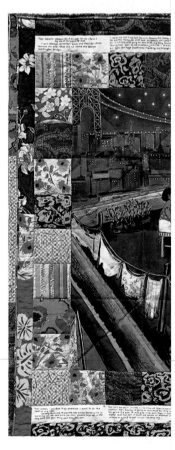

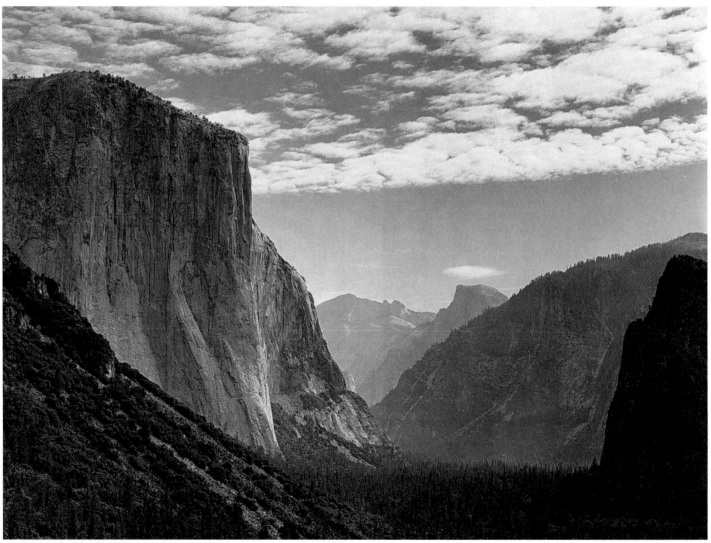

▲ **A**

Ansel Adams. *Yosemite Valley from Inspiration Point.* c. 1936. Photograph. Copyright © 1993
by the Trustees of the Ansel Adams Publishing Rights Trust. All rights reserved.

We ordinarily think of aerial perspective and value changes to show distance as applied to vast landscapes with distant hills, as in **A**. But look at **D**. Of course, the overlapping immediately establishes that the standing woman is behind the figure in the foreground. But notice how the sense of depth is increased because the light dress is similar to the light mirror and wall. If the standing figure were dark, she would tend to merge with the crouching figure, creating a flatter composition. Aerial perspective has many applications.

See also *Value and Space*, page 246, and *Color and Space*, page 272.

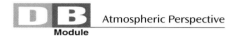
Atmospheric Perspective

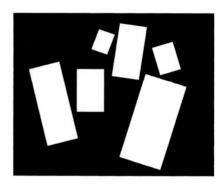

▲ **B**

A feeling of spatial recession can be achieved simply by reducing the size of elements as they apparently recede into the distance.

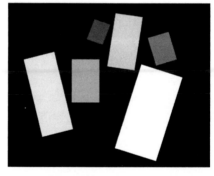

▲ **C**

Spatial recession can be made even more effective if the receding objects blend more and more with the background.

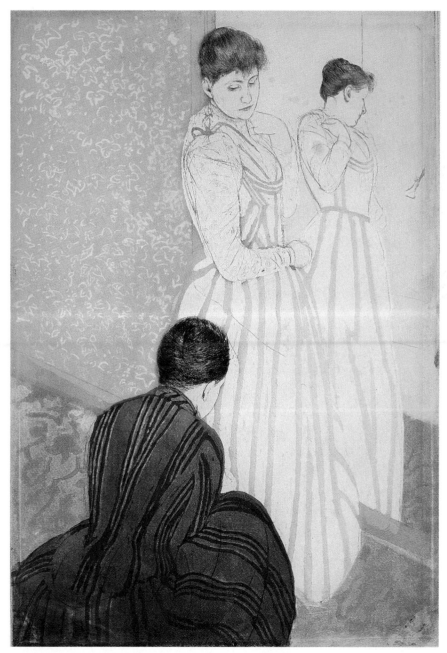

▲ **D**

Mary Cassatt. *The Fitting*. 1890–1891. Drypoint and aquatint on laid paper; plate: 1′ 2³/₄″ × 10″ (37.5 × 25.4 cm), sheet: 1′ 6¹³/₁₆″ × 1′ ¹/₈″ (47.8 × 30.8 cm). National Gallery of Art, Washington, D.C. (Chester Dale Collection, 1963.10.252).

LINEAR PERSPECTIVE

Linear perspective is a complex spatial system based on a relatively simple visual phenomenon: As parallel lines recede, they appear to converge and to meet on an imaginary line called the horizon, or eye level. We have all noticed this effect with railroad tracks or a highway stretching away into the distance. From this everyday visual effect, the whole science of linear perspective has developed. Artists had long noted this convergence of receding parallel lines, but not until the Renaissance was the idea introduced that parallel lines on parallel planes all converge at the same place (a **vanishing point**) on the horizon. Uccello was an early proponent of this spatial system, which can be seen in **A**. The fallen lances are arranged to provide lines pointing to a common vanishing point, establishing the space in which the battle is staged.

Linear Perspective as Unifier

Linear perspective was a dominant device for spatial representation in Western art for several hundred years. It is easy to see why. First, linear perspective does approximate the visual image; it does appear realistic for artists striving to reproduce what the eye sees. Second, by its very nature, perspective acts as a unifying factor. The lines in **A**, receding to a common point, impose an order on a chaotic subject.

Although linear perspective is based on our perception, it is limited to a single fixed vantage point, or a **monocular** depth clue. It is not based on the **parallax** of our two-eyed perception of depth. A strong use of linear perspective can therefore have an artificial quality as seen both in the Uccello and in **B**. Our viewpoint for **B** faces the corner of the gas station, offering a perspective on two sets of planes that are perpendicular to each other. These present two sets of parallel lines that apparently converge at two points on the low horizon line: the right one at the corner of the painting and the left one outside the format.

Linear Perspective in Non-Western Cultures

Although the introduction of, and continued fascination with, linear perspective as a spatial device was mainly a Western development, examples can be found from other cultures. The Japanese woodcut in **C** is an example. The diagonals of the room's floor, walls, and ceiling are clearly receding to a common vanishing point. This print combines a Western system of spatial depiction with the Japanese emphasis on two-dimensional shapes and patterns.

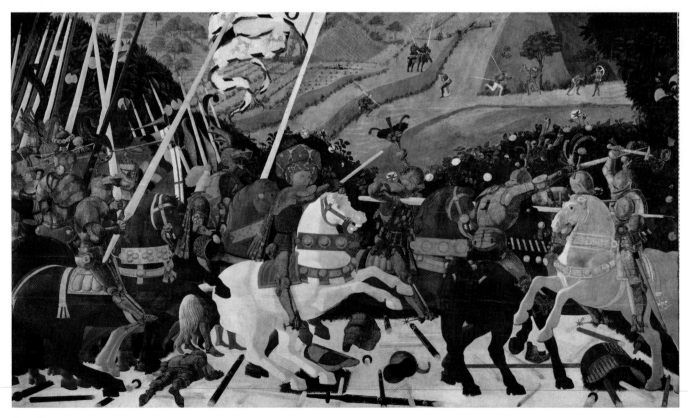

▲ **A**

Paolo Uccello. *The Battle of San Romano in 1432.* Condottiere Niccolo da Tolentino leading the Florentine forces against Siena. National Gallery, London, Great Britain.

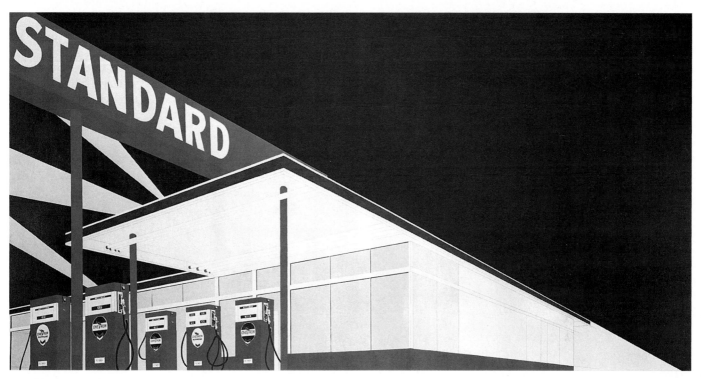

▲ **B**

Edward Ruscha. *Standard Station, Amarillo, Texas.* 1963. Oil on canvas, 5' 4⁷/₈" × 10' 1³/₄" (164.9 × 309.4 cm). Hood Museum of Art, Dartmouth College, Hanover, New Hampshire (gift of James Meeker, Class of 1958, in memory of Lee English, class of 1958, scholar, poet, athlete, and friend).

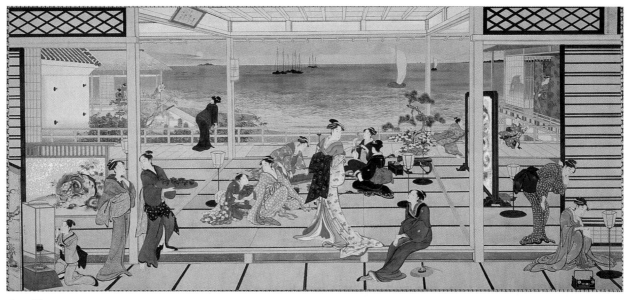

▲ **C**

Kitagawa Utamaro. *Moonlight Revelry at the Dozo Sagami.* Edo Period, Japan. Ink and color on paper, 147.0 × 318.6 cm. Freer Gallery of Art, Smithsonian Institution, Washington, D.C. (gift of Charles Lang Freer, F1903.54).

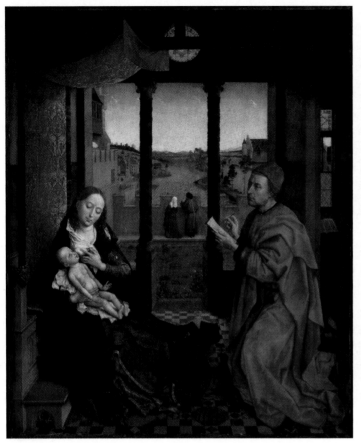

Rogier van der Weyden. *Saint Luke Drawing the Virgin and Child*. c. 1435. Oil and tempera on panel, 4' 6 ¹/₈" × 3' 7 ⁵/₈" (137.5 × 110.8 cm). Museum of Fine Arts, Boston (gift of Mr. and Mrs. Henry Lee Higginson, 1893, 93.153). Photograph © 2007 Museum of Fine Arts, Boston.

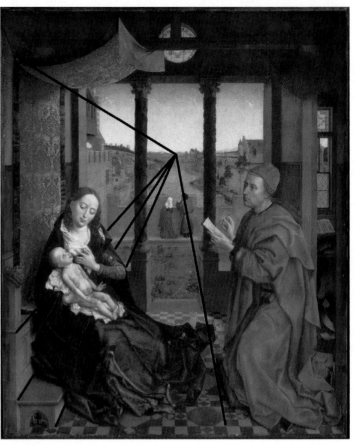

The composition of the painting in **A** involves parallel lines converging at a vanishing point on the horizon.

ONE-POINT PERSPECTIVE

The complete study of linear perspective is a complicated task. Entire books are devoted to this one subject alone, and it cannot be fully described here. The procedures for using linear perspective were rediscovered and developed during the Renaissance. From drawings, we see that in the fifteenth and sixteenth centuries many artists preceded paintings with careful perspective studies of the space involved.

Probably few recent painters have made such a strict use of linear perspective. For the architect, city planner, interior designer, set designer, and so on, an ability to do perspective drawing is essential for presenting their ideas. But it is important for any designer or artist to know the general principles of linear perspective, for it is a valuable tool for representing an illusion of depth.

Positioning the Horizon

The concept of linear perspective starts with the placement of a horizontal line, the "horizon," that corresponds to the "eye level" of the artist. On this line is located the needed number of vanishing points to which lines or edges will be directed. It might seem that working by a "formula" such as linear perspective provides would lead to a certain sameness and monotony in pictures. This is not true, because the artist's choice in the placement of the horizon and vanishing points on the format (or outside it) is almost unlimited. The same scene drawn by the same artist would result in radically different visual compositions by altering these initial choices.

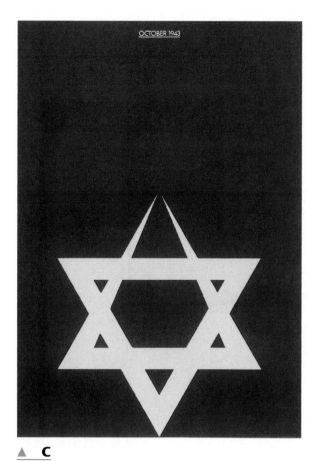

▲ **C**

Per Arnoldi (Denmark). Poster commemorating the
50th anniversary of the Danish Jews' flight to Sweden.
1993. Client: Thanks to Scandinavia, New York.

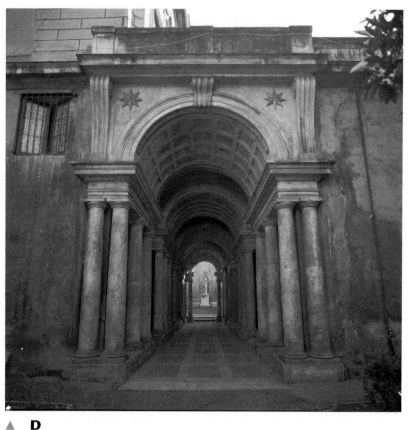

▲ **D**

Francesco Borromini. Arcade, Palazzo Spada, Rome. c. 1635–1650.

Exploring One-Point Perspective

Rogier van der Weyden's painting **(A)** is an example of **one-point perspective**. A single point has been placed on the horizon line, and all the lines of objects at right angles to the plane of the canvas converge toward that point. The lines of the tiled floor, the throne, and architectural details in the landscape, if extended, would meet at this common point **(B)**. The figures are placed in this created volume. In this case the view actually extends to the horizon. The horizon is another term for eye level, which can be found even if our view is more limited. Often the eye level is coincident with the eyes in the figures depicted. In the van der Weyden painting, we can observe that our vantage point is slightly elevated (the horizon line is higher than the eyes of the figures), and we are looking down on the figures.

No diagram is needed to illustrate the one-point perspective used in **C**. This poster, commemorating the flight of Danish Jews to Sweden, transforms one triangle of the Star of David into receding lines suggestive of movement to the distance.

The rules of one-point perspective can also be used to manipulate our experience of actual space. This is the case with Borromini's Arcade for the Palazzo Spada in Rome **(D)**. The columns decrease in size, their spacing gets shorter, and the pavement narrows down the arcade. This very short corridor appears longer due to these systematic reductions in size, shape, and spacing all focused on a single vanishing point of one-point perspective.

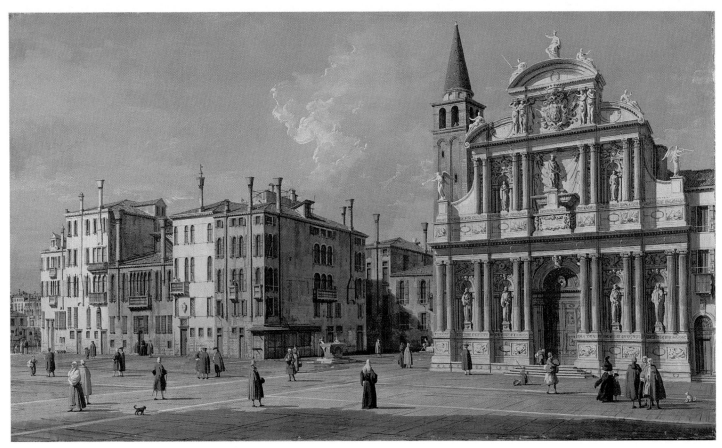

▲ **A**

Giovanni Antonio Canal Canaletto (1697–1798). Campo Santa Maria Zobenigo.
Venice, Italy. Oil on canvas, 1′ 6¹/₂″ × 2′ 6³/₄″ (47 × 78.1 cm). Private collection.

TWO-POINT PERSPECTIVE

One-point perspective presents a very organized and unified
spatial image. **Two-point perspective** probably appears
to us as more natural and lifelike. Here we are not looking
head-on at the scene. Now, it is being viewed from an angle.
No objects are parallel to the picture plane, and all edges
recede to two points on the horizon line. This more nearly
approximates our usual visual experience.

The painting by Canaletto **(A)** illustrates the idea. In the
diagram **(B)** the horizon line is shown on which there are
two points, and the various architectural lines of the different buildings recede to them.

A Static Effect Can Be a Dramatic Element

In a perspective drawing or painting, strict two-point perspective can appear a bit posed and artificial. It assumes
we are standing still and looking without moving. This is
possible and does happen but is not typical of our daily
lives. Our visual knowledge is gained by looking at objects
or scenes from many changing viewpoints. Photography can
capture a still view, and film and video have conditioned us
to rapidly changing points of view. Perhaps for these reasons
linear perspective is not as frequently used in painting today
as it was for centuries. However, painting and drawing still
have the power to share a still and careful observation. The
contemporary painting by Felix de la Concha **(C)** shows
how two-point perspective can be a dramatic element of
composition and can resonate with our daily experience. An
alleyway may seem to be a banal subject, but de la Concha's
attention to the narrow space and surprising facade is
extraordinary.

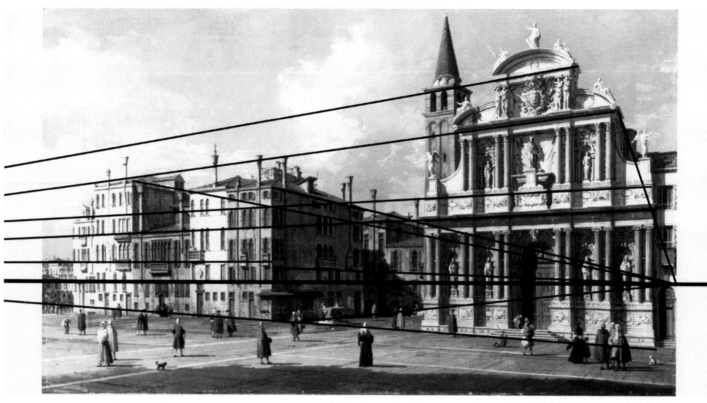

▲ **B**

Diagram superimposed over painting **A**. The angled lines of the architecture would meet at two points on the horizon.

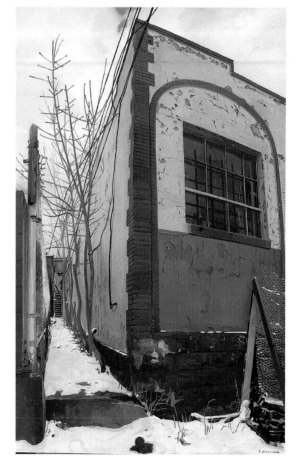

▶ **C**

Felix de la Concha. *Así en el cielo (As in Heaven)*. 2001. Oil on canvas on board, 4′ × 2′ 5 1/2″ (121.9 × 74.9 cm). Karl and Jennifer Salatka Collection, Concept Art Gallery, Pittsburgh, Pennsylvania.

MULTIPOINT PERSPECTIVE

In perspective drawing the vertical edges of forms generally remain vertical. Sometimes a third vanishing point is added above (or below) the horizon so that the vertical parallels also taper and converge. This technique is useful to suggest great height, such as looking up at (or down from) a city skyscraper.

Although city streets or a line of buildings might be laid out in orderly rectangular rows of parallel lines, often in real life a variety of angles will be present. This entails the use of **multipoint perspective**. Different objects will have separate sets of vanishing points if they are not parallel to each other. If they are all on a plane parallel to the ground plane, all vanishing points will still be on a common horizon line. This can reproduce our visual experience where rarely in any scene are all the elements in neat, parallel placement. In the painting by Tooker **(A)**, the long corridors of the subway recede at several different angles from the center foreground. Each area thus has a different vanishing point **(B)**. The anxiety-producing feeling of the subway as a maze is clearly presented.

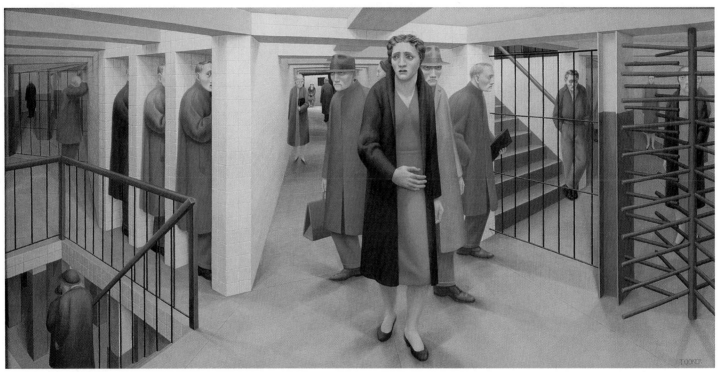

▲ **A**

The angled corridors use several vanishing points. George Tooker. *The Subway.* 1950. Egg tempera on composition board; sight: 1′ 6 ¹/₈″ × 3′¹/₈″ (46 × 91.8 cm), frame: 2′ 2″ × 3′ 8″ (66 × 111.8 cm). Whitney Museum of American Art, New York (purchase with funds from the Juliana Force Purchase Award 50.23).

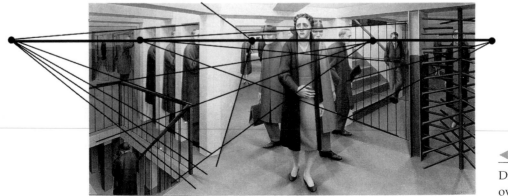

◄ **B**
Diagram superimposed over painting **A**.

For Dynamic Spatial Effect

Multiple vanishing points create a dynamic spatial effect in
a two-dimensional composition even when the composition
is as abstract as the example seen in **C**. The source of this
image may be architectural, but there are no representational
details. The linear perspective leading to three vanishing
points conveys the sense of space. Two vanishing points
are on the horizon line. A third vanishing point (below the
bottom of the picture) is implied by the converging vertical
lines, suggesting a downward view.

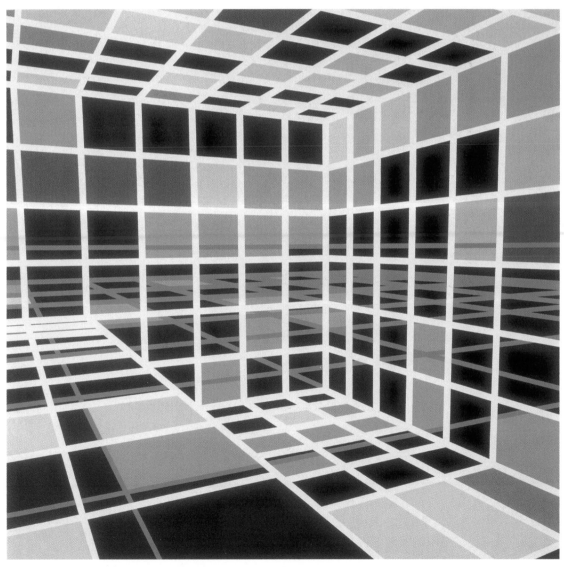

▲ **C**

Sarah Morris. *Pools–Crystal House (Miami)*. 2002. Gloss household paint on canvas,
7′1/4″ × 7′1/4″ (214 × 214 cm). Courtesy Friedrich Petzel Gallery, New York.

A DIFFERENT POINT OF VIEW

To introduce a dramatic, dynamic quality into their pictures, many artists have used what is called **amplified perspective**. This device reproduces the visual image but in the very special view that occurs when an item is pointed directly at the viewer.

Playing with Perspective

A familiar example is the old Army recruiting poster, in which Uncle Sam's pointing finger is thrust forward ("I Want You") and right at the viewer. The same effect can be seen in **A**, in which the figure's legs are thrust directly at us. In this exaggerated example we are presented with the image of the feet being unbelievably large in **juxtaposition** with the body. The photograph heightens a phenomenon that we see in less-dramatic terms every day but to which we unconsciously adjust to conform to our knowledge of the human figure.

In Tony Mendoza's photograph **(B)**, we are presented with an unusual vantage point on a familiar subject. Here the stems of the plants, rather than the flowers, come toward the viewer. This camera angle from below gives us a fresh view and a "bugs-eye" glimpse of the garden.

The contrast of size we see in Yvonne Jacquette's painting in **C** creates an amplified space in a composition that might first capture our attention for its color, pattern, or shapes. The river and harbor make a large, essentially flat shape. The pattern of lights and shadows creates a jewel-like decorative effect. Against this surface composition an amplified perspective evokes a deep space. Individual windows on the foreground tower are as large as the distant image of the Statue of Liberty. This juxtaposition might be hard to hold in one view in actual experience but a painting can render it visible.

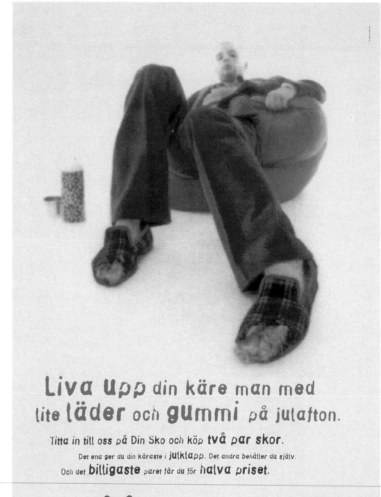
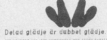

► **A**

Ad for Din Sko shoe store, Sweden. Agency: Inform Advertising Agency, Gothenburg. Art Director: Tommy Ostberg. Photo: Christian Coinberg.

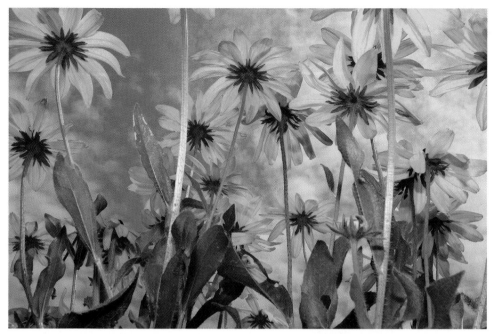

▲ **B**

Tony Mendoza. *Yellow Flowers.*
Photograph on 100% rag paper,
1′ 9″ × 2′ 8″.

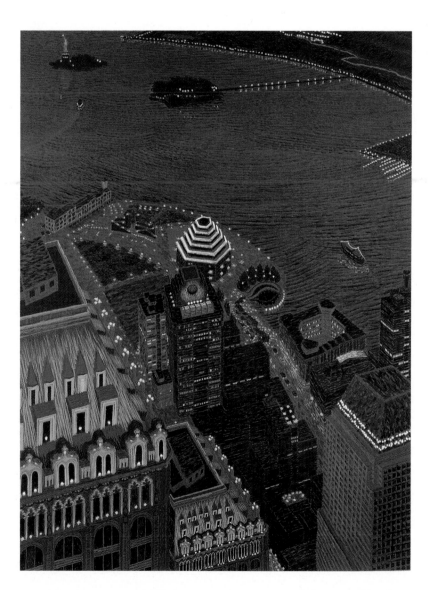

▶ **C**

Yvonne Jacquette. *Mixed Heights and
Harbor from World Trade Center II.* 1998.
Oil on canvas, 5′ 10¹⁄₄″ × 4′ 10³⁄₈″.
Private collection, courtesy of DC
Moore Gallery, New York.

A PICTORIAL DEVICE

Looking at a figure or object from more than one vantage point simultaneously is called **multiple perspective**. Several different views are combined in one image. This device has been used widely in twentieth- and twenty-first-century art, although the idea is centuries old.

Multiple Perspective in Ancient Art

Multiple perspective was a basic pictorial device in Egyptian art, as illustrated in a typical Egyptian painted figure **(A)**. The artist's aim was not necessarily to reproduce the visual image but to give a composite image, combining the most descriptive or characteristic view of each part of the body. In **B** which view of the head is most descriptive, which most certainly a head? The profile obviously says "head" more clearly. But what about the eye **(C)**? The eye in profile is a confusing shape, but the front view is what we know as an

eye. The Egyptians solved this problem by combining a side view of the head with a front view of the eye. Each body part is thus presented in its most characteristic aspect: a front view of the torso, a side view of the legs, and so forth.

Multiple Perspective Today

Since the twentieth century, with the camera able to effortlessly give the fixed visual ("realistic") view, artists have been free to explore other avenues of perception, including multiple perspective. Douglas Cooper employs multiple perspective to capture a dramatic breadth of experiences in one two-dimensional composition **(D)**. The hilly, winding river valley of Pittsburgh is brought together in a mural where the space seems to bend and curve. The straight lines of linear perspective curve when a two-dimensional picture expands to hold more than the view of a single picture plane.

Straight lines yielding to a curved pattern are evident in David Hockney's photographic **montage** of the Brooklyn Bridge **(E)**. The point of view shifts from downward to forward to upward, creating multiple picture planes and multiple perspectives.

As you have noticed, multiple perspective does not give a clear spatial pattern of the position occupied by each element. This aspect has been sacrificed to give a more subjective, **conceptual** view of forms.

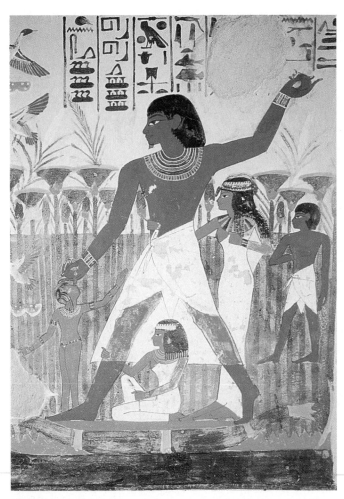

▲ **A**

Detail of Wall Painting in the Tomb of Nakht, Thebes. c. 1410 B.C. Victor R. Boswell, Jr., National Geographic photographer.

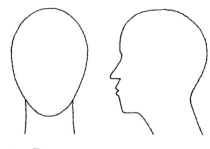

▲ **B**

To the Egyptians the head shown in profile seemed to be the most characteristic view.

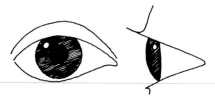

▲ **C**

The front view of the eye gives the clearest, most descriptive view.

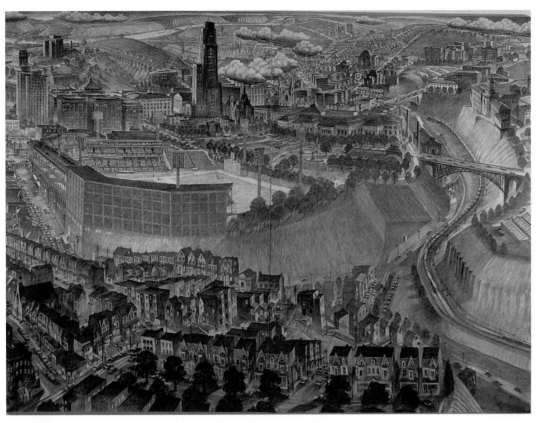

▲ **D**

Douglas Cooper. Portion of *Senator John Heinz Regional History Center Mural.* (1992–1993). Courtesy of the artist.

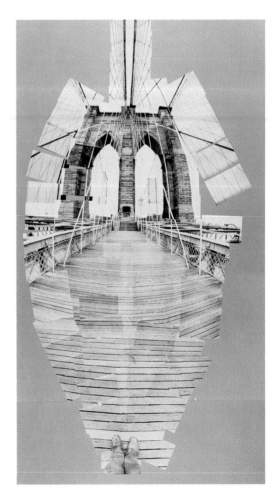

► **E**

David Hockney. *Brooklyn Bridge, November 28, 1982.* Photographic collage, 9′ 1″ × 4′ 10″. Collection © David Hockney.

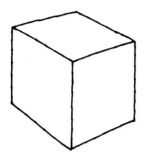

◀ A

In linear perspective, parallel lines gradually draw closer together as they recede into the distance.

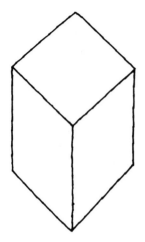

◀ B

In isometric projection, parallel lines remain parallel.

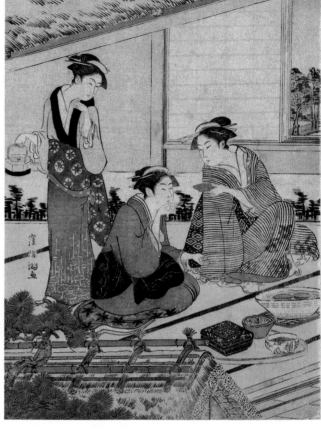

▲ C

Kubo Shunman. *Women in a Tea House*. Late 1780s. Color woodblock print, sheet: 33 × 23 cm. © The Cleveland Museum of Art (bequest of Edward L. Whittemore, 1930.208).

A SPATIAL ILLUSION

For centuries Oriental artists did not make wide use of linear perspective. Another spatial convention was satisfactory for their pictorial purposes. In Oriental art planes recede on the diagonal, but the lines, instead of converging to a vanishing point, remain parallel. Illustration **A** shows a box drawn in linear perspective; **B** shows the box drawn in the Oriental method. In the West we refer to image **B** as an **isometric projection**.

Isometric Projection in the East

Traditional Japanese prints such as **C** illustrate this device. The effect is different from Western perspective but certainly not disturbing. The rather flat decorative effect seems perfectly in keeping with the treatment of the figures, with a strong linear pattern and flat color areas. The artist does not stress three-dimensional solidity or roundness in the figures, so we do not miss this quality in the architecture or the space.

Isometric Projection in the West

Isometric projection, although used extensively in engineering and mechanical drawings, is rarely seen in Western painting. The self-portrait by David Hockney **(D)** uses this device, and the change from the linear perspective is fresh and intriguing. Hockney has explored virtually every method of spatial organization mentioned in this chapter in prints, drawings, paintings, and photography.

The work by Josef Albers **(E)** uses this idea in a purely abstract way. The artist creates a geometric shape drawn in an isometric-type view. The interesting aspect of the design, however, is the shifting, puzzling spatial pattern that emerges. The direction of any plane seems to advance, then recede, then to be flat in a fascinating **ambiguity**.

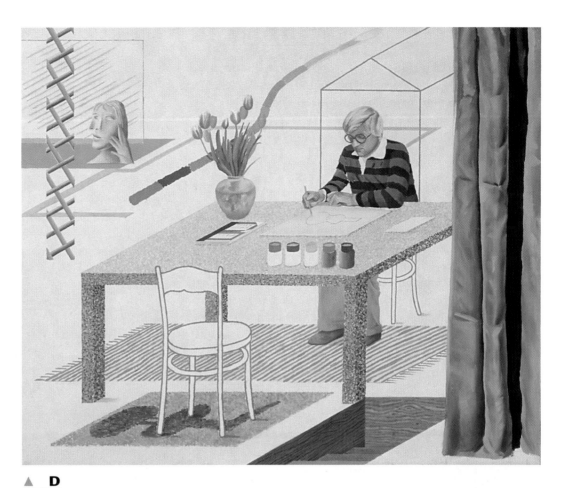

▲ **D**

David Hockney. *Self-Portrait with Blue Guitar.* 1977. Oil on canvas, 5′ × 6′ (1.52 × 1.83 m).

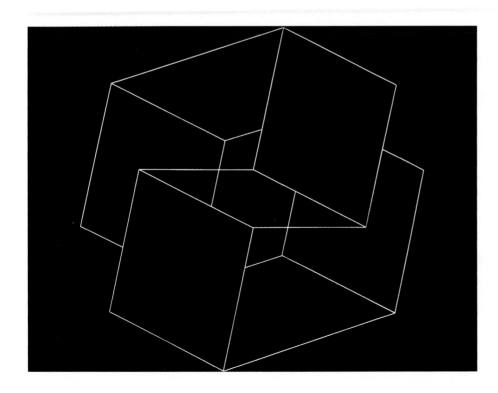

◄ **E**

Josef Albers. *Structural Constellation II.*
c. 1950. Machine-engraved vinylite mounted
on board, 1′ 5″ × 1′ 10¹/₂″ (43.2 × 57.1 cm).
Collection, The Josef Albers Foundation.

THE CONCEPT OF ENCLOSURE

One other aspect of pictorial space is of concern to the artist or designer. This is the concept of enclosure, the use of what is referred to as **open form** or **closed form**. The artist has the choice of giving us a complete scene or merely a partial glimpse of a portion of a scene that continues beyond the format.

Exploring Closed Form

In **A** Chardin puts the focal point in the center of the composition; thus our eyes are not led out of the painting. The still life of musical instruments and sheet music is effectively framed by the curved border of the picture, which echoes the many ovals in the composition. The book on the left and the candle on the right bracket the composition and keep our attention within the picture. This is called closed form.

Exploring Open Form

By contrast, example **B** is clearly open form. The landscape painting by Robert James Foose does not include the entire tree but only part of it. Most of the foliage is outside the picture. The focus is on the lower part of the tree and the reflection in the water. This reflection provides a vertical balance, and the picture feels complete, even if the forms are cropped or incomplete.

The ultimate extension of the open-form concept is illustrated in **C**. This painting breaks out of a rectangular format and effectively destroys any framed, or contained, feeling. In fact, shapes within the painting extend outward, and the white wall creates shapes that cut into the painting but also expand to include a field well beyond the painting's boundary.

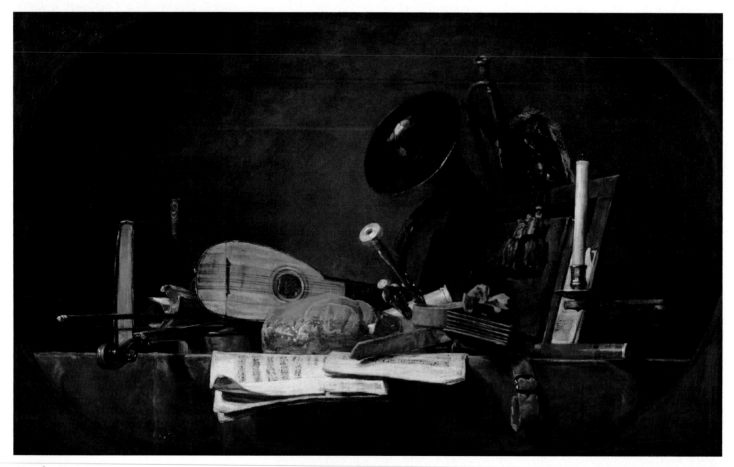

▲ **A**

Jean-Baptiste-Siméon Chardin. *The Attributes of Music.* 1765. Oil on canvas, 2′ 11⁷/₈″ × 4′ 8⁷/₈″ (91 × 145 cm). Musée du Louvre, Paris, France.

It may be most surprising to encounter open form when the subject is the human figure. Figures are often cropped in the action photographs of athletes, and this suggests the dynamics of sports. A cropped figure can also simply suggest a unique point of view. The print by Alex Katz shown in **D** is cropped to form an unexpected composition. The open form implies a figure beyond the picture, while emphasis is given to an unusual focus on the feet.

As you can see, closed form generally gives a rather formal, structured appearance, whereas open form creates a casual, momentary feeling, with elements moving on and off the format in an informal manner.

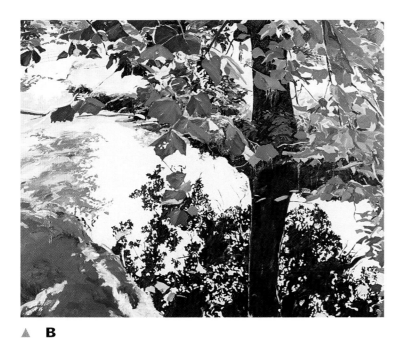

▲ **B**

Robert James Foose. *Light's Course*. 1997.
Oil on linen, 3' 2" × 3' 11" (97 × 119 cm).

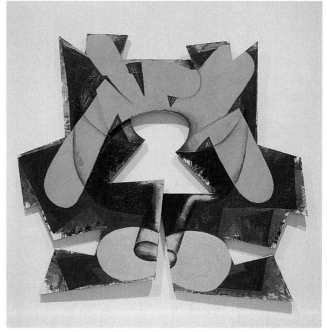

▲ **C**

Elizabeth Murray. *Keyhole*. 1982. Oil on canvas, 8' 3¹/₂" × 9' 2¹/₂". Agnes Gund Collection, New York.

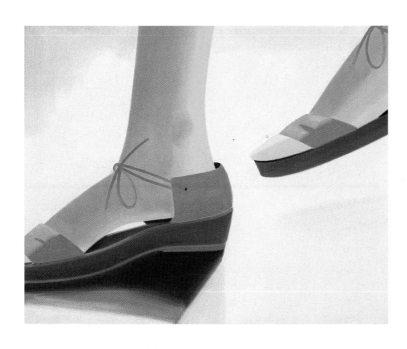

◄ **D**

Alex Katz. *Ada's Red Sandals*. 1987. Oil on canvas, 4' × 5'. Alex Katz Studio II, New York. Art © Alex Katz/Licensed by VAGA, New York, New York.

EQUIVOCAL SPACE

Most art in the twentieth and twenty-first centuries has not been concerned with a purely naturalistic reproduction of the world around us. Photography has provided a way we can all record appearance in a picture. This is true in the area of spatial and depth representation also. Many artists have chosen to ignore the device of overlapping. Instead, they have used what is called **transparency**. When two forms overlap and both are seen completely, the figures are assumed to be "transparent" **(A)**.

Interest in Ambiguity

Transparency does not give us a clear spatial pattern. In **A** we are not sure which plane is on top and which behind. The spatial pattern can change as we look at it. This purposeful

ambiguity is called **equivocal space**, and many artists find it a more interesting visual pattern than the immediately clear spatial organization provided by overlapping in a design.

There is another rationale for the use of transparency. Just because one item is in front of and hides another object does not mean the item in back has ceased to exist. In **B** a bowl of fruit is depicted with the customary visual device of overlapping. In **C** the same bowl of fruit is shown with transparency, and we discover another piece of fruit in the bottom of the bowl. It was always there, simply hidden from our view. So, which design is more realistic? By what standards do you decide?

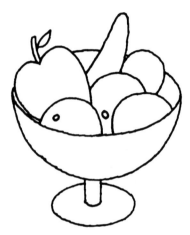

▲ **B**
Overlapping sometimes can be deceptive.

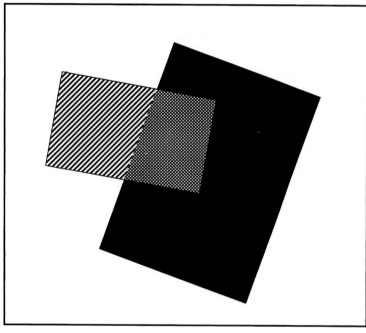

▲ **A**
The use of overlapping with transparency confuses our perception of depth.

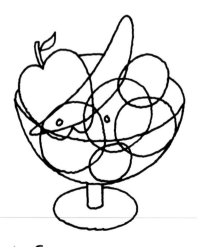

▲ **C**
The use of transparency reveals what is hidden by overlapping.

Exploring Equivocal Space

The sweatshirt design in **D** was created to celebrate a fifth anniversary. The letters spelling "Five" are clear, but they overlap and become transparent with differing patterns and values. The design takes a simple theme and creates an interesting pattern from a few elements.

Spatial ambiguity can also be suggested through the use of open form. A large *X* seems to expand beyond the boundaries of the rectangle in **E**. The same composition can be seen in a moment of figure/ground reversal to be four small triangular shapes against a yellow ground. A spatial ambiguity is created in this reversal.

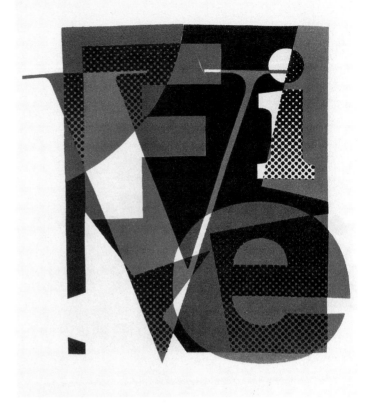

▶ **D**

Sweatshirt design for a fifth anniversary. 1990. Designer: Jennifer C. Bartlett. Design firm: Vickerman-Zachary-Miller (VZM Transystems), Oakland, California.

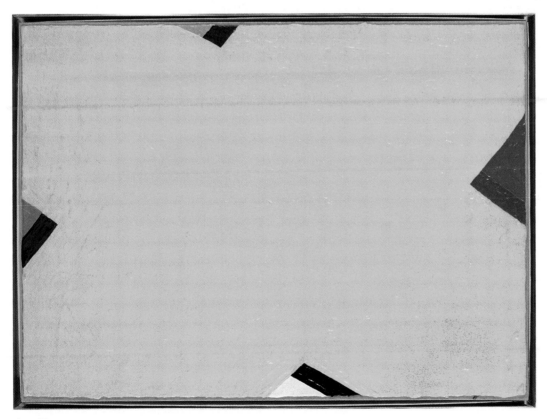

▲ **E**

Al Held. *Yellow.* 1956. Acrylic on paper mounted on board, 57.5 × 77.5 cm. Kunstmuseum Basel, Kupferstichkabinett. (Legat Anne-Marie and Ernst Vischer-Wadler, 1995). Art © Estate of Al Held/Licensed by VAGA, New York, New York.

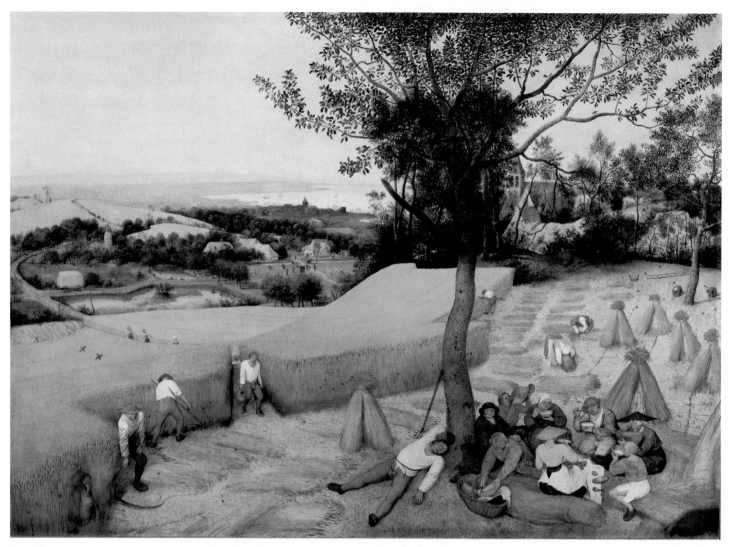

▲ **A**

Pieter Bruegel the Elder. *The Harvesters*. 1565. Oil on wood; overall, including added strips at top, bottom, and right: 3′ 10⁷/₈″ × 5′ 3³/₄″ (119 × 162 cm), original painted surface: 3′ 9⁷/₈″ × 5′ 2⁷/₈″ (116.5 × 159.5 cm). The Metropolitan Museum of Art, Rogers Fund, 1919 (19.164).

COMPLEXITY AND SUBTLETY

Two-dimensional art and design are by definition flat. Unlike the realms of sculpture and architecture, space in two-dimensional art forms can only be implied. This leaves the artist and designer with a range of spatial clues and techniques with a similar range of expressive potential. A flat graphic design may pack a punch for a poster or abstract painting. A complex space may lead a viewer into the subtle depths of a landscape painting.

When we look at the painting by Bruegel **(A)**, we are drawn into space that moves from intimate to vast and deep. In the foreground we observe the details of a scene of workers at leisure. Nearly every spatial device we can think of leads us back through an unfolding and interesting landscape:

Foreground figures and trees are larger.

The trimmed edges of the hayfield follow the rules of linear perspective.

The rolling ground plane offers many instances of overlapping.

The atmosphere softens forms in the distance: value contrast diminishes and colors become cool and subtle.

Bruegel's painting tells us much about life in the sixteenth century, but it also tells us much about the potential for painting to evoke space.

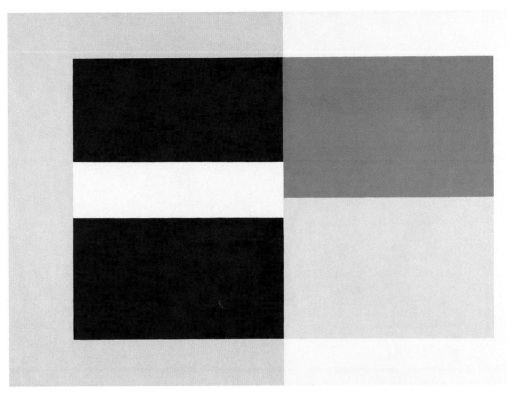

▲ **B**

John McLaughlin. *Y-1958*. 1958. Oil on canvas, 2′ 8″ × 4′.
Addison Gallery of American Art, Phillips Academy,
Andover, Massachusetts (1995.69).

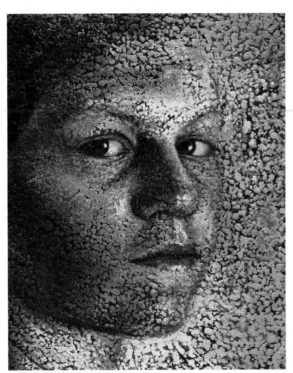

John McLaughlin's painting (**B**) offers a stunning
contrast. By the mid-twentieth century, painting had been
long liberated from illustrative space by photography. That
does not mean that a crisply two-dimensional and geometric
composition can't offer an experience akin to that of space
and depth. The planes can suggest overlap, horizon, boldly
advancing color, subtly dissolving values, and a shifting
sense of which plane advances or retreats. This reading of
the relationships occurs over time, and movement or change
over time implies space.

Susan Moore's painting (**C**) is representational like the
Bruegel but offers a limited space. The figure stands before
a modulated ground, but no other details are provided. The
volume of the figure demands a sense of subtle spatial clues,
and this is evident in the range of edges that separate figure
and ground. Unlike the crisp edges of **B**, Moore's figure
offers a range of defined and soft edges consistent with the
limits of our eye to focus on only one discrete area at a time.

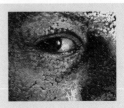

▲ **C**

Edges vary from crisp to soft,
suggesting selected focus and depth
perception. Susan Moore. *Vanity
(Portrait 1)* (detail). 2000. Oil stick on
canvas, 4′ × 3′ 11″.

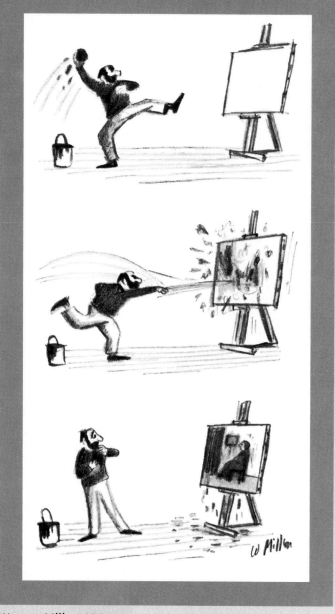

Warren Miller. 1961.
© *The New Yorker Collection* from cartoonbank.com.
All rights reserved.

ILLUSION OF MOTION

FROM STILLNESS
TO MOVEMENT

Relative Stillness

A deceptive stillness characterizes Vermeer's painting *Kitchen Maid* (**A**). This might (at first glance) be seen as the equivalent of a photograph taken at a fast shutter speed, say, 125th of a second. Now consider that the milk is *moving* as the woman pours it and we sense that the duration of the picture might be a brief interval of time longer than a split second. Illustration **B** is another painting that seems to emphasize stillness. The features of the face are in crisp detail while other edges dissolve and marks near the borders of the figure blur the form. These variations evoke depth but also can suggest either our eye movement or the anticipated turning of the figure in space. Even in artworks of quiet stillness we expect or anticipate change.

Almost every aspect of life involves constant change. We humans cannot sit or stand motionless for more than a moment or so; even in sleep we turn and change position. But if we could stop our body movements, the world about us would still continue to change. Thus motion is an important consideration in art.

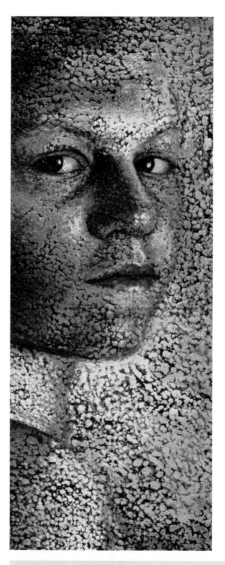

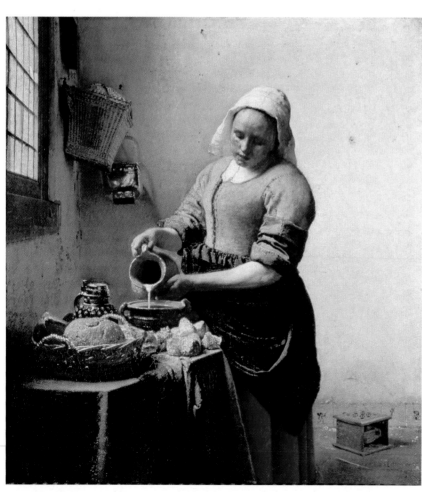

 A

Jan (van Delft) Vermeer. *The Milkmaid*. 1658–1660. Oil on canvas, 45.5 × 41 cm. Rijksmuseum, Amsterdam, The Netherlands.

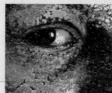

▲ **B**
Contrast in edges and marks at edges can suggest subtle movement of the subject or the viewer. Susan Moore. *Vanity (Portrait 1)* (detail). 2000. Oil stick on canvas, 4' × 3' 11".

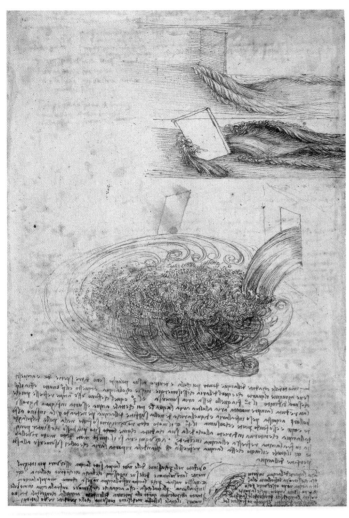

▲ **C**

Leonardo da Vinci. *Study of Flowing Water.* c. 1509–1511.
The Royal Collection, London.

Depicting the Transient

Artists since at least the Renaissance have attempted
to depict movement and elusive imagery. Leonardo's
sketchbooks included drawings of water turbulence **(C)**.
In more recent times, photography has made visible images
that are otherwise invisible to us due to a motion too rapid
for the eye to perceive. Harold Edgerton's photograph of a
bullet piercing an apple **(D)** is one such example. Edgerton
pioneered techniques of strobe lighting, which coordinates
the camera with an instant of light to capture such images.

Certainly technology has evolved beyond photography
to include film and video, and we are familiar with media
that move and change. Sporting events are presented to us
with views previously experienced only by the athletes.
Music videos include rapid cutting and choreography.
Hollywood films and animation convince us that we are
sharing in the action. Artworks share in the use of these
media and include **kinetic** works, computer-mediated
displays, and robotics that move or change either indepen-
dently or in interaction with an audience. Our discussion
in this chapter will focus on the depiction or suggestion
of motion in still forms of art and design.

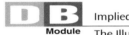

Module   Implied Motion and Time
             The Illusion of Motion

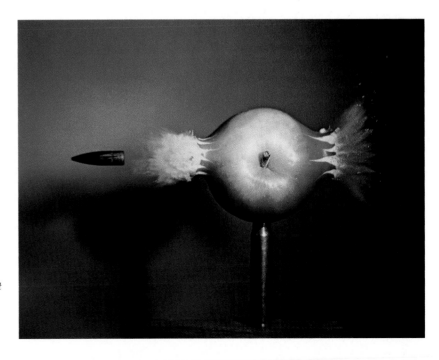

▶ **D**

Harold Edgerton. *Making Applesauce at MIT (.30 Bullet
Piercing an Apple).* 1964. Photograph. © Harold &
Ester Edgerton Foundation, 2007, courtesy of Palm
Press, Inc.

SEEING AND FEELING IMPENDING ACTION

Much of the implication of movement present in art is caused by our memory and experience. We recognize temporary, unstable body positions and realize that change must be imminent. This anticipation is not limited to images of the human figure. The red square in **A** is in a dynamic position poised at an angle as if ready to tumble. Example **B** (a later step in Lissitzky's series) shows that this is what the artist had in mind as all the forms have changed or moved and new ones have entered the space.

Kinesthetic Empathy

In a process called **kinesthetic empathy**, we tend to re-create unconsciously in our own bodies the actions we observe. We actually "feel" in our muscles the exertions of the athlete or dancer; we simultaneously stretch, push, or lean, though we are only watching. This involuntary reaction also applies to static images in art, where it can enhance the feeling of movement.

A feeling of **anticipated movement** can be created by implied lines and gestures. Thus in **C** the standing figure seems ready to strike. The gestures of limbs and flowing fabric (captured in porcelain) heighten the sense of anticipated motion.

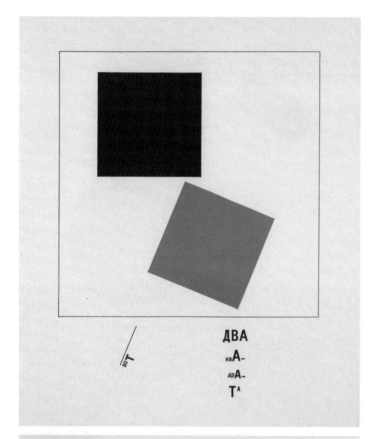

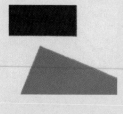

▲ **A**

El Lissitzky. *Of Two Squares: A Suprematist Tale in Six Constructions.* 1922. Illustrated book with letterpress cover and six letterpress illustrations, $10^{15}/_{16}$″ × $8^{7}/_{8}$″ (27.8 × 22.5 cm). Publisher: Skify, Berlin. Gift of the Judith Rothschild Foundation (89.2001.5).

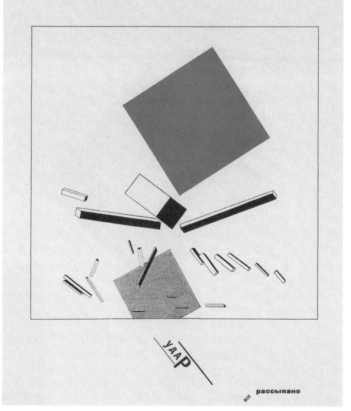

▲ **B**

El Lissitzky. *Of Two Squares: A Suprematist Tale in Six Constructions.* 1922. Illustrated book with letterpress cover and six letterpress illustrations, $10^{15}/_{16}$″ × $8^{7}/_{8}$″ (27.8 × 22.5 cm). Publisher: Skify, Berlin. Gift of the Judith Rothschild Foundation (89.2001.5).

Anticipated Motion by Design

With the advent of rapid forms of transportation and communication in the last century, a significant number of artworks began to reflect an interest in speed or motion. The Italian Futurists, as early as the 1920s, said that the speeding automobile had replaced Venus de Milo as a standard of beauty. Even when parked at the curb, a "street rod" such as the one in **D** anticipates and expresses speed through its long, sweeping lines. This romance with movement and technology led to the streamlining of even utilitarian objects such as toasters and telephones, which would never speed down a highway or fly through the sky.

 Module Actual and Kinetic Motion

▶ **C**

Doccia Porcelain Factory. Sculptor: Giovanni Battista Foggini. Modeler: Gaspero Bruschi. *Mercury and Argus.* 1749. Porcelain, polychrome, and parcel gilt. The Getty Center, Los Angeles, 94.SE.76.

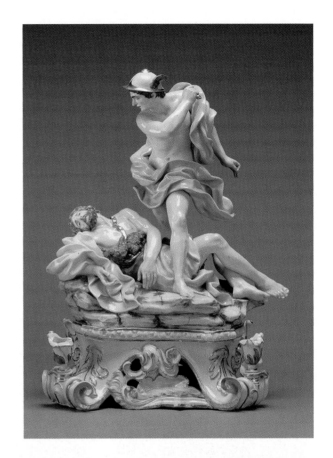

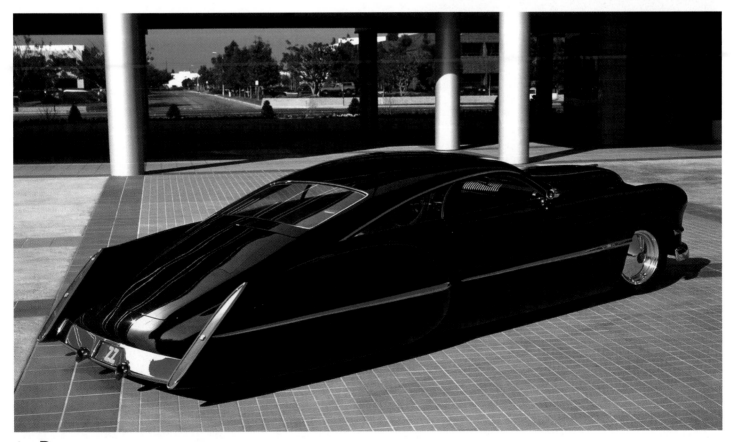

▲ **D**

Larry Erickson and Billy F. Gibbons (designers). *CadZZilla.* 1989. Custom automobile. Design patent DES. 320, 959.

FIGURE REPEATED, FIGURE CROPPED

Figure Repeated

Over the centuries artists have devised various conventions to present an illusion of motion in art. One of the oldest devices is the **repeated figure**. As the thirteenth-century illumination in **A** illustrates, the figure of David from the Bible appears in different positions and situations. Architectural elements divide the format into four areas. In the upper left area, David with his slingshot meets the giant Goliath and prepares for battle. In the upper right, David cuts off the slain giant's head as the Philistine soldiers leave. David presents the head to the King of Israel in the lower left vignette, and in the final scene, David receives the gift of a cloak from an admirer.

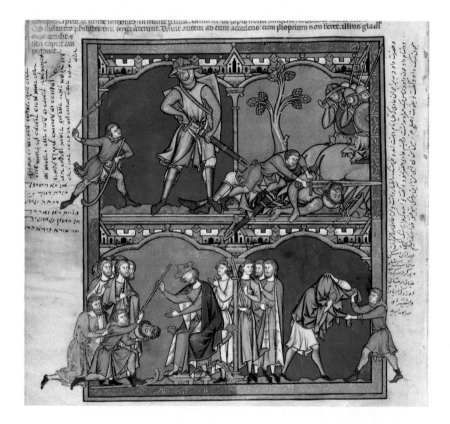

◀ **A**

David slays Goliath and cuts off his head; Abner brings David with the head of Goliath to Saul; Jonathan, smitten with love of David, gives him his garments. Manuscript illumination (M638 f 28v) from Old Testament Miniatures, Paris. c. 1245–1250. Tempera on vellum. The Pierpont Morgan Library, New York.

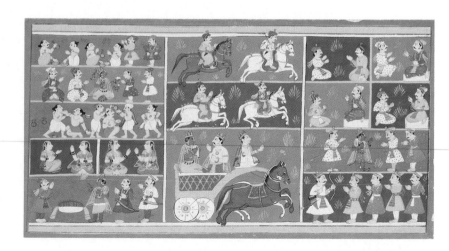

▶ **B**

Krishna Revealing His Nature as Vishnu. Miniature from Malwa, India. c. 1730. Gouache or watercolor on paper, 8″ × 1′ 2³/₄″ (20 × 38 cm). Victoria and Albert Museum, London. Crown Copyright.

This repetitive device was used widely in Oriental cultures as well as in Western medieval art. The figure of Krishna appears over and over in different positions and situations in the Indian miniature **(B)**.

Figure Cropped

A second dramatic way to express motion is by cropping the figure. The composition in **C** effectively crops the lunging basketball player to enhance the feeling of movement. The head and basketball are barely contained in the frame and form a tense line spanning the picture. The forward leg is cropped, heightening the sense of the player bursting through the confines of the frame. In this case the framing rectangle is essential to the suggestion of motion.

Comic strips employ both techniques of figure repetition and figure cropping to create a sense of motion. Bill Watterson's *Calvin and Hobbes* was creative in the use of these devices to bring life to Calvin's real and imagined worlds **(D)**.

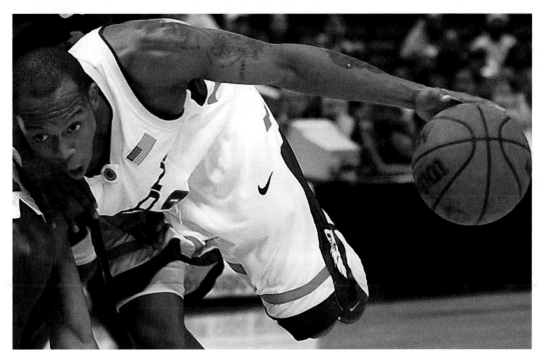

◄ **C**

Taliek Brown of the University of Connecticut. December 10, 2002. Photograph.

▼ **D**

Bill Watterson. *Calvin and Hobbes.* © 1985. Reprinted with permission of Universal Press Syndicate. All rights reserved.

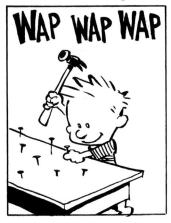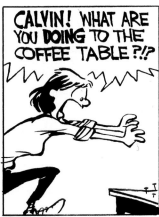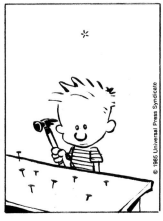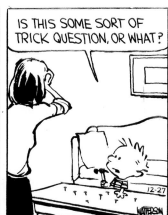

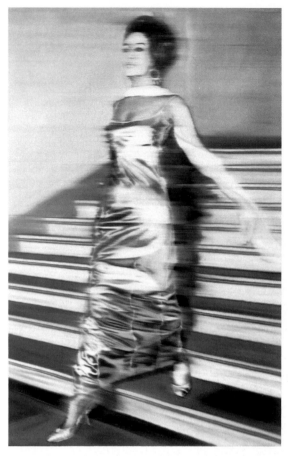

▲ **A**

Gerhard Richter. *Woman Descending the Staircase.* 1965.
6′ 7″ × 4′ 3″ (200.7 × 129.5 cm). The Art Institute of
Chicago (Roy J. and Frances R. Friedman Endowment;
gift of Lannan Foundation, 1997.176).

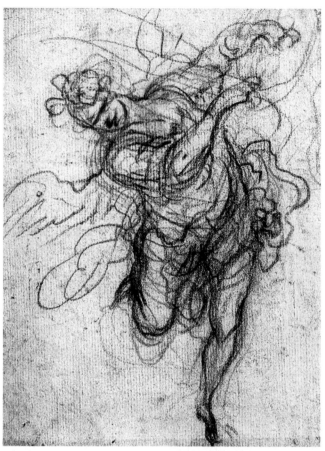

▲ **B**

Anonymous (Italian or Spanish). *Angel (Dancing Figure).*
16th century. Red chalk on cream paper, 6³/₄″ × 5⁵/₁₆″
(17.1 × 13.5 cm). The Metropolitan Museum of Art, gift
of Cornelius Vanderbilt, 1880 (80.3.72).

BLURRED OUTLINES

We readily interpret a photograph, or a painting based on a
photograph, such as **A**, as a symbol of movement because
of the **blurred outlines**. With a fast shutter speed, moving
images are frozen in "stop-action" photographs. When
the shutter speed is relatively slow, the figure becomes a
blurred image that we read as an indication of the subject's
movement. This is an everyday visual experience. When
objects move through our field of vision quickly, we do not
get a clear mental picture of them. A car will pass us on
the highway so fast that we perceive only a colored blur.
Details and edges of the form are lost in the rapidity of the
movement.

The figure in the sixteenth-century Italian drawing in **B**
suggests movement in this way. The dancing figure is drawn
with sketchy, incomplete, and overlapping lines to define her
form and evoke the gestures of the movements.

Bridget Riley's painting **(C)** shows a nonrepresentational
expression of this technique. It is a controlled, simply repetitive pattern of definite, hard-edged curving lines. But when
we stare at it, the edges begin to blur and the lines begin to
"swim" as the black and white areas vibrate. Even the painting's surface appears no longer flat but seems to undulate
and become a rippling surface. This type of painting is called
Op Art, a style of art and design in which static images give
optical illusions of movement.

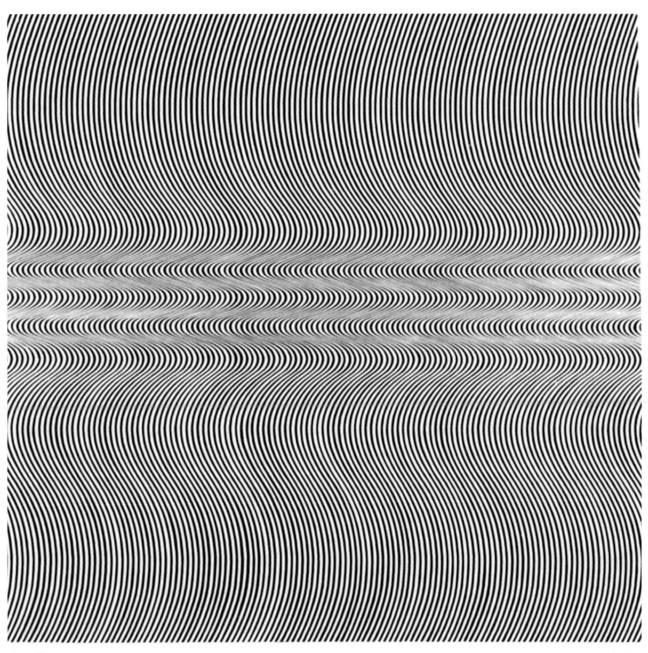

▲ **C**

Bridget Riley. *Current*. 1964. Synthetic polymer paint on composition board, 4′ 10³/₈″ × 4′ 10⁷/₈″
(148.1 × 149.3 cm). The Museum of Modern Art, New York (Philip Johnson Fund).

MULTIPLE IMAGE

Another device for suggesting movement, called **multiple image**, is illustrated in **A**. When we see one figure in an overlapping sequence of poses, the slight change in each successive position suggests movement taking place. The photograph in **A** is from the 1880s. The photographer, Thomas Eakins, was intrigued with the camera's capabilities for answering the visual problem of showing movement and analyzing it.

Illustration **B** shows this idea in a drawing by Ingres. Though Ingres's motive was probably just to try two different positions for the figure, we get a clear suggestion of the figure moving in dancelike gestures.

Lines of Force

Painters of the twentieth and twenty-first centuries have often been concerned with finding a visual language to express the increasingly dynamic quality of the world around us.

Although at first glance very different, Duchamp's famous *Nude Descending a Staircase* (**C**) is much like the Eakins photograph in **A**. Again, multiple images of a figure are shown to suggest a body's movement in progress. Now the body forms are abstracted into simple geometric forms that repeat diagonally down the canvas as the nude "descends." Many curved lines (called **lines of force**) are added to show the pathway of movement. This is a device we commonly see, and immediately understand, in today's comic strips.

Grouping Multiple Images

The group of photographs in **D** is a collection of six similar subjects from different sources. They have the effect of a "multiple image" and create movement across the grid. A sense of motion is created like that of an old film or a flicker book.

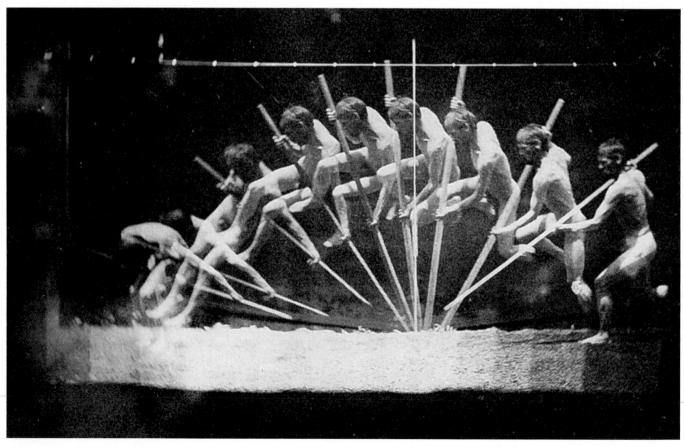

▲ **A**

Thomas Eakins. *Motion Studies, Man Pole-Vaulting*. 1884–1885. Gelatin silver print. The Metropolitan Museum of Art, gift of Charles Bregler, 1941 (41.142.11).

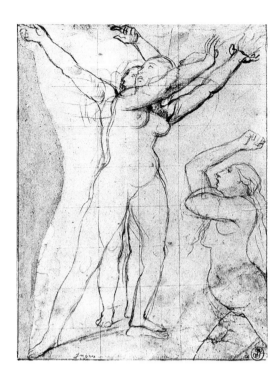

◄ **B**

Jean-August-Dominique Ingres. Study for *The Martyrdom of St. Symphorien*. c. 1826–1834. Pencil on white paper, 30.8 × 23.2 cm. Musée Bonnat, Bayonne, France. N1986; A12246. Photo: Renee-Gabriel Ojéda.

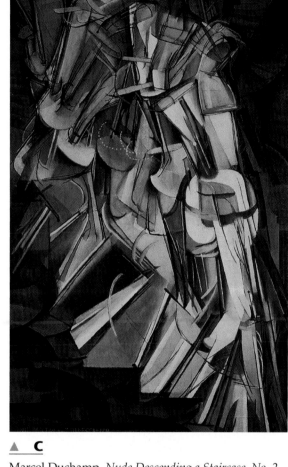

▲ **C**

Marcel Duchamp. *Nude Descending a Staircase, No. 2.* 1912. Oil on canvas, 4′ 10″ × 2′ 11″ (1.47 × 0.89 m). Philadelphia Museum of Art (Louise and Walter Arensberg Collection).

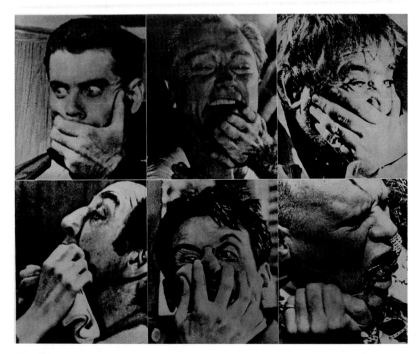

▲ **D**

John Baldessari. *Six Colorful Gags (Male)*. 1991. Photogravure with color aquatint and spit bite aquatint, 3′ 11″ × 4′ 6″. Edition 25. Crown Point Press, San Francisco.

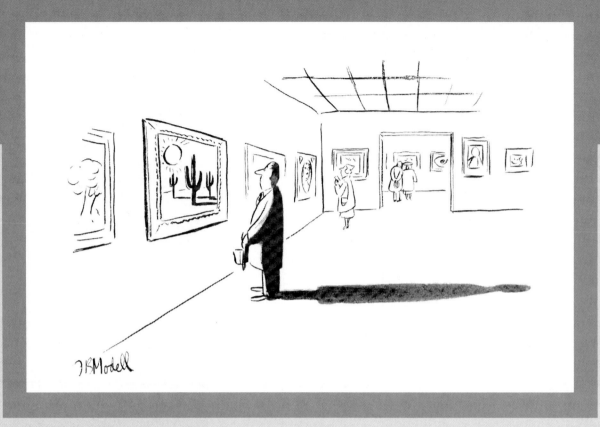

Frank Modell. 1951.
© *The New Yorker Collection* from cartoonbank.com.
All Rights Reserved.

CHAPTER
12

VALUE

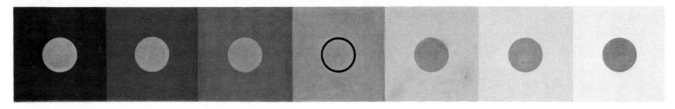

▲ A

A value scale of gray. The center circles are identical in value.

LIGHT AND DARK

Value is simply the artistic term for light and dark. An area's value is its relative lightness or darkness in a given context. Only through changes of light and dark can we perceive anything. Light reveals forms; in a dark room at night we see nothing and bump into furniture and walls. The page you are reading now is legible only because the darkness of the type contrasts with the lightness of the background paper. Even a person (or animal) who is physiologically unable to perceive color can function with only minimal difficulties by using perception based on varying tones of gray.

Illustration **A** is a scale of seven values of gray. These are termed **achromatic** grays, as they are mixtures of only black and white; no color (or chroma) is used.

The Relationship between Light and Dark Areas

The term **value contrast** refers to the relationship between areas of dark and light. Because the scale in **A** is sequential, the contrast between any two adjoining areas is rather slight and is termed *low-value* contrast. The center gray circles are all the same middle value. It is interesting to note how this consistent center gray seems to change visually depending on the background. Indeed, it is hard to believe that the circles on the far left and far right are precisely the same value.

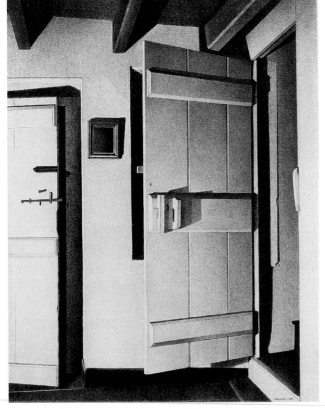

▲ B

Charles Sheeler. *The Open Door.* 1932. Conté crayon on paper, mounted on cardboard, 1′ 11³/₄″ × 1′ 6″ (60.7 × 46.7 cm). The Metropolitan Museum of Art, Edith and Milton Lowenthal Collection, bequest of Edith Abrahamson Lowenthal, 1991 (1992.24.7).

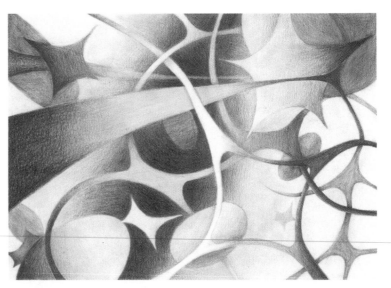

▲ C

Sarah W. Linder. Student drawing. Savannah College of Art and Design/Kristie Bruzenak, Professor of Foundations Studies.

The scale in **A** shows only seven basic steps. Theoretically, between black and white there could be an almost unlimited number of steps. Studies have shown that the average eye can discern about forty variations in value. The artist may use as many or as few values as her or his artistic purposes indicate, though at times the nature of the chosen medium may influence the result. The drawing of the interior in **B** uses a very broad range of values. The artist, Charles Sheeler, drawing with a Conté crayon, skillfully exploited the medium's softness to create many grays and an interesting design of dark and light contrasts. The abstract study in **C** has a similar broad range of values with subtle gradations yielding many value steps. This study emphasizes the play and contrasts of values without an emphasis on representational subject matter.

The Relationship between Value and Color

Value and color are related. Every color is, in itself, also simultaneously a certain value. Pure yellow is a light (high-value) color corresponding to a very light gray in terms of light reflection. Purple is basically a dark, low-value color that would match a very dark gray. A pure red will fall in the middle of the value scale. This is evident in **D** and the companion **E**. The range of values from light to dark is the same as in **B** and **C**, but the number of steps is far fewer—essentially three: light, middle, and dark.

See also *Properties of Color: Value*, page 260.

DB *Value Scale*
Module

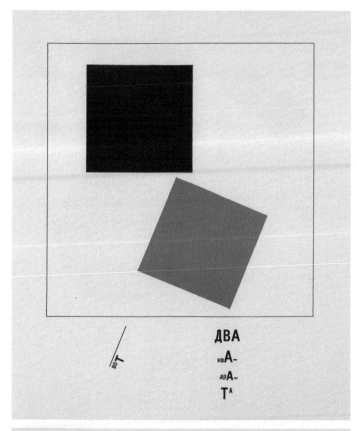

ДВА
кв**А**-
ар**А**-
Тᴬ

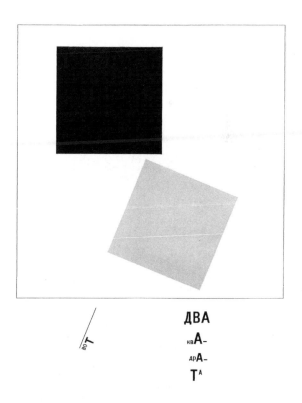

ДВА
кв**А**-
ар**А**-
Тᴬ

▲ **D**

El Lissitzky. *Of Two Squares: A Suprematist Tale in Six Constructions.* 1922. Illustrated book with letterpress cover and six letterpress illustrations, 10 ¹⁵/₁₆″ × 8 ⁷/₈″ (27.8 × 22.5 cm). Publisher: Skify, Berlin. Gift of the Judith Rothschild Foundation (89.2001.5).

▲ **E**

The design is composed of three values: light, middle, and dark. El Lissitzky. *Of Two Squares: A Suprematist Tale in Six Constructions.* 1922. Diagram.

VARIATIONS IN LIGHT AND DARK

In describing paintings or designs, we speak often of their **value pattern**. This term refers to the arrangement and the amount of variation in light and dark, independent of the colors used.

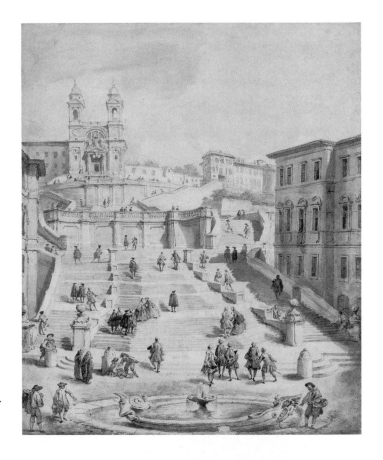

▶ **A**

Giovanni Paolo Pannini. *Scalinata della Trinità dei Monti.* c. 1756–1758. Pen and black ink, brush and gray wash, watercolor, over graphite, 1′ 1 $^{11}/_{16}$″ × 11 $^9/_{16}$″ (34.8 × 29.3 cm). The Metropolitan Museum of Art, Rogers Fund, 1971 (1971.63.1).

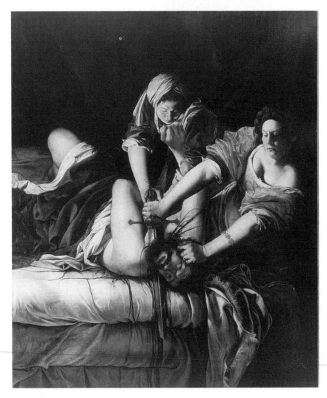

▲ **B**

Artemisia Gentileschi. *Judith Decapitating Holofernes.* c. 1620. Oil on canvas, 5′ 10″ × 5′ (199 × 152.5 cm). Galleria degli Uffizi, Florence, Italy.

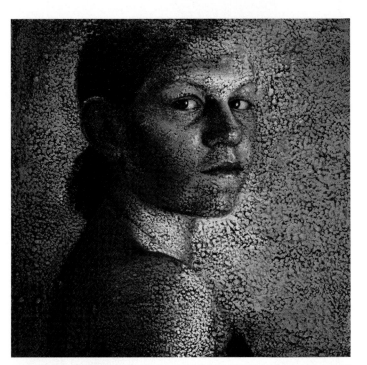

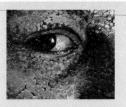

▲ **C**

Susan Moore. *Vanity (Portrait 1).* 2000. Oil stick on canvas, 4′ × 3′ 11″.

High Key or Low Key

When value contrast is minimized and all the values are within a limited range with only small variation, the result is a restrained, subtle effect. The impression is one of understatement, whether the value range is dominated by lights (*high key* is a term used often) or darks (*low key*). In illustration **A** the values are primarily light, with fewer contrasting dark areas. Light even reflects into the shadows. The painting in **B** shows the opposite approach, an extreme contrast of dark and light. This is a Baroque painting, done in a period when artists purposely accentuated value contrasts to portray exciting themes. The violent and gory subject of Artemisia Gentileschi's painting (**B**) receives an aptly emotional visual treatment. The candlelit picture has dramatic, sudden shadows throughout the scene, achieving an almost theatrical effect.

Moore's portrait in **C** shows how a value structure similar to that of **B** can be used to produce a calmer conclusion. The value range and contrasts are similar in both paintings, but the distribution and shapes are different, creating contrasting patterns. The lighter shapes in **B** emerge from the darkness in varied directions with dynamic crossing diagonals. The figure in **C** emerges from a lighter ground in a pattern of mostly graceful curves and counterpoint curves.

The painting by Agnes Martin shown in **D** could not be farther removed from the drama of **B** and is calmer than even **C**. In this case the simple composition of lines creates a quiet meditative feel in a light key. The delicate line weight and grid composition produce an allover pattern across the pale canvas.

 Descriptive and Expressive Properties of Value

▲ **D**

Agnes Martin. *Morning*. 1965. Acrylic and pencil on canvas, 182.6 x 181.9 cm. © ARS, New York. Tate Gallery, London, Great Britain.

CREATING A FOCAL POINT

A valuable use of dark-and-light contrast is to create a focal point or center of attention in a design. A visual emphasis or "starting point" is often desired. A thematically important character or feature can be visually emphasized by value contrast. High dark-and-light contrast instantly attracts our attention because of **value emphasis**. By planning high contrast in one area and subdued contrast elsewhere, the artist can ensure where the viewer's eye will be directed first.

Homer's watercolor of a leaping trout **(A)** emphasizes the trout through value contrast. The light underbelly stands out against the dark background, and the darker tail stands out against the backdrop of reflected light on the water.

The etching in **B** places emphasis on the light window at the right-hand side of the composition. Our eye follows the path of the gentle light to the softly illuminated figure grouping of the Holy Family. All other features of the interior melt into the darkness as we move away from that spot.

An Experiment in Value Contrast

Strong contrast of value creates an equal emphasis in both **C** and **D**. These photographs have precisely the same vantage point and appear almost like a positive and negative of the same image. In reality the artist has collaborated with nature to produce two striking images of contrast. In **C** a wet sycamore stick is seen against the snow. The photograph in **D** shows the same stick the next day, stripped of its bark, against the ground after the snow has melted away. In each case the form of the branch stands in contrast to the ground, but for very different reasons!

Value before Color

All these images, of course, exist in color. But the black-and-white reproductions here are valuable to show the artists' reliance on value contrast, irrespective of the particular colors involved. Most artists are as aware of the value pattern they create as the pattern of various colors. The artistic choice is often not green or red but how dark (or light) a green or red to use.

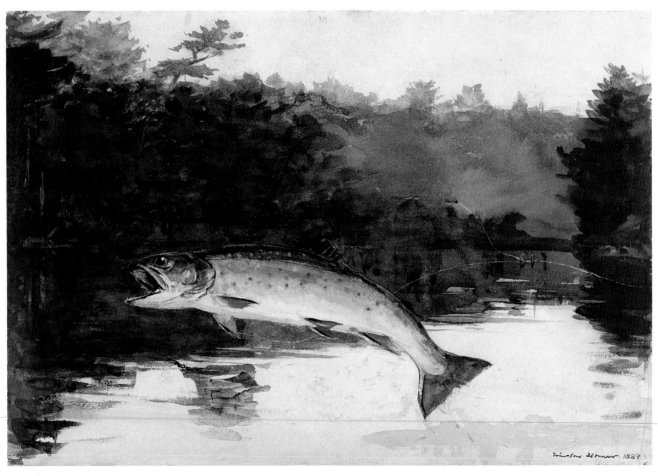

▲ **A**

Winslow Homer. *Leaping Trout.* 1889. Watercolor on paper, 1' 1⁷/₈" × 1' 7". Portland Museum of Art, Portland, Maine (bequest of Charles Shipman Payson, 1881.1).

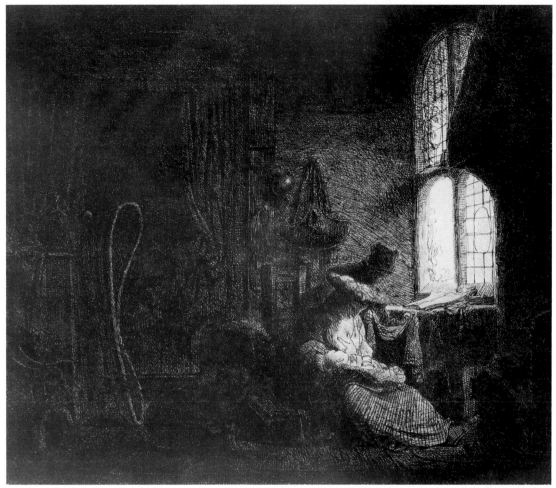

▲ **B**

Ferdinand Bol. *Holy Family in an Interior.* 1643. Etching, drypoint and engraving; sheet: 7³/₁₆″ × 8¹/₂″ (18.21 × 21.59 cm). The Metropolitan Museum of Art, The Elisha Whittelsey Collection, The Elisha Whittelsey Fund, 1995 (1995.100).

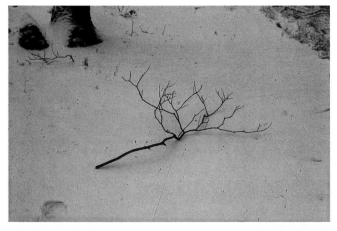

▲ **C**

Andy Goldsworthy. Photograph, January 1981. *Sycamore stick placed on snow/raining heavily.* Middleton Woods, Yorkshire. From *Andy Goldsworthy: A Collaboration with Nature* (New York: Harry N. Abrams, 1990).

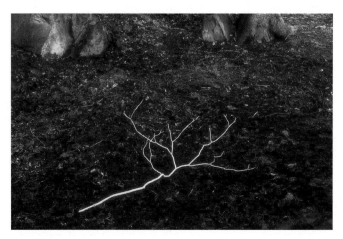

▲ **D**

Andy Goldsworthy. Photograph, January 1981. *Snow gone by next day, bark stripped, chewed and scraped off.* Middleton Woods, Yorkshire. From *Andy Goldsworthy: A Collaboration with Nature* (New York: Harry N. Abrams, 1990).

USING VALUE TO SUGGEST SPACE

One of the most important uses of gradations of dark and light is to suggest volume or space.

On a flat surface, value can be used to impart a three-dimensional quality to shapes. During the Renaissance the word **chiaroscuro** was coined to describe the artistic device of using light and dark to imply depth and volume in a painting or drawing. Chiaroscuro is a combination of the Italian words for "light" and "dark." A drawing using only line is very effective in showing shapes. By varying the weight of the line, an artist may imply dimension or solidity, but the effect is subtle. When areas of dark and light are added, we begin to feel the three-dimensional quality of forms. This is apparent in Michelangelo's *Madonna and Child* (**A**). The baby has been shaded in dark and light, giving it a feeling of volume and three dimensions, especially in comparison with the figure of the Madonna. Being drawn just in line, she remains a fairly flat portrayal. The watercolor in **B** shows how effectively the feeling of volume and space can be presented. Here the representational source is undulating paper, but the subject is space and light.

Value and Atmospheric Perspective

Much art has been, and is, concerned with producing a simulation of our three-dimensional world. On a two-dimensional piece of paper or canvas, an illusion of space is desired—and perhaps not just the roundness of a head but a whole scene receding far into the distance. Here again the use of value can be an effective tool of the artist. High-value contrast seems to come forward, to be actually closer, whereas areas of lesser contrast recede or stay back, suggesting distance. Notice how effectively Caspar Friedrich has used this technique in his painting (**C**). The figure on the rocks in front is sharply dark against the rest of the picture. Then each receding rock, wave, and bit of land becomes progressively lighter and closer to the value of the sky. An illusion of great depth is thus created by manipulating the various values. This technique does reproduce what our eyes see: Far-off images visually become grayer and less distinct as the distance increases. In art, this is called **aerial**, or *atmospheric,* **perspective**.

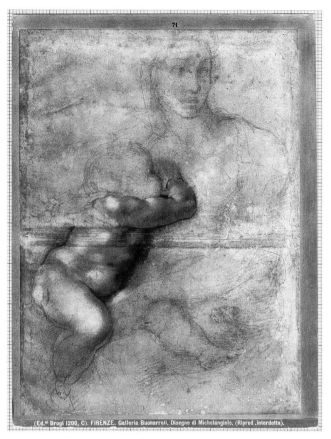

▲ **A**

Michelangelo. *Madonna and Child.* 1535–1540(?). Black and red chalk and white pigment on prepared paper, 1′ 9³/₈″ × 1′ 3⁵/₈″ (54 × 40 cm). Casa Buonarotti, Florence, Italy.

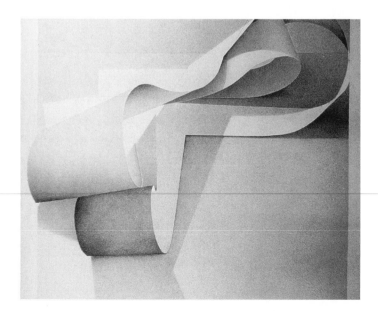

▶ **B**

Sue Hettmansperger. *Untitled Drawing.* 1975. Watercolor and pencil, 1′ 11″ × 2′ 1″ (58 × 64 cm). Collection of North Carolina National Bank.

Physical Space and Psychological Space

In **D** the artist, Sue Coe, has used the values to create zones of light and darkness. Coe creates both the literal space of the hotel room and the troubled psychological space that Charlie Parker occupied in his short life. Although the composition is divided into two contrasting areas, there is a remarkable range of values in each.

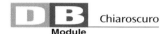 Chiaroscuro
Module

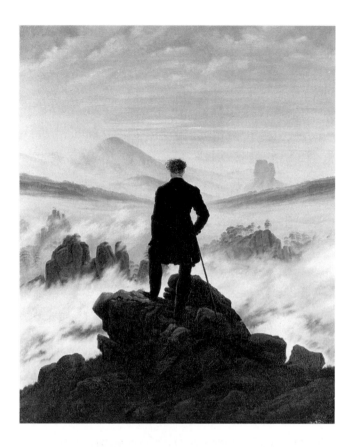

▶ **C**

Caspar David Friedrich. *The Wanderer Above the Sea of Mist.* c. 1817–1818. Oil on canvas, 2′ 4³/₈″ × 2′ 5³/₈″ (94.8 × 74.8 cm). Kunsthalle, Hamburg.

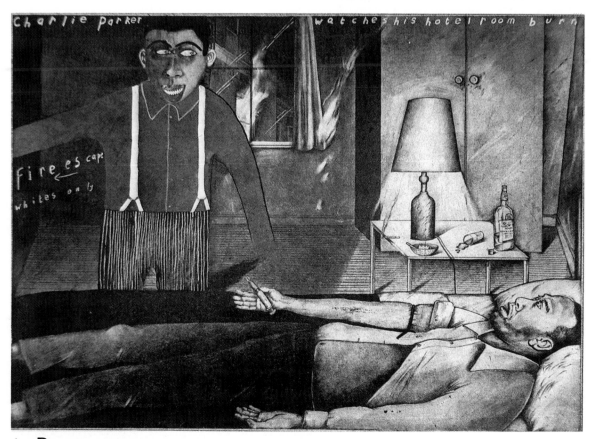

▲ **D**

Sue Coe. *Charlie Parker Watches His Hotel Room Burn.* 1984. Photo etching, 10¹/₂″ × 1′ 2″. © 1984 Sue Coe. Courtesy Galerie St. Etienne, New York.

AN OVERVIEW

The use of value in a work of art is what we would commonly call **shading**. However, to say that an artist uses shading does little to describe the final work, as there are so many techniques and hence many visual effects available. Artistic aims vary from producing a naturalistic rendition of some visual image to creating a completely nonobjective work that uses dark and light simply to provide added visual interest to the design. Even with a similar purpose, works about the same subject done by the same artist will be very different depending on the chosen medium and technique. These examples can show you just a few of the almost unlimited possibilities.

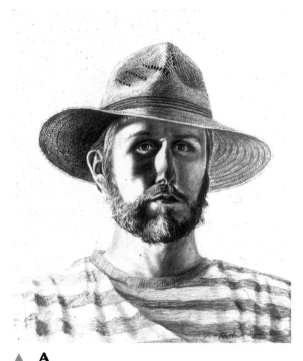

▲ **A**

Walter Hatke. *Self-Portrait.* 1973. Graphite on paper.

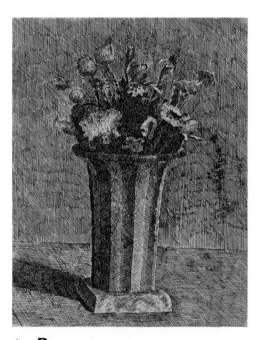

▲ **B**

Georgio Morandi. *Striped Vase with Flowers.* 1924. Etching on zinc, 239 × 204 mm. Museo Morandi, Bologna, Italy.

▶ **C**

Giovanni Domenico Tiepolo. *St. Ambrose Addressing the Young St. Augustine.* c. 1747–1750. Black chalk, pen, and brown ink with brown wash on paper, 7⁵/₈″ × 10⁷/₈″. Arkansas Arts Center Foundation Collection: Purchased with a gift from Helen Porter and James T. Dyke, 1993 (93.035).

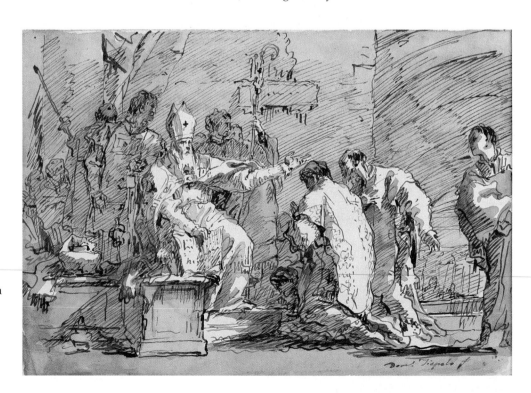

Choosing the Medium

Pencil, charcoal, chalk, and Conté crayon are familiar media to art students. Being soft media they are capable of providing (if desired) gradual changes of dark to light. The Hatke drawing (**A**) shows the subtle and gradual transitions possible. Areas of contrast sit alongside subtle shifts in value, and the artist leads us gracefully from a predominantly light ground to the darkest values in the shadow.

Experimenting with Technique

A medium such as black ink, by its nature, gives decidedly sharp value contrast. But this can be altered in several ways. The artist may use what is called **cross-hatching** (black lines of various densities that, seen against the white background, can give the impression of different grays). Again, variations are possible. These lines may be done with careful, repetitive precision or in a more atmospheric manner as in **B**.

An artist may also choose the technique of **wash drawing**, in which dark ink or watercolor is mixed with water, diluting the medium to produce desired shades of gray (or brown). The **mixed-media** drawing shown in **C** creates value shapes in this manner. The value created by the wash contrasts with the bright lighter values. Darker values are created by combining parallel hatching of dark ink lines within the middle value wash.

Visual Grays

The use of dots to create visual grays is a very common procedure, though we may not realize it. All the black-and-white halftones we see daily in newspapers, books, and magazines are actually areas of tiny black dots in various concentrations to produce visual grays. This is a photomechanical process, but the same effect can be seen in Seurat's drawing (**D**). Here the dots are created by the artist scraping a soft Conté crayon over a heavily textured white paper. Again, dots of black produce visual grays.

Using the same concept, **E** presents a definite visual feeling of grays and, hence, dimension and volume. But this "drawing" is accomplished by computer manipulation of a photograph. The grays are created by the positioning of hundreds of small numerals of various densities that combine with the white background to give us the impression of many different grays.

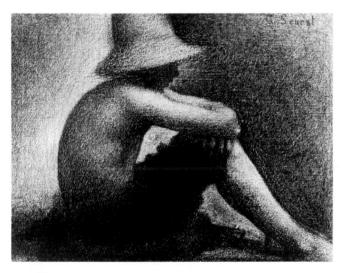

▲ **D**

Georges Seurat. *Seated Boy with Straw Hat (Study for The Bathers)*. 1882. Conté crayon, 9¹/₂″ × 1′ ¹/₄″ (24.13 × 31.1 cm). Yale University Art Gallery, New Haven (Everett V. Meeks Fund).

▶ **E**

Spread from catalog featuring fashion by R. Newbold, a Paul Smith subsidiary, Autumn/ Winter 1996. Art Director: Alan Aboud. Photographer: Sandro Sodano. Computer Manipulation: Nick Livesey, Alan Aboud, Sandro Sodano.

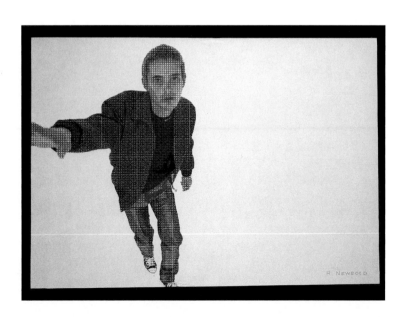

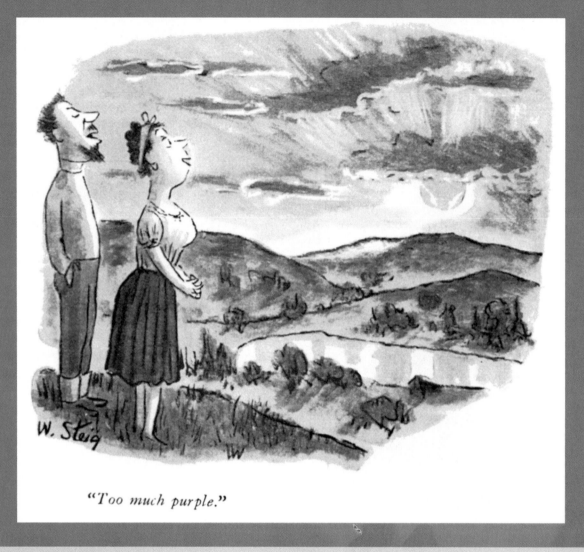

"Too much purple."

COLOR

COLOR THEORY

It is not only the professional artist or designer who deals with color. All of us make color decisions almost every day. We constantly choose items to purchase of which the color is a major factor. Our world today is marked by bold uses of color in every area of ordinary living. We can make color choices for everything from home appliances to bank checks—it seems that most things we use have blossomed into bright colors. Fashion design, interior design, architecture, industrial design—all fields in art are now increasingly concerned with color.

Therefore, everyone can profit by knowing some basic color principles. Unfortunately, the study of color can be rather complex. The word *color* has so many aspects that it means different things to a physicist, optician, psychiatrist, poet, lighting engineer, and painter; and the analysis of color becomes a multifaceted report in which many experts competently describe their findings. Shelves of books in the library on the topic attest that a comprehensive study of color from all viewpoints is impossible in a limited space.

The Essentials

However, any study of color must start with a few important, basic facts. The essential fact of color theory is that color is a property of light, not an object itself. Sir Isaac Newton illustrated this property of light in the seventeenth century when he put white light through a prism. The prism broke up white light into the familiar rainbow of hues **(A)**. Objects have no color of their own but merely the ability to reflect certain rays of white light, which contains all the colors. Blue objects absorb all the rays except the blue ones, and these are reflected to our eyes. Black objects absorb all the rays; white objects reflect all of them. The significance of this fact for the artist is that as light changes, color will change.

Color Mixing

But although color indeed comes from light, the guidelines of color mixing and usage are different depending on whether the color source is light or pigments and dyes. Rays of light are direct light, whereas the color of paint is reflected light. Color from light combines and forms new visual sensations based on what is called the **additive system**. On the other hand, pigments combine in the **subtractive system**. This term is appropriate. Blue paint is "blue" because when light hits its surface the pigment absorbs (or "subtracts") all the color components except the blue that is reflected to our eyes. Artists should be aware of both systems. The painter, of course, will be mainly concerned with the subtractive, whereas the stage lighting designer, photographer, and often the interior designer will be concerned with the additive.

Lights projected from different sources mix according to the additive method. The diagram in **B** shows the three **primary colors** of light—red, green, and blue—and the colors produced where two hues overlap. The three primaries combined will produce white light. Complementary (or opposite) hues in light (red/cyan, blue/yellow, green/magenta) when mixed will again produce an achromatic (neutral) gray or white. Where light from a cyan (blue-green) spotlight overlaps with light from a red spotlight, the visual sensation is basically white. Combining these two colors in paint would produce a dark neutral "mud"—anything but white.

This latter mixture of pigments functions according to the subtractive system. The red paint reflects little or no blue-green, and the blue-green paint reflects little or no red. When mixed together they act like two filters that now combine to reflect less light, thus approaching black (or a dark neutral) as the result. All paint mixture is to some degree subtractive; that is, the mixture is always weaker than at least one of the parent colors.

Because this book is primarily for use in studio art classes, where the usual medium is paint, the information in this chapter refers mainly to the subtractive system of color usage.

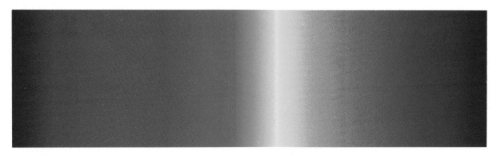

▲ **A**

The spectrum of colors is created by passing white light through a prism.

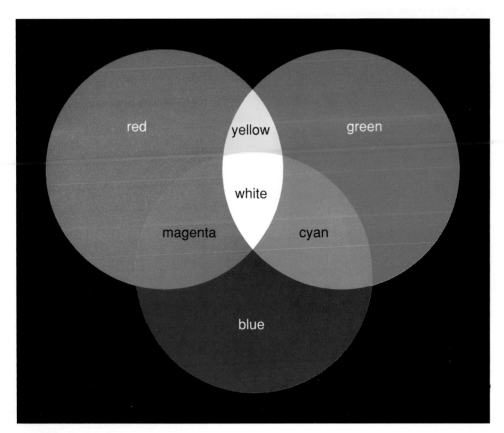

▲ **B**

Colors of light mix according to the additive process.

LIGHT AND COLOR PERCEPTION

In any discussion of color, it is important to acknowledge that color is a product of light. Therefore, as light changes, the color we observe will change. What color is grass? Green? Grass may be almost gray at dawn, yellow-green at noon, and blue-black at midnight. The colors of things are constantly changing with the light. Though this is a simple visual fact, our mind insists that the grass is green despite the visual evidence to the contrary, a psychological compensation called **color constancy**. This **constancy effect** is useful from the standpoint of human adaptation and survival. Imagine the problems if we questioned the colors of things with each new perception. Yet it is just this kind of questioning that has led artists such as Monet to reveal the range of color sensations around us. Monet's two paintings of poplars along the River Epte (**A** and **B**) are typical of this artist's reinvestigation of the same setting under different circumstances. Season, time of day, and weather conditions all contribute to different light and a difference in the color we perceive.

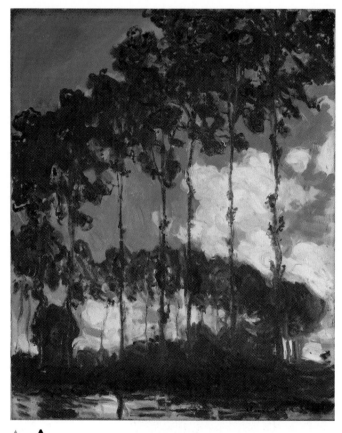

▲ **A**

Claude Monet. *Poplars on the Epte.* 1891. Oil on canvas, 92.4 × 73.7 cm. Tate Gallery, London, England.

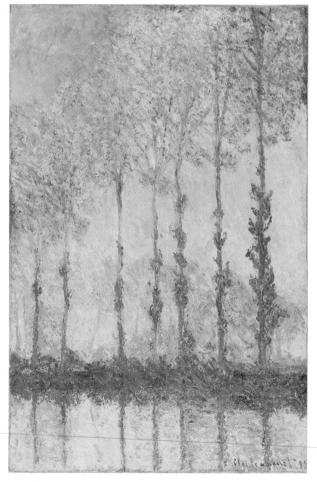

▲ **B**

Claude Monet. *Poplars.* 1891. Oil on canvas, 3′ 3 3/8″ × 2′ 1 5/8″ (100 × 65 cm). Philadelphia Museum of Art.

Observing Color in Our Surroundings

The changing color of the landscape under varying light conditions is easy to understand based on our daily experiences. Such changes occur all around us in subtle ways as well. The Italian painter Morandi revisited the same still-life objects over a period of years. The simple confines of his studio set a stage for careful observation of color nuance and light.

The paintings shown in **C** and **D** (from 1939 and 1948, respectively) include an object in common. This "white" object takes on a slightly yellow cast in the 1939 painting and a slightly violet complexion in the 1948 painting. The light may have been different, or, quite simply, Morandi's perception may have been altered by new insights or the influence of surrounding elements.

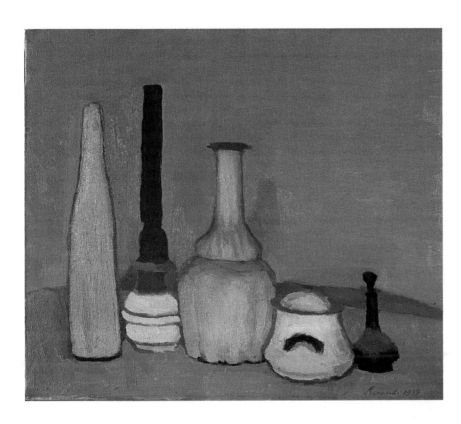

◄ **C**

Giorgio Morandi. *Still Life*. 1939. Oil on canvas, 41.5 × 47.3 cm. Museo Morandi, Bologna, Italy.

► **D**

Giorgio Morandi. *Still Life*. 1948. Oil on canvas, 35.9 × 50 cm. Museo Morandi, Bologna, Italy.

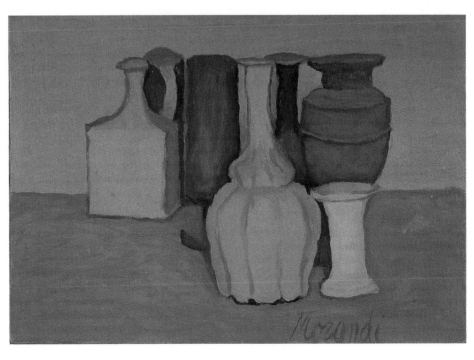

INFLUENCE OF CONTEXT

Color has a basic, instinctive, visual appeal. Great art has been created in black and white, but few artists have totally ignored the added visual interest that color lends. The uninhibited use of color was a primary characteristic of art in the twentieth century. Some artists used color primarily as an emotional element, and many artists used color in a strictly intuitive way. However, there were artists who studied color per se and thereby added immeasurably to our knowledge of color and color use.

Today's artists and students (and authors) owe a great debt to the twentieth-century artist Josef Albers, who as a painter and teacher devoted a career to the study of color and color relationships. His books and paintings have contributed invaluably to our knowledge of color. Many of the concepts in this discussion are reflections of his research and teaching.

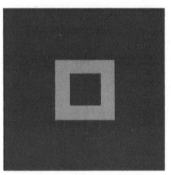  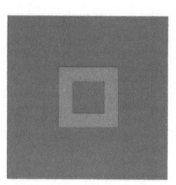 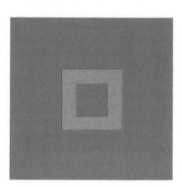

▲ **A**

The red-purple squares, although seemingly different, are identical.

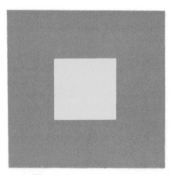 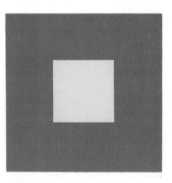

▲ **B**

A brilliant, vibrant color will not show much change despite different surroundings.

Color and Its Surroundings

Related to the concept of color changing with the light is one other important color phenomenon: Our perception of colors changes according to their surroundings. Even in the same light, a color will appear different depending on the colors that are adjacent to it. Rarely do we see a color by itself. Normally colors are seen in conjunction with others, and the visual differences are often amazing. A change in value (dark and light) is a common occurrence. Illustration **A** shows that not only the value but also the color changes. The smaller "pink" squares are identical; the visual differences are

caused by the various background colors these squares are placed against. In **B**, however, the two yellow areas, despite different background colors, still look about the same. With pure, vibrant colors, optical changes will be very slight. Grayed, neutral colors are constantly changing in different contexts, as you can see in **C**.

These manipulations of our perception are not mere "tricks." Illustrations **A** and **C** are not exceptions to our everyday experiences: They are examples of contextual influences that surround our every perception.

 C

The gray sample looks different
against the two background colors.

HUE

The first property of color is what we call **hue**. Hue simply refers to the name of the color. Red, orange, green, and purple are hues. Although the words *hue* and *color* are often used as synonyms, there is a distinction between the two terms. *Hue* describes the visual sensation of the different parts of the color **spectrum**. However, one hue can be varied to produce many colors. So even though there are relatively few hues, there can be an almost unlimited number of colors.

Pink, rose, scarlet, maroon, and crimson are all colors, but the hue in each case is red. We are all aware that in the world of commercial products, color names abound; plum, adobe, colonial blue, desert sunset, Mayan gold, and avocado are a few examples. These often romantic images are extremely inexact terms that mean only what the manufacturers think they mean. The same hue (or color) can have dozens of different commercial names. You will even notice that the same hue can have different names in different color systems. "Blue," for instance, may be a blue-violet in one system and a cyan in another. One system may use the term *purple* and another *violet*. Try to see past the names given to the colors and look instead at the relationships.

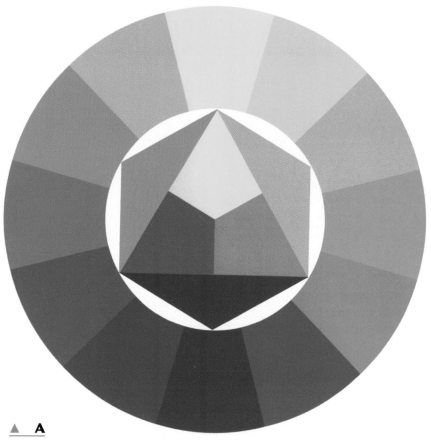

▲ **A**

The twelve-step color wheel of Johannes Itten.

Color Wheels

The most common organization for the relationships of the basic colors is the **color wheel** shown in **A**. The wheel system dates to the early eighteenth century, and this version is one updated by Johannes Itten in the twentieth century. This particular organization uses twelve hues, which are divided into three categories.

The three primary colors are red, yellow, and blue. From these, all other colors can theoretically be mixed. The three **secondary colors** are mixtures of the two primaries: Red and yellow make orange; yellow and blue make green; blue and red make violet. The six **tertiary colors** are mixtures of a primary and an adjacent secondary: Blue and green make blue-green, red and violet make red-violet, and so on.

The color wheel of twelve hues is the one still most commonly used. If you look closely, however, you will notice that the complements are not consistent with those shown in the illustration of additive and subtractive primaries. Furthermore, if you try mixing colors based on this wheel (such as blue and red to make violet), you will find the results to be dull and unsatisfactory. The color wheel shown in **B** is based on the Munsell Color System, and this version has ten equal visual steps. Mixtures of complements on this wheel will more closely produce neutrals (when tested as light mixtures on a computer, for example), and the positions of the colors are more useful in predicting paint mixtures as well.

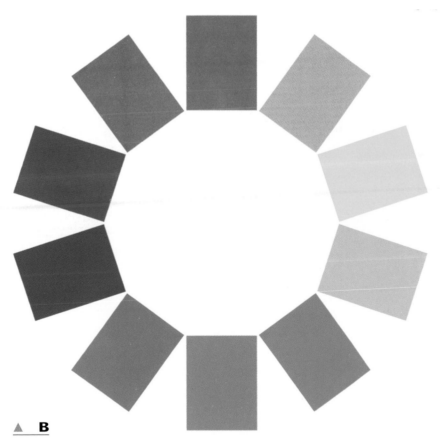

▲ **B**
Munsell color wheel. Courtesy of Gretag Macbeth, New Windsor, New York.

VALUE

The second property of color is **value**, which refers to the lightness or darkness of the hue. In pigment, adding white or black paint to the color alters value. Adding white lightens the color and produces a **tint**, or high-value color. Adding black darkens the color and produces a **shade**, or low-value color. Individual perception varies, but most people can distinguish at least forty tints and shades of any color.

"Normal" Color Values Differ

Not all the colors on the color wheel are shown at the same value. Each is shown at normal value, with the pure color unmixed and undiluted. The normal values of yellow and of blue, for example, are radically different **(A)**. Because yellow is a light, or high-value, color, a yellow value scale shows many more shades than tints. The blue scale shows more tints, because normal blue is darker than a middle value.

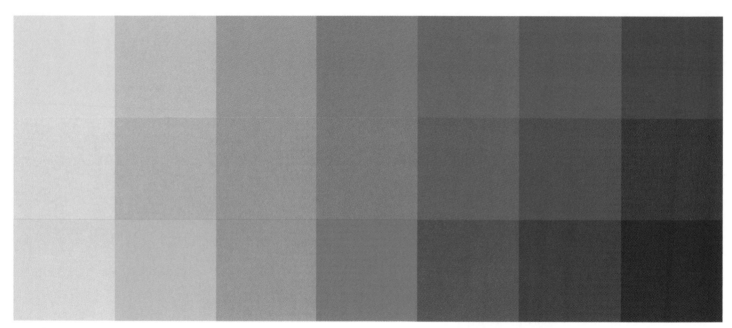

▲ **A**

Value scales for blue, gray, and yellow with equal visual steps.

Changing Color Values

When working with paint and pigments, the value of a color can be altered by thinning the color with medium. The more transparent color will be a lighter value when applied over a white background. The value of a color can also be altered by mixture with other hues: A naturally dark violet will darken a yellow, for example.

Value, like color itself, is variable and depends entirely on surrounding hues for its visual sensation. In **B** the center green area appears much lighter and more luminous on the black background than on the white.

Color Interaction

It is well known that colors are changed by their context. Amounts and repetition are also critical factors in color interaction. The same green shown in **B** takes on a different complexion when it is "woven" through the black or white as shown in **C**. In this case the white and green interact in a mixture effect (best perceived from a distance), producing a lighter value field of color than the green and black pattern.

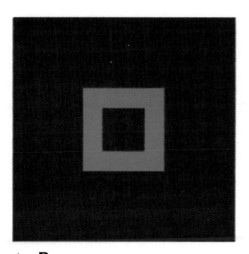
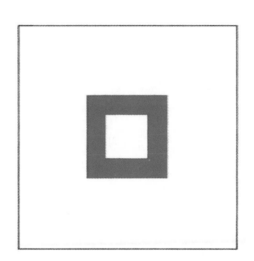

▲　**B**

The same color will appear to change in value, depending upon the surrounding color.

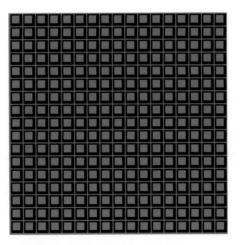
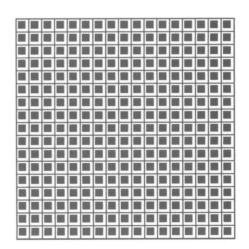

▲　**C**

The visual mixture of green with black and white.

INTENSITY/
COMPLEMENTARY COLORS

The third property of color is **intensity**, which refers to the brightness of a color. Because a color is at full intensity only when pure and unmixed, a relationship exists between value and intensity. Mixing black or white with a color changes its value and at the same time affects its intensity. To see the distinction between the two terms, look at the two tints (high value) of red in example **A**. The tints have about the same degree of lightness, yet one might be called "rose," the other "shocking pink." The two colors have very different visual effects, and the difference comes from brightness or intensity. Intensity is sometimes called **chroma**, or *saturation*.

▲ **A**

Two tints of red at the same value have different intensities.

▶ **B**

Complementary colors neutralize each other in mixture.

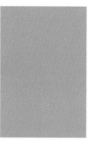
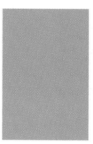

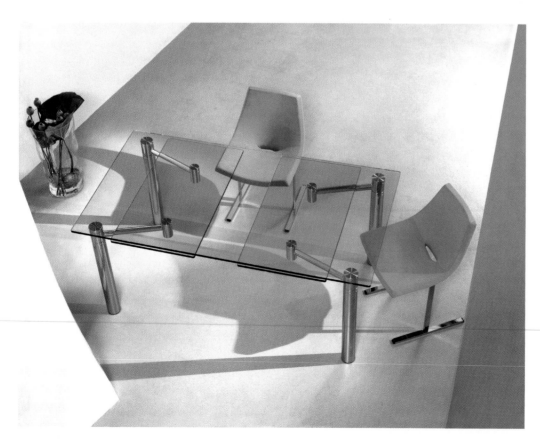

◀ **C**

Casanova Table and Side Chairs. Domus Design Collection, New York.

How to Lower Intensity

There are two ways to lower the intensity of a color, to make a color less bright, more neutral, and duller. One way is to mix gray with the color. Depending on the gray used, you can dull a color without changing its value. The second way is to mix a color with its **complement**, the color directly across from it on the color wheel. Illustration **B** shows an intensity scale involving the complementary colors blue and orange. Neutralized (low-intensity) versions of a color are often called *tones*. In **B** we see two intensity levels of blue and two intensity levels of orange with gray in the middle. As progressively more orange is added to the blue, the blue becomes duller, more grayed. The same is true of the orange, which becomes browner when blue is added. Note this effect in the photograph of orange chairs seen through the blue glass table **(C)**.

The Degas painting in **D** is characterized by varying intensities of a single hue. The warm red-orange ranges in intensity to include flesh tones and browns. When other hues are not present, the effect of intensity is even more obvious.

How to Increase Intensity

Complementary colors are direct opposites in position and in character. Mixing complementary colors together neutralizes them, but when complementary colors are placed next to each other, they intensify each other's brightness. When blue and orange are side by side, each color appears brighter than in any other context. This effect is called **simultaneous contrast**, meaning that each complement simultaneously intensifies the visual brilliance of the other, so that the colors appear to vibrate. Artists use this visual effect when they wish to produce brilliant color.

Afterimage

Another phenomenon that defines complementary color is the **afterimage** effect. Stare at an area of intense color for a minute or so, and then glance away at a white piece of paper or wall. Suddenly, an area of the complementary color will seem to appear. For example, when you look at a white wall after staring at a red shape, a definite blue-green area in somewhat the same shape will seem to take form on the wall.

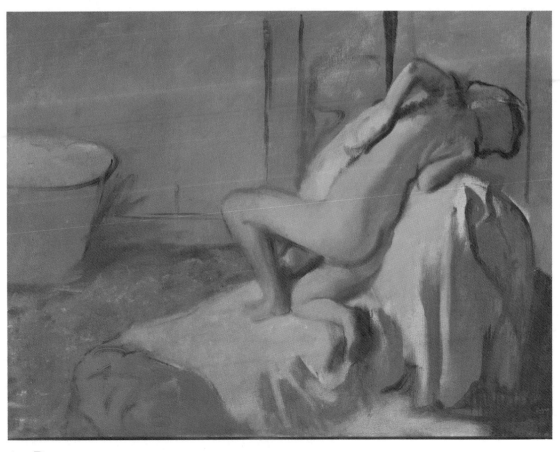

▲ **D**

Edgar Degas. *After the Bath, Woman Drying Herself.* c.1896. Oil on canvas, 2' 11" × 3' 9²/₃" (89 × 116 cm). Philadelphia Museum of Art (Purchased, Estate of the late George D. Widener, 1980-6-1).

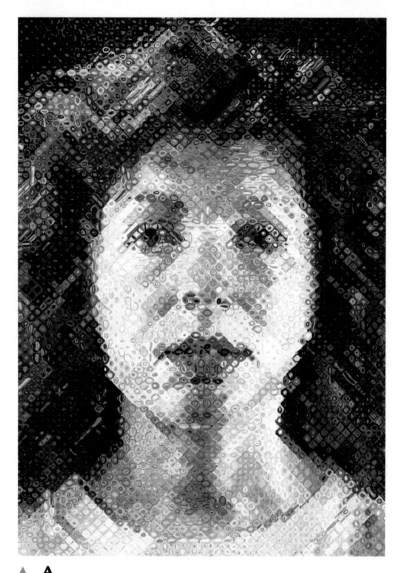

▲ **A**

Chuck Close. *April*. 1990–1991.Oil on canvas, 8' 4" × 7'.
Courtesy Pace Wildenstein, New York.

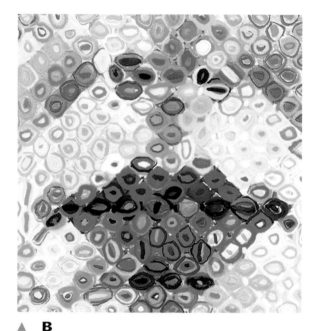

▲ **B**

Chuck Close. *April* (detail). 1990–1991. Oil on canvas,
8' 4" × 7'. Courtesy Pace Wildenstein, New York.

TECHNIQUES THAT SUGGEST LIGHT

Pigments combine along certain guidelines to create new
colors. However, muddy or dull colors are often the result.
Even when mixing adjacent colors on the color wheel you
may find the results to be less intense than you anticipated,
and the farther apart the hues, the more subtractive (darker
and duller) the mixture. To understand this process, think
of the pigments as acting like filters, which in combination
(or mixture) allow less light or color to reflect off the colored
surface to the viewer's eye.

Visual Color Mixing Techniques

Pigment simply will never reproduce the luminous and
brilliant quality of light. Recognizing this, artists have
struggled with the problem and tried various techniques
to overcome it. One attempt is called **visual color mixing**
or **optical mixture**. Rather than mixing two colors on the
palette, artists place two pure colors side by side in small
areas so the viewer's eye (at a certain distance) will do the
mixing. Or perhaps they drag a brush of thick pigment of
one color loosely across a field of another color. The uneven
paint application allows bits and pieces of the background
to show through. Again, the pure colors are mixed in our
perception, not on the canvas.

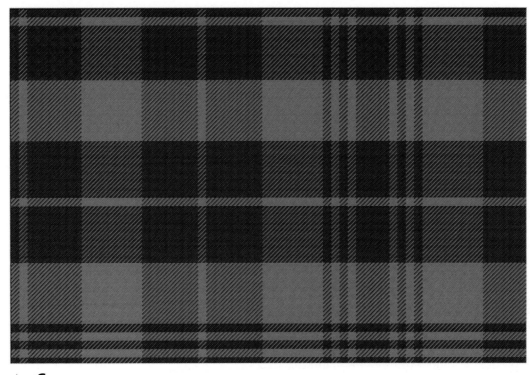

▲ **C**

Black Watch Plaid for Band Regimental Tartan (#396). House of Tartan, Ltd., Perthshire, Scotland.

Visual Mixing in Art and Television

Visual mixing is often associated with the post-Impressionist era of the late nineteenth century and can be observed in the works of artists such as Seurat and van Gogh. The techniques of **pointillism** and *divisionism* both use small bits of juxtaposed color to produce different color sensations. In a way, these artists anticipated the truly additive color mixing that occurs on a color television screen. A TV screen is composed of thousands of luminous pixels. The colors we see are a visual mix of the light primaries red, blue, and green. Such luminosity is not possible with the surface of painting. Still, artists continue to explore the possibilities of visual mixture, as can be seen in *April* **(A)** by the contemporary painter Chuck Close. The large scale of this portrait assures that we will always be aware of the pattern of color bits and that they will not absolutely merge into a mixture. In fact, this technique is usually most luminous when that is the case.

This particular painting by Close has large, obvious units of color, as can be seen in the detail **(B)**. Earlier paintings by the artist employed smaller, more subtle dots and dashes. The larger marks in the newer work allow us to easily see the components of the "mixture." It is evident that the closer the value of the color bits, the more easily they merge.

Visual Mixing in Other Art Forms

The basic idea of visual mixing is used in many areas. In creating mosaics, stirring a bowl of red and blue tiles will not, of course, produce purple tesserae. Instead, small pieces of pure-colored tiles are interspersed to produce the effect of many other intermediate colors. The same process is employed in creating tapestries. Weavers working with a limited number of colored yarns or threads can intermingle them, so that at a distance the eye merges them and creates an impression of many hues, values, or intensities. Illustration **C** is a plaid, or tartan, fabric that demonstrates this phenomenon. From a distance the material can seem to be a pattern of many colors and values. Close inspection might reveal that just three colored threads have been woven in various densities to produce all the visual variations.

A version of the pointillist technique is now used every day in a photomechanical adaptation in the printing of color pictures. The numerous colors we see in printed reproductions, such as those on these pages, are usually produced by just four basic colors in a small dot pattern. The dots in this case are so tiny that we are totally unaware of them unless we use a magnifying glass to visually enlarge them.

IDENTIFYING COLOR WITH THE SENSES

"Cool" colors? **"Warm" colors**? These may seem odd adjectives to apply to the visual sensation of color, as cool and warm are sensations of touch, not sight. Nevertheless, we are all familiar with the terms and continually refer to colors this way. Because of the learned association of color with objects, we continue to relate colors to physical sensations. Hence, red and orange (fire) and yellow (sunlight) become identified as warm colors. Similarly, blue (sky, water) and green (grass, plants) are always thought of as cool colors.

A Psychological Effect

Touching an area of red will assuredly not burn your hand, but looking at red will indeed induce a feeling of warmth. The effect may be purely psychological, but the results are very real. Perhaps you have read of the workers in an office painted blue complaining of the chill and actually getting colds. The problem was solved not by raising the thermostat but by repainting the office in warm tones of brown. The painting by Archibald Motley in **A** creates a nighttime scene dominated by the dark values of intense blue. This blue might even evoke the cool relief that night brings after a hot summer day.

Color Context Makes a Difference

We generally think of the colors yellow through red-violet as the warm side of the color wheel and yellow-green through violet as the cool segment. The visual effects are quite variable, however, and again depend a great deal on the context in which we see the color. In **B** the green square appears very warm surrounded by a background of blue. But in **C** the identical green, when placed on an orange background, shifts and becomes a cooler tone.

Creating Depth and Volume

Because warm colors tend to advance whereas cool colors seem to recede, the artist may use the warm/cool relationship to establish a feeling of depth and volume. Probably no group of artists has investigated and expanded our ideas of color more than the Impressionists. The blue and purple shadows (instead of gray or black) that so shocked the nineteenth-century public seem to us today perfectly logical and reasonable.

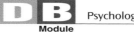

Psychological Dimensions of Color

▶ **A**

Archibald J. Motley Jr. *Gettin' Religion.* 1948. Oil on canvas, 2' 7⁷/₈" × 3' 3¹/₄". Collection Archie Motley and Valerie Gerrard Browne, Evanston, Illinois. Chicago History Museum.

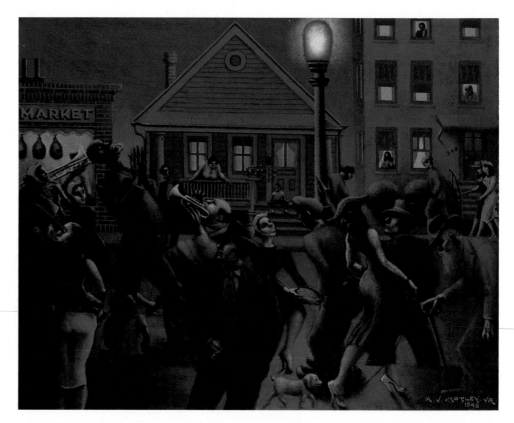

The contrast of warm and cool evokes a feeling of light. This can be seen in **D**. Few details are evident in the cityscape veiled by the curtains, but we readily understand the "logic" of the view and the suggestion of light. The cityscape takes on the cool color of the sky in the distance, and the near buildings show the warmth of sunlight. The artist intensifies this warm and cool theme with the contrast between the woman's blue robe and the orange she holds in her hand. The warm colors are repeated in the flowers and the color of her hair.

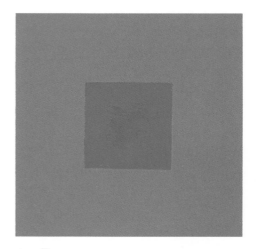

▲ **B**

A colored area on a cool background
will appear warmer in tone.

▲ **C**

The same color surrounded by
a warm background seems cool.

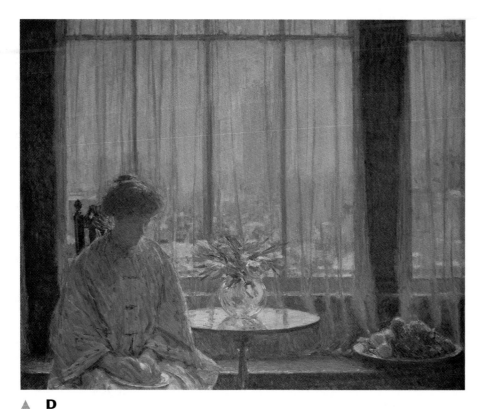

▲ **D**

Childe Hassam. *The Breakfast Room, Winter Morning.* 1911. Oil on canvas.
© Worcester Art Museum, Massachusetts / The Bridgeman Art Library.

COLOR DOMINANCE

Areas of emphasis in a work of art create visual interest and, naturally, have been carefully planned by the artist. Color is very often the means chosen to provide this emphasis—color is probably the most direct device to use. When planning emphasis, we might think of using a larger size somewhere, or perhaps changing a shape, or isolating one element by itself. As the diagrams in **A** show, the use of color dominates these other devices. You will notice that the accented color is not a radically different hue or very different in value or intensity. Such contrasts, of course, would heighten the effect. But **A** shows that color by its very character commands attention.

Color as Attention-Grabber

Sometimes the artist or designer may wish to create a definite focal point or center of attention that the observer will see first. A bright or vivid color, such as the yellow in the dental floss advertisement **(B)** creates an emphasis that the shape or position of the words "boy bands" would not achieve in black and white. In this case the focus is not on the product which is more subtly presented in the foreground. A memorable and humorous reference to dental floss is suggested by emphasizing an irritant to be flossed out.

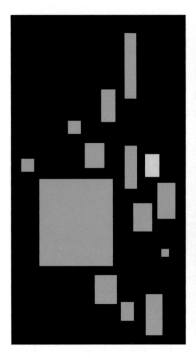
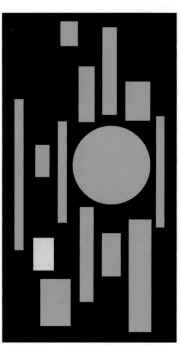
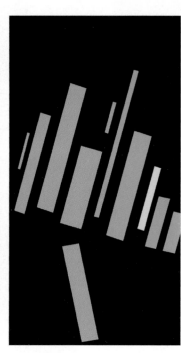

◀ **A**

Color is so strong a visual element that it will dominate other devices to establish emphasis.

▶ **B**

"Music." P&G—Glide Dental Floss Campaign. Saatchi & Saatchi, New York. Creative Director: Tony Granger, Jan Jacobs, Leo Premutico. Art Director: Menno Kluin. Copywriter: Icaro Doria. Photo: Jenny van Sommers.

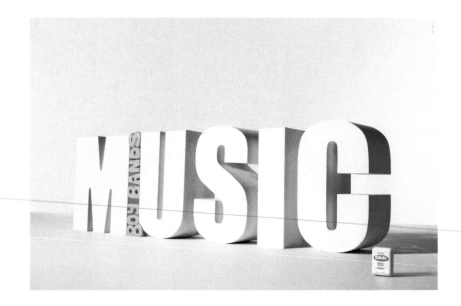

The unusual arrangement of autumn leaves in *Elm* by Andy Goldsworthy in **C** shows how color can create an emphasis so strong that it dominates other elements. In this case Goldsworthy tore similar dark and yellow leaves and mated a dark half to a yellow half of another similarly shaped leaf. These mated leaves form the boundary, which contains many other yellow leaves set off against the field of darker and duller older leaves. The result emphasizes the yellow shape and gives the appearance of the dark leaves having been painted within that rough circle.

In each of the above examples yellow is the dominant hue and attention grabber. In **A** yellow provides emphasis in a cluster of green shapes. In **B** yellow dominates a predominantly light valued composition, and in **C** the fact that yellow is a light hue asserts dominance in an otherwise dark composition.

The very strong emphasis that color can provide is one reason some artists consider color to be the most powerful of the visual elements. You can see the origins of such modern design considerations in Lissitzky's now familiar composition **(D)** featuring the dominant red square.

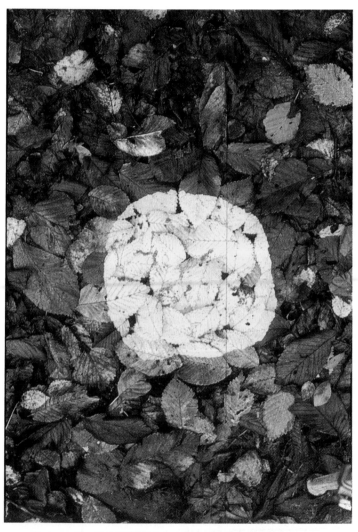

▲ **C**

Andy Goldsworthy. *Elm*. Middleton Woods, Yorkshire. 1980. From *Andy Goldsworthy: A Collaboration with Nature* (New York: Harry N. Abrams, 1990).

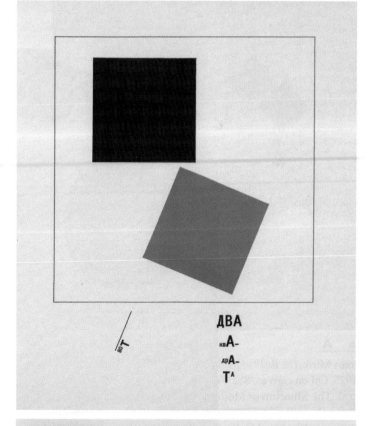

▲ **D**

El Lissitzky. *Of Two Squares: A Suprematist Tale in Six Constructions.* 1922. Illustrated book with letterpress cover and six letterpress illustrations, 10¹⁵/₁₆″ × 8⁷/₈″ (27.8 × 22.5 cm). Publisher: Skify, Berlin. Gift of the Judith Rothschild Foundation (89.2001.5).

COLOR'S SPATIAL PROPERTIES

There is a direct relationship between color and a visual impression of depth, or pictorial space. Colors have an innate advancing or receding quality because of slight muscular reactions in our eyes as we focus on different colors. Intense, warm colors (red, orange, yellow) seem to come forward; cool colors (blue, green) seem to go back. The design of numbers in various colors (**A**) illustrates this principle. When we look at this design, we can see that some numbers immediately pop forward and actually seem closer than others. Some numbers appear to stay back, with others seeming to be far in the background. Relative size can influence this effect, with larger items automatically seeming closer. But notice that size is not really a consideration here. There are numbers of equal size and weight that advance or retreat based solely on their color. Colors closest in hue or value to the dark brown ground will tend to recede.

Atmospheric Perspective

Another aspect of the relationship of color and spatial illusion is that the dust in the earth's atmosphere breaks up the color rays from distant objects and makes them appear bluish (**B**). As objects recede, any brilliance of color becomes more neutral, finally seeming to be gray-blue. The strange landscape in **C** gives a feeling of great distance. The overlapping planes of the receding fragments change in color and value. The photograph has concentrated warm browns and oranges in the close foreground. Then, as distance increases, the elements become pale and cooler in color. Value and color contrasts are more pronounced in the foreground and more subtle in the distance. In this case (**C**) the image shows the effect of atmospheric perspective but is definitely *not* the reassuring blue sky and hills of a pastoral landscape such as **B**.

Using Color to Emphasize Flatness

In contrast, David Hockney in *Mulholland Drive: The Road to the Studio* (**D**) consciously flattens and compresses space by his use of color. Hills, groves of trees, and the towers of power lines are obvious images from the landscape, but the shapes, colors, and patterns are laid out like a crazy quilt. Even the maplike patterns at the top add emphasis to the essential flatness of the arrangement. In this case, hot oranges work as both foreground and background. You can see blue along the bottom or "foreground" of the painting as well as farther up or "back" in the landscape.

See also *Devices to Show Depth: Aerial Perspective,* page 204, and *Value and Space,* page 246.

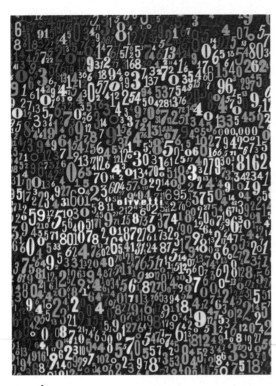

▲ **A**
Giovanni Pintori. Advertisement for Olivetti calculators. 1949. Associazione Archivio Storico Olivetti, Ivrea, Italy.

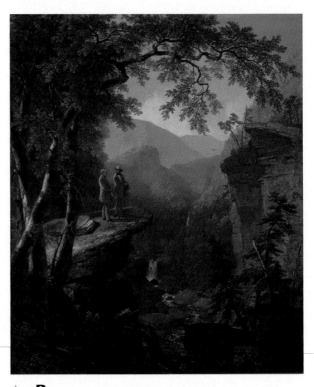

▲ **B**
Asher B. Durand. *Kindred Spirits.* 1849. Oil on canvas, 3′ 8″ × 3′. Courtesy Crystal Bridges Museum of American Art, Bentonville, Arkansas.

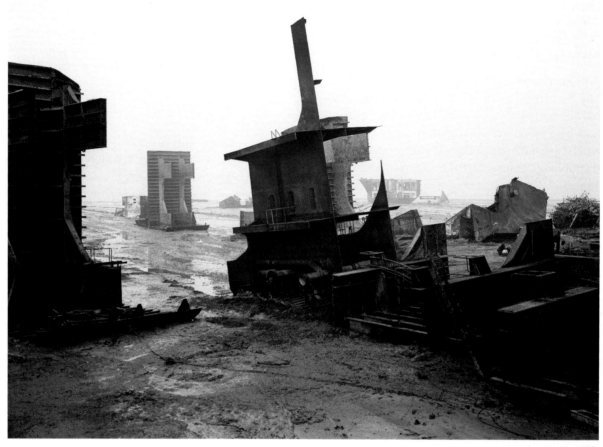

▲ **C**

Edward Burtynsky. *Shipbreaking #10, Chittagong, Bangladesh.*
2000. Photograph. Charles Cowles Gallery, New York.

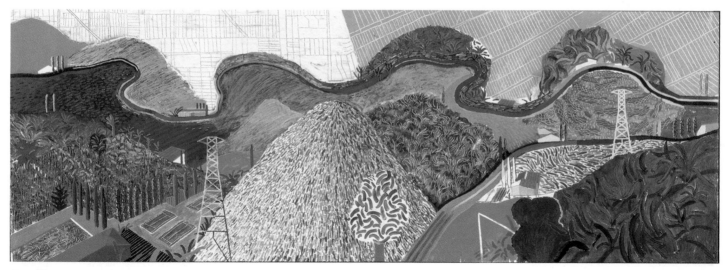

▲ **D**

David Hockney. *Mulholland Drive: The Road to the Studio.* 1980. Acrylic on canvas, 7′ 2″ × 20′ 3″ (218.44 × 617.22 cm).
Los Angeles County Museum of Art (purchased with funds from the F. Patrick Burns Bequest).

MONOCHROMATIC/ANALOGOUS

Certain color schemes are thought of as **color harmonies**. These schemes are organized by simple color relationships.

Monochromatic Color Scheme

A **monochromatic** color scheme involves the use of only one hue. The hue can vary in value, and pure black or white may be added. Painter Mark Tansey has varied the values in **A** by a process of wiping away the paint to reveal the white "ground" underneath. The use of monochrome unites the montage of images that come together in this painting. Tansey also uses monochrome as a way to emphasize textural difference over color difference and to suggest the qualities of an old photograph.

Illustration **B** is a predominantly monochromatic photograph and layout. A bit of brown at the bottom offers the only hue contrast to the values of blue. In this case a monochromatic scheme puts the emphasis on shapes in the composition.

Analogous Color Scheme

An **analogous** color scheme combines several hues that sit next to each other on the color wheel. Again, the hues may vary in value. The Navajo textile **(C)** shows the related, harmonious feeling that analogous color lends to a design. This blanket includes colors adjacent to red on the color wheel.

Tonality

Color unity is described by another term. We often speak of the *tonality* of a design or painting. **Tonality** refers to the dominance of a single color or the visual importance of a hue that seems to pervade the whole color structure despite the presence of other colors. Monochromatic patterns (as value studies in one color) give a uniform tonality, because only one hue is present. Analogous color schemes can also produce a dominant tonality, as **D** shows. When colors are chosen from one part of the color wheel, they will share one hue in common. In **D** a bit of red seems to be in every color, although this is not strictly monochrome. The hues range from warmer reds (a presence of yellow) to cooler browns, and pinks.

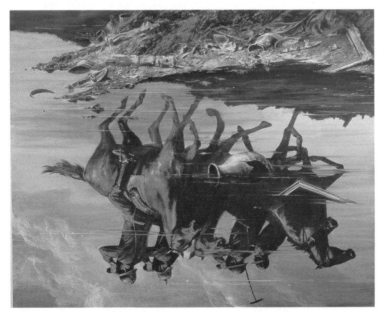

▲ **A**

Mark Tansey. *Forward Retreat*. 1986. Oil on canvas, 7′ 10″ × 9′ 8″ (2.4 × 2.9 m). Collection of Eli Broad Family Foundation, Santa Monica, California. Courtesy Gagosian Gallery, New York.

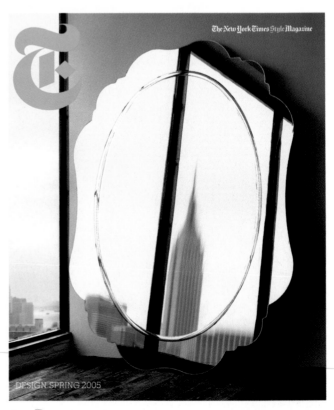

▲ **B**

The New York Times, Style magazine. Spring 2005.

▶ **C**

Navajo blanket/rug. c. 1885–1895.
4′ 7″ × 6′ 10″ (140.5 × 207.8 cm).
Natural History Museum of Los
Angeles County (William Randolph
Hearst Collection, A.5141.42–153).

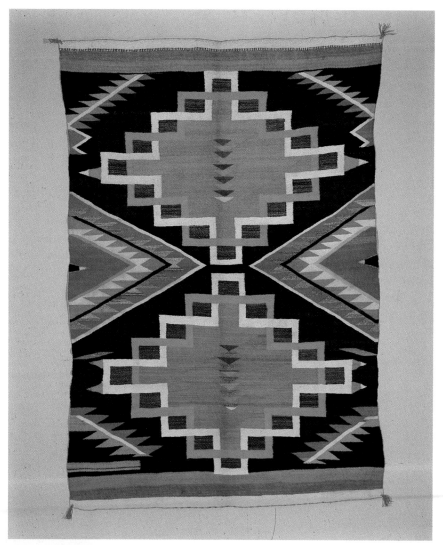

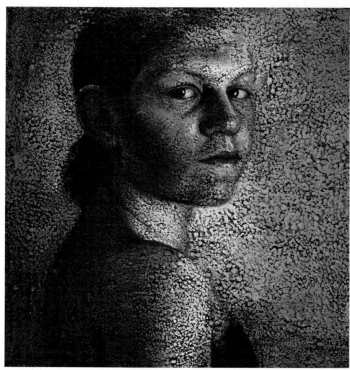

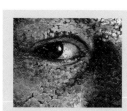

◀ **D**

Susan Moore. *Vanity (Portrait 1)*. 2000.
Oil stick on canvas, 4′ × 3′ 11″.

COMPLEMENTARY/TRIADIC

A **complementary** color scheme, as the term implies, joins colors opposite each other on the color wheel. This combination produces a sense of contrast, as in Stuart Davis's painting titled *Visa* (**A**). This painting has the graphic qualities of a billboard or sign. The complementary contrast of magenta letters and green background makes use of the eye-catching devices of advertising.

Split Complementary Color Scheme

A split complementary color scheme is related to the complementary scheme but employs colors adjacent to one of the complementary pairs. For example, the sky in **B** is balanced by a range of yellows and oranges near the complementary opposite of the blue. It is more common to find a complex solution such as **B** than a simple complementary pair.

Triadic Color Scheme

A **triadic** color scheme involves three hues equally spaced on the color wheel. Red, yellow, and blue would be the most common example. These hues form a triangle on the color wheel and suggest balance. This is true even when the red, yellow, and blue are subtle as in Vermeer's painting *Girl with a Pearl Earring* (**C**). Red, yellow, and blue often appear in combination with the simple contrast of black and white as they do in this picture.

Planning Color Schemes

These color schemes or harmonies are probably more common to such design areas as interiors, posters, and packaging than to painting. In painting, color often is used intuitively, and many artists would reject the idea that they work by formula. But knowing these harmonies can help designers consciously plan the visual effects they want a finished pattern to have. Moreover, color can easily provide a visual unity that might not be obvious in the initial pattern of shapes. Even though design aims vary, often the more complicated and busy the pattern of shapes is, the more useful will be a strict control of the color. The reverse is also true.

D B Complementary versus Analogous Colors
Module

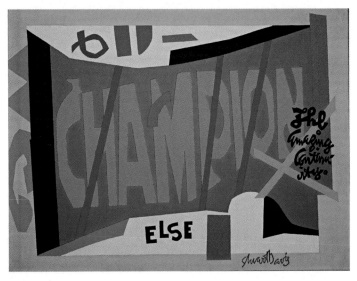

▲ **A**

Stuart Davis. *Visa.* 1951. Oil on canvas, 3′ 4″ × 4′ 4″. The Museum of Modern Art, New York (gift of Mrs. Gertrud A. Mellon, 9.1953). Art © Estate of Stuart Davis/ Licensed by VAGA, New York, New York.

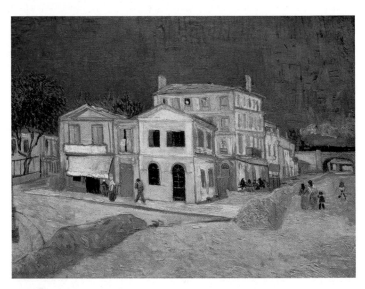

▲ **B**

Vincent van Gogh. *The Yellow House.* 1888. Oil on canvas, 72 × 91.5 cm. © Van Gogh Museum, Amsterdam, The Netherlands/The Bridgeman Art Library.

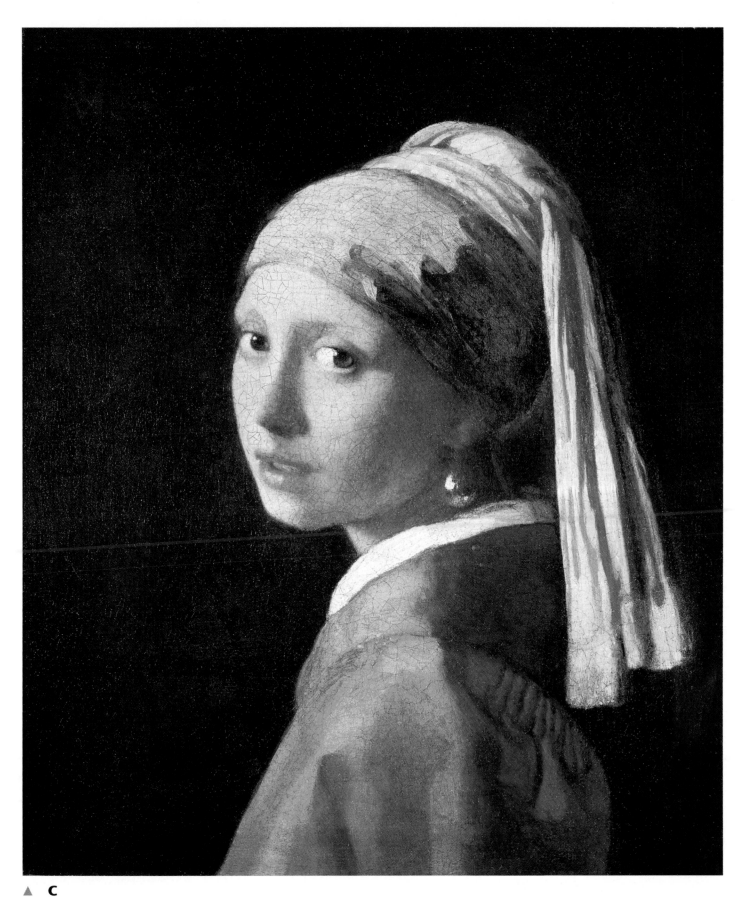

▲ **C**

Jan Vermeer. *Girl with a Pearl Earring.* c. 1665–1666. Oil on canvas, 1′ 5$^1/_2$″ × 1′ 3$^3/_8$″
(44.5 × 39 cm). Royal Cabinet of Paintings, Mauritshuis, The Hague.

UNEXPECTED COMBINATIONS

Color discord is the opposite of color harmony. A combination of discordant colors can be visually disturbing. Discordant colors have no basic affinity for each other (as you would find with analogous colors), nor do they seem to balance each other (as with a complementary contrast).

The term *discord* conveys an immediate negative impression. Discord in life, in a personal relationship, may not be pleasant, but it often provides a stimulus or excitement. In the same manner, discord can be extremely useful in art and design.

Using Discord to Add Interest

Mild discord results in exciting, eye-catching color combinations. The world of fashion has exploited the idea to the point that mildly discordant combinations are almost commonplace. A discordant color note in a painting or design may contribute visual surprise and also may better express certain themes or ideas. A poster may better attract attention by its startling colors.

▲ **A**

Pure orange and red-purple.

▲ **B**

The same colors with closer values.

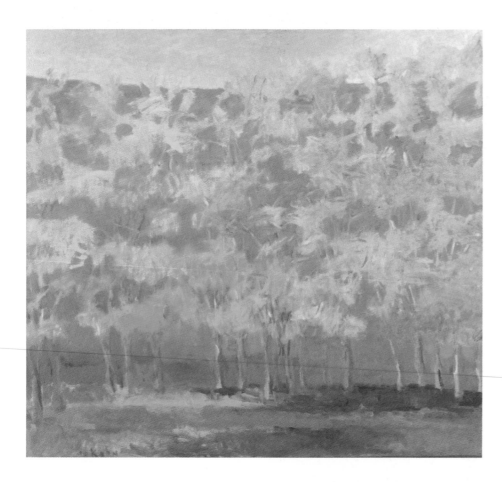

◀ **C**

Wolf Kahn. *Color/Tree Symphony.* 1994. Oil on canvas, 4′ 3¹/₂″ × 4′ 8¹/₂″. Grace Borgenicht Gallery, New York. Art © Estate of Wolf Kahn/Licensed by VAGA, New York, New York.

Once, rules were taught about just which color combinations were harmonious and which were definitely to be avoided because the colors did not "go together." A combination of pink and orange was unthinkable; even blue and green patterns were suspect. Today these rules seem silly, and we approach color more freely, seeking unexpected combinations.

The color pair of orange and red-purple shown in **A** is one that has been called discordant. This is typical of color pairings that are widely separated on the color wheel but not complements. In **B** the effect is even more discordant when the red-purple is lightened to the same value as the orange.

Wolf Kahn **(C)** takes full advantage of this red-purple and orange color pairing to create *Color/Tree Symphony*. The colors conjure the intense impact of autumn foliage and seem to create light.

Colors in Conflict

Certain color pairings are almost difficult to look at. In fact, our eye experiences a conflict in trying to perceive them simultaneously. Red and cyan literally have a vibrating edge when their values are equal and their intensities are high **(D)**. You will find this to be true for a range of colors when they are paired at equal value, but the **vibrating color** effect is strongest with reds opposed to blues and greens. Annie May Young exploits this almost electric effect in her quilt shown in **E**.

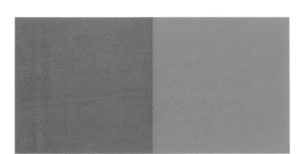

▲ **D**

Red and cyan will have a vibrating edge when values are equal and intensities are high.

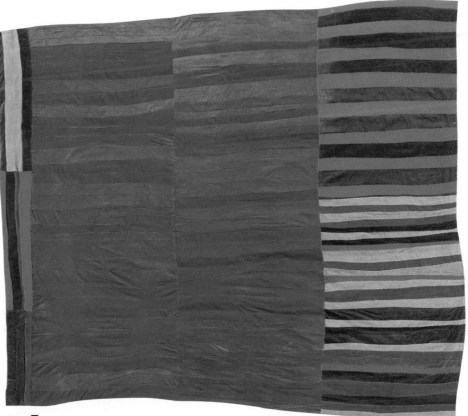

▲ **E**

Annie Mae Young. *Quilt*. c. 1965. Cotton stiff material: corduroy sheeting, polyester dress and pants material, wool, 7′ 7″ × 6′ 9″. By permission of the artist.

LOCAL, OPTICAL, ARBITRARY

There are three basic ways in which color can be used in painting. An artist may use what is called **local color**. This refers to identifying the color of an object under ordinary daylight. Local color is the **objective** color that we "know" objects are: Grass is green, bananas are yellow, apples are red. The use of local color reinforces, or takes advantage of, our preconceptions of an object's color.

Light Affects Color

Visually, the red of an apple can change radically, depending on the illumination. Because color is a property of light, the color of any object changes at sunset, under moonlight, or by different city lights. Even atmospheric effects can visually change the local color of distant objects, such as faraway mountains that appear blue. An artist reproducing these visual effects is using optical color. Lighting directors for theater and dance consciously manipulate lighting to evoke mood, create space, and give emphasis to principal actors as in **A**.

Subjective Use of Color

In arbitrary color, the color choices are subjective rather than based on the colors seen in nature. The artist selects colors for design, aesthetic, or emotional reasons. Large patches of color make up the composition of Milton Avery's *White Rooster* **(B)**. The blue tree and salmon-colored sky are bold subjective color choices. Arbitrary color is sometimes difficult to pinpoint, because many painters take some artistic liberties in using color. Has the artist disregarded the colors he saw, or has he merely intensified and exaggerated the visual reference? This latter use is termed *heightened color*. Gauguin's painting in **C** intensifies the red earthen pathway, bringing it close in saturation to the woman's dress.

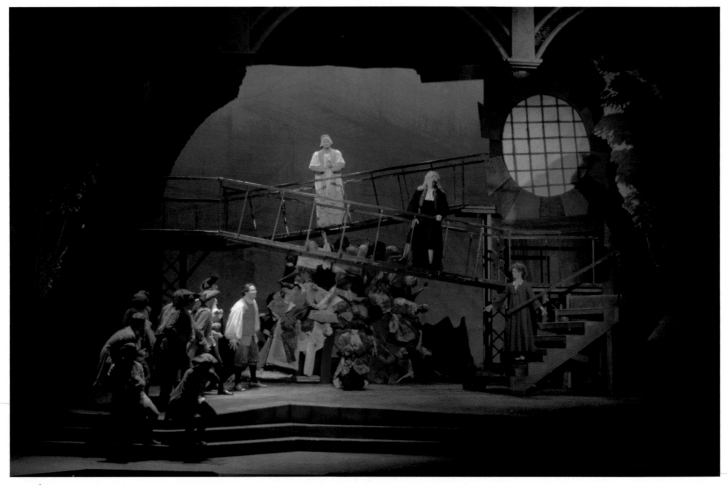

▲ **A**

Scene from *Candide* by Leonard Bernstein and Richard Wilbur. The Ohio State University Department of Theatre.

Pure arbitrary (or subjective) color is often seen in twentieth-century and contemporary painting. Just as art in general has moved away from naturalism, so too has arbitrary color tended to become an important interest. Even color photographers—with filters, infrared film, and various darkroom techniques—have experimented widely in the area of unexpected color effects.

These categories of color use obviously apply to paintings with identifiable subject matter. In nonobjective art, the forms have no apparent reference to natural objects, so the color is also nonobjective. Purely aesthetic considerations determine the color choices.

 Local versus Optical Color

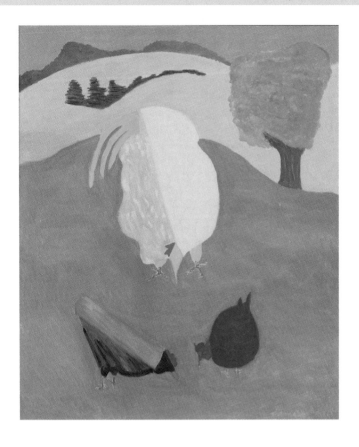

▶ **B**

Milton Avery. *White Rooster.* 1947. Oil on canvas, 5′ 1 1/2″ × 4′ 2 3/4″. The Metropolitan Museum of Art, gift of Joyce Blaffer von Bothmer, in memory of Mr. and Mrs. Robert Lee Blaffer, 1975 (1975.210).

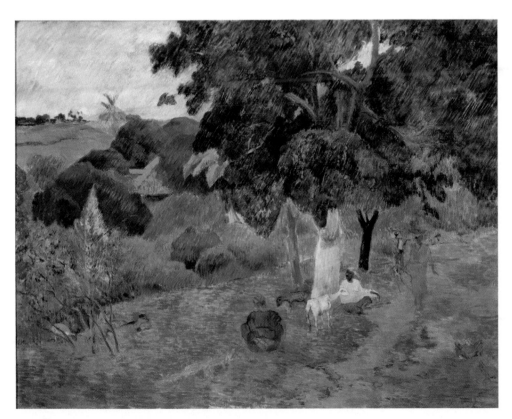

▲ **C**

Paul Gauguin. *Allées et Venues, Martinique (Coming and Going).* 1887. Oil on canvas, 2′ 4 1/2″ × 3′ 1/4″ (72.5 × 92 cm). © Carmen Thyssen-Bornemisza Collection on loan to the Museo Thyssen-Bornemisza (CTB.1979.88).

EMOTIONAL COLOR

COLOR EVOKES A RESPONSE

"Ever since our argument, I've been blue."

"I saw red when she lied to me."

"You're certainly in a black mood today."

"I was green with envy when I saw their new house."

These statements are emotional. The speakers are expressing an emotional reaction, and somehow a color reference makes the meaning clearer, because color appeals to our emotions and feelings. For artists who wish to arouse an emotional response in the viewer, **emotional color** is the most effective device. Even before we "read" the subject matter or identify the forms, the color creates an atmosphere to which we respond.

▶ **A**

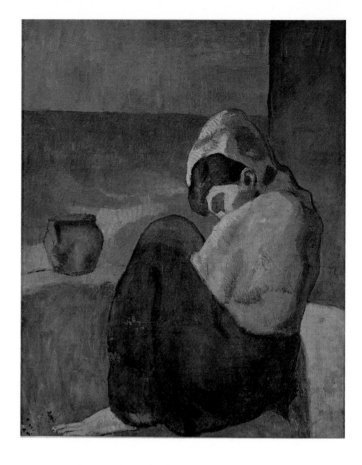

Pablo Picasso. *Crouching Woman*. 1902. Oil on canvas, 2' 11" × 2' 4" (90 × 71 cm). Staatsgalerie, Stuttgart.

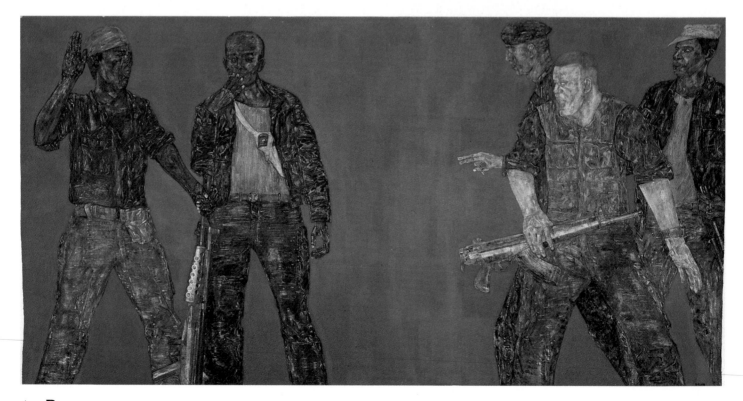

▲ **B**

Leon Golub. *Mercenaries IV*. 1980. Acrylic on linen, 10' × 19' 2 1/2" (3 × 6 m). Private collection, courtesy of the artist.
Art © Estate of Leon Golub / Licensed by VAGA, New York, New York. Courtesy Ronald Feldman Fine Arts.

Colors Evoke Emotions

In a very basic instance, we commonly recognize so-called warm and cool colors. Yellows, oranges, and reds give us an instinctive feeling of warmth and evoke warm, happy, cheerful reactions. Cooler blues and greens are automatically associated with quieter, less-outgoing feelings and can express melancholy **(A)** or depression. These examples are generalities, of course, for the combination of colors is vital, and the artist can also influence our reactions by the values and intensities of the colors selected.

Theme and Context

Paintings in which color causes an emotional reaction and relates to the thematic subject matter are very common. The flat red background in Leon Golub's *Mercenaries IV* **(B)** is evocative of blood and impending violence associated with the threatening image of the mercenaries. The intense red seems to push these figures at us, heightening our emotional response to the subject matter. The "dirty" colors and complementary greens also contribute to the emphasis on conflict and violence.

With a change of context, the same hue can evoke a different response. Red is also a dominant color in Hans Hofmann's *The Golden Wall* **(C)**, and once again the red seems to push the other shapes toward us. The nonobjective shapes of intense color and modulations in the red field create a vibrant, joyous quality in this painting quite different from Golub's *Mercenaries IV.*

The power of color to evoke an emotional response is undeniable. The context or situation the artist creates in a composition determines whether the effect is inventive or merely a cliché.

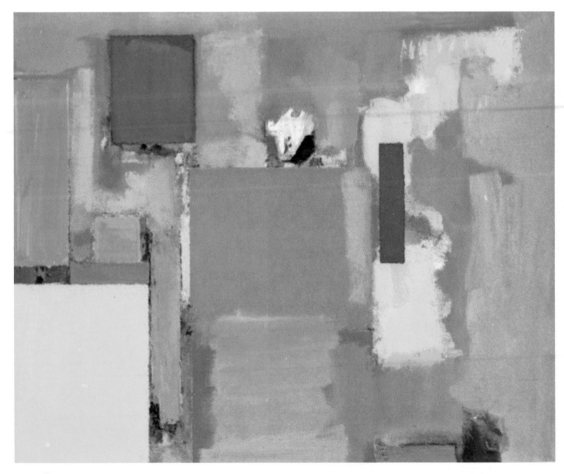

▲ **C**

Hans Hofmann. *The Golden Wall.* 1961. Oil on canvas, 5′ × 6′1/2″ (151 × 182 cm). Photograph © 1993. The Art Institute of Chicago (Mr. and Mrs. Frank G. Logan Prize Fund, 1962.775).

CONCEPTUAL QUALITIES OF COLOR

"Don't worry, he's true-blue."

"I caught him red-handed."

"So I told her a little white lie."

"Why not just admit you're too yellow to do it?"

We frequently utter statements that employ color references to describe character traits or human behavior. These color references are symbolic. The colors in the preceding statements symbolize abstract concepts or ideas: fidelity, sin, innocence, and cowardice. The colors do not stand for tangibles like fire, grass, water, or even sunlight. They represent mental, conceptual qualities. The colors chosen to symbolize various ideas are often arbitrary, or the initial reasons for their choice have become so deeply buried in history we no longer remember them. Can we really explain why green means "go" and red signifies "stop"?

Cultural Differences

A main point to remember is that symbolic color references are cultural: They are not the same worldwide but vary from one society to another. What is the color of mourning that one associates with a funeral? Our reply might be black, but the answer would be white in India, violet in Turkey, brown in Ethiopia, and yellow in Burma. What is the color of royalty? We think of purple (dating back to the Egyptians), but the royal color was yellow in dynastic China and red in ancient Rome (a custom continued today in the cardinals' robes of the Catholic Church). What does a bride wear? White is our response, but yellow is the choice in Hindu India, and red is the choice in China.

Different eras and different cultures invent different color symbols. The symbolic use of color was very important in ancient art for identifying specific figures or deities to an illiterate public. Not only the ancients used color in this manner—in the countless pictures of the Virgin Mary throughout centuries of Western art, she is almost always shown in a blue robe over a red or white garment **(A)**.

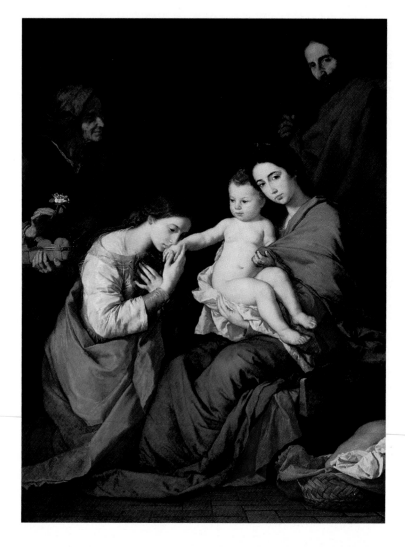

◀ **A**

Jusepe de Ribera. *The Holy Family with Saints Anne and Catherine of Alexandria.* 1648. Oil on canvas, 6′ 10 1/2″ × 5′ 3/4″ (209.6 × 154.3 cm). The Metropolitan Museum of Art, Samuel D. Lee Fund, 1934 (34.73).

Symbolic Color Today

Symbolic color designations are less important in art than they once were. Perhaps we are more conscious today of symbolic color as it is used in advertising, such as green to evoke an association with environmental responsibility or black to connote sophistication. Until recently black was taboo for food packaging—now it may suggest a premium product.

Color symbolism can still be powerful to a large audience, however. The red and white stripes of the American flag shift to the black and white stripes of prison garb in David Hollenbach's indictment of the American justice system **(B)**.

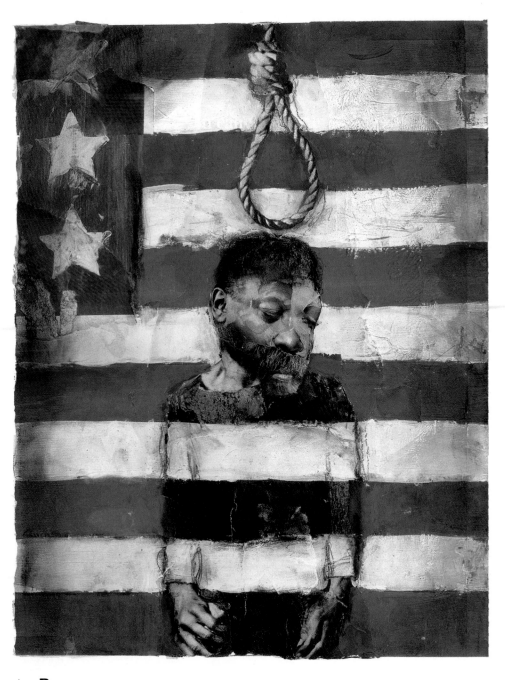

▲ **B**

David Hollenbach. Client: *The American Prospect.* "The Judge as Lynch Mob," *Communication Arts Illustration Annual* 43 (July 2002), p. 51.

A CONTINUING DEBATE

We customarily think of an artist as working with color, but consider the vast area of drawings, prints, and photographs produced using pure value and no color. Also consider fields such as sculpture and architecture. Here, though color is present, the main design consideration has often been value because of the usual monotone of the materials involved. Texture, which is so important an element in these fields, is essentially a variation in light and dark visual patterns. It would seem that an artist in almost any field or specialization should be skillful in manipulating both color and value.

Artists Speak about Color

Do color and value work together or at cross-purposes? This question has been argued over the centuries. Some critics have maintained that the emphasis in a work should be on one or the other. Some artists of the past seem to have thought this way also. Leonardo da Vinci called color the "greatest enemy of art," and Titian supposedly said that an artist needs only three colors. Obviously, these artists emphasized value changes rather than contrast of pure color. The **Fauves** and **Expressionists** of the twentieth century would undoubtedly agree with van Gogh's statement, "Coloring is what makes a painter a painter."

Defining New Periods

Historically it seems that, for whatever reason, many artists have often chosen to put the emphasis on either color or value. Art historians outlining the stylistic changes in art have described shifts in this area as indicative of a new period.

This changing of color/value emphasis among different artists and different periods would explain why some works seem so inadequate when shown in a black-and-white illustration. Although a Renaissance painting may be satisfactory, if not satisfying, shown only in value, a book on Impressionism would be impossible without any illustrations in color. The sparkle and brilliance of the original paintings would be lost.

Relationship between Color and Value

A comparison between a black-and-white reproduction and a color one can be useful in revealing the relationship between the value structure and the color structure of a composition. The value structure of the Matisse painting **(A)** shows a fairly bland assortment of similar grays. When we see the same painting reproduced in color **(B)**, the contrast of pink and green becomes vivid and the pale orange and blue come to life.

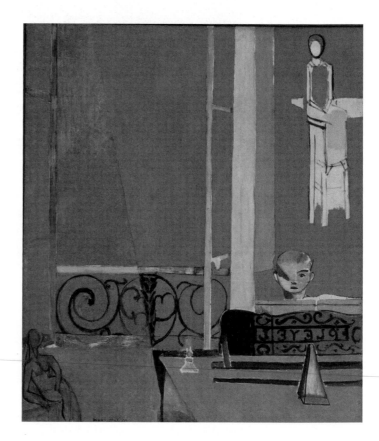

▶ **A**

The values of the pink and green shapes are close to the value of the expanse of gray.

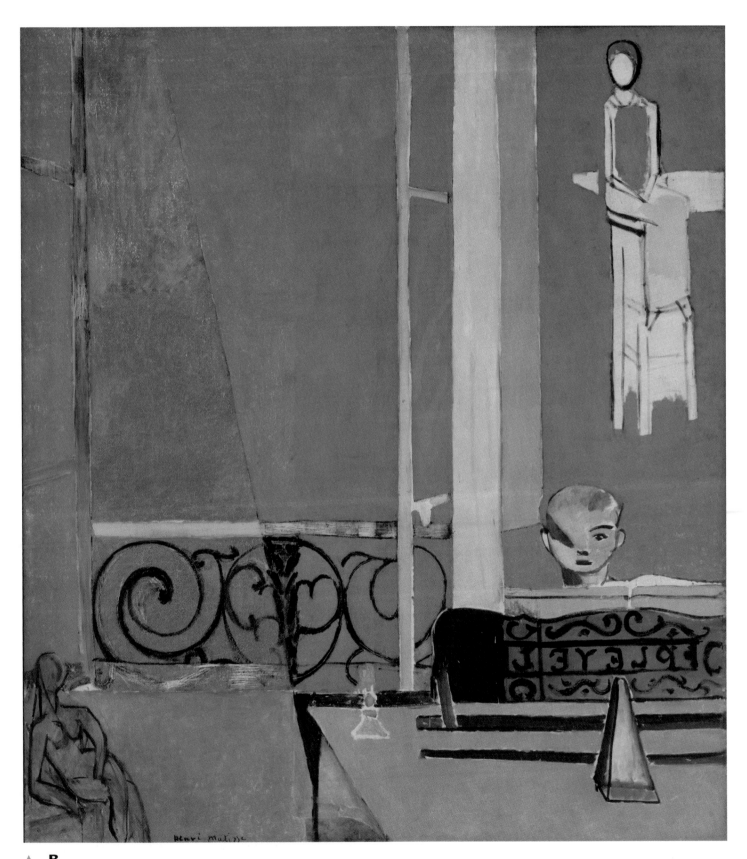

▲ **B**

Henri Matisse. *The Piano Lesson*. Issy-les-Moulineaux. Late summer 1916. Oil on canvas, 8′ 1/2″ × 6′ 11 3/4″. The Museum of Modern Art, New York, Mrs. Simon Guggenheim Fund (125.1946).

Abstraction A visual representation that may have little resemblance to the real world. Abstraction can occur through a process of simplification or distortion in an attempt to communicate an essential aspect of a form or concept.

Achromatic Black, gray, or white with no distinctive hues.

Additive system A color mixing system in which combinations of different wavelengths of light create visual sensations of color.

Aerial perspective The perception of less-distinct contours and value contrasts as forms recede into the background. Colors appear to be washed out in the distance or take on the color of the atmosphere. Also called *atmospheric perspective*.

Aesthetics A branch of philosophy concerned with the beautiful in art and how the viewer experiences it.

Afterimage Occurs after staring at an area of intense color for a certain amount of time and then quickly glancing away toward a white surface, where the complementary color seems to appear.

Allover pattern A composition that distributes emphasis uniformly throughout the two-dimensional surface by repetition of similar elements.

Alternating rhythm A rhythm that consists of successive patterns in which the same elements reappear in a regular order. The motifs alternate consistently with one another to produce a regular (and anticipated) sequence.

Ambiguity Obscurity of motif or meaning.

Amplified perspective A dynamic and dramatic illusionistic effect created when an object is pointed directly at the viewer.

Analogous colors A color scheme that combines several hues located next to each other on the color wheel.

Analysis A measure of the attributes and relationships of an artwork or design.

Anamorphic Term used to describe an image that has been optically distorted.

Anticipated movement The implication of movement on a static two-dimensional surface caused by the viewer's past experience with a similar situation.

Art deco A decorative style, popular in the 1920s, characterized by its geometric patterns and reflecting the rise of industry and mass production in the early twentieth century.

Art nouveau A late nineteenth-century style that emphasized organic shapes.

Assemblage An assembly of found objects composed as a piece of sculpture. See **Collage**.

Asymmetrical balance Balance achieved with dissimilar objects that have equal visual weight or equal eye attraction.

Axis A line of reference around which a form or composition is balanced.

Balance The equilibrium of opposing or interacting forces in a pictorial composition.

Bilateral symmetry Balance with respect to a vertical axis.

Biomorphic Describes shapes derived from organic or natural forms.

Blurred outline A visual device in which most details and the edges of a form are lost in the rapidity of the implied movement.

Calligraphy Elegant, flowing lines suggestive of writing with an aesthetic value separate from its literal content.

Caryatid An architectural column in the form of a human figure.

Chiaroscuro The use of light and dark values to imply depth and volume in a two-dimensional work of art.

Chroma See **Intensity**.

Chromatic Relating to the hue or saturation of color.

Classical Suggestive of Greek and Roman ideals of beauty and purity of form, style, or technique.

Closed form The placement of objects by which a composition keeps the viewer's attention within the picture.

Collage An artwork created by assembling and pasting a variety of materials onto a two-dimensional surface.

Color constancy A psychological compensation for changes in light when observing a color. A viewer interprets the color to be the same under various light conditions.

Color discord A perception of dissonance in a color relationship.

Color harmony Any one of a number of color relationships based on groupings within the color wheel. See also **Analogous colors**, **Color triad**, and **Complementary**.

Color symbolism Employing color to signify human character traits or concepts.

Color triad Three colors equidistant on the color wheel.

Color wheel An arrangement of colors based on the sequence of hues in the visible spectrum.

Complementary A color scheme incorporating opposite hues on the color wheel. Complementary colors accentuate each other in juxtaposition and neutralize each other in mixture.

Composition The overall arrangement and organization of visual elements on the two-dimensional surface.

Conceptual Artwork based on an idea. An art movement in which the idea is more important than the two- or three-dimensional artwork.

Constancy effect An aspect of human perception that allows us to see size or color or form as consistent even if circumstances change appearances.

Content An idea conveyed through the artwork that implies the subject matter, story, or information the artist communicates to the viewer.

Continuation A line or edge that continues from one form to another, allowing the eye to move smoothly through a composition.

Continuity The visual relationship between two or more individual designs.

Contour A line used to follow the edges of forms and thus describe their outlines.

Cool color A color closer to blue on the color wheel.

Critique A process of criticism for the purpose of evaluating and improving art and design.

Cross contour Lines that appear to wrap around a form in a pattern that is at an angle to the outline of the form.

Cross-hatching A drawing technique in which a series of lines are layered over each other to build up value and to suggest form and volume.

Crystallographic balance Balance with equal emphasis over an entire two-dimensional surface so that there is always the same visual weight or attraction wherever you may look. Also called *allover pattern*.

Cubist (Cubism) A form of abstraction that emphasizes planes and multiple perspectives.

Curvilinear Rounded and curving forms that tend to imply flowing shapes and compositions.

Description A verbal account of the attributes of an artwork or design.

Design A planned arrangement of visual elements to construct an organized visual pattern.

Distortion A departure from an accepted perception of a form or object. Distortion often manipulates established proportional standards.

Draftsmanship The quality of drawing or rendering.

Earthworks Artworks created by altering a large area of land using natural and organic materials. Earthworks are usually large-scale projects that take formal advantage of the local topography.

Emotional color A subjective approach to color use to elicit an emotional response in the viewer.

Enigmatic Puzzling or cryptic in appearance or meaning.

Equilibrium Visual balance between opposing compositional elements.

Equivocal space An ambiguous space in which it is hard to distinguish the foreground from the background. Your perception seems to alternate from one to the other.

Expressionism An artistic style in which an emotion is more important than adherence to any perceptual realism. It is characterized by the exaggeration and distortion of objects in order to evoke an emotional response from the viewer.

Eye level See **Horizon line**.

Facade The face or frontal aspect of a form.

Fauve A French term meaning "wild beast" and descriptive of an artistic style characterized by the use of bright and intense expressionistic color schemes.

Figure Any positive shape or form noticeably separated from the background, or the negative space.

Focal point A compositional device emphasizing a certain area or object to draw attention to the piece and to encourage closer scrutiny of the work.

Folk art Art and craft objects made by people who have not been formally trained as artists.

Form When referring to objects, it is the shape and structure of a thing. When referring to two-dimensional artworks, it is the visual aspect of composition, structure, and the work as a whole.

Formal Traditional and generally accepted visual solutions.

Fresco A mural painting technique in which pigments mixed in water are used to form the desired color. These pigments are then applied to wet lime plaster, thereby binding with and becoming an integral part of a wall.

Gestalt A unified configuration or pattern of visual elements whose properties cannot be derived from a simple summation of its parts.

Gesture A line that does not stay at the edges but moves freely within forms. These lines record movement of the eye as well as implying motion in the form.

Golden mean A mathematical ratio in which width is to length as length is to length plus width. This ratio has been employed in design since the time of the ancient Greeks. It can also be found in natural forms.

Golden rectangle The ancient Greek ideal of a perfectly proportioned rectangle using a mathematical ratio called the Golden mean.

Graphic Forms drawn or painted onto a two-dimensional surface; any illustration or design.

Grid A network of horizontal and vertical intersecting lines that divide spaces and create a framework of areas.

Ground The surface of a two-dimensional design that acts as the background or surrounding space for the "figures" in the composition.

Harmony The pleasing combination of parts that make up a whole composition.

Hieratic scaling A composition in which the size of figures is determined by their thematic importance.

Horizon line The farthest point we can see where the delineation between the sky and ground becomes distinct. The line on the picture plane that indicates the extent of illusionistic space and on which are located the vanishing points.

Hue A property of color defined by distinctions within the visual spectrum or color wheel. "Red," "blue," "yellow," and "green" are examples of hue names.

Idealism An artistic theory in which the world is not reproduced as it is but as it should be. All flaws, accidents, and incongruities of the visual world are corrected.

Illustration A picture created to clarify or accompany a text.

Imbalance Occurs when opposing or interacting forms are out of equilibrium in a pictorial composition.

Impasto A painting technique in which pigments are applied in thick layers or strokes to create a rough three-dimensional paint surface on the two-dimensional surface.

Implied line An invisible line created by positioning a series of points so that the eye will connect them and thus create movement across the picture plane.

Impressionism An artistic style that sought to re-create the artist's perception of the changing quality of light and color in nature.

Informal balance Synonymous with **asymmetrical balance**. It gives a less-rigid, more casual impression.

Installation A mixed-media artwork that generally takes into account the environment in which it is arranged.

Intensity The saturation of hue perceived in a color.

Interpretation A subjective conclusion regarding the meaning, implication, or effect of an artwork or design.

Isometric projection A spatial illusion that occurs when lines receding on the diagonal remain parallel instead of converging toward a common vanishing point. Used commonly in Oriental and Far Eastern art.

Juxtaposition When one image or shape is placed next to or in comparison to another image or shape.

Kinesthetic empathy A mental process in which the viewer consciously or unconsciously re-creates or feels an action or motion he or she only observes.

Kinetic Artworks that actually move or have moving parts.

Legato A connecting and flowing rhythm.

Line A visual element of length. It can be created by setting a point in motion.

Line quality Any one of a number of characteristics of line determined by its weight, direction, uniformity, or other features.

Linear perspective A spatial system used in two-dimensional artworks to create the illusion of space. It is based on the perception that if parallel lines are extended to the horizon line, they appear to converge and meet at a common point, called the vanishing point.

Lines of force Lines that show the pathway of movement and add strong visual emphasis to a suggestion of motion.

Local color The identifying color perceived in ordinary daylight.

Lost-and-found contour A description of a form in which an object is revealed by distinct contours in some areas whereas other edges simply vanish or dissolve into the ground.

Mandala A radial concentric organization of geometric shapes and images commonly used in Hindu and Buddhist art.

Medium The tools or materials used to create an artwork.

Minimalism An artistic style that stresses purity of form above subject matter, emotion, or other extraneous elements.

Mixed media The combination of two or more different media in a single work of art.

Module A specific measured area or standard unit.

Monochromatic A color scheme using only one hue with varying degrees of value or intensity.

Monocular Pertaining to vision from one eye only.

Montage A recombination of images from different sources to form a new picture.

Multiple image A visual device used to suggest the movement that occurs when a figure is shown in a sequence of slightly overlapping poses in which each successive position suggests movement from the prior position.

Multiple perspective A depiction of an object that incorporates several points of view.

Multipoint perspective A system of spatial illusion with different vanishing points for different sets of parallel lines.

Naturalism The skillful representation of the visual image, forms, and proportions as seen in nature with an illusion of volume and three-dimensional space.

Negative shape A clearly defined shape within the ground that is defined by surrounding figures or boundaries.

Negative space Unoccupied area or empty space surrounding the objects or figures in a composition.

Nonobjective A type of artwork with absolutely no reference to, or representation of, the natural world. The artwork is the reality.

Objective Having to do with reality and fidelity to perception.

One-point perspective A system of spatial illusion in two-dimensional art based on the convergence of parallel lines to a common vanishing point usually on the horizon.

Op Art A style of art and design that emphasizes optical phenomena.

Opaque A surface impenetrable by light.

Open form The placement of elements in a composition so that they are cut off by the boundary of the design. This implies that the picture is a partial view of a larger scene.

Optical mixture Color mixture created by the eye as small bits of color are perceived to blend and form a mixture.

Overlapping A device for creating an illusion of depth in which some shapes are in front of and partially hide or obscure others.

Pattern The repetition of a visual element or module in a regular and anticipated sequence.

Parallax The resolution of two images from binocular (two-eyed) vision.

Picture plane The two-dimensional surface on which shapes are organized into a composition.

Plane The two-dimensional surface of a shape.

Pointillism A system of color mixing (used in painting and drawing) based on the juxtaposition of small bits of pure color. Also called *divisionism* (see **Optical mixture**).

Pop art An art movement originating in the 1960s that sought inspiration from everyday popular culture and the techniques of commercial art.

Positive shape Any shape or object distinguished from the background.

Primary colors The three colors from which all other colors theoretically can be mixed. The primaries of pigments are traditionally presented as red, yellow, and blue, whereas the primaries of light are red, blue, and green.

Progressive rhythm Repetition of a shape that changes in a regular pattern.

Proportion Size measured against other elements or against a mental norm or standard.

Proximity The degree of closeness in the placement of elements.

Psychic line A mental connection between two points or elements. This occurs when a figure is pointing or looking in a certain direction, which causes the eye to follow toward the intended focus.

Radial balance A composition in which all visual elements are balanced around and radiate from a central point.

Realism An approach to artwork based on the faithful reproduction of surface appearances with a fidelity to visual perception.

Rectilinear Composed of straight lines.

Repeated figure A compositional device in which a recognizable figure appears within the same composition in different positions and situations so as to relate a narrative to the viewer.

Repetition Using the same visual element over again within the same composition.

Representational An image suggestive of the appearance of an object that actually exists.

Rhythm An element of design based on the repetition of recurrent motifs.

Saturation See **Intensity**.

Secondary color A mixture of any two primary colors.

Shade A hue mixed with black.

Shading Use of value in artwork.

Shape A visually perceived area created either by an enclosing line or by color and value changes defining the outer edges.

Silhouette The area between the contours of a shape.

Simultaneous contrast The effect created by two complementary colors seen in juxtaposition. Each color seems more intense in this context.

Site specific A work of art in which the content and aesthetic value is dependent on the artwork's location.

Spectrum The range of visible color created when white light is passed through a prism.

Staccato Abrupt changes and dynamic contrast within the visual rhythm.

Static Still, stable, or unchanging.

Subject The content of an artwork.

Subjective Reflecting a personal bias.

Subtractive system A color mixing system in which pigments (physical substances) are combined to create visual sensations of color. Wavelengths of light absorbed by the substance are subtracted, and the reflected wavelengths constitute the perceived color.

Suprematism A Russian art movement of the early twentieth century that emphasized nonobjective form.

Surrealism An artistic style that stresses fantastic and subconscious approaches to art making and often results in images that cannot be rationally explained.

Symbol An element of design that communicates an idea or meaning beyond that of its literal form.

Symmetry A quality of a composition or form wherein a precise correspondence of elements exists on either side of a center axis or point.

Tactile texture The use of materials to create a surface that can be felt or touched.

Tertiary color A mixture of a primary and an adjacent secondary color.

Texture The surface quality of objects that appeals to the tactile sense.

Tint A hue mixed with white.

Tonality A single color or hue that dominates the entire color structure despite the presence of other colors.

Transparency A situation in which an object or form allows light to pass through it. In two-dimensional art, two forms overlap, but they are both seen in their entirety.

Triadic A color scheme involving three equally spaced colors on the color wheel.

Trompe l'oeil A French term meaning "to fool the eye." The objects are in sharp focus and delineated with meticulous care to create an artwork that almost fools the viewer into believing that the images are the actual objects.

Two-point perspective A scene that is viewed through an angle, with no objects parallel to the picture plane and with edges receding to two points on the horizon line.

Unity The degree of agreement existing among the elements in a design.

Value A measure of relative lightness or darkness.

Value contrast The relationship between areas of dark and light.

Value emphasis Use of a light-and-dark contrast to create a focal point within a composition.

Value pattern The arrangement and amount of variation in light and dark values independent of any colors used.

Vanishing point In linear perspective, the point at which parallel lines appear to converge on the horizon line. Depending on the view there may be more than one vanishing point.

Vernacular A prevailing or commonplace style in a specific geographical location, group of people, or time period.

Vertical location A spatial device in which elevation on the page or format indicates a recession into depth. The higher an object, the farther back it is assumed to be.

Vibrating colors Colors that create a flickering effect at their border. This effect usually depends on an equal value relationship and strong hue contrast.

Visual color mixing Placing small units of color side by side so that the eye perceives the mixture rather than the individual component colors.

Visual texture A two-dimensional illusion suggestive of a tactile quality.

Volume The appearance of height, width, and depth in a form.

Warm color A color closer to the yellow-to-red side of the color wheel.

Wash drawing A technique of drawing in water-based media.

General

Berger, John. *Ways of Seeing.* London: British Broadcast Corporation, 1987.

Buser, Thomas. *Experiencing Art Around Us.* Belmont, CA: Wadsworth/Thomson, 2006.

Canaday, John. *What Is Art?* New York: Alfred A. Knopf, 1980.

Dondis, Donis A. *A Primer of Visual Literacy.* Cambridge, MA: MIT Press, 1973.

Faulkner, Ray, Edwin Ziegfeld, and Howard Smagula. *Art Today: An Introduction to the Visual Arts,* 6th ed. Fort Worth, TX: Harcourt Brace College Publishers, 1987.

McCarter, R. William, and Rita Gilbert. *Living with Art,* 2nd ed. New York: McGraw-Hill, 1988.

Preble, Duane, and Sarah Preble. *Artforms: An Introduction to the Visual Arts,* 5th ed. New York: HarperCollins, 1993.

Roth, Richard, and Susan Roth. *Beauty Is Nowhere: Ethical Issues in Art and Design.* Amsterdam: Gordon and Breach, 1998.

Tufte, Edward R. *Visual Explanations: Images and Quantities, Evidence and Narrative.* New Haven, CT: Graphics Press, 1996.

Art History

Arnason, H. H. *History of Modern Art,* 3rd rev. ed. New York: Harry N. Abrams, 1986.

Gardner, Louise, et al. *Art through the Ages,* 11th ed. Fort Worth, TX: Harcourt Brace College Publishers, 2001.

Janson, H. W. *History of Art,* 4th rev. and enl. ed. New York: Harry N. Abrams, 1991.

Smagula, Howard. *Currents,* 2nd ed. Englewood Cliffs, NJ: Prentice-Hall, 1989.

General Design

Bevlin, Marjorie Elliot. *Design through Discovery,* 6th ed. Fort Worth, TX: Harcourt Brace College Publishers, 1994.

Bothwell, Dorr, and Marlys Frey. *Notan: DarkLight Principle of Design.* New York: Dover, 1991.

Collier, Graham. *Form, Space and Vision: An Introduction to Drawing and Design,* 4th ed. Englewood Cliffs, NJ: Prentice-Hall, 1985.

De Lucio-Meyer, J. *Visual Aesthetics.* New York: Harper & Row, 1974.

De Sausmarez, Maurice. *Basic Design: The Dynamics of Visual Form.* Blue Ridge Summit, PA: TAB Books, 1990.

Hoffman, Armin. *Graphic Design Manual.* New York: Van Nostrand Reinhold, 1977.

Hurlburt, Allen. *The Design Concept.* New York: Watson-Guptill Publications, 1981.

Hurlburt, Allen. *The Grid.* New York: Van Nostrand Reinhold, 1982.

Hurlburt, Allen. *Layout: The Design of the Printed Page.* New York: Watson-Guptill Publications, 1989.

Itten, Johannes. *Design and Form: The Basic Course at the Bauhaus,* 2nd rev. ed. New York: Van Nostrand Reinhold, 1975.

Kepes, Gyorgy. *Language of Vision.* Chicago: Paul Theobald, 1969.

Kerlow, Isaac Victor, and Judson Rosebush. *Computer Graphics.* New York: Van Nostrand Reinhold, 1986.

Maier, Manfred. *Basic Principles of Design.* New York: Van Nostrand Reinhold, 1977.

Mante, Harald. *Photo Design: Picture Composition for Black and White Photography.* New York: Van Nostrand Reinhold, 1971.

Margolin, Victor. *Design Discourse.* Chicago: University of Chicago Press, 1989.

Mau, Bruce. *Life Style.* New York: Phaidon Press, 2005.

McKim, Robert H. *Thinking Visually.* New York: Van Nostrand Reinhold, 1980.

Murphy, Pat. *By Nature's Design.* San Francisco: Chronicle Books, 1993.

Myers, Jack Frederick. *The Language of Visual Art.* Orlando, FL: Holt, Rinehart and Winston, 1989.

Stoops, Jack, and Jerry Samuelson. *Design Dialogue.* Worcester, MA: Davis Publications, 1983.

Wilde, Richard. *Problems, Solutions: Visual Thinking for Graphic Communications.* New York: Van Nostrand Reinhold, 1989.

Wong, Wucius. *Principles of Three-Dimensional Design.* New York: Van Nostrand Reinhold, 1977.

Wong, Wucius. *Principles of Two-Dimensional Design.* New York: Van Nostrand Reinhold, 1972.

Visual Perception

Arnheim, Rudolf. *Art and Visual Perception: A Psychology of the Creative Eye, the New Version,* 2nd rev. and enl. ed. Berkeley: University of California Press, 1974.

Bloomer, Carolyn M. *Principles of Visual Perception,* 2nd ed. New York: Van Nostrand Reinhold, 1989.

Ehrenzweig, Anton. *The Hidden Order of Art: A Study in the Psychology of Artistic Imagination.* Berkeley: University of California Press, 1976.

Gombrich, E. H. *Art and Illusion: A Study in the Psychology of Pictorial Representation.* Princeton, NJ: Princeton University Press, 1961.

Space

Carraher, Ronald G., and Jacqueline B. Thurston. *Optical Illusions and the Visual Arts.* New York: Van Nostrand Reinhold, 1966.

Coulin, Claudius. *Step-by-Step Perspective Drawing: For Architects, Draftsmen and Designers.* New York: Van Nostrand Reinhold, 1971.

D'Amelio, Joseph. *Perspective Drawing Handbook.* New York: Leon Amiel, Publisher, 1964.

Doblin, Jay. *Perspective: A New System for Designers,* 11th ed. New York: Whitney Library of Design, 1976.

Ivins, William M., Jr. *On the Rationalization of Sight: With an Examination of Three Renaissance Texts on Perspective to Which Is Appended "De Artificiali Perspectiva" by Viator (Pelerin).* New York: Da Capo Press, 1973.

Luckiesh, M. *Visual Illusions: Their Causes, Characteristics and Applications.* New York: Dover Publications, 1965.

Montague, John. *Basic Perspective Drawing,* 2nd ed. New York: Van Nostrand Reinhold, 1993.

Mulvey, Frank. *Graphic Perception of Space.* New York: Van Nostrand Reinhold, 1969.

White, J. *The Birth and Rebirth of Pictorial Space,* 3rd ed. Cambridge, MA: Harvard University Press, 1987.

Texture

Battersby, Marton. *Trompe-l'Oeil: The Eye Deceived.* New York: St. Martin's Press, 1974.

O'Connor, Charles A., Jr. *Perspective Drawing and Applications.* Englewood Cliffs, NJ: Prentice-Hall, 1985.

Proctor, Richard M. *The Principles of Pattern: For Craftsmen and Designers.* New York: Van Nostrand Reinhold, 1969.

Wescher, Herta. *Collage.* New York: Harry N. Abrams, 1968.

Color

Albers, Josef. *Interaction of Color,* rev. ed. New Haven, CT: Yale University Press, 1975.

Birren, Faber. *Creative Color: A Dynamic Approach for Artists and Designers.* New York: Van Nostrand Reinhold, 1961.

Birren, Faber. *Ostwald: The Color Primer.* New York: Van Nostrand Reinhold, 1969.

Birren, Faber. *Principles of Color,* rev. ed. West Chester, PA: Schiffer Publishing, Limited, 1987.

Birren, Faber, ed. *Itten: The Elements of Color.* New York: Van Nostrand Reinhold, 1970.

Birren, Faber, ed. *Munsell: A Grammar of Color.* New York: Van Nostrand Reinhold, 1969.

De Grandis, Luigina. *Theory and Use of Color.* New York: Harry N. Abrams, 1987.

Fabri, Frank. *Color: A Complete Guide for Artists.* New York: Watson-Guptill, 1967.

Gerritsen, Frank J. *Theory and Practice of Color.* New York: Van Nostrand Reinhold, 1974.

Itten, Johannes. *The Art of Color,* rev. ed. New York: Van Nostrand Reinhold, 1984.

Kippers, Harald. *Color: Origin, Systems, Uses.* New York: Van Nostrand Reinhold, 1973.

Pentak, Stephen, and Richard Roth. *Color Basics.* Belmont, CA: Wadsworth/Thomson, 2003.

Rhode, Ogden N. *Modern Chromatics: The Student's Textbook of Color with Application to Art and Industry,* new ed. New York: Van Nostrand Reinhold, 1973.

Varley, Helen, ed. *Color.* Los Angeles: Knapp Press, 1980.

Verity, Enid. *Color Observed.* New York: Van Nostrand Reinhold, 1980.

Zelanski, Paul, and Mary Pat Fisher. *Color.* Englewood Cliffs, NJ: Prentice-Hall, 1989.

Society (ARS), New York/VG Bild-Kunst, Bonn. **147E** By permission of Mark Feldstein and Dover Publications. **149B** © 2007 Artists Rights Society (ARS), New York/VG Bild-Kunst, Bonn.

Chapter 8: Opener © *The New Yorker Collection*. 1968 Charles E. Martin from cartoonbank.com. All Rights Reserved. **153B** Erich Lessing/Art Resource, NY. **153C** © Estate of Roy Lichtenstein **156A** Painting by Russell Connor/ Copyright © 1992, *The New Yorker Magazine*, Inc. Reprinted by permission. All Rights Reserved. **158B** Alinari/Art Resource, NY. **160A** Photo: Salander-O'Reilly Galleries, NY. **161D** © 2007 Artists Rights Society (ARS), New York. Digital Image © The Museum of Modern Art/Licensed by SCALA/Art Resource, NY. **162A** Collection of Walker Art Center, Minneapolis, Minnesota. Gift of Elizabeth McFadden. **163B** Photo: Rick Hall. **164A** Photo: CNAC/MNAM/Dist. Réunion des Musées Nationaux/ Art Resource, NY . **164B** Courtesy Rocio Romero LLC, Perryville, MO; photo Julio Pereira. **167C** Copyright Aaron Siskind Foundation. **167D** © 2007 Richard Serra/Artists Rights Society (ARS), New York. Photo © Kate Pentak. **169C** © 2007 Artists Rights Society (ARS), New York/VG Bild-Kunst, Bonn. Digital Image © The Museum of Modern Art/Licensed by SCALA/Art Resource, NY. **170B** Photo: Gérard Blot. Réunion des Musées Nationaux/Art Resource, NY. **171C** Image © The Metropolitan Museum of Art. **171D** Courtesy of Locks Gallery, Philadelphia. **173C** © 2007 Estate of Pablo Picasso/Artists Rights Society (ARS), New York. Photo © The Art Institute of Chicago.

Chapter 9: Opener © *The New Yorker Collection*. 1968 Lee Lorenz from cartoonbank.com. All Rights Reserved. **176A** © Adrienne Salinger. **176B** © Margaret Courtney-Clarke/CORBIS. **177C** © 2007 The Josef and Anni Albers Foundation/Artists Rights Society (ARS), New York. Photo: Katya Kallsen © President and Fellows of Harvard College. **177D** © 2007 The Josef and Anni Albers Foundation/Artists Rights Society (ARS), New York. **178A** Secondhand Rose. **180A** The Victorian Design Book: A Complete Guide to Victorian House Trim (Ottawa: Lee Valley Tools Ltd., 1984). **180B** The Victorian Design Book: A Complete Guide to Victorian House Trim (Ottawa: Lee Valley Tools Ltd., 1984). **181D** Photo: The New York Public Library/Art Resource, NY. **183B** © Chester Higgins Jr. All Rights Reserved. **184A** Gérald Blot/Réunion des Musées Nationaux, Paris/Art Resource, NY. **185B** Stephen Pitkin. **185C** Photo: Mansfield Bascom/Wharton Esherick Museum. **186A** Digital Image © The Museum of Modern Art/ Licensed by SCALA/Art Resource, NY. **187C** Smithsonian American Art Museum, Washington DC/Art Resource, NY. **189B** Courtesy of Locks Gallery, Philadelphia. **189C** Digital Image © The Museum of Modern Art/ Licensed by SCALA/Art Resource, NY. **189D** © 2007 Artists Rights Society (ARS), New York/VG Bild-Kunst, Bonn. Digital Image © The Museum of Modern Art/Licensed by SCALA/Art Resource, NY.

Chapter 10: Opener By permission of Sidney Harris, ScienceCartoonsPlus .com. **194A** Robert Burley © Design Archive, Toronto. **194B** © Michel Taupin. **195C** © Michel Taupin. **196A** Photo © The Art Institute of Chicago. **197D** © 2007 Artists Rights Society (ARS), New York/VG Bild-Kunst, Bonn. Digital Image © The Museum of Modern Art/Licensed by SCALA/Art Resource, NY. **197E** © 2007 Artists Rights Society (ARS), New York/VG Bild-Kunst, Bonn. Digital Image © The Museum of Modern Art/Licensed by SCALA/Art Resource, NY. **198B** Lee Stalsworth/ Hirshhorn Museum and Sculpture Garden. **199C** Photograph © 1996 The Metropolitan Museum of Art. **200C** © 2007 The Jacob and Gwendolyn Lawrence Foundation, Seattle/Artists Rights Society (ARS), New York. Photo: Lee Stalworth/Hirshhorn Museum and Sculpture Garden. **202B** Faith Ringgold © 1998. **203C** Photo: Smithsonian American Art Museum, Washington D.C./Art Resource, NY. **203D** Museum of the City of New York, Berenice Abbott Collection. **205D** Image © 2003 Board of Trustees, National Gallery of Art, Washington. **206A** Photo: Erich Lessing/Art Resource, NY. **207B** Hood Museum of Art, Dartmouth College, Hanover, NH. P.976.281. **207C** Freer Gallery of Art, Smithsonian Institution, Washington, D.C. Gift of Charles Lang Freer, F1903.54. **209C** Thanks to Scandinavia, NY. Source: Page 122, Print, Jan/Feb. 1996. **209D** Mairani/ Grazia Neri. **210A** ©The Metropolitan Museum of Art, by permission of the collector. **211C** Photo: Concept Art Gallery and Sukolsky Burnelle Inc., Pittsburgh, PA. **212A** Whitney Museum of American Art, NY, 50.23. By permission of the artist, Courtesy of DC Moore Gallery, NY. **215C** Private Collection, Courtesy of DC Moore Gallery, New York. **216A** Victor R. Boswell/National Geographic Society Image Collection. **217D** Historical Society of Western Pennsylvania. **217E** © David Hockney. **219D** © David Hockney. **219E** © 2007 The Josef and Anni Albers Foundation/Artists Rights Society (ARS), NY. **220A** Réunion des Musées Nationaux/Art Resource, NY. **221B** By permission of the artist. **221C** Photo: Jim Strong **224A** © 1998 The Metropolitan Museum of Art. **225B** Addison Gallery of American Art, Phillips Academy, Andover, Massachusetts. **225C** Courtesy of Locks Gallery, Philadelphia.

Chapter 11: Opener © *The New Yorker Collection*. 1961 Warren Miller from cartoonbank.com. All Rights Reserved. **228A** Photo: Erich Lessing/Art Resource, NY . **228B** Courtesy of Locks Gallery, Philadelphia. **229C** The Royal Collection © 2007, Her Majesty Queen Elizabeth II. **230A** © 2007 Artists Rights Society (ARS), New York/VG Bild-Kunst, Bonn. Digital Image © The Museum of Modern Art/Licensed by SCALA/Art Resource, NY. **230B** © 2007 Artists Rights Society (ARS), New York/VG Bild-Kunst, Bonn. Digital Image © The Museum of Modern Art/Licensed by SCALA/Art Resource, NY. **231D** © Gizmachine, Inc. 1989. All Rights Reserved; photo: Timothy Remus. **232A** Photo: The Pierpont Morgan Library/Art Resource, NY. **232B** V&A Images/Victoria and Albert Museum. **233C** AP/Wide World Photos. **233D** Calvin and Hobbes. © 1985 Watterson. Reprinted with permission of Universal Press Syndicate. All rights reserved. **234A** By permission of Gerhard Richter, Koln; photo © The Art Institute of Chicago. **234B** Image © The Metropolitan Museum of Art. **235C** © 2007 Bridget Riley. All rights reserved. Courtesy Karsten Schubert, London. Digital Image © The Museum of Modern Art/Licensed by SCALA/Art Resource, NY. **236A** Image © The Metropolitan Museum of Art. **237B** Réunion des Musées Nationaux, Paris/Art Resource, NY. **237C** © 2007 Artists Rights Society (ARS), New York/ADAGP, Paris/Succession Marcel Duchamp. Photo: Philadelphia Museum of Art/Art Resource, NY. **237D** Photo: John Baldessari.

Chapter 12: Opener © *The New Yorker Collection*. 1951. Frank Modell from cartoonbank.com. All Rights Reserved. **240B** Image © The Metropolitan Museum of Art. **240C** Photo © Sarah W. Linder. **241D** © 2007 Artists Rights Society (ARS), New York/VG Bild-Kunst, Bonn. Digital Image © The Museum of Modern Art/Licensed by SCALA/Art Resource, NY. **241E** © 2007 Artists Rights Society (ARS), New York/VG Bild-Kunst, Bonn. **242A** Photograph © 1995 The Metropolitan Museum of Art. **242B** Alinari/Art Resource, NY. **242C** Courtesy of Locks Gallery, Philadelphia. **243D** Tate London/Art Resource, NY. **245B** Image © The Metropolitan Museum of Art. **245C** Selected ancillaries (abridged editions, teacher's editions, student guides, manuals, instructor resource guides, etc.); not allowed **245D** Selected ancillaries (abridged editions, teacher's editions, student guides, manuals, instructor resource guides, etc.); not allowed **246A** Alinari/Art Resource, NY. **246B** Collection of North Carolina National Bank. **247C** Bildarchiv Preussischer Kulturbesitz/Art Resource, NY. **248A** © Walter Hatke **248B** © 2007 Artists Rights Society (ARS), New York/SIAE, Rome. Photo: Luciano Calzolari, Bologna, Italy.

Chapter 13: Opener © *The New Yorker Collection*. 1957 William Steig from cartoonbank.com. All Rights Reserved. **254A** Photo: Tate Gallery, London/ Art Resource, NY. **255C** © 2007 Artists Rights Society (ARS), New York/ SIAE, Rome. Photo: Luciano Calzolari, Bologna, Italy. **255D** © 2007 Artists Rights Society (ARS), New York/SIAE, Rome. Photo: Luciano Calzolari, Bologna, Italy. **264A** Photo: Ellen Page Wilson, Courtesy Pace Wildenstein, New York. © Chuck Close, Courtesy Pace Wildenstein, New York. **264B** Photo: Ellen Page Wilson, Courtesy Pace Wildenstein, New York. © Chuck Close, Courtesy Pace Wildenstein, New York. **265C** House of Tartan Ltd. Perthshire, Scotland. **269C** © 2007 Artists Rights Society (ARS), New York/VG Bild-Kunst, Bonn. Digital Image © The Museum of Modern Art/ Licensed by SCALA/Art Resource, NY. **269D** Selected ancillaries (abridged editions, teacher's editions, student guides, manuals, instructor resource guides, etc.); not allowed **270A** © 2007 Successió Joan Miró/Artists Rights Society (ARS), New York/ADAGP, Paris. Digital Image © The Museum of Modern Art/Licensed by SCALA/Art Resource, NY. **270B** © 2007 Successió Joan Miró/Artists Rights Society (ARS), New York/ADAGP, Paris. Digital Image (© The Museum of Modern Art/Licensed by SCALA/ Art Resource, NY. **272A** Reprinted with permission: Ing. C. Olivetti & C., S.p.A.; G Pintori, Artist. **273C** Edward Burtynsky/Toronto Image Works. **273D** © 1980 David Hockney; photo © 2006 Museum Associates/LACMA. **274B** Copyright © by the New York Times Co. Reprinted with permission. **275D** Courtesy of Locks Gallery, Philadelphia. **276A** Digital Image © The Museum of Modern Art/Licensed by SCALA/Art Resource, NY. **277C** Mauritshuis, The Hague/Art Resource, NY. **280A** Scenic Design by Dan Gray, Lighting Design by Mary Tarantino, Costume Design by Kristine Kearney. **281B** © 2007 Milton Avery Trust/Artists Rights Society (ARS), New York. Photo © 1980 The Metropolitan Museum of Art. **282B** © 2007 Estate of Pablo Picasso/Artists Rights Society (ARS), New York. **283C** © 2007 Estate of Hans Hofmann/Artists Rights Society (ARS), New York. Photo © The Art Institute of Chicago. **284A** Photograph © 1979 The Metropolitan Museum of Art. **285B** By permission of Frank Sturges for David Hollenbach. **286A** © 2007 Succession H. Matisse, Paris/Artists Rights Society (ARS), New York. **287B** © 2007 Succession H. Matisse, Paris/Artists Rights Society (ARS), New York. Photo © The Museum of Modern Art/New York.